THE MAGUS

A COMPLETE SYSTEM OF

OCCULT PHILOSOPHY

BOOKS 1 & 2

Printed or published to the highest ethical standard

THE MAGUS

A COMPLETE SYSTEM OF OCCULT PHILOSOPHY

BOOKS 1 & 2

Francis Barrett

England

1801

TABLE OF CONTENTS

The Magus, Book I

THE MAGUS,

OR

CELESTIAL INTELLIGENCER;

BEING
A COMPLETE SYSTEM OF OCCULT PHILOSOPHY. IN TWO
BOOKS;

CONTAINING THE ANTIENT AND MODERN PRACTICE OF THE
CABALIFTIC ART, NATURAL AND CELEFTIAL MAGIC, &C.;
FHEWING THE WONDERFUL EFFECTS THAT MAY BE
PERFORMED BY A KNOWLEDGE OF THE
CELESTIAL INFLUENCES, THE OCCULT PROPERTIES OF
METALS, HERBS, AND STONES,

AND THE
APPLICATION OF ACTIVE TO PASSIVE PRINCIPLES.
EXHIBITING THE SCIENCES OF NATURAL MAGIC; ALCHYMY,
OR HERMETIC PHILOSOPHY;

ALSO
THE NATURE CREATION, AND FALL OF MAN;
HIS NATURAL AND FUPERNATURAL GIFTS; THE MAGICAL
POWER INHERENT IN THE SOUL, &C.; WITH A GREAT VARIETY
OF RARE EXPERIMENTS IN NATURAL MAGIC:

THE CONSTELLATORY PRACTICE, OR TALISMANIC MAGIC;
THE NATURE OF THE ELEMENTS. STARS, PLANETS, SIGNS, &C.;
THE
CONFTRUCTION AND COMPOFITION OF ALL SORTS OF MAGIC
SEALS, IMAGES, RINGS, GLAFFES, &C.;

THE VIRTUE AND EFFICACY OF NUMBERS, CHARACTERS, AND
FIGURES, OF GOOD AND EVIL SPIRITS.
MAGNETISM, AND CABALISTICAL OR CEREMONIAL MAGIC;
IN WHICH, THE FECRET MYFTERIES OF THE CABALA ARE
EXPLAINED; THE OPERATIONS OF GOOD AND EVIL SPIRITS;

1

ALL KINDS OF CABALIFTIC FIGURES, TABLES, SEALS, AND NAMES, WITH THEIR UFE, &C.
THE TIMES, BONDS, OFFICES, AND CONJURATION OF SPIRITS.
TO WHICH IS ADDED
BIOGRAPHIA ANTIQUA, OR THE LIVES OF THE MOST EMINENT PHILOSOPHERS, MAGI, &C.
THE WHOLE ILLUSTRATED WITH A GREAT VARIETY OF CURIOUS ENGRAVINGS, MAGICAL AND CABALISTICAL FIGURES, &C.

BY FRANCIS BARRETT, F.R.C.

Professor of Chemistry, natural and occult Philosophy, the Cabala, &c., &c.

LONDON:

1801.

Francis Barrett.
Student in Chemistry, Metaphysicks.
Natural & Occult Philosophy &c. &c.

PREFACE

IN this Work, which we have written chiefly for the information of those who are curious and indefatigable in their enquiries into occult knowledge, we have, at a vast labour and expence, both of time and charges, collected whatsoever can be deemed curious and rare, in regard to the subject of our speculations in Natural Magic--the Cabala--Celestial and Ceremonial Magic--Alchymy--and Magnetism; and have divided it into two Books, sub-divided into Parts: to which we have added a third Book, containing a biographical account of the lives of those great men who were famous and renowned for their knowledge; shewing upon whose authority this Science of Magic is founded, and upon what principles. To which we have annexed a great variety of notes, wherein we have impartially examined the probability of the existence of Magic, both of the good and bad species, in the earliest, as well as in the latter, ages of the world. We have exhibited a vast number of rare experiments in the course of this Treatise, many of which, delivered in the beginning, are founded upon the simple application of actives to passives; the others are of a higher speculation.

In our history of the lives of Philosophers, &c. we have omitted nothing that can be called interesting or satisfactory. We have taken our historical characters from those authors most deserving of credit; we have given an outline of the various reports tradition gives of them; to which are annexed notes, drawn from the most probable appearance of truth, impartially describing their characters and actions; leaning neither to the side of those who doubt every thing, nor to them whose credulity takes in every report to be circumstantially true.

At this time, the abstruse sciences of Nature begin to be more investigated than for a century past, during which space they have been almost totally neglected; but men becoming more enlightened, they begin to consider the extraordinary effects that were wrought by ancient philosophers, in ages that were called dark. Many, therefore, have thought that time, nature, causes, and effects, being the same, with the additional improvements of mechanical and liberal arts, we may, with their knowledge of Nature, surpass them in the producing of wonderful effects; for which cause many men are naturally impelled, without education or other advantage, to dive into the contemplation of Nature; but the study thereof being at first difficult, they have recourse to lay out a great deal of money in collecting various books: to remedy which inconvenience and expence, the Author undertook to compose THE MAGUS, presuming that his labours herein will meet with the general approbation of either the novitiate or adept: for whose use and instruction it is now published.

But to return to the subject of our Book: we have, in the First Part, fully explained what Natural Magic is; and have shewn that, by the application of actives to passives, many wonderful effects are produced that are merely natural, and done by manual operations. We have procured every thing that was valuable and scarce respecting this department of our work, which we have introduced under the title of Natural Magic; and a variety of our own experiments likewise. In the possession of this work, the laborious and diligent student will find a complete and delectable companion; so that he who has been searching for years, for this author and the other, will in this book find the marrow of them all.

But I would advise, that we do not depend too much upon our own wisdom in the understanding of these mysteries; for all earthly wisdom is foolishness in the esteem of God--I mean all the wisdom of man, which he pretends to draw from any other source than God alone.

We come next to the Second Part of our First Book, treating of the art called the Constellatory Practice, or Talismanic Magic; in which we fully demonstrate the power and efficacy of Talismans, so much talked of, and so little understood, by most men: we therefore explain, in the clearest and most intelligible, manner, how Talismans may be made, for the execution of various purposes, and by what means, and from what source they become vivified, and are visible instruments of great and wonderful effects. We likewise shew the proper and convenient times; under what constellations and aspects of the planets they are to be formed, and the times when they are most powerful to act; and, in the next place, we have taught that our own spirit is the vehicle of celestial attraction, transferring celestial and spiritual virtue into Seals, Images, Amulets, Rings, Papers, Glasses, &c. Also, we have not forgot to give the most clear and rational illustration of sympathy and antipathy--attraction and repulsion. We have likewise proved how cures are performed by virtue of sympathetic powers and medicines--by seals, rings, and amulets, even at unlimited distances, which we have been witnesses of and are daily confirmed in the true and certain belief of. We know how to communicate with any person, and to give him intimation of our purpose, at a hundred or a thousand miles distance; but then a preparation is necessary, and the parties should have their appointed seasons and hours for that purpose; likewise, both should be of the same firm constancy of mind, and a disciple or brother in art. And we have given methods whereby a man may receive true and certain intimation of future things (by dreams), of whatsoever his mind has before meditated upon, himself being properly disposed. Likewise, we have recited the various methods used by the antients for the invocation of astral spirits, by circles, crystals, &c.; their forms of exorcism, incantations, orations, bonds, conjurations; and have given a general display of the instruments of their art; all of which we have collected out of the works of the most famous magicians, such as Zoroaster, Hermes, Apollonius, Simon of the Temple, Trithemius, Agrippa, Porta (the Neapolitan), Dee, Paracelsus, Roger Bacon, and a great many others; to which we have subjoined our own notes, endeavouring to point out the difference of these arts, so as to free the name of Magic from any scandalous imputation; seeing it is a word originally significative not of any evil, but of every good and laudable science, such as a man might profit by, and become both wise and happy; and the practice so far from being offensive to God or man, that the very root or ground of all magic takes its rise from the Holy Scriptures, viz.--"The fear of God is the beginning of all wisdom;"--and charity is the end: which fear of God is the beginning of Magic; for Magic is wisdom, and on this account the wise men were called Magi. The magicians were the first Christians; for, by their high and excellent knowledge, they knew that that Saviour which was promised, was now born man--that Christ was our Redeemer, Advocate, and Mediator; they were the first to acknowledge his glory and majesty; therefore let no one be offended at the venerable and sacred title of Magician--a title which every wise man merits while he pursues that path which Christ himself trod, viz. humility, charity, mercy, fasting, praying, &c.; for the true magician is the truest Christian, and nearest disciple of our blessed Lord, who set the example we ought to follow; for he says--"If ye have faith, &c.;" and "This kind comes not by fasting and prayer, &c.;" and "Ye shall tread upon scorpions, &c.;" and again, "Be wise as serpents, and harmless as doves."--Such instructions as these are frequently named, and given in many places of the Holy Scriptures. Likewise, all the Apostles confess the power of working miracles through faith in the name of Christ Jesus, and that all wisdom is to be attained through him; for he says, "I am the light of the world!"

We have thought it adviseable, likewise, to investigate the power of numbers, their sympathy with the divine names of God; and, seemly the whole universe was created by number, weight, and measure, there is no small efficacy in numbers, because nothing more clearly represents the Divine Essence to human understanding than numbers; seeing that in all the Divine holy names there is still a conformity of numbers, so that the conclusion of this our First Book forms a complete system of mathematical magic; in which I have collected a vast number of curious seals from that famous magician Agrippa, and likewise from Paracelsus, noting them particularly, as I have found them correspondent with true science on experiment.

The Second Book forms a complete treatise on the mysteries of the Cabala and Ceremonial Magic; by the study of which, a man (who can separate himself from material objects, by the mortification of the sensual appetite--abstinence from drunkenness, gluttony, and other bestial passions, and who lives pure and temperate, free from those actions which degenerate a man to a brute) may become a recipient of Divine light and knowledge; by which they may foresee things to come, whether to private families, or kingdoms, or states, empires, battles, victories, &c.; and likewise be capable of doing much good to their fellow-creatures: such as the healing of all disorders, and assisting with the comforts of life the unfortunate and distressed.

We have spoken largely of prophetic dreams and visions in our Cabalistic Magic, and have given the tables of the Cabala, fully set down for the information of the wise; some few most secret things being reserved by the Author for his pupils only, not to be taught by publication.

The Third Book forms a complete Magical Biography, being collected from most antient authors, and some scarce and valuable manuscripts; and which has been. the result of much labour in acquiring. Therefore, those who wish to benefit in those studies, must shake off the drowsiness of worldly vanity, all idle levity, sloth, intemperance, and lust; so that they may be quiet, clean, pure, and free from every distraction and perturbation of mind, and worthily use the knowledge he obtains from his labours.

Therefore, my good friend, whosoever thou art, that desirest to accomplish these things, be but persuaded first to apply thyself to the ETERNAL WISDOM, entreating him to grant thee understanding, then seeking knowledge with diligence, and thou shalt never repent thy having taken so laudable a resolution, but thou shalt enjoy a secret happiness and serenity of mind, which the world can never rob thee of.

Wishing thee every success imaginable in thy studies and experiments, hoping that thou wilt use the benefits that thou mayest receive to the honour of our Creator and for the profit of thy neighbour, in which exercise thou shalt ever experience the satisfaction of doing thy duty; remember our instructions--to be silent: talk only with those worthy of thy communication--do not give pearls to swine; be friendly to all, but not familiar with all; for many are, as the Scriptures mention--wolves in sheep clothing.

ADVERTISEMENT

AS an Introduction to the Study of Natural Magic, we have thought fit to premise a short discourse on the Influence of the Stars, and on Natural Magic in general, showing how far the influences of the heavenly bodies are useful to our purposes, and likewise to what extent we may admit those influences; rejecting some speculations concerning the planetary inclinations, as far as they appertain to questionary abuses, that seem to us idle, and of no validity, or yet founded on any principles of sound philosophy, or corresponding to the word of God in the Scriptures. In which discourse we have fully set down our reasons for rejecting some parts of astrology, and admitting others which are founded on good principles, and coinciding with the Scriptures and Natural Philosophy: our purpose being to clear the understanding of errors, and not to enforce any thing but what appears to be substantiated by nature, truth, and experiment.

INTRODUCTION TO THE STUDY OF NATURAL MAGIC.

OF THE INFLUENCES OF THE STARS.

IT has been a subject of ancient dispute whether or not the stars, as second causes, do so rule and influence man as to ingraft in his nature certain passions, virtues, propensities, &c., and this to take root in him at the very critical moment of his being born into this vale of misery and wretchedness; likewise, if their site and configuration at this time do shew forth his future passions and pursuits; and by their revolutions, transits, and directed aspects, they point out the particular accidents of the body, marriage, sickness, preferments, and such like; the which I have often revolved in my mind for many years past, having been at all times in all places a warm advocate for stellary divination or astrology: therefore in this place it is highly necessary that we examine how far this influence extends to man, seeing that I fully admit that man is endowed with a free-will from God, which the stars can in no wise counteract. And as there is in man the power and apprehension of all divination, and wonderful things, seeing that we have a complete system in ourselves, therefore are we called the microcosm, or little world; for we carry a heaven in ourselves from our beginning, for God hath sealed in us the image of himself; and of all created beings we are the epitome, therefore we must be careful, lest we confound and mix one thing with another. Nevertheless, man, as a pattern of the great world, sympathizes with it according to the stars, which, agreeably to the Holy Scriptures, are set for times and seasons, and not as causes of this or that evil, which may pervade kingdoms or private families, although they do in some measure foreshew them, yet they are in no wise the cause; therefore I conceive in a wide different sense to what is generally understood that "Stars rule men, but a wise man rules the stars:" to which I answer, that the stars do not rule men, according to the vulgar and received opinion; as if the stars should stir up men to murders, seditions, broils, lusts, fornications, adulteries, drunkenness, &c., which the common astrologers hold forth as sound and true doctrine; because, they say, Mars and Saturn, being conjunct, do this and much more, and many other configurations and afflictions of the two great infortunes (as they are termed), when the benevolent planets Jupiter, Venus, and Sol, happen to be detrimented or afflicted; therefore, then, they say men influenced by them are most surely excited to the commission of the vices before named; yet a wise man may, by the liberty of his own free-will, make those affections and inclinations void, and this they call "To rule the stars;" but let them know, according to the sense here understood, first, it is not in a wise man to resist evil inclinations, but of the grace of God, and we call none wise but such as are endued with grace; for, as we have said before, all natural wisdom from the hands of man is foolishness in the sight of God; which was not before understood to be a wise man fenced with grace; for why should he rule the stars, who has not any occasion to fear conquered inclinations?--therefore a natural wise man is as subject to the slavery of sin as others more ignorant than himself, yet the stars do not incline him to sin. God created the heavens without spot, and pronounced them good, therefore it is the greatest absurdity to suppose the stars, by a continual inclining of us to this or that misdeed, should be our tempters, which we eventually make them, if we admit they cause inclinations; but know that it is not from without, but within, by sin, that evil inclinations do arise: according to the Scriptures, "Out of the heart of man proceed evil cogitations, murmurs, adulteries, thefts, murders, &c." Because, as the heavens and apprehension of all celestial virtues are scaled by God in the soul and spirit of man; so when man becomes depraved by sin and the indulgence of his gross and carnal appetite, he then becomes the scat of the Infernal Powers, which may be justly deemed a hell; for then the bodily and fleshly sense obscures the bright purity and thinness of the spirit, and he becomes the instrument of our spiritual enemy in the exercise of all infernal lusts and passions.

Therefore it is most necessary for us to know that we are to beware of granting or believing any effects from the influences of the stars more than they have naturally; because there are many whom I have lately conversed with, and great men, too, in this nation, who readily affirm that the stars are the causes of any kinds of diseases, inclinations, and fortunes; likewise that they blame the stars for all their misconduct and misfortunes.

Nevertheless, we do not by these discourses prohibit or deny all influence to the stars; on the contrary, we affirm there is a natural sympathy and antipathy amongst all things throughout the whole universe, and this we shall shew to be displayed through a variety of effects; and likewise that the stars, as signs, do foreshew great mutations, revolutions, deaths of great men, governors of provinces, kings, and emperors; likewise the weather, tempests, earthquakes, deluges, &c.; and this according to the law of Providence. The lots of all men do stand in the hands of the Lord, for he is the end and beginning of all things; he can remove crowns and sceptres, and displace the most cautious arrangements and councils of man, who, when he thinks himself most secure, tumbles headlong from the seat of power, and lies grovelling in the dust.

Therefore our astrologers in most of their speculations seek without a light, for they conceive every thing may be known or read in the stars; if an odd silver spoon is but lost, the innocent stars are obliged to give an account of it; if an old maiden loses a favourite puppy, away she goes to an oracle of divination for information of the whelp. Oh! vile credulity, to think that those celestial bodies take cognizance of, and give in their configurations and aspects, continual information of the lowest and vilest transactions of dotards, the most trivial and frivolous questions that are pretended to be resolved by an inspection into the figure of the heavens. Well does our legislature justly condemn as juggling impostors all those idle vagabonds who infest various parts of this metropolis, and impose upon the simple and unsuspecting, by answering, for a shilling or half-crown fee, whatever thing or circumstance may be proposed to them, as if they were God's vicegerents on earth, and his deputed privy counsellors.

They do not even scruple ever to persuade poor mortals of the lower class, that they shew images in glasses, as if they actually confederated with evil spirits: a notable instance I will here recite, that happened very lately in this city. Two penurious Frenchmen, taking advantage of the credulity of the common people, who are continually gaping after such toys, had so contrived a telescope or optic glass as that various letters and figures should be reflected in an obscure manner, shewing the images of men and women, &c.; so that when any one came to consult these jugglers, after paying the usual fee, they, according to the urgency of the query, produced answers by those figures or letters; the which affrights the inspector into the glass so much, that he or she supposes they have got some devilish thing or other in hand, by which they remain under the full conviction of having actually beheld the parties they wished to see, though perhaps they may at the same time be residing many hundreds of miles distance therefrom; they, having received this impression from a pre-conceived idea of seeing the image of their friend in this optical machine, go away, and anon report, with an addition of ten hundred lies, that they have been witness of a miracle. I say this kind of deception is only to be acted with the vulgar, who, rather than have their imaginations balked, would swallow the most abominable lies and conceits. For instance, who would suppose that any rational being could be persuaded that a fellow-creature of proper size and stature should be able by any means to thrust his body into a quart bottle?--the which thing was advertised to the public by a merry knave (not thinking there were such fools in existence), to be done by him in a public theatre. Upwards of 600 persons were assembled to behold the transaction, never doubting but the fellow meant to keep his word, when to the great mortification and disgrace of this long-headed audience, the conjuror came forth amidst a general stir and buz of "Ay, now! see! now! see! he is just going to jump in."--"Indeed," says the conjuror, "ladies and gentlemen, I am not; for if you were such fools as to believe such an absurdity, I am not wise enough to do it:"-- therefore, making his bow, he disappeared, to the great discomfort of these wiseheads, who straightway withdrew in the best manner they could.

As for the telescope magicians, they were taken into custody by the gentlemen of the police office, in Bow Street; nor would their familiar do them the kindness to attempt their rescue.

But to have done with these things that are unworthy our notice as philosophers, and to proceed to matters of a higher nature: it is to be noted what we have before said, in respect of the influences of the stars, that Ptolemy, in his quadrapartite, in speaking of generals, comes pretty near our ideas on the subject of planetary influence, of which we did not at any time doubt, but do not admit (nay, it is not necessary, seeing there is an astrology in Nature), that each action of our life, our afflictions, fortunes, accidents, are deducible to the influential effects of the planets: they proceed from ourselves; but I admit that our thoughts, actions, cogitations, sympathize with the stars upon the principle of general sympathy. Again, there is a much stronger sympathy between persons of like constitution and temperament, for each mortal creature possesses a Sun and system within himself; therefore, according to universal sympathy, we are affected by the general influence or universal spirit of the world, as the vital principle throughout the universe: therefore we are not to look into the configurations of the stars for the cause or incitement of men's bestial inclinations, for brutes have their specifical inclinations from the propagation of their principle by seed, not by the sign of the horoscope; therefore as man is oftentimes capable of the actions and excesses of brutes, they cannot happen to a man naturally from any other source than the seminal being infused in his composition; for seeing likewise that the soul is immortal, and endued with free-will, which acts upon the body, the soul cannot be inclined by any configuration of the stars either to good or evil; but from its own immortal power of willingly being seduced by sin, it prompts to evil; but enlightened by God, it springs to good, on, the soul feeds while in this frail body; but what further concerns the soul of man in this, and after this, we shall fully investigate the natural magic of the soul, in which we have fully treated every point of enquiry that has been suggested to us by our own imagination, and by scientific experiments have proved its divine virtue originally scaled therein by the Author of its being.

Sufficient it is to return to our subject relative to astrology, especially to know what part of it is necessary for our use, of which we will select that which is pure and to our purpose, for the understanding and effecting of various experiments in the course of our works, leaving the tedious calculation of nativities, the never-ceasing controversies and cavillations of its professors, the dissensions which arise from the various modes of practice; all which we leave to the figure-casting plodder, telling him, by-the-by, that whatever he thinks he can foreshew by inspecting the horoscope of a nativity, by long, tedious, and night-wearied studies

13

and contemplations; I say, whatever he can shew respecting personal or national mutations, changes, accidents, &c. &c., all this we know by a much easier and readier method; and can more comprehensively, clearly, and intelligibly, shew and point out, to the very letter, by our Cabal, which we know to be true, without deviation, juggling, fallacy, or collusion, or any kind of deceit or imposture whatsoever; which Cabal or spiritual astrology we draw from the Fountain of Knowledge, in all simplicity, humility, and truth; and we boast not of ourselves, but of Him who teaches us through his divine mercy, by the light of whose favour we see into things spiritual and divine: in the possession of which we are secure amidst the severest storms of hatred, malice, pride, envy, hypocrisy, levity, bonds, poverty, imprisonment, or any other outward circumstance; we should still be rich, want nothing, be fed with delicious meats, and enjoy plentifully all good things necessary for our support: all this we do not vainly boast of, as figurative, ideal, or chimerical; but real, solid, and everlasting, in the which we exult and delight, and praise his name forever and ever: Amen.

All which we publicly declare to the world for the honour of our God, being at all times ready to do every kindness we can to our poor neighbour, and, as far as in us lies, to comfort him, sick or afflicted; in doing which we ask no reward: it is sufficient to us that we can do it, and that we may be acceptable to Him who says--"I am the light of the world; to whom with the Father, and Holy Spirit, be ascribed all power, might, majesty, and dominion: Amen."

To the faithful and discreet Student of Wisdom.

Greeting:

TAKE our instructions; in all things ask counsel of God, and he will give it; offer up the following prayer daily for the illumination of thy understanding: depend for all things on God, the first cause; with whom, by whom, and in whom, are all things: see thy first care be to know thyself; and then in humility direct thy prayer as follows.

A Prayer or Oration to God.

ALMIGHTY and most merciful God, we thy servants approach with fear and trembling before thee, and in all humility do most heartily beseech thee to pardon our manifold and blind transgressions, by us committed at any time; and grant, O, most merciful Father, for his sake who died upon the cross, that our minds may be enlightened with the divine radiance of thy holy wisdom; for seeing, O, Lord of might, power, majesty, and dominion, that, by reason of our gross and material bodies, we are scarce apt to receive those spiritual instructions that we so earnestly and heartily desire. Open, O, blessed Spirit, the spiritual eye of our soul, that we may be released from this darkness overspreading us by the delusions of the outward senses, and may perceive and understand those things which are spiritual. We pray thee, oh, Lord, above all to strengthen our souls and bodies against our spiritual enemies, by the blood and righteousness of our blessed Redeemer, thy Son, Jesus Christ; and through him, and in his name, we beseech thee to illuminate the faculties of our souls, so that we may clearly and comprehensively hear with our ears, and understand with our hearts; and remove far from us all hypocrisy, deceitful dealing, profaneness, inconstancy, and levity; so that we may, in word and act, become thy faithful servants, and stand firm and unshaken against all the attacks of our bodily enemies, and likewise be proof against all illusions of evil spirits, with whom we desire no communication or interest; but that we may be instructed in the knowledge of things, natural and celestial: and as it pleased thee to bestow on Solomon all wisdom, both human and divine; in the desire of which knowledge he did so please thy divine majesty, that in a dream, of one night, thou didst inspire him with all wisdom and knowledge, which he did wisely prefer before the riches of this life; so may our desire and prayer be graciously accepted by thee; so that, by a firm dependence on thy word, we may not be led away by the vain and ridiculous pursuits of worldly pleasures and delights, they not being durable, nor of any account to our immortal happiness. Grant us, Lord, power and strength of intellect to carry on this work, for the honour and glory of thy holy name, and to the comfort of our neighbour; and without design of hurt or detriment to any, we may proceed in our labours, through Jesus Christ, our Redeemer: Amen.

OF NATURAL MAGIC IN GENERAL.

BEFORE we proceed to particulars, it will not be amis to speak of generals; therefore, as an elucidation, we shall briefly show what sciences we comprehend under the title of Natural Magic; and to hasten to the point, we shall regularly proceed from theory to practice; therefore, Natural Magic undoubtedly comprehends a knowledge of all Nature, which we by no means can arrive at but by searching deeply into her treasury, which is inexhaustible; we therefore by long study, labour, and practice, have found out many valuable secrets and experiments, which are either unknown, or are buried in the ignorant knowledge of the present age. The wise ancients knew that in Nature the greatest secrets lay hid, and wonderful active powers were dormant, unless excited by the vigorous faculty of the mind of man; but as, in these latter days, men have themselves almost wholly up to vice and luxury, so their understandings have become more and more depraved; 'till, being swallowed up in the gross senses, they become totally unfit for divine contemplations and deep speculations in Nature; their intellectual faculty being drowned in obscurity and dulness, by reason of their sloth, intemperance, or sensual appetites. The followers of Pythagoras enjoined silence, and forbade the eating of the flesh of animals; the first, because they were cautious, and aware of the vanity of vain babbling and fruitless cavillations: they studied the power of numbers to the highest extent; they forbade the eating of flesh not so much on the score of transmigration, as to keep the body in a healthful and temperate state, free from gross humours; by these means they qualified themselves for spiritual matters, and attained unto great and excellent mysteries, and continued in the exercise of charitable arts, and the practice of all moral virtues: yet, seeing they were heathens, they attained not unto the high and inspired lights of wisdom and knowledge that were bestowed on the Apostles, and others, after the coming of Christ; but they mortified their lusts, lived temperately, chaste, honest, and virtuous; which government is so contrary to the practice of modern Christians, that they live as if the blessed word had come upon the earth to grant them privilege to sin. However, we will leave Pythagoras and his followers, to hasten to our own work; whereof we will first explain the foundation of Natural Magic, in as clear and intelligible a manner as the same can be done.

The First Principles of Natural Magic: Book the First

CHAPTER 1. NATURAL MAGIC DEFINED...

NATURAL MAGIC DEFINED--OF MAN--HIS CREATION--DIVINE IMAGE--AND OF THE SPIRITUAL AND MAGICAL VIRTUE OF THE SOUL.

NATURAL MAGIC is, as we have said, a comprehensive knowledge of all Nature, by which we search out her secret and occult operations throughout her vast and spacious elaboratory; whereby we come to a knowledge of the component parts, qualities, virtues, and secrets of metals, stones, plants, and animals; but seeing, in the regular order of the creation, man was the work of the sixth day, every thing being prepared for his vicegerency here on earth, and that it pleased the omnipotent God, after he had formed the great world, or macrocosm, and pronounced it good, so he created man the express image of himself; and in man, likewise, an exact model of the great world. We shall describe the wonderful properties of man, in which we may trace in miniature the exact resemblance or copy of the universe; by which means we shall come to the more easy understanding of whatever we may have to declare concerning the knowledge of the inferior nature, such as animals, plants, metals, and stones; for, by our first declaring the occult qualities and properties that are hid in the little world, it will serve as a key to the opening of all the treasures and secrets of the macrocosm, or great world: therefore, we shall hasten to speak of the creation of man, and his divine image; likewise of his fall, in consequence of his disobedience; by which all the train of evils, plagues, diseases, and miseries, were entailed upon his posterity, through the curse of our Creator, but deprecated by the mediation of our blessed Lord, Christ.

THE CREATION, DISOBEDIENCE, AND FALL OF MAN.

ACCORDING to the word of God, which we take in all things for our guide, in the 1st chapter of Genesis, and the 26th verse, it is said--"God said, let us make man in our image, after our likeness; and let them have dominion over the fish of the sea, and over the fowl of the air, and over the cattle, and over all the earth, and over every creeping thing that creepeth upon the earth."--Here is the origin and beginning of our frail human nature; hence every soul was created by the very light itself, and Fountain of Life, after his own express image, likewise immortal, in a beautiful and well-formed body, endued with a most excellent mind, and dominion or unlimited monarchy over all Nature, every thing being subjected to his rule, or command; one creature only being excepted, which was to remain untouched and consecrated, as it were, to the divine mandate: "Of every tree of the garden thou mayest freely eat; But of the tree of the knowledge of good and evil, thou shalt not eat of it; for in the day that thou eatest of it, thou shalt surely die." Gen. ii. ver. 16. Therefore Adam was formed by the finger of God, which is the Holy Spirit; whose figure or outward form was beautiful and proportionate as an angel; in whose voice (before he sinned) every sound was the sweetness of harmony and music: had he remained in the state of innocency in which he was formed, the weakness of mortal man, in his depraved state, would not have been able to bear the virtue and celestial shrillness of his voice. But when the deceiver found that man, from the inspiration of God, had began to sing so shrilly, and to repeat the celestial harmony of the heavenly country, he counterfeited the engines of craft: seeing his wrath against him was in vain, he was much tormented thereby, and began to think how he might entangle him into disobedience of the command of his Creator, whereby he might, as it were, laugh him to scorn, in derision of his new creature, man.

Van Helmont, in his Oriatrike, chap. xcii., speaking of the entrance of death into human nature, &c., finely touches the subject of the creation, and man's disobedience: indeed, his ideas so perfectly coincide with my own, that I have thought fit here to transcribe his philosophy, which so clearly explains the text of Scripture, with so much of the light of truth on his side, that it carries along with it the surest and most positive conviction.

"Man being essentially created after the image of God, after that, he rashly presumed to generate the image of God out of himself; not, indeed, by a certain monster, but by something which was shadowly like himself. With the ravishment of Eve, he, indeed, generated not the image God like unto that which God would have inimitable, as being divine; but in the vital air of the seed he generated dispositions; careful at some time to receive a sensitive, discursive, and motive soul from the Father of Light, yet mortal, and to perish; yet, nevertheless, he ordinarily inspires, and of his own goodness, the substantial spirit of a mind showing forth his own image: so that man, in this respect, endeavoured to generate his own image; not after the manner of brute beasts, but by the copulation of seeds, which at length should obtain, by request, a soulified light from the Creator; and the which they call a sensitive soul.

"For, from thence hath proceeded another generation, conceived after a beast-like manner, mortal, and uncapable of eternal life, after the manner of beasts; and bringing forth with pains, and subject to diseases, and death; and so much the more sorrowful, and full of misery, by how much that very propagation in our first parents dared to invert the intent of God.

"Therefore the unutterable goodness forewarned them that they should not taste of that tree; and otherwise he foretold, that the same day they should die the death, and should feel all the root of calamities which accompanies death."

Deservedly, therefore, hath the Lord deprived both our parents of the benefit of immortality; namely, death succeeded from a conjugal and brutal copulation; neither remained the spirit of the Lord with man, after that he began to be flesh.

Further; because that defilement of Eve shall thenceforth be continued in the propagation of posterity, even unto the end of the world, from hence the sin of the despised fatherly admonition, and natural deviation from the right way, is now among other sins for an impurity, from an inverted, carnal, and well nigh brutish generation, and is truly called original sin; that is, man being sowed in the pleasure of the concupiscence of the flesh, shall therefore always reap a necessary death in the flesh of sin; but, the knowledge of good and evil, which God placed in the dissuaded apple, did contain in it a seminary virtue of the concupiscence of the flesh, that is, an occult forbidden conjunction, diametrically opposite to the state of innocence, which state was not a state of stupidity; because He was he unto whom, before the corruption of Nature, the essences of all living creatures whatsoever were made known, according to which they were to be named from their property, and at their first sight to be essentially distinguished: man, therefore, through eating of the apple, attained a knowledge that he had lost his radical innocency; for, neither before the eating of the apple was he so dull or stupified that he knew not, or did not perceive himself naked; but, with the effect of shame and brutal concupiscence, he then first declared he was naked.

For that the knowledge of good and evil signifies nothing but the concupiscence of the flesh, the Apostle testifies; calling it the law, and desire of sin. For it pleased the Lord of heaven and earth to insert in the apple an incentive to concupiscence; by which he was able safely to abstain, by not eating of the apple, therefore dissuaded therefrom; for otherwise he had never at any time been tempted, or stirred up by his genital members. Therefore the apple being eaten, man, from an occult and natural property ingrafted in the fruit, conceived a lust, and sin became luxurious to him, and from thence was made an animal seed, which, hastening into the previous or foregoing dispositions of a sensitive soul, and undergoing the law of other causes, reflected itself into the vital spirit of Adam; and, like an ignis-fatuus, presently receiving an archeus or ruling spirit, and animal idea, it presently conceived a power of propagating an animal and mortal seed, ending into life.

Furthermore, the sacred text hath in many places compelled me unto a perfect position, it making Eve an helper like unto Adam; not, indeed, that she should supply the name, and room of a wife, even as she is called, straightway after sin, for she was a virgin in the intent of the Creator, and afterwards filled with misery: but not, as long as the state of purity presided over innocency, did the will of man overcome her; for the translation of man into Paradise did foreshew another condition of living than that of a beast; and therefore the eating of the apple doth by a most chaste name cover the concupiscence of the flesh, while it contains the "knowledge of good and evil" in this name, and calls the ignorance thereof the state of innocence: for, surely, the attainment of that aforesaid knowledge did nourish a most hurtful death, and an irrevocable deprivation of eternal life: for if man had not tasted the apple, he had lived void of concupiscence, and offsprings had appeared out of Eve (a virgin) from the Holy Spirit.

But the apple being eaten, "presently their eyes were opened," and Adam began lustfully to covet copulation with the naked virgin, and defiled her, the which God had appointed for a naked help unto him. But man prevented the intention of God by a strange generation in the flesh of sin; whereupon there followed the corruption of the former nature, or the flesh of sin, accompanied by concupiscence: neither doth the text insinuate any other mark of "the knowledge of good and evil," than that they "knew themselves to be naked," or, speaking properly, of their virginity being corrupted, polluted with bestial lust, and defiled. Indeed, their whole "knowledge of good and evil" is included in their shame within their privy parts alone; and therefore in the 8th of Leviticus, and many places else in the Holy Scriptures, the privy parts themselves are called by no other etymology than that of shame; for from the copulation of the flesh their eyes were opened, because they then knew that the good being lost, had brought on them a degenerate nature, shamefulness, an intestine and inevitable obligation of death; sent also into their posterity.

Alas! too late, indeed they understood, by the unwonted novelty and shamefulness of their concupiscence, why God had so lovingly forbade the eating of the apple. Indeed, the truth being agreeable unto itself, doth attest the filthiness of impure Adamical generation; for the impurity which had received a contagion from any natural issues whatsoever of menstrues or seed, and that by its touching alone is reckoned equal to that which should by degrees creep on a person from a co-touching of dead carcases, and to be expiated by the same ceremonious rite that the text might agreeably denote, that death began by the concupiscence of the flesh lying hid in the fruit forbidden; therefore, also, the one only healing medicine, of so great an impurity contracted by touching, consisted in washing: under the similitude or likeness thereof, faith and hope, which in baptism are poured on us, are strengthened.

For as soon as Adam knew that by fratricide the first born of mortals, whom he had begotten in the concupiscence of the flesh, had killed his brother, guiltless and righteous as he was; and foreseeing the wicked errors of mortals that would come from thence, he likewise perceived his own miseries in himself; certainly knowing that all these calamities had happened unto him from the sin of concupiscence drawn from the apple, which were unavoidably issuing on his posterity, he thought within himself that the most discreet thing he could do, was hereafter wholly to abstain from his wife, whom he had violated; and therefore he mourned, in chastity and sorrow, a full hundred years; hoping that by the merit of that abstinence, and by an opposition to the concupiscence of the flesh, he should not only appease the wrath of the incensed Deity, but that he should again return into the former splendour and majesty of his primitive innocence and purity. But the repentance of one age being finished, it is most probable the mystery of Christ's incarnation was revealed unto him; neither that man ever could hope to return to the brightness of his ancient purity by his own strength, and much less that himself could reprieve his posterity from death; and that, therefore, marriage was well pleasing, and was after the fall indulged unto him by God because he had determined thus to satisfy his justice at the fulness of times, which should, to the glory of his own name, and the confusion of Satan, elevate mankind to a more sublime and eminent state of blessedness.

From that time Adam began to know his wife, viz. after he was an hundred years old, and to fill the earth, by multiplying according to the blessing once given him, and the law enjoined him--"Be fruitful and multiply."--Yet so, nevertheless, that although. matrimony, by reason of the great want of propagation, and otherwise impossible coursary succession of the primitive divine generation, be admitted as a sacrament of the faithful.

If, therefore, both our first parents, after the eating of the apple, were ashamed, they covered only their privy parts; therefore that shame doth presuppose, and

accuse of something committed against justice--against the intent of the Creator--
and against their own proper nature: by consequence, therefore, that Adamical
generation was not of the primitive constitution of their nature, as neither of the
original intent of the Creator; therefore, when God foretels that the earth shall
bring forth thistles and thorns, and that man shall gain his bread by the sweat of
his brow, they were not execrations, but admonitions, that those sort of things
should be obvious in the earth: and, because that beasts should bring forth in
pain--should plow in sweat--should eat their food with labour and fear, that the
earth should likewise bring forth very many things besides the intention of the
husbandman; therefore, also, that they ought to be nourished like unto brute
beasts, who had begun to generate after the manner of brute beasts.

It is likewise told Eve, after her transgression, that she should bring forth in pain.
Therefore, what hath the pain of bringing forth common with the eating of the
apple, unless the apple had operated about the concupiscence of the flesh, and by
consequence stirred up copulation; and the Creator had intended to dissuade it,
by dehorting from the eating of the apple. For, why are the genital members of
women punished with pains at child-birth, if the eye in seeing the apple, the
hands in cropping it, and the mouth in eating of it, have offended? for was it not
sufficient to have chastised the life with death, and the health with very many
diseases?--Moreover, why is the womb afflicted, as in brutes, with the manner of
bringing forth, if the conception granted to beasts were not forbidden to man?

After their fall, therefore, their eyes were opened, and they were ashamed: it
denotes and signifies that, from the filthiness of concupiscence, they knew that
the copulation of the flesh was forbidden in the most pure innocent chastity of
nature, and that they were overspread with shame, when, their eyes being opened,
their understandings saw that they had committed filthiness most detestable.

But on the serpent and evil spirit alone was the top and summit of the whole
curse, even as the privilege of the woman, and the mysterious prerogative of the
blessing upon the earth, viz. That the woman's seed should bruise the head of the
serpent. So that it is not possible that to bring forth in pain should be a curse; for

24

truly with the same voice of the Lord is pronounced the blessing of the woman, and victory over the infernal spirit.

Therefore Adam was created in the possession of immortality. God intended not that man should be an animal or sensitive creature, nor be born, conceived, or live as an animal; for of truth he was created unto a living soul, and that after the true image of God; therefore he as far differed from the nature of an animal, as an immortal being from a mortal, and as a God-like creature from a brute.

I am sorry that our school-men, many of them, wish, by their arguments of noise and pride, to draw man into a total animal nature (nothing more), drawing (by their logic) the essence of a man essentially from an animal nature: because, although man afterwards procured death to himself and posterity, and therefore may seem to be made nearer the nature of animal creatures, yet it stood not in his power to be able to pervert the species of the divine image: even so as neither was the evil spirit, of a spirit, made an animal, although he became nearer unto the nature of an animal, by hatred and brutal vices. Therefore man remained in his own species wherein he was created; for as often as man is called an animal, or sensitive living creature, and is in earnest thought to be such, so many times the text is falsified which says, "But the serpent was more crafty than all the living creatures of the earth, which the Lord God had made;" because he speaks of the natural craft and subtilty of that living and creeping animal. Again, if the position be true, man was not directed into the propagation of seed or flesh, neither did he aspire unto a sensitive soul; and therefore the sensible soul of Adamical generation is not of a brutal species, because it was raised up by a seed which wanted the original ordination and limitation of any species; and so that, as the sensitive soul in man arose, besides the intent of the Creator and Nature; so it is of no brutal species, neither can it subsist, unless it be continually tied to the mind, from whence it is supported in its life.

Wherefore, while man is of no brutal species, he cannot be an animal in respect to his mind, and much less in respect to his soul, which is of no species.

25

Therefore know, that neither evil spirit, nor whole nature also, can, by any means or any way whatever, change the essence given unto man from his Creator, and by his foreknowledge determined that he should remain continually such as he was created, although he, in the mean time, hath clothed himself with strange properties, as natural unto him from the vice of his own will; for as it is an absurdity to reckon man glorified among animals, because he is not without sense or feeling, so to be sensitive does not shew the inseparable essence of an animal.

Seeing, therefore, our first parents had both of them now felt the effect throughout their whole bodies of the eating, of the apple, or concupiscence of the flesh in their members in Paradise, it shamed them; because their members, which, before, they could rule at their pleasure, were afterwards moved by a proper incentive to lust.

Therefore, on the same clay, not only mortality entered through concupiscence, but it presently after entered into a conceived generation; for which they were, the same day, also driven out of Paradise: hence followed an adulterous, lascivious, beast-like, devilish generation, and plainly incapable of entering into the kingdom of God, diametrically opposite to God's ordination by which means death, and the threatened punishment, corruption, became inseparable to man and his posterity.

Therefore, original sin was effectively bred from the concupiscence of the flesh, but occasioned only by the apple being eaten, and the admonition despised: but the stimulative to concupiscence was placed in the dissuaded tree, and that occult lustful property radically inserted and implanted in it. But when Satan (besides his hope, and the deflowering of the virgin, nothing hindering of it) saw that man was not taken out of the way, according to the forewarning (for he knew not that the Son of God had constituted himself a surety, before the Father, for man) he, indeed, looked at the vile, corrupted, and degenerated nature of man, and saw that a power was withdrawn from him of uniting himself to the God of infinite majesty, and began greatly to rejoice. That joy was of short duration, for, by and by, he likewise knew that marriage was ratified by Heaven--that the divine

26

goodness yet inclined to man--and that Satan's own fallacies and deceits were thus deceived: hence conjecturing that the Son of God was to restore every defect of contagion, and, therefore, perhaps, to be incarnated. He then put himself to work how, or in what manner, he should defile the stock that was to be raised up by matrimony with a mortal soul, so that he might render every conception of God in vain: therefore he stirred up not only his fratricides, and notoriously wicked persons, that there might be evil abounding at all times; but he procured that Atheism might arise, and that, together with Heathenism, it might daily increase, whereby indeed, if he could not hinder the co-knitting of the immortal mind with the sensitive soul, he might, at least, by destroying the law of Nature, bring man unto a level with himself under infernal punishment: but his special care and desire was to expunge totally the immortal mind out of the stock of posterity.

Therefore he (the Devil) stirs up, to this day, detestable copulations in Atheistical libertines: but he saw from thence, that nothing but brutish or savage monsters proceeded, to be abhorred by the very parents themselves; and that the copulation with women was far more plausible to men; and that by this method the generation of men should constantly continue; for he endeavoured to prevent the hope of restoring a remnant, that is, to hinder the incarnation of the Son of God; therefore he attempted, by an application of active things, to frame the seed of man according to his own accursed desire; which, when he had found vain and impossible for him to do, he tried again whether an imp or witch might not be fructified by sodomy; and when this did not fully answer his intentions every way, and he saw that of an ass and a horse a mule was bred, which was nearer a-kin to his mother than his father; likewise that of a coney and dormouse being the father, a true coney was bred, being distinct from his mother, only having a tail like the dormouse; he declined these feats, and betook himself to others worthy, indeed, only of the subtile craft of the Prince of Darkness.

Therefore Satan instituted a connexion of the seed of man with the seed and in the womb of a junior witch, or sorceress, that he might exclude the dispositions unto an immortal mind from such a new, polished conception: and afterwards came forth an adulterous and lascivious generation of Faunii, Satyrs, Gnomes,

Nymphs, Sylphs, Driades, Hamodriades, Neriads, Mermaids, Syrens, Sphynxes, Monsters, &c., using the constellations, and disposing the seed of man for such like monstrous prodigious generations.

And, seeing the Faunii and Nymphs of the woods were preferred before the others in beauty, they afterwards generated their offspring amongst themselves, and at length began wedlocks with men, feigning that, by these copulations, they should obtain an immortal soul for them and their offspring; but this happened through the persuasions and delusions of Satan to admit these monsters to carnal copulation, which the ignorant were easily persuaded to and therefore these Nymphs are called Succubii: although Satan afterwards committed worse, frequently transchanging himself, by assuming the persons of both Incubii and Succubii, in both sexes; but they conceived not a true young by the males, except the Nymphs alone. The which, indeed, seeing the sons of God (that is, men) had now, without distinction, and in many places, taken to be their wives, God was determined to blot out the whole race begotten by these infernal and detestable marriages, through a deluge of waters, that the intent of the evil spirit might be rendered frustrate.

Of which monsters before mentioned, I will here give a striking example from Helmont: for he says, a merchant of Ægina, a countryman of his, sailing various times unto the Canaries, was asked by Helmont for his serious judgment about certain creatures, which the mariners frequently brought home from the mountains, as often as they went, and called them Tude-squils; [24:1] for they were dried dead carcasses, almost three-footed, and so small that a boy might easily carry one of them upon the palm of his hand, and they were of an exact human shape; but their whole dead carcass was clear or transparent as any parchment, and their bones flexible like gristles; against the sun, also, their bowels and intestine were plainly to be seen; which thing I, by Spaniards there born, knew to be true. I considered that, to this day, the destroyed race of the Pygmies were there; for the Almighty would render the expectations of the evil spirit, supported by the abominable actions of mankind, void and vain; and he has, therefore, manifoldly saved us from the craft and subtilty of the Devil, unto whom eternal punishments are due, to his extreme and perpetual confusion, unto the everlasting sanctifying of the Divine Name.

24:1 Stude-quills, or Stew'd quills.

CHAPTER 2. OF THE WONDERS OF NATURAL MAGIC...

OF THE WONDERS OF NATURAL MAGIC, DISPLAYED IN A VARIETY OF SYMPATHETIC AND OCCULT OPERATIONS THROUGHOUT THE FAMILIES OF ANIMALS, PLANTS, METALS, AND STONES, TREATED OF MISCELLANEOUSLY.

THE wonders of Animal Magic we mean fully to display under the title of Magnetism. But here we hasten to investigate by what means, instruments, and effects, we must apply actives to passives, to the producing of rare and uncommon effects; whether by actions, amulets, alligations and suspensions--or rings, papers, unctions, suffumigations, allurements, sorceries, enchantments, images, lights, sounds, or the like. Therefore, to begin with things more simple:-- If any one shall, with an entire new knife, cut asunder a lemon, using words expressive of hatred, contumely, or dislike, against any individual, the absent party, though at an unlimited distance, feels a certain inexpressible and cutting anguish of the heart, together with a cold chilliness and failure throughout the body;-- likewise of living animals, if a live pigeon be cut through the heart, it causes the heart of the party intended to affect with a sudden failure; likewise fear is induced by suspending the magical image of a man by a single thread;--also, death and destruction by means similar to these; and all these from a fatal and magical sympathy.

Likewise of the virtues of simple animals, as well as manual operations, of which we shall speak more anon:--The application of hare's fat pulls out a thorn;-- likewise any one may cure the tooth-ache with the stone that is in the head of the toad; also, if any one shall catch a living frog before sun-rise, and he or she spits in the mouth of the frog, will be cured of an asthmatic consumption;--likewise the right or left eye of the same animal cures blindness; and the fat of a viper cures a bite of the same. Black hellebore easeth the head-ache, being applied to the head, or the powder snuffed lip the nose in a moderate quantity. Coral is a well-known preservative against witchcraft and poisons, which if worn now, in this time, as much round children's necks as usual, would enable them to combat many diseases which their tender years are subjected to, and to which, with fascinations, they often fall a victim. I know how to compose coral amulets, or talismans, which, if suspended even by a thread, shall (God assisting) prevent all harms and accidents of violence from fire, or water, or witchcraft, and help them to withstand all their diseases.

Paracelsus and Helmont both agree, that in the toad, although so irreverent to the sight of man, and so noxious to the touch, and of such strong violent antipathy to the blood of man, I say, out of this hatred Divine Providence hath prepared us a remedy against manifold diseases most inimical to man's nature. The toad hath a natural aversion to man; and this scaled image, or idea of hatred, he carries in his head, eyes, and most powerfully throughout his whole body: now that the toad may be highly prepared for a sympathetic remedy against the plague or other disorders, such as the ague, falling sicknesses, and various others; and that the terror of us, and natural inbred hatred may the more strongly be imprinted and higher ascend in the toad, we must hang him up aloft in a chimney, by the legs, and set under him a dish of yellow wax, to receive whatsoever may come down, or fall from his mouth; let him hang in this position, in our sight, for three or four days, at least till he is dead; now we must not omit frequently to be present in sight of the animal, so that his fears and inbred terror of us, with the ideas of strong hatred, may encrease even unto death.

So you have a most powerful remedy in this one toad, for the curing of forty thousand persons infected with the pest or plague.

Van Helmont's process for making a preservative amulet against the plague is as follows:--

"In the month of July, in the decrease of the moon, I took old toads, whose eyes abounded with white worms hanging forth into black heads, so that both his eyes were totally formed with worms, perhaps fifty in number, thickly compacted together, their heads hanging out; and as oft as any one of them attempted to get out, the toad, by applying his fore-foot, forbade its utterance. These toads being hung up, and made to vomit in the manner before mentioned, I reduced the insects and other matters ejected from the toad, with the waxen dish being added thereto; and the dried carcass of the toad being reduced into powder I formed the whole into troches, with gum-dragon; which, being borne about the left breast, drove speedily away all contagion; and being fast bound to the place affected, thoroughly drew out the poison: and these troches were more potent after they had returned into use divers times than when new. I found them to be a most powerful amulet against the plague; for if the serpent eateth dust all the days of his life, because he was the instrument of sinning; so the toad eats earth, (which he vomits up) all the days of his life; and, according to the Adeptical philosophy, the toad bears an hatred to man, so that he infects some herbs that are useful to man with his poison, in order for his death. But this difference note between the toad and the serpent: the toad, at the sight of man, from a natural quality sealed in him, called antipathy, conceives a great terror or astonishment; which terror from man imprints on this animal a natural efficacy against the images of the affrighted archeus in man For, truly the terror of the toad kills and annihilates the ideas of the affrighted archeus in man, because the terror in the toad is natural, therefore radical."

For the poison of the plague is subdued by the poison of the toad, not by an action primarily destructive, but by a secondary action; as the pestilent idea of hatred or terror extinguishes the ferment, by whose mediation the poison of the plague subsists, and proceeds to infect: for seeing the poison of the plague is the product of the image of the terrified archeus established in a fermental, putrified odour, and mumial air, this coupling ferments the appropriate mean, and immediately the subject of the poison is taken away.

Therefore the opposition of the amulet formed from the body, &c., of the toad, takes away and prevents the baneful and most horrible effects of the pestilential poison and ferment of the plague.

Hence it is conjectured that he is an animal ordained by God, that the idea of his terror being poisonous indeed to himself, should be to us, and to our plague, a poison in terror. Since, therefore, the toad is most fearful at the beholding of man, which in himself, notwithstanding, forms the terror conceived from man, and also the hatred against man, into an image and active real being, and not consisting only in a confused apprehension; hence it happens that a poison ariseth in the toad, which kills the pestilent poison of terror in man; to wit, from whence the archeus waxeth strong, he not only perceiving the pestilent idea to be extinguished in himself; but, moreover, because he knoweth that something inferior to himself is terrified, dismayed, and doth fly. Again, so great is the fear of the toad, that if he is placed directly before thee, and thou dost behold with an intentive furious look, so that he cannot avoid thee, for a quarter of an hour, he dies, 27:1 being fascinated with terror and astonishment.

OF THE SERPENT.

HIPPOCRATES, by the use of some parts of this animal, attained to himself divine honours; for therewith he cured pestilence and contagion, consumptions, and very many other diseases; for he cleansed the flesh of a viper. The utmost part of the tail and head being cut off, he stripped off the skin, casting away the bowels and gall; he reserved of the intestines only the heart and liver; he drew out all the blood, with the vein running down the back-bone; he bruised the flesh and the aforesaid bowels with the bones, and dried them in a warm oven until they could be powdered, which powder he sprinkled on honey; being clarified and boiled, until he knew that the fleshes in boiling had cast aside their virtue, as well in the broth as in the vapours; he then added unto this electuary the spices of his country to cloak the secret. But this cure of diseases by the serpent contains a great mystery, viz. that as death crept in by the serpent of old, itself ought to be mitigated by the death of the serpent; for Adam, being skilful in the properties of all beasts, was not ignorant also that the serpent was more crafty than other living creatures, and that the aforesaid balsam, the remedy of death, lay hid in the serpent; wherefore the spirit of darkness could not more falsely deceive our first parents than tinder the guileful serpent's form; for they foolishly imagined they should escape the death, so sorely threatened by God, by the serpent's aid.

Amber is an amulet:--a piece of red amber worn about one, is a preservative against poisons and the pestilence.

Likewise, a sapphire stone is as effectual. Oil of amber, or amber dissolved in pure spirit of wine, comforts the womb being disordered: if a suffumigation of it be made with the warts of the shank of a horse, it will cure many disorders of that region.

The liver and gall of an eel, likewise, being gradually dried and reduced to powder, and taken in the quantity of a filbert-nut in a glass of warm wine, causes a speedy and safe delivery to women in labour. The liver of a serpent likewise effects the same.

Rhubarb, on account of its violent antipathy to choler, wonderfully purges the same. Music is a well-known specific for curing the bite of a tarantula, or any venomous spider; likewise, water cures the hydrophobia. Warts are cured by paring off the same; or by burying as many pebbles, secretly, as the party has warts. The king's-evil may be cured by the heart of a toad worn about the neck, first being dried.--Hippomanes excites lust by the bare touch, or being suspended on the party. If any one shall spit in the hand with which he struck, or hurt, another, so shall the wound be cured;--likewise, if any one shall draw the halter wherewith a malefactor was slain across the throat of one who hath the quinsey, it certainly cures him in three days; also, the herb cinque-foil being gathered before sun-rise, one leaf thereof cures the ague of one day; three leaves, cures the tertian; and four, the quartan ague. Rape seeds, sown with cursings and imprecations, grows the fairer, and thrives; but if with praises, the reverse. The juice of deadly nightshade, distilled, and given in a proportionate quantity, makes the party imagine almost whatever you chuse. The herb nip, being heated in the hand, and afterwards you hold in your hand the hand of any other party, they shall never quit you, so long as you retain that herb. The herbs arsemart, comfrey, flaxweed, dragon-wort, adder's-tongue, being steeped in cold water, and if for some time being applied on a wound, or ulcer, they grow warm, and are buried in a muddy place, cureth the wound, or sore, to which they were applied. Again, if any one pluck the leaves of asarabacca, drawing them upwards, they will purge another, who is ignorant of the drawing, by vomit only; but if they are wrested downward to the earth, they purge by stool. A sapphire, or a stone that is of a deep blue colour, if it be rubbed on a tumour, wherein the plague discovers itself, (before the party is too far gone) and by and by it be removed from the sick, the absent jewel attracts all the poison or contagion therefrom. And thus much is sufficient to be said concerning natural occult virtues, whereof we speak in a mixed and miscellaneous manner coming to more distinct heads anon.

27:1 I have tried this experiment upon the toad, and other reptiles of his nature, and was satisfied of the truth of this affirmation.

CHAPTER 3. OF AMULETS, CHARMS, AND ENCHANTMENTS

THE instrument of enchanters is a pure, living, breathing spirit of the blood, whereby we bind, or attract, those things which we desire or delight in; so that, by an earnest intention of the mind, we take possession of the faculties in a no less potent manner than strong wines beguile the reason and senses of those who drink them; therefore, to charm, is either to bind with words, in which there is great virtue, as the poet sings--

"Words thrice she spake, which caus'd, at will, sweet sleep
"Appeas'd the troubled waves, and roaring deep."

Indeed, the virtue of man's words are so great, that, when pronounced with a fervent constancy of the mind, they are able to subvert Nature, to cause earthquakes, storms, and tempests. I have, in the country, by only speaking a few words, and used some other things, caused terrible rains and claps of thunder. Almost all charms are impotent without words, because words are the speech of the speaker, and the image of the thing signified or spoken of; therefore, whatever wonderful effect is intended, let the same be performed with the addition of words significative of the will or desire of the operator; for words are a kind of occult vehicle of the image conceived or begotten, and sent out of the body by the soul; therefore, all the forcible power of the spirit ought to be breathed out with vehemency, and an arduous and intent desire; and I know how to speak, and convey words together, so as they may be carried onward to the hearer at a vast distance, no other body intervening, which thing I have done often. Words are also oftentimes delivered to us, seemingly by others, in our sleep, whereby we seem to talk and converse; but then no vocal conversations are of any effect, except they proceed from spiritual and occult causes: such spirits have often manifested singular things to me, while in sleep, the which, in waking, I have thought nought of, until conviction of the truth taught me credulity in such like matters. In the late change of Administration, I knew, at least five days before it actually terminated, that it would be as I described to a few of my friends. These things are not alike manifested to every one; only, I believe, to those who have long seriously attended to contemplations of this abstruse nature; but there are those who will say it is not so, merely because they themselves cannot comprehend such things.

However, not to lose time, we proceed. There are various enchantments, which I have proved, relative to common occurrences of life, viz. a kind of binding to that effect which we desire: as to love, or hatred; or to those things we love, or against those things we hate, in all which there is a magical sympathy above the power of reasoning; therefore, those abstruse matters we feel, are convinced of, and reflect upon, and draw them into our use. I will here set down, while speaking of these things, a very powerful amulet for the stopping, immediately, a bloody-flux; for the which (with a faith) I dare lay down my life for the success, and entire cure.

An Amulet for Flux of Blood.

"In the blood of Adam arose death--in the blood of Christ death is extinguished-- in the same blood of Christ I command thee, O, blood, that thou stop fluxing!" 31:1

In this one godly superstition there will be found a ready, cheap, easy remedy for that dreadful disorder the bloody-flux, whereby a poor miserable wretch will reap more real benefit than in a whole shop of an apothecary's drugs. These four letters are a powerful charm, or amulet, against the common ague; likewise, let them be written upon a piece of clean and new vellum, at any time of the day or night, and they will be found a speedy and certain cure, and much more efficacious than the word Abracadabra: however, as that ancient charm is still (amongst some who pretend to cure agues, &c.) in some repute, I will here set down the form and manner of its being written; 32:1 likewise it must be pronounced, or spoken, in the same order as it is written, with the intent or will of the operator declared at the same time of making it.

31:1 Let the party who pronounces these words hold the other's hand.

CHAPTER 4. OF UNCTIONS, PHILTERS, POTIONS, &C.-- THEIR MAGICAL VIRTUES

UNGUENTS, or unctions, collyries, philters, &c., conveying the virtues of things natural to our spirits, do multiply, transform, transfigure, and transmute it accordingly; they also transpose those virtues, which are in them, into it, so that it not only acts upon its own body, but also upon that which is near it, and affects that (by visible rays, charms, and by touching it) with some agreeable quality like to itself. For, because our spirit is the pure, subtil, lucid, airy, and unctuous vapour of the blood, nothing, therefore, is better adapted for collyriums than the like vapour, which are more suitable to our spirit in substance; for then, by reason of their likeness, they do more stir up, attract, and transform the spirit. The same virtue have other ointments, and confections. Hence, by the touch, often plague, sickness, faintings, poisoning, and love, is induced, either by the hands or clothes being anointed; and often by kissing, things been held in the mouth, love is likewise excited.

Now the sight, as it perceives more purely and clearer than the other senses, seals in us the marks of things more acutely, and does, most of all, and before all others, agree with our fantastic spirit; as is apparent in dreams, when things seen do more often present themselves to us than things heard, or any thin coming under the other senses. Therefore, when collyriums transform the visual spirits, that spirit easily affects the imagination, which, being affected with divers species and forms, transmits the same, by the same spirit, unto the outward sense of sight, by which there is formed in it a perception of such species and forms, in that manner, as if it were moved by external objects, that there appear to be seen terrible images, spirits, and the like. There are some collyriums which make us see the of images of spirits of the air, or elsewhere; which I can make of the gall of a man, and the eyes of a black cat, and some other things. The same is made, likewise, of the blood of a lapwing, bat, and a goat; and if a smooth shining piece of steel be smeared over with the juice of mugwort, and be made to fume, it causes invocated spirits to appear. There are some perfumes, or suffumigations and unctions, which make men speak in their sleep, walk, and do those things that are done by men that are awake, and often what, when awake, they cannot, or dare not do; others, again, make men hear horrid or delightful sounds, noises, and the like.

And, in some measure, this is the cause why mad and melancholy men believe they hear and see things equally false and improbable, falling into most gross and pitiful delusions, fearing where no fear is, and angry where there is none to contend. Such passions as these we can induce by magical vapours, confections, perfumes, collyries, unguents, potions, poisons, lamps, lights, &c.; likewise by mirrors, images, enchantments, charms, sounds, and music; also by divers rites, observations, ceremonies, religion, &c.

32:1

It is here to be particularly noticed by us, that, in forming of a charm, or amulet, it will be of no effect except the very soul of the operator is strongly and intensely exerted and impressed, as it were, and the image of the idea sealed on the charm, or amulet for, without this, in vain will be all the observation of times, hours and constellations therefore, this I have thought fit to mention, once for all, that it may be almost always uppermost in the mind of the operator, for, without this one thing being observed and noticed, many who form seals, &c., do fall short of the wished for effect.

ABRACADABRA
BRACADABRA
RACADABRA
ACADABRA
CADABRA
ADABRA
DABRA
ABRA
BRA
RA
A

CHAPTER 5. OF MAGICAL SUSPENSIONS AND ALLIGATIONS...

OF MAGICAL SUSPENSIONS AND ALLIGATIONS--SHEWING HOW, AND BY WHAT POWER, THEY RECEIVE VIRTUE, AND ARE EFFICACIOUS IN NATURAL MAGIC.

WHEN the soul of the world, by its virtue, doth make all things (that are naturally generated, or artificially made) fruitful, by sealing and impressing on them celestial virtues for the working of some wonderful effect, then things themselves not only applied by collyry, or suffume, or ointment, or any other such like way; but when they are conveniently bound to, or wrapped up, or suspended about the neck, or any other way applied, although by ever so easy a contact, they do impress their virtue upon us: by these alligations, &c., therefore, the accidents of the body and mind are- changed into sickness or health, valour, fear, sadness or joy, and the like; they render those that carry them, gracious, terrible, acceptable, rejected, honoured, beloved, or hateful and abominable.

Now these kind of passions are conceived to be infused no otherwise than is manifest in the grafting of trees, where the vital life and virtue is communicated from the trunk to the twig engrafted into it, by way of contact and alligation; so in the female palm-tree, when she comes near to the male, her boughs bend to the male, which the gardener seeing, he binds them together by ropes across, but soon becomes straight, as if by the continuation of the rope she had received a propagating virtue from the male. And it is said, if a woman takes a needle, and bewray it with dung, and put it up in earth in which the carcass of a man has been buried, and carry it about her in a piece of cloth used at a funeral, no man can defile her as long as she carries that.

Now by these examples we see how, by certain alligations of certain things, also suspensions, or by the most simple contact or continuation of any thread, we may be able to receive some virtues thereby; but it is necessary to know the certain rule of magical alligation and suspension; and the manner that the art requires is this, viz. that they must be done under a certain and suitable constellation; and they must be done with wire, or silken threads, or sinews of certain animals; and those things that are to be wrapped up, are to be done in the leaves of herbs, or skins of animals, or membraneous parchments, &c. For, if you would procure the solary virtue of any thing, this is to be wrapped up in bay leaves, or the skin of a lion, hung round the neck with gold, silk, or purple or yellow thread: while the sun reigns in the heavens, so shalt thou be endued with the virtue of that thing. So if a saturnine quality or thing be desired, thou shalt in like manner take that thing, while Saturn reigns, and wrap it up in the skin of an ass, or in a cloth used at a funeral, especially if melancholy or sadness is to be induced, and with a sad, or ash, or leaden, or black silk or thread, hang it about thy neck; and so in the same manner we must proceed with the rest.

CHAPTER 6. OF ANTIPATHIES

IT is necessary, in this place, to speak of the antipathies of natural things, seeing it is requisite, as we go on, to have a thorough knowledge of that obstinate contrariety of Nature, where any thing shuns its contrary, and drives it, as it were, out of its presence. Such antipathy as this has the root rhubarb against choler; treacle against poison; the sapphire stone against hot biles, feverish heats, and diseases of the eyes; the amethyst against drunkenness; the jasper against the bloody-flux and offensive imaginations; the emerald, and agnus castus against lust; achates or agates against poison; piony against the falling sickness; coral against the ebullition of black choler, and pains of the stomach; the topaz against spiritual heats, such as are covetousness, lust, and all manner of love excesses. The same antipathy is there, also, of pismires against the herb organ, and the wing of a bat, and the heart of a lapwing, from the presence of which they fly. Also, the organ is contrary to a certain poisonous fly which cannot resist the sun, and resists salamanders, and loaths cabbage with such a deadly hatred that they cannot endure each other. So they say cucumbers hate oil. And the gall of a crow makes even men fearful, and drives them from the place wherein it is placed. A diamond disagrees with a loadstone; that being present, it suffers no iron to be drawn to it. Sheep avoid frog-parsley as a deadly thing; and, what is more wonderful, Nature hath depictured the sign of this antipathy upon the livers of sheep, in which the very figure of frog-parsley doth naturally appear. Again, goats hate garden-basil, as if there was nothing more pernicious. And, amongst animals, mice and weasels disagree; so a lizard is of a contrary nature to a scorpion, and induces great terror to the scorpion with its very sight, and they are therefore killed with the oil of them; which oil will likewise cure the wounds made by scorpions. There is a great enmity between scorpions and mice; therefore if a mouse be applied to the bite of a scorpion, he cures it. Nothing is so much an enemy to snakes as crabs; and if swine be hurt by them, they are cured by crabs; the sun, also being in Cancer, serpents are tormented. Also, the scorpion and crocodile kill one another; and if the bird ibis does but touch a crocodile with one of his feathers, he makes him unmoveable. The bird called a bustard flies away at the sight of a horse; and a hart at the sight of a ram, or a viper. An elephant trembles at the hearing of the grunting of a hog; so doth a lion at the crowing of a cock; and a panther will not touch them that are anointed with the fat of a hen, especially if garlick has been put into it. There is also an enmity between foxes and swans; bulls and jackdaws. And some birds are at a perpetual variance, as daws and owls; kites and crows; turtle and ring-tail; egepis and eagles; also, harts and dragons. Amongst water animals, there is a great antipathy between dolphins and whirlpools; the mullet and pike; lamprey and conger; pourcontrel and lobster, which latter, but seeing the former, is nearly struck dead with fear; but the lobster tears the conger. The civet-cat cannot resist the panther; and if the skins of both be hung up against each other, the skin or hairs of the panther will fall off. Apollo says, in his hieroglyphics, if any one be girt about with the skin of a civet-cat, he may pass safe through his enemies. The lamb flies from the wolf; and if the tall, skin, or head of lupus be hung up in the sheeps'-cot, they cannot eat their meat for very fear. And Pliny mentions the bird called the marlin, that breaks the eggs of the crow, whose young are annoyed by the fox; that she also will pinch the whelps of the fox, and the fox likewise, which, when the crow sees, they help the fox against her as against a common enemy. The linnet lives in, and eats thistles; yet she hates the ass, because he eats the thistles and flowers of them. There is so great an enmity between the little bird called esalon and the ass, that their blood will not mix; and that, at the simple braying of the ass, both the esalon's eggs and young perish together. There is, also, a total antipathy of the olive-tree to the harlot; that, if she plant it, it will neither thrive nor prosper, but wither. A lion fears lighted torches, and is tamed by nothing sooner. The wolf fears not sword or spear, but a stone; by the throwing of which a wound being made, worms breed in the wolf. A horse fears a camel so much that he cannot endure the picture of that beast. An elephant, when he rages, is quieted by seeing a cock. A snake is afraid of a naked man, but pursues one clothed. A mad bull is tamed by being tied to a fig-tree. Amber attracts all things to it but garden-basil, and things smeared with oil, between which there is a natural antipathy.

CHAPTER 7. OF THE OCCULT VIRTUES OF THINGS...

OF THE OCCULT VIRTUES OF THINGS WHICH ARE INHERENT IN THEM ONLY IN THEIR LIFE-TIME, AND SUCH AS REMAIN IN THEM EVEN AFTER DEATH.

IT is expedient for us to know that there are some things which retain virtue only while they are living, others even after death. So in the cholic, if a live duck be applied to the belly, it takes away the pain, and the duck dies. If you take the heart out of any animal, and, while it is warm, bind it to one that has a quartan fever, it drives it away. So if any one shall swallow the heart of a lapwing, swallow, weasel, or a mole, while it is yet living and warm with natural heat, it improves his intellect, and helps him to remember, understand, and foretel things to come. Hence this general rule,--that whatever things are taken for magical uses from animals, whether they are stones, members, hair, excrements, nails, or any thing else, they must be taken from those animals while they are yet alive, and, if it is possible, that they may live afterwards. If you take the tongue of a frog, you put the frog into water again;--and Democritus writes, that if any one shall take out the tongue of a water-frog, no other part of the animal sticking to it, and lay it upon the place where the heart beats of a woman, she is compelled, against her will, to answer whatsoever you shall ask of her. Also, take the eyes of a frog, which must be extracted before sun-rise, and bound to the sick party, and the frog to be let go again blind into the water, the party shall be cured of a tertian ague; also, the same will, being bound with the flesh of a nightingale in the skin of a hart, keep a person always wakeful without sleeping. Also, the roe of the fork fish being bound to the navel, is said to cause women an easy child-birth, if it be taken from it alive, and the fish put into the sea again. So the right eye of a serpent being applied to the soreness of the eyes, cures the same, if the serpent be let go alive. So, likewise, the tooth of a mole, being taken out alive, and afterwards let go, cures the tooth-ache; and dogs will never bark at those who have the tail of a weasel that has escaped. Democritus says, that if the tongue of the cameleon be taken alive, it conduces to good success in trials, and likewise to women in labour;

but it must be hung up on some part of the outside of the house, otherwise, if brought into the house, it might be most dangerous.

There are very many properties that remain after death; and these are things in which the idea of the matter is less swallowed up, according. to Plato, in them: even after death, that which is immortal in them will work some wonderful things:--as in the skins we have mentioned of several wild beasts, which will corrode and eat one another after death; also, a drum made of the rocket-fish drives away all creeping things at what distance soever the sound of it is heard; and the strings of an instrument made of the guts of a wolf, and being strained upon a harp or lute, with strings made of sheep-guts, will make no harmony.

CHAPTER 8. OF THE WONDERFUL VIRTUES OF SOME KIND OF PRECIOUS STONES

IT is a common opinion of magicians, that stones inherit great virtues, which they receive through the spheres and activity of the celestial influences, by the medium of the soul or spirit of the world. Authors very much disagree in respect of the probability of their actually having such virtues in potentia, some debating warmly against any occult or secret virtue lying hid in them; others, as warmly, shewing the causes and effects of these sympathetic properties. However, to leave these trifling arguments to those who love cavil and contentions better than I do, and, as I have neither leisure nor inclination to enter the lists with sophists, and tongue-philosophers; I say, that these occult virtues are disposed throughout the animal, vegetable, and mineral kingdoms, by seeds, or ideas originally emanating from the Divine mind, and through supercelestial spirits and intelligence always operating, according to their proper offices and governments allotted them; which virtues are infused, as we before said, through the medium of the Universal Spirit, as by a general and manifest sympathy and antipathy established in the law of Nature. Amongst a variety of examples, the loadstone is one most remarkable proof of the sympathy and antipathy we speak of. However to hasten to the point. Amongst stones, those which resemble the rays of the sun by their golden sparklings, (as does the glittering stone ætites) prevent the failing-sickness and poisons, if worn on the finger; so the stone which is called oculis solis, or eye of the sun, being in figure like to the apple of the eye, from which shines forth a ray, comforts the brain, and strengthens sight; the carbuncle, which shines by night, hath a virtue against all airy and vaporous poisons; the chrysolite stone, of a light green colour, when held against the sun, there shines in it a ray like a star of gold; this is singularly good for the lungs, and cures asthmatical complaints; and if it be bored through, and the hollow filled with the mane of an ass, and bound to the left arm, it chases away all foolish and idle imaginations and melancholy fears, and drives away folly. The stone called iris, which is like crystal in colour, being found with six corners, when held in the shade, and the sun suffered to shine through it, represents a natural rainbow in the air. The stone heliotropium, green, like a jasper or emerald, beset with red specks, makes the wearer constant, renowned, and famous, and conduces to long life; there is, likewise, another wonderful property in this stone, and that is, that it so dazzles the eyes of men, that it causes the bearer to be invisible; but then there must be applied to it the herb bearing the same name, viz. heliotropium, or the sun-flower; and these kind of virtues Albertus Magnus, and William of Paris, mention in their writings. The jacinth also possesses virtue from the sun against poisons, pestilences, and pestiferous vapours; likewise it renders the bearer pleasant and acceptable; conduces, also, to gain money; being simply held in the mouth, it wonderfully cheers the heart, and strengthens the mind. Then there is the pyrophilus, of a red mixture, which Albertus Magnus reports that Æsculapius makes mention of in one of his epistles to Octavius Cæsar, saying, "There is a certain poison, so intensely cold, which preserves the heart of man, being taken out, from burning; so that if it be put into the fire for any time, it is turned into a stone, which stone is called pyrophilus:" it possesses a wonderful virtue against poison; and it infallibly renders the wearer thereof renowned and dreadful to his enemies. Apollonius is reported to have found a stone called pantaura, (which will attract other stones, as the loadstone does iron) most powerful against all poisons: it is spotted like the panther, and therefore some naturalists have given this stone the name of pantherus: Aaron calls it evanthum; and some, on account of its variety, call it pantochras.

CHAPTER 9. OF THE MIXTURES OF NATURAL THINGS ONE WITH ANOTHER...

OF THE MIXTURES OF NATURAL THINGS ONE WITH ANOTHER, AND THE PRODUCING OF MONSTROUS ANIMALS, BY THE APPLICATION OF NATURAL MAGIC.

MAGICIANS, students, and observers of the operations of Nature, know how, by the application of active forms to a matter fitly disposed, and made, as it were, a proper recipient, to effect many wonderful and uncommon things that seem strange, and above Nature, by gathering this and that thing beneficial and conducive to that effect which we desire; however, it is evident that all the powers and virtues of the inferior bodies are not found comprehended in any one single thing, but are dispersed amongst many of the compounds here amongst us; wherefore it is necessary, if there be a hundred virtues of the sun dispersed through so many animals, plants, metals, or stones, we should gather all these together, and bring them all into one form, in which we shall see all the said virtues, being united, contained. Now there is a double virtue in commixing: one, viz. which was once planted in its parts, and is celestial; the other is obtained by a certain artificial mixture of things, mixed among themselves, according to a due proportion, such as agree with the heavens under a certain constellation; and this virtue descends by a certain similitude or likeness that is in things amongst themselves, by which they are drawn or attracted towards their superiors, and as much as the following do by degrees correspond with them that go before, where the patient is fitly applied to its agent. So from a certain composition of herbs, vapours, and such like, made according to the rules of Natural and Celestial Magic, there results a certain common form; of which we shall deliver the true and infallible rules and experiments in our Second Book, where we have written expressly on the same.

We ought, likewise, to understand that by how much more noble and excellent the form of any thing is, by so much the more it is prone, and apt to receive, and powerful to act. Then the virtue of things do indeed become wonderful; viz. when they are applied to matters, mixed and prepared in fit seasons to give them life, by procuring life for them from the stars, our own spirit powerfully co-operating therewith; for there is so great a power in prepared matters, which we see do then receive life, when a perfect mixture of qualities do break the former contrariety; for so much the more perfect life things receive, by as much the temper and composition is free from contrariety. Now the heavens, as a prevailing cause, do, from the beginning of every thing, (to be generated by the concoction and perfect digestion of the matter) together with life, bestow celestial influences and wonderful gifts, according to the capacity that is in that life and sensible soul to receive more noble and sublime virtues. For the celestial virtue otherwise lies asleep, as sulphur kept from flame; but in living bodies it doth always burn, as kindled sulphur, which, by its vapour, fills all the places that are near.

There is a book called, "A Book of the Laws of Pluto," which speaks of monstrous generations, which are not produced according to the laws of Nature. Of these things which follow we know to be true; viz. of worms are generated gnats; of a horse, wasps; of a calf and ox, bees. Take a living crab, his legs being broken off, and he buried under the earth, a scorpion is produced. If a duck be dried into powder, and put into water, frogs are soon generated; but if he be baked in a pie, and cut into pieces, and be put in a moist place under ground, toads are generated. Of the herb garden-basil, bruised, and put between two stones, are generated scorpions. Of the hairs of a menstruous woman, put under dung, are bred serpents; and the hair of a horse's tail, put into water, receives life, and is turned into a most pernicious worm. And there is an art wherewith a hen, sitting upon eggs, may be generated the form of a man, which I myself know how to do, and which magicians call the mandrake, and it hath in it wonderful virtues.

You must, therefore, know which and what kind of matters are either of art or nature, begun or perfected, or compounded of more things, and what celestial influences they are able to receive. For a congruity of natural things is sufficient for the receiving of influence from celestial because, nothing hindering, the celestials send forth their light upon inferiors they suffer no matter to be destitute of their virtue. Wherefore as much matter as is perfect and pure is, as we before said, fitted to receive celestial influences; for that is the binding and continuing of the matter of the soul to the world, which doth daily flow in upon things natural, and all things which Nature hath prepared, that it is impossible that a prepared matter should not receive life, or a more noble form.

CHAPTER 10. OF THE ART OF FASCINATION...

OF THE ART OF FASCINATION, BINDING, SORCERIES, MAGICAL CONFECTIONS, LIGHTS, CANDLES, LAMPS, &c. &c.; BEING THE CONCLUSION OF THE NATURAL MAGIC. [43:1]

WE have so far spoken concerning the great virtues, and wonderful efficacy, of natural things; it remains now that we speak of a wonderful power and faculty of fascination; Or, more properly, a magical and occult binding of men into love or hatred, sickness or health;--also, the binding of thieves, that they cannot steal in any place; or to bind them that they cannot remove, from whence they may be detected;--the binding of merchants, that they cannot buy nor sell;--the binding of an army, that they cannot pass over any bounds;--the binding of ships, so that no wind, though ever so strong, shall be able to carry them out of that harbour;--the binding of a mill, that it cannot, by any means whatsoever, be turned to work;-- the binding of a cistern, or fountain, that the water cannot be drawn up out of them;--the binding of the ground, so that nothing will bring forth fruit, or flourish in it; also, that nothing can be built upon it;--the binding of fire, that, though it be ever so strong, it shall burn no combustible thing that is put to it;-- also, the binding of lightnings and tempests, that they shall do no hurt;--the binding of dogs, that they cannot bark;--also, the binding of birds and wild beasts, that they shall not be able to run or fly away; and things familiar to these, which are hardly creditable, yet known by experience. Now how it is that these kind of bindings are made and brought to pass, we must know. They are thus done: by sorceries, collyries, unguents, potions, binding to and hanging up of talismans, by charms, incantations, strong imaginations, affections, passions, images, characters, enchantments, imprecations, lights, and by sounds, numbers, words, names, invocations, swearings, conjurations, consecrations, and the like.

OF SORCERIES.

THE force of sorceries are, no doubt, very powerful; indeed, they are able to confound, subvert, consume, and change all inferior things; likewise there are sorceries by which we can suspend the faculties of men and beasts. Now, as we have promised, we will shew what some of these kind of sorceries are, that, by the example of these, there may be a way opened for the whole subject of them. Of these, the first is menstruous blood, which, how much power it has in sorcery, we will now consider:--First, if it comes over new wine, it will turn it sour; and if it does but touch a vine, it will spoil it for ever; and, by its very touch, it renders all plants and trees barren, and those newly set, die; it burns up all the herbs in the garden, and makes fruit fall from trees; it makes dim the brightness of a looking-glass, dulls the edges of knives and razors, dims the beauty of polished ivory, and makes iron rusty; it likewise makes brass rusty, and to smell very strong; by the taste, it makes dogs run mad, and, being thus mad, if they once bite any one, that wound is incurable; it destroys whole hives of bees, and drives them away, if it does but touch them; it makes linen black that is boiled with it; it makes mares cast their foals by touching them with it, and women miscarry; it makes asses barren if they cat of the corn touched by it. The ashes of menstruous clothes cast upon purple garments, that are to be washed, change their colour, and likewise take away the colour of flowers. It also drives away tertian and quartan agues, if it be put into the wool of a black ram, and tied up in a silver bracelet; as also if the soles of the patient's feet be anointed therewith, and especially if it be done by the woman herself, the patient not knowing what she uses. It likewise cures the falling sickness; but most especially it cures them that are afraid of water or drink after they are bitten by a mad dog, if only a menstruous cloth be put under the cup. Likewise, if a menstruous woman shall walk naked, before sun-rise, in a field of standing corn, all hurtful things perish; but if after sun-rise, the corn withers; also, they are able to expel hail, rain, thunders, and lightnings; more of which Pliny mentions. Know this, that if they happen at the decrease of the moon, they are a much greater poison than in the increase, and yet much greater if they happen between the decrease and change; but if they happen in the eclipse of the sun or moon, they are a most incurable and violent poison. But they are of the greatest force when they happen in the first years of the virginity, for then if they but touch the door-posts of a house, no mischief can take effect in it. And some say that the threads of any garment touched therewith cannot be burnt, and if they are cast into a fire, it will spread no farther. Also it is noted, that the root of piony being given with castor, and smeared over with a menstruous cloth, it certainly cureth the falling sickness.

Again, let the stomach of a hart be roasted, and to it be put a perfume made with a menstruous cloth; it will make cross-bows useless for the killing of any game. The hairs of a menstruous woman, put under dung, breeds serpents; and if they are burnt, will drive away serpents with the fume. So great and powerful a poison is in them, that they are a poison to poisonous creatures.

We next come to speak of hippomanes, which, amongst sorceries, are not accounted the least: and this is a little venemous piece of flesh, the size of a fig, and black, which is in the forehead of a colt newly foaled, which, unless the mare herself doth presently eat, she will hardly ever love her foles, or let them suck; and this is a most powerful philter to cause love, if it be powdered, and drank in a cup with the blood of him that is in love: such a potion was given to Medea by Jason.

There is another sorcery which is called hippomanes, viz. a venomous liquor issuing out of the share of a mare at the time she lusts after the horse. The civet-cat, also, abounds with sorceries; for the posts of a door being touched with her blood, the arts of jugglers and sorcerers are so invalid that evil spirits can by no means be called up, or compelled to talk with them:--This is Pliny's report. Also, those that are anointed with the oil of her left foot, being boiled with the ashes of the ancle bone of the same and the blood of a weasel, shall become odious to all. The same, also, is to be done with the eye being decocted. If any one hath a little of the strait-gut of this animal about him, and it is bound to the left arm, it is a charm; that if he does but look upon a woman, it will cause her to follow him at all opportunities; and the skin of this animal's forehead withstands witchcraft.

We next come to speak of the blood of a basilisk, which magicians call the blood of Saturn.--This procures (by its virtue) for him that carries it about him, good success of petitions from great men; likewise makes him amazingly successful in the cure of diseases, and the grant of any privilege. They say, also, that a tike, if it be taken out of the left car of a dog, and it be altogether black, if the sick person shall answer him that brought it in, and who, standing at his feet, shall ask him concerning his disease, there is certain hope of life; and that he shall die if he make him no answer. They say, also, that a stone bitten by a mad dog causes discord, if it be put into drinks; and if any one shall put the tongue of a dog, dried, into his shoe, or some of the powder, no dog is able to bark at him who hath it; and more powerful this, if the herb hound's-tongue be put with it. And the membrane of the secundine of a bitch does the same; likewise, dogs will not bark at him who hath the heart of a dog in his pocket.

The red toad (Pliny says) living in briers and brambles, is full of sorceries, and is capable of wonderful things: there is a little bone in his left side, which being cast into cold water, makes it presently hot; by which, also, the rage of dogs are restrained, and their love procured, if it be put in their drink, making them faithful and serviceable; if it be bound to a woman, it stirs up lust. On the contrary, the bone which is on the right side makes hot water cold, and it binds it so that no heat can make it hot while it there remains. It is a certain cure for quartans, if it be bound to the sick in a snake's skin; and like wise cures all fevers, the St. Anthony's fire, and restrains love and lust. And the spleen and heart are effectual antidotes against the poisons of the said toad. Thus much Pliny writes.

Also it is said, that the sword with which a man is slain hath wonderful power; for if the snaffle of a bridle, or bit, or spurs, be made of it, with these a horse ever so wild is tamed, and made gentle and obedient. They say, if we dip a sword, with which any one was beheaded, in wine, that it cures the quartan, the sick being given to drink of it. There is a liquor made, by which men are made as raging and furious as a bear, imagining themselves in every respect to be changed into one; and this is done by dissolving or boiling the brains and heart of that animal in new wine, and giving any one to drink out of a skull, and, while the force of the draught operates, he will fancy every living creature to be a bear like to himself; neither can any thing divert or cure him till the fumes and virtue of the liquor are entirely expended, no other distemper being perceivable in him.

The most certain cure of a violent head-ache, is to take any herb growing upon the top of the head of an image; the same being bound, or hung about one with a red thread, it will soon allay the violent pain thereof.

OF MAGICAL LIGHTS, CANDLES, LAMPS, &c.

THERE are made, artificially, some kinds of lamps, torches, candles, and the like, of some certain and appropriate materials and liquors opportunely gathered and collected for this purpose, which, when they are lighted and shine alone, produce some wonderful effects. There is a poison from mares, after copulation, which, being lighted in torches composed of their fat and marrow, doth represent on the walls a monstrous deformity of horses' heads, which thing is both easy and pleasant to do: the like may be done of asses and flies. And the skin of a serpent or snake, lighted in a green lamp, makes the images of the same to appear; and grapes produce the same effect, if, when they are in their flowers, you shall take a phial, and bind it to them, filled with oil, and shall let them remain so till they are ripe, and then the oil be lighted in a lamp, you shall see a prodigious quantity of grapes; and the same in other fruits. If centaury be mixed with honey and the blood of a lapwing, and be put in a lamp, they that stand about will be of a gigantic stature; and if it be lighted in a clear evening, the stars will seem scattered about.

The ink of the cuttle-fish being put into a lamp, makes Blackamoors appear. So, also, a candle made of some saturnine things, such as man's fat and marrow, the fat of a black cat, with the brains of a crow or raven, which being extinguished in the mouth of a man lately dead, will afterwards, as often as it shines alone, bring great horror and fear upon the spectators about it.

Of such like torches, candles, lamps, &c., (of which we shall speak further in our Book of Magnetism and Mummies) Hermes speaks largely of; also Plato and Chyrannides; and, of the later writers, Albertus Magnus makes particular mention of the truth and efficacy of these, in a treatise on these particular things relative to lights, &c.

OF THE ART OF FASCINATION, OR BINDING BY THE LOOK OR. SIGHT.

WE call fascination a binding, because it is effected by a look, glance, or observation, in which we take possession of the spirit, and overpower the same, of those we mean to fascinate or suspend; for it comes through the eyes, and the instrument by which we fascinate or bind is a certain, pure, lucid, subtil spirit, generated out of the ferment of the purer blood by the heat of the heart, and the firm, determined, and ardent will of the soul which directs it to the object previously disposed to be fascinated. This doth always send forth by the eyes rays or beams, carrying with them a pure subtil spirit or vapour into the eye or blood of him or her that is opposite. So the eye, being opened and intent upon any one with a strong imagination, doth dart its beams, which are the vehicle of the spirit, into whatever we will affect or bind, which spirit striking the eye of them who are fascinated, being stirred up in the heart and soul of him that sends them forth, and possessing the breast of them who are struck, wounds their hearts, infects their spirits, and overpowers them.

Know, likewise, that in witches, those are most bewitched, who, with often looking, direct the edge of their sight to the edge of the sight of those who bewitch or fascinate them; whence arose the saying of "Evil eyes, &c." For when their eyes are reciprocally bent one upon the other, and are joined beams to beams, and lights to lights, then the spirit of the one is joined to the spirit of the other, and then are strong ligations made; and most violent love is stirred up, only with a sudden looking on, as it were, with the darting a look, or piercing into the very inmost of the heart, whence the spirit and amorous blood, being thus wounded, are carried forth upon the lover, and enchanter; no otherwise than the spirit and the blood of him that is murdered is upon the murderer, who, if standing near the body killed, the blood flows afresh, which thing has been tried by repeated experiments.

So great power is there in fascination that many uncommon and wonderful things are thereby effected, especially when the vapours of the eyes are subservient to the affection; therefore collyries, ointments, alligations, &,c. are used to affect and corroborate the spirit in this or that manner: to induce love, they use venereal collyriums, as hippomanes, blood of doves, &c. To induce fear, they use martial collyriums, as the eyes of wolves, bear's fat, and the civet-cat. To procure misery, or sickness, they use saturnine, and so on.

Thus much we have thought proper to speak concerning Natural Magic, in which we have, as it may be said, only opened the first chamber of Nature's storehouse; indeed we should have inserted many more things here, but as they fall more properly under the heads of Magnetism, Mummy, &c., to which we refer the reader, we shall take our leave of the reader for the present, that we may give him time to breathe, likewise to digest what he has here feasted upon; and, while he is preparing to enter the unlocked chambers of Magic and Nature, we will procure him a rich service of most delicious meats, fit for the hungry and thirsty traveller through the vast labyrinths of wisdom and true science.

END OF THE NATURAL MAGIC.

THE Author having, under the title of Natural Magic, collected and arranged every thing that was curious, scarce, and valuable, as well his own experiments, as those in which he has been indefatigable in gathering from the science and practice of Magical Authors, and those the most ancient and abstruse, as may be seen in the list at the end of the Book, where he has put down the names of the authors, from which he has translated many things that were never yet published in the English language, particularly Hermes, Tritemius, Paracelsus, Bacon, Dee, Porta, Agrippa, &c. &c. &c.; from whom he has not been ashamed to borrow what he thought and knew would be valuable and gratifying to the sons of Wisdom, in addition to many other rare and uncommon experiments relative to this art.

43:1 The latter part of this Chapter serves as a rule to be observed in the composition of all kinds of mixed experiments; and it is as appropriate to the materials collected for talismans, seals, &c. treated of in our Celestial Magic, Book II.--F. B.

The Jewel of Alchymy

THE

TRUE SECRET OF THE PHILOSOPHERS' STONE;

OR,

JEWEL OF ALCHYMY.

WHEREIN
THE PROCESS OF MAKING THE GREAT ELIXIR

is discovered;

BY WHICH BASE METALS MAY BE TURNED INTO PURE GOLD; CONTAINING THE MOST EXCELLENT AND PROFITABLE INSTRUCTIONS IN THE

HERMETIC ART;

DISCOVERING THAT VALUABLE AND SECRET MEDICINE OF THE PHILOSOPHERS,

To make Men Healthy, Wise, and Happy.

BY F. BARRETT,

STUDENT OF CHEMISTRY, NATURAL PHILOSOPHY, &c., 1801.

EPISTLE TO MUSEUS

"Thou, O, Museus! whose mind is high,
"Observe my words, and read them with thine eye
"These secrets in thy sacred breast repone,
"And in thy journey think of God alone;
"The Author of all things, that cannot die
"Of whom we now shall speak---------"

I TELL thee here, Museus, to observe our words, and read them with thine eye, that is, the eye of thine understanding; for, know, there are many that hear us speak, that read not the meaning of our words. Wherefore shouldst thou contemplate these mysteries with so much constancy of mind, if thou didst not perceive in them some great good most desirable?--Listen, then, O, young man, and hear our words! We will shew thee the dangerous precipice of vanity and head-long desire--we will describe to thee the stubborn and fatal will of our passions, even with tears of contrition, and heartfelt compassion for thy inexperience--we will lead thee, as it were, by the hand, through those labyrinths of vice, wherewith thou art daily surrounded; and, however prejudiced thou mightest be against the receiving of our doctrine, yet, be assured, we have in our possession the magical virtue and power of binding thee to our principles, and making thee happy, in spite of thyself. Here is a great secret! thou shalt say--every man wishes to be happy--which I grant; but my answer is--most men prevent their own happiness; they destroy it, by suffering themselves to be governed by the outward principle of the flesh, thinking the greatest good to be in the satisfying of their carnal appetites, or in the amassing together heaps of wealth, whereby they thrust down the meek and poor, raising up the standards of Pride, Envy, and Oppression. These things every day's experience confirms; nay, there are some so blind, that, in the possession of much wealth, they think there is nothing beyond it; insomuch, that they triumph in lust, oppression, revenge, and contumely. But how is it, thou wilt say, that, seeing man is a reasonable being, he can possibly give up his government so easily?--I say, when man suffers the unreasonable and bestial part to deprave him, then he immediately becomes a slave, (and the vilest of slavery is that which deprives man of his social virtues;) for then, although in the possession of great worldy things, such as houses, estates, and all other temporal gifts, yet he becomes an immediate instrument to the Prince of this World and the Powers of Darkness, seeing that those riches he inherits are merely given him in this life, to bestow upon others those necessaries and comforts which he himself does not feel the want of, and by which he might, if not blinded by his passions and lusts, secure himself an eternal and incorruptible treasure. But he who possesses treasures without mercy, liberality, bounty, charity, &c., robs the Eternal Author of all good, of the honour due unto him, and, in short, is working destruction to his own soul; his riches, instead of benefitting himself and others, eventually and finally terminates as a curse: while he lives here he is a scourge to society; and, after he leaves this, it is plain enough pointed out in the New Testament what will he his situation and condition.

Therefore, thou young man, that hast but a few years to live, study how to attain the stone we teach of: it will protract the beauty of thy youth, though thou shouldst live for centuries--it will ever supply thee with the means of comforting the afflicted; insomuch, that when thou hast attained this truly desirable and most perfect talisman, thy life will become soft and pleasant; no cares, nor corroding pangs--no self-torment will ever invade thy mind; neither shalt thou want the means to be happy, in respect of the possession of the goods of this life, but shalt have abundantly. But how, and from what source, all this is to proceed--out of what thing, or matter thou shalt attain thy wished-for end--the studying of the ensuing Treatise will sufficiently shew.

TO THE READER

ALTHOUGH we do not, in any point of science, arrogate perfection in ourselves, yet something we have attained by dear experience, by diligent labour, and by study, worthy of being communicated for the instruction of either the licentious libertine, or the grave student--the observer of Nature; and this, our Work, we concentrated into a focus: it is, as it were, a spiritual essence drawn from a large quantity of matter; for we can say, with propriety, that this little Treatise is truly spiritual, and essential to the happiness of man: therefore, to those who wish to be happy, with every good intention we commend this Work to be their constant companion and study, in which, if they persevere, they shall not fail of their desires in the attainment of the true Philosophers' Stone.

PART THE FIRST

OF ALCHYMY, ITS DIVINE ORIGIN, &c.--DIFFICULTY OF ATTAINING A PERFECTION IN THE ART--WHAT AN ADEPT IS-- OF THE CABALA--THE ROSIE CRUCIANS ADEPTISTS-- POSSIBILITY OF BEING AN ADEPT--LIKEWISE, THAT THE LAPIS PHILOSOPHORUM EXISTS IN NATURE, AND THAT PROVED BY SUFFICIENT AUTHORITY, AND THAT THEY ARE NOT ALL IMPOSTORS WHO ARE ALCHYMISTS, OR PRETEND TO IT--THE MADNESS OF THE SCHOOLS PROVED, AND THE FOOLISHNESS OF THEIR WISDOM--THE TRIUMPH OF CHEMICAL PHILOSOPHY, OR THE HERMETIC ART PREFERABLE TO ANY OTHER.

IT is not necessary here to enter into a long detail of the merits of Alchymical Authors and Philosophers; suffice it to say, that Alchymy, the grand touch-stone of natural wisdom, is of Divine origin: it was brought down from Heaven by the Angel Uriel. Zoroaster, the first philosopher by fire, made pure gold from all the seven metals; he brought the sun ten times brighter from the bed of Saturn, and fixed it with the moon, who thereby copulating, begot a numerous offspring of an immortal nature, a pure living spiritual sun, burning in the refulgency of its own divine light, a seed of a sublime and fiery nature, a vigorous progenitor. This Zoroaster was the father of alchymy, illumined divinely from above; he knew every thing, yet seemed to know nothing; his precepts of art were left in hieroglyphics, yet in such sort that none but the favourites of Heaven ever reaped benefit thereby. He was the first who engraved the pure Cabala in most pure gold, and, when he died, resigned it to his Father who liveth eternally, yet begot him not: that Father gives it to his sons, who follow the precepts of Wisdom with vigilance, ingenuity, and industry, and with a pure, chaste, and free mind.

Hermes, Trismegistus, Geber, Artephius, Bacon, Helmont, Lully, and Basil Valentine, have written most profoundly, yet abstrusely, and all declare not the thing sought for. Some say they were forbid; others that they declared it obviously and intelligibly, yet some few little points they kept to themselves. However far off the main point they lead us, of this be sure,--that something valuable is to be drained, as it were, out of each.

Geber is good--Artephius is better--but Flammel is best of all;--and better still than these is the instructions we give; for with them a man (following our directions) shall never want gold; therefore to be an adept is possible, but first "seek the kingdom of God, and all these things shall be added unto you." This is truth incontrovertible, and herein lies a vast secret--"seek and ye shall find;"--but remember, whatsoever ye ask, that shall ye receive.

The cabala, in its utmost purity, is contained in the many precepts given in this book. The cabala enables us to understand--to bring our understandings to act, and, by that means, to attain knowledge;--knowledge makes us the children of God--God makes whom he pleases adepts in wisdom. To be an adept, according to God's will, is no contemptible calling.

The noble and virtuous Brethren of the Rosy Cross holds this truth sacred that "Virtue flies from no man;" therefore how desirable a thing is Virtue. She teaches us, first, wisdom, then charity, love, mercy, faith, and constancy; all these appertain to Virtue; therefore it is physically possible for any well-inclined man to become an adept, provided he lays aside his pride of reasoning, all obstinacy, blindness, hypocrisy, incredulity, superstition, deceit, &c.

An adept, therefore, is one who not only studies to do God's will upon earth, in respect of his moral and religious duties; but who studies, and ardently prays to his benevolent Creator to bestow on him wisdom and knowledge from the fulness of his treasury; and he meditates, day and night, how he may attain the true aqua vita--how he may be filled with the grace of God; which, when he is made so happy, his spiritual and internal eye is open to a glorious prospect of mortal and immortal riches:--he wants not food, raiment, joy, or any other thing-- he is filled with the celestial spiritual manna--he enjoys the marrow and fat things of the earth--he treads the wine-press, not of the wrath, but of the mercy of God-

-he lives to the glory of God, and dies saying "Holy, holy, holy Lord of Sabaoth! blessed is thy name, now and for evermore! Amen."

Therefore, to be an adept, as we have before hinted, is to know thyself, fear God, and love thy neighbour as thyself; and by this thou shalt come to the fulfilment of thy desires, O, man; but by no other means under the scope of Heaven.

When thy soul shall be made drunk by the divine ambrosial nectar, then shall thy understanding be more clear than the noontide sun;--then, by thy strong and spiritualized intellectual eye, shalt thou see into the great treasury of Nature, and thou shalt praise God with thy whole heart;--then wilt thou see the folly of the world; and thou shalt unerringly accomplish thy desire, and shalt possess the true Philosophers' stone, to the profit of thy neighbour. I say, thou shalt visibly and sensibly, according to thy corporal faculties; not imaginary, not delusively, but real.

Helmont, an author of no mean repute, avouches that he has actually seen the stone which converts base metals into gold; that he has seen it with his eyes., and handled it with his fingers: taken from his own relation of the fact; notwithstanding Kircher's declamation against the possibility of obtaining it, noting them all who professed alchymy to be a set of impostors and jugglers, giving no better an exposition of their process of transmutation than this--"An Alchymist," says Kircher, "procures or desires a crucible to be brought, wherein is put lead or any other base metal, which, while in fusion, he (the Alchymist) stirs about with an iron rod, and then," he says, "he drops in, from between his fingers, a bit of gold; and after stirring up for some time, and essay being made, gold is found." This is, indeed, a very lame method of exploding alchymy; but, however, to leave Kircher as much in the dark as he was, we shall give you Van Helmont's declaration, a philosopher of much greater note than this pseudo-chemist Kircher. Van Helmont says--"I have divers times handled that stone with my hands, and have seen a real transmutation of saleable quicksilver with mine eyes, which, in proportion, did exceed the powder which made the gold in some thousand degrees.

"It was of the colour that is in saffron, being weighty in its powder, and shining like bruised glass, when it should be the less exactly beaten. But there was once given unto me the fourth part of one grain, (I call, also, a grain the six hundredth part of an ounce). This powder I involved in wax, scraped off a certain letter, lest, in casting it into the crucible, it should be dispersed, through the smoak of the coals; which pellet of wax I afterwards cast into the three-cornered vessel of a crucible upon a pound of quicksilver, hot and newly bought; and presently the whole quicksilver, with some little noise, stood still from flowing, and resided like a lump; but the heat of that argent vive was as much as might forbid melted lead from recoagulating. The fire being straightway after increased under the bellows, the metal was melted; the which, the vessel of fusion being broken, I found to weigh eight ounces of the most pure gold.

"Therefore, a computation being made, a grain of that powder doth convert nineteen thousand two hundred grains of impure and volatile metal, which is obliterable by the fire, into true gold.

"For that powder, by uniting the aforesaid quicksilver unto itself, preserved the same, at one instant, from an eternal rust, putrefaction, death, and torture of the fire, howsoever most violent it was, and made it as an immortal thing, against any vigour or industry of art and fire, and transchanged it into the virgin purity of gold; at leastwise one only fire of coals is required herein."

By which we see that so learned and profound a philosopher as Van Helmont could not so easily have been made to believe that there existed a possibility of transmutation of base metals into pure gold, without he had actually proved the same by experiment.

Again, let the standing monuments of Flammel's liberal bounty to the poor, through this mean, to be seen at Paris every day, stand as a testimony to the truth of the existing possibility of transmutation. Likewise, Helmont mentions a stone that he saw, and had in his possession, which cured all disorders, the plague not excepted. I shall relate the circumstance in his own words, which are as follow:--

"There was a certain Irishman, whose name was Butler, being some time great with James, King of England, he being detained in the prison of the Castle of Vilvord; and taking pity on one Baillius, a certain Franciscan Monk, a most famous preacher of Gallo-Britain, who was also imprisoned, having an erisipelas in his arm; on a certain evening, when the Monk did almost despair, he swiftly tinged a certain little stone in a spoonful of almond-milk, and presently withdrew it thence. So he says to the keeper--'Reach this supping to that Monk; and how much soever he shall take thereupon, he shall be whole, at least within a short hour's space.'--Which thing even so came to pass, to the great admiration of the keeper and the sick man, not knowing from whence so sudden health shone upon him, seeing that he was ignorant that he had taken any thing: for his left arm, being before hugely swollen, fell down as that it could scarcely be discerned from the other. On the morning following, I, being entreated by some great men, came to Vilvord, as a witness of his deeds; therefore I contracted a friendship with Butler.

"Soon afterwards, I saw a poor old woman, a laundress, who, from the age of sixteen years, had laboured with an intolerable megrim, cured in my presence. Indeed he, by the way, lightly dipped the same little stone in a spoonful of oil of olives, and presently cleansed the same stone by licking it with his tongue, and laid it up into his snuff-box; but that spoonful of oil he poured into a small bottle of oil, whereof one only drop he commanded to be anointed on the head of the aforesaid old woman, who was thereby straightway cured, and remained whole; which I attest I was amazed, as if he was become another Midas; but he, smiling, said--

'My most dear friend, unless thou come hitherto, so as to be able, by one only remedy, to cure every disease, thou shalt remain in thy young beginnings, however old thou shalt become.'--I easily assented to this, because I had learned that from the secrets of Paracelsus; and being now more confirmed by sight and hope. But I willingly confess, that that new mode of curing was unaccustomed and unknown to me: I therefore said, that a young Prince of our Court, Viscount of Gaunt, brother to the Prince of Episuoy, of a very great House, was so wholly prostrated by the gout, that he thenceforth lay only on one side, being wretched, and deformed with many knots: he, therefore, taking hold of my right hand, said-- 'Wilt thou that I cure the young man? I will cure him for thy sake.'--'But,' I replied, 'he is of that obstinacy, that he had rather die, than drink one only medicinal potion.'

'Be it so,' said Butler; 'for neither do I require any other thing, than that he do, every morning, touch this little stone, thou seest, with the top of his tongue; for after three weeks from thence, let him wash the painful and unpainful knots with his own urine, and thou shalt soon afterwards see him cured, and soundly walking. Go thy ways, and tell him, with joy, what I have said.'

"I therefore, being glad, returned to Brussels, and told him what Butler had said.

"But the Potentate answered--'Go, tell Butler that if he shall restore me as thou hast said, I will give him as much as he shall require;--demand the price, and I will willingly sequester that which is deposited for his security.--And when I declared the thing to Butler, on the day following, he was very wrath, and said--'That Prince is mad, or witless and miserable, and therefore will I never help him: for neither do I stand in need of his money--neither do I yield--nor am I inferior to him.'--Nor could I ever induce him, afterwards, to perform what before he had promised; wherefore I began to doubt whether the things I had before seen were dreams.

"It happened, in the mean time, that a friend, overseer and master of the glass-furnace at Antwerp, being exceeding fat, most earnestly requested of Butler that he might be freed from his fatness; unto whom Butler offered a small piece of that little stone, that he might once every morning lick, or speedily touch it with the top of his tongue: and, within three weeks, I saw his breast made more strait, or narrow, by one span, and him to have lived no less whole afterwards. Wherefore I began again to believe that the aforesaid gouty Prince might have been cured, according to the manner Butler had promised.

"In the mean time, I sent to Vilvord, to Butler, for a remedy, in the case of poison given me by a secret enemy; for I miserably languished--all my joints were pained; and my pulse, vehement, being at length become an intermitting one, did accompany the faintings of my mind, and extinguishment of my strength.

"Butler, being still detained in prison, commanded my household-servant, whom I had sent, that forthwith he should bring unto him a small bottle of oil of olives; and his little stone, aforesaid, being tinged therein, as at other times, he sent that oil unto me; and told the servant, that with one only small drop of the oil, I should anoint only one place of the pain, or all the places, if I would; the which I did, and yet felt no help thereby. In the mean time, my enemy, according to his lot, being about to die, bade that pardon should be craved of me for his sin; so I knew that I had taken poison, the which I suspected; and therefore, also, I procured with all care to extinguish the slow venom, which, through the grace of God favouring me, I escaped.

"Seeing that, afterwards, many other cures were performed upon certain gentlewomen, I asked Butler why so many women should be cured, but that I (while that I sharply conflicted with death itself, being also environed with pains of all my joints and organs) should not feel any ease?--But he asked with what disease I had laboured?--And when he understood that poison had given a beginning to the disease, he said,--that, as the cause had come from within to without, the oil ought to be taken into the body, or the stone to be touched with the tongue; because the grief being cherished within, it was not local or external; and also observed, that the oil did, by degrees, uncloath itself with the efficacy of healing, because the little stone being lightly tinged in it, it had not pithily charged the oil throughout its whole body, but had only ennobled it with a delible or obliterable besprinkling of its odour: for truly that stone did present, in the eyes and tongue, sea-salt spread abroad, or rarified; and it is sufficiently known that salt is not to be very intimately mixed with oil.

"This same man, also, cured an Abbess, who, for eighteen years, had had her right arm swelled, with an entire deprivation of motion, and the fingers thereof stiff and unmoveable, only by the touching of her tongue with this admirable stone.

"But very many being present witnesses of these same wonders, did suspect some hidden sorcery, or diabolical craft; for the common people have it for an ancient custom, that whatsoever honest thing their ignorance has determined not to comprehend, they do, for a privy shift of their ignorance, refer the same to be the juggling of an evil spirit. But I could never decline so far, because the remedy was supposed to be natural; for neither words, ceremonies, nor any other suspected thing, was required. For neither is it lawful, according to man's power of understanding, to refer the glory of God, shewn forth in Nature, unto the devil. For none of those people had required aid of Butler, as from necromancy any way suspected; yea, the thing was at first made trial of with smiling, and without faith and confidence; yet this easy method of curing shall long remain suspected by many; for the wit of the vulgar being inconstant and idle, they do more readily consecrate so great a bounty of restitution unto diabolical contrivance, than to Divine Goodness, the framer, lover, saviour, refresher of human nature, and the father of the poor. And these vile prejudices are not only inherent in the common people, but also in those that are learned, who rashly search into the beginning of healing, being not yet instructed, or observing the common and blockish rules; because they are always wise as children, who have never gone over their mother's threshold, being: afraid of every fable. For they who have not hitherto known the whole circuit of diseases to be included within the spirit of life, which maketh the assault; or if they hereafter, reading my studies by the way, shall imprint on themselves this moment or concernment of healing; nevertheless, because they have been already before accustomed from the very beginnings of their studies, to the precepts of the humorists, they will easily, at length, depart from me, and leap back to the favourite bigotry and ancient opinions of the schools."

But now we will hasten to the manner of preparation necessary to qualify a man for the attainment of these sublime gifts.

OF THE PREPARATION OF A MAN TO QUALIFY HIM FOR THE SEARCH OF THIS TREASURE...

Of the Preparation of a Man to qualify him for the Search of this Treasure; and of the first Matter (prima materia) of the Stone.

LESSON I.

THE preparation for this work is simply this:--Learn to cast away from thee all vile affections--all levity and inconstancy of mind; let all thy dealings be free from deceit and hypocrisy; avoid the company of vain young men; hate all profligacy, and profane speaking.

LESSON II.

Keep thy own, and thy neighbours' secrets; court not the favours of the rich; despise not the poor, for he who does will be poorer than the poorest.

LESSON III.

Give to the needy and unfortunate what little thou canst spare; for he that has but little, whatever he spares to the miserable, God shall amply reward him.

LESSON IV.

Be merciful to those who offend thee, or who have injured thee; for what must that man's heart be, who would take heavy vengeance on a slight offence? Thou shalt forgive thy brother until seventy times seven.

LESSON V.

Be not hasty to condemn the actions of others, lest thou shouldst, the next hour, fall into the very same error; despise scandal and tattling; let thy words be few.

LESSON VI.

Study day and night, and supplicate thy Creator that he would be pleased to grant thee knowledge and understanding; and that the pure spirits may have communication with, and influence, in thee.

LESSON VII.

Be not overcome with drunkenness; for, be assured, that half the evils that befall mankind originate in drunkenness: for too great a quantity of strong liquors deprive men of their reason; then, having lost the use of the faculty of their judgment, they immediately become the recipient of all evil influences, and are justly compared to weathercocks, that are driven hither and thither by every gust of wind; so those who drown the reasonable power, are easily persuaded to the lightest and most frivolous pursuits, and, from these, to vices more gross and reprobate; for the ministers of darkness have never so favourable an opportunity of insinuating themselves into the minds and hearts of men, as when they are lost in intoxication. I pray you to avoid this dreadful vice.

LESSON VIII.

Avoid gluttony, and all excess--it is very pernicious, and from the Devil these are the things that constantly tempt man, and by which he falls a prey to his spiritual adversary; for he is rendered incapable of receiving any good or divine gift. Besides, the divine and angelic powers or essences delight not to be conversant about a man who is defiled, and stinking with debauchery and excess.

LESSON IX.

Covet not much gold, but learn to be satisfied with enough; for to desire more than enough, is to offend the Deity.

LESSON X.

Read often these ten preparatory Lessons to fit thee for the great work, and for the receiving of higher things; for the more pure thou art in heart and mind, by so much quicker shall you perceive those high secrets we teach, and which are entirely hid from the discernment of the vicious and depraved, because it never can happen that such a source of treasure can be attained merely to satisfy our more gross, earthly, and vain desires and inclinations, because here nothing must be thought to be grasped, or wrested out of this book, but to the fulfilling of a good end and purpose. When thou shalt have so far purified thy heart, as we have spoken is indispensably necessary for the receiving of every good thing, thou shalt then see with other eyes than thou dost at present--thy spiritual eye will be opened, and thou shalt read man as plain as thou wilt our books; but, for all this, depend not on the strength of thy own wisdom, for even then, when we think our hearts secure, if we do not watch them that they sleep not, the Devil, or his ministers, immediately take us at this unguarded moment, and tempts us into the actual commission of some sin or other: either he excites our appetite for lust and concupiscence, or any other deadly sin; therefore, using our blessed Redeemer's words--"What I say unto you, I say unto you all--watch!"

Perhaps, I do not doubt but, there are some that will say, when they look at our works, this fellow is all rant, all preaching--he tells us what we knew before as well as himself. To such I say, let them read our book but twice; if they do not gather something that they will acknowledge precious, (nay, be convinced that it is precious, to their own satisfaction) I will burn these writings, and they shall be no more remembered by me.

To conclude this Part: we say that the First Matter (Prima Materia) Adam brought with him out of Paradise, and left it, as an inheritance, to us his successors; had he remained in his original purity, he would have been permitted to have used it

74

himself; but the eternal fiat was passed, that he was to "earn his bread by the sweat of his brow;" therefore he could not effect what was afterwards performed by some of his offspring.

Hermes Trismegistus, that ancient philosopher, wrote touching the attainment of this stone, which he pronounced to be of all benefit to man, and one of the greatest blessings he could possess; and although his writings contain much of the excellency of truth, being wrapped up in such symbolical figures, it renders them exceedingly difficult to be understood, yet, if comprehended, they, no doubt, contain some very great secrets by which mortal man may profit.

Now it belongs to our purpose to know what it is from which we must extract the first matter of this stone, to go on with our process, because we must have materials to work upon; for all philosophers agree that, the first matter being found, we may proceed without much difficulty. For the first matter, (I shall speak as plainly as possible) first, the grand question in debate is--Where is it to be found?--I say it is to be found in ourselves. We all possess this first matter, from the beggar to the king; every mothers' son carries it about him; and, could our ingenious chemists but find a process for the extracting, how well would all their labours be repaid. The next question naturally comes to us--How are we to draw, or attract the secret matter of the stone out of ourselves?--Not by any common means; and yet it is to be drawn into very action, and that by the most simple means, and in a manner that the attaining of the philosophers' stone would very soon follow it. I pray you, my friend, look into thyself, and endeavour to find out in what part of thy composition is the prima materia of the lapis philosophorum, or out of what part of thy substance can the first matter of our stone be drawn out. Thou sayest, it must either be in the hair, sweat, or excrement. I say in none of these thou shalt ever be able to find it, and yet thou shalt find it in thyself.

Many great philosophers and chemists, whom I have the pleasure to know, affirm that, admitting of the possibility of transmutation, it (i. e. the first matter) must be taken from the purest gold. To this I say it must not; neither has it any thing at all to do with extrinsical gold. They will say then that the pure ens of gold may be drawn from gold itself. True, it may so; but then I would ask if they could ever produce more gold than that out of which the soul or essence was extracted; if they have, they have indeed found out a secret beyond the powers of our comprehension; because it is against reason to suppose that if a pound of gold yields a drachm of the soul or essence, that that only will tinge any more than a pound of purified lead, or ☿ because we have tried various experiments, and I have, in some of my first essays, turned both lead and mercury into good gold; but no more than that out of which the soul was extracted. But, however, not to lose our time in vain and ridiculous disputation, know that whatever prodigious things or experiments have been tried with respect to the first matter, by external subjects, either in the mineral, animal, or vegetable kingdoms, as they are called, I say in us is the power of all wonderful things, which the supreme Creator has, of his infinite mercy, implanted in our souls; out of her is to be extracted the first matter, the true argent vive, the ☿ of the philosophers, the true ens of ☉, viz. a spiritual living gold, or waterish mercury, or first matter, which, by being maturted, is capable of transmuting a thousand pts. of impure metal into good and perfect gold, which endure fire, test, or cupel.

PART THE SECOND

OF THE MANNER OF EXTRACTING THE FIRST MATTER OF THE PHILOSOPHERS' STONE, AND THE USE IT IS PUT TO IN PURIFYING THE IMPERFECT METALS, AND TRANSMUTING THEM INTO GOOD GOLD.

LESSON XI.

TAKE the foregoing instructions as thy principal instrument, and know that our soul has the power, when the body is free, as we before said, of any pollution, the heart void of malice and offence; I say the soul is then a free agent, and has the power, spiritually and magically, to act upon any matter whatsoever; therefore I said the first matter is in the soul; and the extracting of it, is to bring the dormant power of the pure, living, breathing spirit and eternal soul into act. Note well that every agent has its power of acting upon its patient. Every essence that is distilled forth is received into a recipient, but that recipient must first be made clean. Even so must the soul and heart of man: the vile affections must be thrown away, and trampled under foot; then shalt thou be able to proceed in thy work, which do in the manner following.

LESSON XII.

The expence thou must be at will be but a trifle: all the instruments necessary are but three, viz. a crucible, an egg philosophical, and a retort with its receiver. Put your fine gold, in weight about 5 dwts., file it up, put it into your philosophic egg, pour upon it the twice of its weight of the best Hungarian ☿, close up the egg with an Hermetic seal, put it for three months in horse-dung, take it out at the end of that time, and see what kind of form thy gold and ☿ has assumed; take it out, pour on it half its weight of good spirit of sal ammon., set them in a pot full of sand over the fire in the retort, let them distil into a pure essence, add to one pt. of this ☿ two pts. of thy water of life, or prima materia, put them into thy philosophical. egg, and

LESSON XIII.

set them into horse-dung for another three months; then take them out, and see what thou hast--a pure etherial essence, which is the living gold; pour this pure spiritual liquor upon a drachm of molten fine gold, and you will find that which will satisfy thy hunger and thirsting after this secret; for the increase of thy gold will seem to thee miraculous, as indeed it is. Take it to a jeweller's or goldsmith's; let him try it in thy presence, and thou wilt have reason to bless God for his mercy to thee. Do thy duty as he has commanded thee, and use all the benefit thou shalt receive, in actions worthy of thy nature.

LESSON XIV.

When thy spiritual eve is opened, and thou shalt begin to see to what end thou wert created, thou Shalt want no necessary thing either for thy comfort or support; only keep in the rules we have prescribed in the beginning of this little treatise--Fear God, and love thy neighbour as thyself; be not hasty to reveal any secrets thou mayest learn, for the good spirits, both day and night, will be thy instructors, and will continually reveal thee many secrets. Think not that thou canst either profit or benefit so much by the instruction of those who profess great advantages in classical education and high schooling; be assured they are, in spiritual knowledge, much in the dark: for he who desires not spiritual knowledge cannot attain it by, any means, but by, first, coming to God; secondly, by purifying his own heart; thirdly, by submitting himself to the will of the Holy Spirit, to guide and direct him in all truth, to the attaining of all knowledge, both human and divine; and by arrogating nothing to our own power or strength, but by referring all to the mercy and goodness of God.--Amen.

The Celestial Intelligencer

CONTAINING

THE CONSTELLATORY PRACTICE,

OR

TALISMANIC MAGIC.

SHEWING

The true Properties of the Elements, Meteors, Stars, Planets, &c., &c.;
likewise the Nature of Intelligences, Spirits, Dæmons, and Devils; the
Construction and Composition of all Sorts of Magic Seals, Images, Rings,
Glasses, Pictures, &c, &c.; the Power and Composition of Numbers,
Mathematical Figures, and Characters of Spirits both good and evil.

THE WHOLE OF THE ABOVE ILLUSTRATED BY A GREAT VARIETY OF

Beautiful Figures, Types, Letters, Seals, Images, Magic Characters, &c.

FORMING A COMPLETE SYSTEM OF DELIGHTFUL KNOWLEDGE AND ABSTRUSE SCIENCE;

Such as is warranted never before to have been published in the English
Language.

BY FRANCIS BARRETT,

STUDENT OF CHEMISTRY, OCCULT PHILOSOPHY, THE CABALA,

&c. &c. &c.

1801.

CHAPTER 1. OF THE FOUR ELEMENTS AND THEIR NATURAL QUALITIES

IT is necessary that we should know and understand the nature and quality of the four elements, in order to our being perfect in the principles and ground-work of our studies in the Talismanic, or Magical Art.

Therefore, there are four elements, the original grounds of all corporeal things, viz. fire, earth, water, and air, of which elements all inferior bodies are compounded; not by way of being heaped up together, but by transmutation and union; and when they are destroyed, they are resolved into elements. But there are none of the sensible elements that are pure; but they are, more or less, mixed, and apt to be changed the one into the other: even as earth, being moistened and dissolved, becomes water, but the same being made thick and hard, becomes earth again; and being evaporated through heat it passes into air, and that being kindled into fire, and this being extinguished, into air gain, but being cooled after burning, becomes earth again, or else stone, or sulphur; and this is clearly demonstrated by lightning. Now every one of these elements have two specifical properties: the former whereof it retains as proper to itself; in the other, as a mean, it agrees with that which comes directly after it. For fire is hot and dry--earth, cold and dry;--water, cold and moist--and air, hot and moist. And so in this manner the elements, according to two contrary qualities, are opposite one to the other: as fire to water, and earth to air. Likewise, the elements are contrary one to the other n another account: two are heavy, as earth and water--and the others are light, as fire and air; therefore the Stoics called the former, passives--but the latter, actives. And Plato distinguishes them after another manner, and assigns to each of them three qualities, viz. to the fire, brightness, thinness, and motion--to the earth, darkness, thickness, and quietness; and, according to these qualities, the elements of fire and earth are contrary. Now the other elements borrow their qualities from these, so that the air receives two qualities from the fire,--thinness, and motion; and the earth one, viz. darkness. In like manner water receives two qualities of the earth,--darkness and thickness; and the fire one, viz. motion. But fire is twice as thin as air, thrice more moveable, and four times brighter; the air is twice more bright, thrice more thin, and four times more moveable. Therefore, as fire is to air, so is air to water, and water to the earth; and again, as the earth is to the water, so is water to air, and air to fire. And this is the root and foundation of all bodies, natures, and wonderful works; and he who can know, and thoroughly understand these qualities of the elements, and their mixtures, shall bring to pass wonderful and astonishing things in magic.

Now each of these elements have a threefold consideration, so that the number of four may make up the number of twelve; and, by passing by the number of seven into ten, there may be a progress to the supreme unity upon which all virtue and wonderful things do depend. Of the first order are the pure elements, which are neither compounded, changed, or mixed, but are incorruptible; and not OF which, but THROUGH which, the virtues of all natural things are brought forth to act. No man is able fully to declare their virtues, because they can do all things upon all things. He who remains ignorant of these, shall never be able to bring to pass any wonderful matter.

Of the second order are elements that are compounded, changeable, and impure; yet such as may, by art, be reduced to their pure simplicity; whose virtue, when they are thus reduced, doth, above all things, perfect all occult and common operations of Nature; and these are the foundation of the whole of Natural Magic.

Of the third order, are those elements which originally and of themselves are not elements, but are twice compounded, various and changeable into another. These are the infallible medium, and are called the middle nature, or soul of the middle nature; very few there are that understand the deep mysteries thereof. In them is, by means of certain numbers, degrees, and orders, the perfection of every effect in what thing soever, whether natural, celestial, or supercelestial: they are full of wonders and mysteries, and are operative as in Magic natural, so divine. For from these, through them, proceeds the binding, loosing, and transmutation of all things--the knowledge and foretelling of things to come--also, the expelling of evil, and the gaining of good spirits. Let no one, therefore, without these three sorts of elements, and the true knowledge thereof, be confident that he can work any thing in the Occult Science of Magic and Nature.

But whosoever shall know how to reduce those of one order into another, impure into pure, compounded into simple, and shall understand distinctly the nature, virtue, and power of them, in number, degrees, and order, without dividing the substance, he shall easily attain to the knowledge and perfect operation of all natural things, and celestial secrets likewise; and this is the perfection of the Cabala, which teaches all these before mentioned; and, by a perfect knowledge thereof, we perform many rare and wonderful experiments.

CHAPTER 2. OF THE PROPERTIES AND WONDERFUL NATURE OF FIRE AND EARTH

THERE are two things, (says Hermes) viz. fire and earth, which are sufficient for the operation of all wonderful things: the former is active, and the latter passive. Fire, in all things, and through all things, comes and goes away bright; it is in all things bright, and at the same time occult, and unknown. When it is by itself (no other matter coming to it, in which it should manifest its proper action) it is boundless and invisible; of itself sufficient for every action that is proper to it;-- itself is one, and penetrates through all things; also spread abroad in the heavens, and shining. But in the infernal place, straitened, dark, and tormenting; and in the midway it partakes of both. It is in stones, and is drawn out by the stroke of the steel; it is in earth, and causes it, after digging up, to smoke; it is in water, and heats springs and wells; it is in the depths of the sea, and causes it, being tossed with the winds, to be hot; it is in the air, and makes it (as we often see) to burn. And all animals, and all living things whatsoever, as also vegetables, are preserved by heat;--and every thing that lives, lives by reason of the inclosed heat. The properties of the fire that is above, are heat, making all things fruitful; and a celestial light, giving life to all things. The properties of the infernal fire are a parching heat, consuming all things; and darkness; making all things barren. The celestial and bright fire drives away spirits of darkness;--also, this our fire, made with wood, drives away the same, in as much as it hath an analogy with, and is the vehiculum of, that superior light; as also of him who saith, "I am the light of the world," which is true fire--the Father of lights, from whom every good thing that is given comes;--sending forth the light of his fire, and communicating it first to the sun and the rest of the celestial bodies, and by these, as by mediating instruments, conveying that light into our fire. As, therefore, the spirits of darkness are stronger in the dark--so good spirits, which are angels of lights, are augmented not only .by that light (which is divine, of the sun, and celestial), but also by the light of our common fire. Hence it was that the first and most wise institutors of religions and ceremonies, ordained that prayers, singings, and all manner of divine worships whatsoever, should not be performed without lighted candles or torches: hence, also, was that significant saying of Pythagoras--"Do not speak of God without a light!"--And they commanded that, for the driving away of wicked spirits, lights and fires should be kindled by the carcasses of the dead, and that they should not be removed until the expiations were, after a holy manner, performed, and then buried. And the great Jehovah himself, in the old law, commanded that all his sacrifices should be offered with fire and that fire should always be burning upon the altar, which custom the Priests of the Altar did always observe and keep amongst the Romans. Now the basis and foundation of all the elements is the earth; for that is the object, subject, and receptacle of all celestial rays and influences: in it are contained the seeds, and seminal virtues of all things; and therefore, it is said to be animal, vegetable, and mineral. It, being made fruitful by the other elements and the heavens, brings forth all things of itself. It receives the abundance of all things, and is, as it were, the first fountain from whence all things spring;--it is the centre, foundation, and mother of all things. Take as much of it as you please, separated, washed, depurated, and subtilized, and if you let it lie in the open air a little while, it will, being full and abounding with heavenly virtues, of itself bring forth plants, worms, and other living things; also stones, and bright sparks of metals. In it are great secrets: if, at any time it shall be purified, by the help of fire, [77:1] and reduced into its simple nature by a convenient washing, it is the first matter of our creation, and the truest medicine that can restore and preserve us.

77:1 Agrippa here, speaking of the element of earth being reduced to its utmost simplicity, by being purified by fire and a convenient washing, means, that it is the first and principal ingredient necessary to the production of the Philosopher's stone, either of animals or metals.

CHAPTER 3. OF THE WATER AND AIR

THE other two elements, viz. water and air, are not less efficacious than the former; neither is Nature wanting to work wonderful things in them. There is so great a necessity of water, that without it nothing can live--no herb nor plant whatsoever without the moistening of water, can bring forth; in it is the seminary virtue of all things, especially of animals, whose seed is manifestly waterish. The seeds, also, of trees and plants, although they are earthy, must, notwithstanding, of necessity be rotted in water before they can be fruitful; whether they be imbided with the moisture of the earth, or with dew, or rain, or any other water that is on purpose put to them.--For Moses writes, that only earth and water can bring forth a living soul; but he ascribes a two-fold production of things to water, viz. of things swimming in the water, and of things flying in the air above the earth; and that those productions that are made in and upon the earth are partly attributed to the very water the same scripture testifies, where it saith, that the plants and the herbs did not grow, because God had not caused it to rain upon the earth. Such is the efficacy of this element of water, that spiritual regeneration cannot be done without it, as Christ himself testified to Nicodemus. Very great, also, is the virtue of it in the religious worship of God, in expiations and purifications; indeed the necessity of it is no less than that of fire. Infinite are the benefits, and divers are the uses, thereof as being that, by virtue of which all things subsist, are generated, nourished, and in creased. Hence it was that Thales of Miletus, and Hesiod, concluded that water was the beginning of all things; and said it was the first of all the elements, and the most potent; and that, because it hath the mastery over all the rest. For, as Pliny saith--"Waters swallow up the earth--extinguish flames--ascend on high--and, by the stretching forth of the clouds, challenge the heavens for their own; the same, falling down, becomes the cause of all things that grow in the earth." Very many are the wonders that are done by waters, according to the writings of Pliny, Solinus, and many other historians.

Josephus also makes relation of the wonderful nature of a certain river betwixt Arcea and Raphanea, cities of Syria, which runs with a full channel all the

Sabbath-day, and then on a sudden stops, as if the springs were stopped, and all the six days you may pass over it dry-shod; but again, on the seventh day, no man knowing the reason of it, the waters return again, in abundance as before! wherefore the inhabitants thereabout called it the Sabbath-day River) because of the seventh day, which was holy to the Jews.--The Gospel, also, testifies of a sheep-pool, into which whosoever stepped first after the water was troubled by the Angel, was made whole of whatsoever disease he had. The same virtue and efficacy, we read, was in a spring of the Ionian Nymphs, which was in the territories belonging to the town of Elis, at a village called Heradea, near the river Citheron, which whosoever stepped into, being diseased, came forth whole, and cured of all his diseases. Pausanias also reports, that in Lyceus, a mountain of Arcadia, there was a spring called Agria, to which, as often as the dryness of the region threatened the destruction of fruits, Jupiter, Priest of Lyceus, went; and, after the offering of sacrifices, devoutly praying to the waters of the spring, holding a bough of an oak in his hand, put it down to the bottom of the hallowed spring; then, the waters being troubled, a vapour ascending from thence into the air, was blown into clouds, which being joined together, the whole heaven was overspread: which being, a little after, dissolved into rain, watered all the country most wholesomely.--Moreover, Ruffus, a physician of Ephesus, besides many other authors, wrote strange things concerning the wonders of waters, which, for aught I know, are found in no other author.

It remains, that I speak of the air.--This is a vital spirit passing through all beings--giving life and subsistence to all things--moving and filling all things. Hence it is that the Hebrew doctors reckon it not amongst the elements; but count it as a medium, or glue, joining things together, and as the resounding spirit of the world's instrument. It immediately receives into itself the influence of all celestial bodies, and then communicates them to the other elements, as also to all mixed bodies. Also, it receives into itself, as if it were a divine looking-glass, the species of all things, as well natural as artificial; as also of all manner of speeches, and retains them; and carrying them with it, and entering into the bodies of men, and other animals, through their pores, makes an impression upon them, as well when they are asleep as when they are awake, and affords matter for divers strange dreams and divinations.--Hence, they say, it is that a man, passing by a place where a man was slain, or the carcass newly hid, is moved with fear and dread; because the air, in that place, being full of the dreadful species of man-slaughter, doth, being breathed in, move and trouble the spirit of the man with the like species; whence it is that he becomes afraid. For every thing that makes a sudden impression astonishes Nature. Whence it is that many philosophers were of opinion, that air is the cause of dreams, and of many other impressions of the mind, through the prolonging of images, or similitudes, or species (which proceed from things and speeches, multiplied in the very air), until they come to the senses, and then to the phantasy and soul of him that receives them; which, being freed from cares, and no way hindered, expecting to meet such kind of species, is informed by them. For the species of things, although of their own proper nature they are carried to the senses of men, and other animals in general, may, notwithstanding, get some impression from the heavens whilst they are in the air; by reason of which, together with the aptness and disposition of him that receives them, they may be carried to the sense of one, rather than of another. And hence it is possible, naturally, and far from all manner of superstition (no other spirit coming between), that a man should be able, in a very small time, to signify his mind unto another man, abiding at a very long and unknown distance from him-- although he cannot precisely give an estimate of the time when it is, yet, of necessity, it must be within twenty-four hours;--and I, myself, know how to do it, and have often done it. The same also, in time past, did the Abbot Tritemius both know and do.--Also, when certain appearances (not only spiritual, but also natural) do flow forth from things, that is to say, by a certain kind of flowings forth of bodies from bodies, and do gather strength in the air, they shew themselves to us as well through light as motion--as well to the sight as to other senses--and sometimes work wonderful things upon us, as Platonius proves and teacheth. And we see how, by the south-wind, the air is condensed into thin clouds, in which, as in a looking-glass, are reflected representations at a great distance, of castles, mountains, horses, men, and other things, which when the clouds are gone, presently vanish.--And Aristotle, in his Meteors, shews that a rainbow is conceived in a cloud of the air, as in a looking-glass.--And Albertus says, that the effigies of bodies may, by the strength of Nature, in a moist air, be easily represented; in the same manner as the representations of things are in things.--And Aristotle tells of a man, to whom it happened, by reason of the weakness of his sight, that the air that was near to him became, as it were, a looking-glass to him, and the optic-beam did reflect back upon himself, and could not penetrate the air, so that, whithersoever he went, he thought he saw his own image, with his face towards him, go before him.--In like manner, by the artificialness of some certain looking-glasses, may be produced at a distance, in the air, besides the looking-glasses, what images we please; which, when ignorant men see, they think they see the appearances of spirits or souls--when, indeed, they are nothing else but semblances a-kin to themselves, and without life. And it is well-known, if in a dark place, where there is no light but by the coming in of a beam of the sun some where through a little hole, a white paper or plain looking-glass be set up against the light, that there may be seen upon them whatsoever things are done without, being shined upon by the sun. And there is another slight or trick yet more wonderful:--if any one shall take images, artificially painted, or written letters, and, in a clear night, set them against the beams of the full moon, those resemblances being multiplied in the air, and caught upward, and reflected back together with the beams of the moon, another man, that is privy to the thing, at a long distance, sees, reads, and knows them in the very compass and circle of the moon; which art of declaring secrets is, indeed, very profitable for towns and cities that are besieged, being a thing which Pythagoras long since did, and which is not unknown to some in these days; I will not except myself. And all these things, and many more, and much greater than these, are grounded in the very nature of the air, and have their reasons and causes declared in mathematics and optics. And as these resemblances are reflected back to the sight, so also are they, sometimes, to the hearing, as is manifest in echo. But there are many more secret arts than these, and such whereby any one may, at a remarkable distance, hear, and understand distinctly, what another speaks or whispers.

CHAPTER 4. OF COMPOUND, OR MIXED BODIES...

OF COMPOUND, OR MIXED BODIES--IN WHAT MANNER THEY RELATE TO THE ELEMENTS--AND HOW THE ELEMENTS RELATE TO THE SOULS, SENSES, AND DISPOSITIONS OF MEN.

THE next in order, after the four simple elements, are the four kinds of perfect bodies compounded of them, viz. metals, stones, plants, and animals; and although in the generation of each of these, all the elements combine together in the composition, yet every one of them follows and resembles one of the elements which is most predominant: for all stones, being earthy, are naturally heavy, and are so hardened with dryness that they cannot be melted;--but metals are watery, and may be melted, which naturalists and chemists find to be true, viz. that they are composed or generated of a viscous water, or watery argent vive. Plants have such an affinity with the air, that unless they are out in it, and receive its benefit, they neither flourish nor increase. So also animals, as the Poet finely expresses it--

"Have, in their natures, a most fiery force,
"And also spring from a celestial source:"

and fire is so natural to them that, being extinguished, they soon die.

Now, amongst stones, those that are dark and heavy, are called earthy--those which are transparent, of the watery element, as crystal, beryl, and pearls--those which swim upon the water and are spongious, as the pumice-stone, sponge, and sophus, are called airy--and those are attributed to the element of fire, out of which fire is extracted, or which are resolved into fire; as thunder-stones, fire-stones, asbestos. Also, amongst metals;--lead and silver are earthy; quicksilver is watery; copper and tin, airy; gold and iron, fiery. In plants, also, the roots resemble earth--the leaves, water--flowers, the air--and seed, the fire, by reason of their multiplying spirit. Besides, some are hot, some cold, some moist, others dry, borrowing their names from the qualities of the elements. Amongst animals, also, some are, in comparison of others, earthy, because they live in the very bowels of the earth, as worms, moles, and many other reptiles; others watery, as fish; others which always abide in the air, therefore airy; others, again, fiery, as salamanders, crickets; and such as are of a fiery heat, as pigeons, ostriches, eagles, lions, panthers, &c. &c.

Now, in animals, the bones resemble earth--vital spirit, the fire--flesh, the air--and humours, the water; and these humours also resemble the elements, viz. yellow choler, the fire--the blood, the air--phlegm, the water—and black choler, or melancholy, the earth. And, lastly, in the soul itself, the understanding resembles the fire--reason, the air--imagination, the water-- and the senses the earth. And these senses again are divided amongst themselves, according to the elements: for the sight is fiery, because it cannot perceive without the help of fire and light--the hearing is airy, for a sound is made by the striking of the air--the smell and taste resemble water, without the moisture of which there is neither smell nor taste-and, lastly, the feeling is wholly earthly, because it takes gross bodies for its object. The actions, also, and operations of man are governed by the elements: for the earth signifies a slow and firm motion; the water, fearfulness, sluggishness, and remiss ness in working; air signifies cheerfulness, and an amiable disposition; but fire, a fierce, working, quick, susceptible disposition. The elements are, therefore, the first and original matter of all things; and all things are of and according to them and they in and through all things diffuse their virtues.

CHAPTER 5. THAT THE ELEMENTS ARE IN THE HEAVENS, IN THE STARS, IN DEVILS, ANGELS, INTELLIGENCES, AND, LASTLY, IN GOD HIMSELF

IN the original and exemplary world, all things are all in all; so also in this corporeal world. And the elements are not only in these inferior things; but are in the heavens, in stars, in devils, in angels, and likewise in God himself, the maker and original example of all things.

Now it must be understood that in these inferior bodies the elements are gross and corruptible; but in the heavens they are, with their natures and virtues, after a celestial and more excellent manner than in sublunary things: for the firmness of the celestial earth is there without the grossness of water; and the agility of air without exceeding its bounds; the heat of fire without burning, only shining, giving light and life to all things by its celestial heat.—Now amongst the stars, or planets, some are fiery, as Mars, and the Sun--airy, as Jupiter, and Venus--watery, as Saturn, and Mercury--and earthy, such as inhabit the eighth orb, and the Moon (which by many is accounted watery), seeing that, as if it were earth, it attracts to itself the celestial waters, with which being imbibed it does, on account of its proximity to us, pour forth and communicate to our globe.

There are, likewise, amongst the signs, some fiery, some airy, some watery, and some earthy. The elements rule them, also, in the heavens, distributing to them these four threefold considerations of every element, according to their triplicities, viz. the beginning, middle, and end.

Likewise, devils are distinguished according to the elements: for some are called earthy devils, others fiery, some airy, and others watery. Hence, also, those four infernal rivers: fiery Phlegethon, airy Cocytus, watery Styx, earthy Acheron. Also, in the Gospel, we read of comparisons of the elements: as hell fire, and eternal fire, into which the cursed shall be commanded to go;--and in Revelations, of a lake of fire:--and Isaiah, speaking of the damned, says that the Lord will smite them with corrupt air;--and in Job, they shall skip from the waters of the snow to the extremity of heat; and, in the same, we read, that the earth is dark, and covered with the darkness of death, and miserable darkness.

And these elements are placed in the angels of heaven, and the blessed intelligences: there is in them a stability of their essence, which is an earthy virtue, in which is the stedfast seat of God. By the Psalmist they are called waters, where he says--"Who rulest the waters that are higher than the heavens;"--also, in them their subtile breath is air, and their love is shining fire; hence they are called in Scripture, the wings of the wind; and, in another place, the Psalmist speaks of them thus--"Who makest angels thy spirits, and thy ministers a flaming fire!"-- Also, according to the different orders of spirits or angels, some are fiery, as seraphims, authorities, and powers--earthy, as cherubim--watery, as thrones and archangels--airy, as dominions and principalities.

And do we not read of the original Maker of all things, that the earth shall be opened and bring forth a Saviour?--Likewise it is spoken of the same, that he shall be a fountain of living water, cleansing and regenerating and the same spirit breathing the breath of life; and the same, according to Moses' and Paul's testimony--a consuming fire.

That the elements are, therefore, to be found every where, and in all things, after their manner, no man will dare to deny: first, in these inferior bodies, feculent and gross; and in celestials, more pure and clear; but in super-celestials, living, and in all respects blessed. Elements, therefore, in the exemplary world, are ideas of things to be produced; in intelligences, they are distributed powers; in the heavens, they are virtues; and in inferior bodies, are gross forms.

CHAPTER 6. THAT THE WISDOM OF GOD WORKS BY THE MEDIUM OF SECOND CAUSES...

THAT THE WISDOM OF GOD WORKS BY THE MEDIUM OF SECOND CAUSES (I. E. BY THE INTELLIGENCES, BY THE HEAVENS, ELEMENTS, AND CELESTIAL BODIES) IS PROVED BEYOND DISPUTE IN THIS CHAPTER.

IT is to be noted, that God, in the first place, is the end and beginning of all virtue: he gives the seal of the ideas to his servants, the intelligences, who, as faithful officers, sign all things entrusted to them with an ideal virtue; the heavens and stars, as instruments, disposing the matter, in the mean while, for the receiving of those forms which reside in Divine Majesty, and to be conveyed by stars. And the Giver of forms distributes them by the ministry of his intelligences, which he has ordained as rulers and comptrollers over his works; to whom such a power is entrusted, in things committed to them, that so all virtue in stones, herbs, metals, and all other things, may come from the intelligences, the governors. Therefore the form and virtue of things come first from the ideas--then from the ruling and governing intelligences--then from the aspects of the heavens disposing--and, lastly, from the tempers of the elements disposed, answering the influences of the heavens, by which the elements themselves are ordered or disposed. These kinds of operations, therefore, are performed in these inferior things by express forms; and in the heavens, by disposing virtues; in intelligences, by mediating rules; in the original cause, by ideas and exemplary forms; all which must of necessity agree in the execution of the effect and virtue of every thing.

There is, therefore, a wonderful virtue and operation in every herb and stone, but greater in a star; beyond which, even from the governing intelligences, every thing, receives and obtains many things for itself, especially from the Supreme Cause, with whom all things mutually and exactly correspond, agreeing in an harmonious consent.

Therefore there is no other cause of the necessity of effects, than the connection of all things with the First Cause, and their correspondency with those divine patterns and eternal ideas, whence every thing hath its determinate and particular place in the exemplary world, from whence it lives and receives its original being; and every virtue of herbs, stones, metals, animals, words, speeches, and all things that are of God, are placed there.

Now the First Cause (which is God), although he doth, by intelligences and the heavens, work upon these inferior things, does sometimes (these mediums being laid aside, or their officiating being suspended) work those things immediately by himself--which works are then called miracles. But whereas secondary causes do, by the command and appointment of the First Cause, necessarily act, and are necessitated to produce their effects; if God shall, notwithstanding, according to his pleasure, so discharge and suspend them that they shall wholly desist from the necessity of that command, then they are called the greatest miracles of God. For instance: the fire of the Chaldean furnace did not burn the children; the sun stood still at the command of Joshua, and became retrograde one whole day; also, at the prayer of Hezekiah, it went back ten degrees; and when our Saviour Christ was crucified, it became darkened, though at full moon.

And the reason of these operations can by no rational discourse, no magic or science, occult or profound soever, be found out or understood; but are to be learned by Divine oracles only. 87:1

87:1 The foregoing Chapter, if well considered, will open the intellect to a more easy comprehension of the Magical Science of Nature, &c.; and will facilitate, in a wonderful degree, our studies in these sublime mysteries.

CHAPTER 7. OF THE SPIRIT OF THE WORLD

NOW seeing that the soul is the essential form, intelligible and incorruptible, and is the first mover of the body, and is moved of itself; but that the body, or matter, is of itself unable and unfit for motion, and does very much degenerate from the soul, it appears that there is need of a more excellent medium:--now such a medium is conceived to be the spirit of the world, or that which some call a quintessence; because it is not from the four elements, but a certain first thing, having its being above and beside them. There is, therefore, such a kind of medium required to be, by which celestial souls may be joined to gross bodies, and bestow upon them wonderful gifts. This spirit is, in the same manner, in the body of the world, as our spirit is in our bodies; for as the powers of our soul are communicated to the members of the body by the medium of the spirit, so also the virtue of the soul of the world is diffused, throughout all things, by the medium of the universal spirit; for there is nothing to be found in the whole world that hath not a spark of the virtue thereof. Now this spirit is received into things, more or less, by the rays of the stars, so far as things are disposed, or made fit recipients of it. By this spirit, therefore, every occult property is conveyed into herbs, stones, metals, and animals, through the sun, moon, planets, and through stars higher than the planets. Now this spirit may be more advantageous to us if we knew how to separate it from the elements; or, at least, to use those things chiefly which are most abounding with this spirit. For those things in which the spirit is less drowned in a body, and less checked by matter, do much more powerfully and perfectly act, and also more readily generate their like; for in it are all generative and seminal virtues. For which cause the alchymist endeavours to separate this spirit from gold and silver, which, being rightly separated and extracted, if it shall be afterwards projected upon any metal, turns it into gold or silver; which is no way impossible or improbable, when we consider that by art that may be done in a short time, what Nature, in the bowels of the earth (as in a matrix), perfects in a very long space of time.

CHAPTER 8. OF THE SEALS AND CHARACTERS IMPRESSED BY CELESTIALS UPON NATURAL THINGS

ALL stars have their peculiar natures, properties, and conditions, the seals and characters whereof they produce through their rays even in these inferior things, viz. in elements, in stones, in plants, in animals, and their members; whence every thing receives from an harmonious disposition, and from its star shining upon it, some particular seal or character stamped upon it, which is the significator of that star or harmony, containing in it a peculiar virtue, different from other virtues of the same matter, both generically, specifically, and numerically. Every thing, therefore, hath its character impressed upon it by its star for some peculiar effect, especially by that star which doth principally govern it; and these characters contain in them the particular natures, virtues, and roots of their stars, and produce the like operations upon other things on which they are reflected; and stir up and help the influences of their stars, whether they be planets, or fixed stars and figures, or celestial constellations, viz. as often as they shall be made in a fit matter, and in their due and accustomed times; which the ancient wise men (considering such as laboured much in finding out occult properties of things) did set down, in writing, the images of the stars, their figures, seals, marks, characters, such as Nature herself did describe by the rays of the stars in these inferior bodies: some in stones, some in plants, some in joints and knots of trees and their boughs, and some in various members of animals. For the bay-tree, lote-tree, and marigold, are solary herbs, and their roots and knots being cut, they show the characters of the sun; and in stones the character and images of celestial things are often found. But there being so great a diversity of things, there is only a traditional knowledge of a few things which human understanding is able to reach; therefore very few of those things are known to us, which the ancient philosophers and chiromancers attained to, partly by reason and partly by experience; and there yet lie hid many things in the treasury of Nature, which the diligent student and wise searcher shall contemplate and discover.

CHAPTER 9. TREATING OF THE VIRTUE AND EFFICACY OF PERFUMES...

TREATING OF THE VIRTUE AND EFFICACY OF PERFUMES, OR SUFFUMIGATIONS, AND VAPOURS; AND TO WHAT PLANETS THEY ARE PROPERLY AND RIGHTLY ATTRIBUTED.

IT is necessary, before we come to the operative or practical part of Talismanic Magic, to show the compositions of fumes or vapours, that are proper to the stars, and are of great force for the opportunely receiving of celestial gifts, under the rays of the stars--inasmuch as they strongly work upon the air and breath; for our breath is very much changed by such kind of vapours, if both vapours be of the other like. The air being also, through the said vapours, easily moved, or infected with the qualities of inferiors, or celestial (daily quickly penetrating our breast and vitals), does wonderfully reduce us to the like qualities. Let no man wonder how great things suffumigations can do in the air; especially when they shall, with Porphyry, consider that, by certain vapours exhaled from proper suffumigations, ærial spirits are raised; also thunder and lightnings, and the like: as the liver of a cameleon being burnt on the house top, will raise showers and lightnings; the same effect has the head and throat, if they are burnt with oaken wood. There are some suffumigations under the influences of the stars, that cause images of spirits to appear in the air, or elsewhere: for if coriander, smallage, henbane, and hemlock be made to fume, by invocations spirits will soon come together, being attracted by the vapours which are most congruous to their own natures; hence they are called the herbs of the spirits. Also it is said, that if a fume be made of the root of the reedy herb sagapen, with the juice of hemlock and henbane, and the herb tapsus barbatus, red sanders, and black poppy, it will likewise make strange shapes appear; but if a suffume be made of smallage, it chases them away, and destroys their visions. Again, if a perfume is made of calamint, piony, mint, and palma christi, it drives away all evil spirits and vain imaginations. Likewise, by certain fumes, animals are gathered together, and put to flight. Pliny mentions concerning the stone liparis, that, with the fume thereof, all beasts are attracted together. The bones in the upper part of the throat of a hart, being burnt, bring serpents together; but the horn of the hart, being burnt, chases away the same; likewise, a fume of peacock's feathers does the same. Also, the lungs of an ass, being burnt, puts all poisonous things to flight; and the fume of the burnt hoof of a horse drives away mice; the same does the hoof a mule; and with the hoof of the left-foot flies are driven away. And if a house, or ally place, be smoaked with the gall of a cuttle-fish, made into a confection with red storax, roses, and lignum aloes, and then there be some sea-water or blood cast into that place, the whole house will seem to be full of water or blood.

Now such kind of vapours as these, we must conceive, do infect a body, and infuse a virtue into it which continues long, even as the poisonous vapour of the pestilence, being kept for two years in the walls of a house, infects the inhabitants; and as the contagion of pest or leprosy lying hid in a garment, will, long after, infect him that wears it.

Now there are certain suffumigations used to almost all our instruments of magic (of which hereafter), such as images, rings, &c. For some of the magicians say, that if any one shall hide gold, or silver, or any other such like precious thing (the moon being in conjunction with the sun), and shall perfume the place with coriander, saffron, henbane, smallage, and black poppy, of each the same quantity, and bruised together, and tempered with the juice of hemlock, that thing which is so hid shall never be taken away therefrom, but that spirit shall continually keep it; and if any one shall endeavour to take it away by force, they shall be hurt, or struck with a frenzy. And Hermes says, there is nothing like the fume of spermaceti for the raising up of spirits; therefore if a fume be made of that, lignum aloes, pepperwort, musk, saffron, and red storax, tempered together with the blood of a lapwing or bat, it will quickly gather airy spirits to the place where it is used; and if it be used above the graves of the dead, it will attract spirits and ghosts thither.

Now the use of suffumigations is this: that whenever we set about making any talisman, image, or the like, under the rule or dominion of any star or planet, we should by no means omit the making of a suffumigation appropriate to that planet or constellation under which we desire to work any effect or wonderful operation; as for instance:--when we direct any work to the sun, we must suffume with solary things; if to the moon, with lunary things; and so of the rest. And we must be careful to observe, that as there is a contrariety, or antipathy, in the natures of the stars and planets and their spirits, so there is also in suffumigations: for there is an antipathy between lignum aloes and sulphur frankincense and quicksilver; and spirits that are raised by the fume of lignum aloes, are laid by the burning of sulphur. For the learned Proclus gives an example of a spirit that appeared in the form of a lion, furious and raging: by setting a white cock before the apparition it soon vanished away; because there is so great a contrariety between a cock and a lion;--and let this suffice for a general observation in these kind of things. We shall proceed with showing distinctly the composition of the several fumes appropriated to the seven planets.

CHAPTER 10. OF THE COMPOSITION OF SOME PERFUMES APPROPRIATED TO THE SEVEN PLANETS

THE SUN. ☉

WE make a suffumigation for the sun in this manner:--

Take of saffron, ambergris, musk, lignum aloes, lignum balsam, the fruit of the laurel, cloves, myrrh, and frankincense; of each a like quantity; all of which being bruised, and mixed together, so as to make a sweet odour, must be incorporated with the brain of an eagle, or the blood of a white cock, after the manner of pills, or troches.

THE MOON. ☽

For the moon, we make a suffume of the head of a frog dried, and the eyes of a bull, the seed of white poppies, frankincense, and camphire, which must be incorporated with menstruous blood, or the blood of a goose.

SATURN. ♄

For saturn take the seed of black poppies, henbane, mandrake root, loadstone, and myrrh, and mix them up with the brain of a cat and the blood of a bat.

JUPITER. ♃

Take the seed of ash, lignum aloes, storax, the gum Benjamin, the lapis lazuli, the tops of peacocks' feathers, and incorporate with the blood of a stork, or swallow, or the brain of a hart.

MARS. ♂

Take uphorbium, bdellium, gum armoniac, the roots of both hellebores, the loadstone, and a little sulphur, and incorporate them altogether with the brain of a hart, the blood of a man, and the blood of a black cat.

VENUS. ♀

Take musk, ambergris, lignum aloes, red roses, and red coral, and make them up with sparrow's brains and pigeon's blood.

MERCURY. ☿

Take mastich, frankincense, cloves, and the herb cinquefoil, and the agate stone, and incorporate them all with the brain of a fox, or weasel, and the blood of a magpie.

GENERAL FUMES OF THE PLANETS.

To Saturn are appropriated for fumes, odoriferous roots: as pepper-wort root, &c., and the frankincense tree. To Jupiter, all odoriferous fruits: as nutmegs, cloves, &c. To Mars, all odoriferous woods: as sanders, Cyprus, lignum balsam, and lignum aloes. To the Sun, all gums: as frankincense, mastich benjamin, storax, laudanum, ambergris, and musk. To Venus, flowers: as roses, violets, saffron, and the like. To Mercury, all the parings of wood or fruit: as cinnamon, lignum cassia, mace, citron peel, and bayberries, and whatever seeds are odoriferous. To the Moon, the leaves of all vegetables: as the leaf indum, the leaf of the myrtle, and bay tree. Know, also, that according to the opinion of all magicians, in every good matter (as love, good-will, &c.), there must be a good perfume, odoriferous and precious;--and in evil matters (as hatred, anger, misery, and the like), there must be a stinking fume that is of no worth.

101

The twelves Signs of the Zodiac also have their proper suffumigations, viz., Aries, myrrh; Taurus, pepper-wort; Gemini, mastich; Cancer, camphire; Leo, frankincense; Virgo, sanders; Libra, galbanum; Scorpio, oppoponax; Sagittarius, lignum aloes; Capricorn, benjamin; Aquarius, euphorbium; Pisces, red storax. But Hermes describes the most powerful fume to be, that which is compounded of the seven aromatics, according to the powers of the seven planets: for it receives from Saturn, pepper-wort; from Jupiter, nutmeg; from Mars, lignum-aloes; from the Sun, mastich; from Venus, saffron; from Mercury, cinnamon; and from the Moon, myrtle.

By a close observation of the above order of suffumigations, conjoined with other things, of which we shall speak hereafter (necessary to the full accomplishment of Talismanic Magic), many wonderful effects may be caused, especially if we keep in eye what was delivered in the first part of our Magic, viz. that the soul of the operator must go along with this; otherwise, in vain is suffumigation, seal, ring, image, picture, glass, or any other instrument of magic: seeing that it is not merely the disposition, but the act of the disposition, and firm and powerful intent or imagination that gives the effect.--We shall now hasten to speak, generally, of the construction of rings magical, and their wonderful and potent virtues and operations.

CHAPTER 11. OF THE COMPOSITION AND MAGIC VIRTUE OF RINGS

RINGS, when they are opportunely made, impress their virtues upon us insomuch that they affect the spirit of him that carries them with gladness or sadness; and render him bold or fearful, courteous or terrible, amiable or hateful; inasmuch, also as they fortify us against [94:1] sickness, poisons, enemies, evil spirits, and all manner of hurtful things; and often, where the law has no effect, these little trifles greatly assist and corroborate the troubled spirit of the wearer, and help him, in a wonderful manner, to overcome his adversaries, while they do wonder how it is that they cannot effect any hurtful undertaking against him. These things, I say, are great helps against wrathful, vicious, worldly-minded men, inasmuch as they do terrify, hurt, and render invalid the machinations of those who would otherwise work our misery or destruction. All which we are neither afraid nor ashamed to declare, well knowing that these things will be hid from the wicked and profane, so as that they cannot draw the same into any abuse, or privy mischief toward their neighbour; we having reserved some few things in this art to ourselves--not willing to throw pearls before swine, And however simple and plain we may describe some certain experiments and operations (so as that the great-mouthed school philosophers may mutter or scoff thereat), yet there is nothing delivered in this book but what may be, by an understanding thereof, brought into effect, and, likewise, out of which some good may be derived. But to proceed.

The manner of making of these rings is thus:--when any star ascends in the horoscope (fortunately), with a fortunate aspect or conjunction of the moon, we proceed to take a stone and herb, that is under that star, and likewise make a ring of the metal that is corresponding to the star; and in the ring under the stone, put the herb or root, not forgetting to inscribe the effect, image, name, and character, as also the proper suffume. But I shall speak more of these in another place, where I speak of images and characters. Therefore, in making of rings magical, these things are unerringly to be observed as we have ordered;--if any one is willing to work any effect or experiment in magic, he must by no means neglect the necessary circumstances which we have so uniformly delivered. I have read, in Philostratus Jarchus, that a Prince of the Indians bestowed seven rings, marked with the virtues and names of the seven planets, to Appollonius, of which he wore one every day, distinguishing according to the names of the days; by the benefit of which he lived above one hundred and thirty years, as also always retained the beauty of his youth. In like manner, Moses, the Lawgiver and Ruler of the Hebrews, being skilled in the Egyptian Magic, is said, by Josephus, to have made rings of love and oblivion. There was also, as saith Aristotle, among the Cireneans, a ring of Battas, which could procure love and honour. We read, also, that Eudamus, a certain philosopher, made rings against the bites of serpents, bewitchings, and evil spirits. The same doth Josephus relate of Solomon. Also we read, in Plato, that Gygus, King of Lydia, had a ring of wonderful and strange virtues; the seal of which, when he turned it toward the palm of his hand, no body could see him, but he could see all things; by the opportunity of which ring, he ravished the Queen, and slew the King his master, and killed whomsoever he thought stood in his way; and in these villanies nobody could see him; and at length, by the benefit of this ring, he became King of Lydia. [96:1]

94:1 The Author will engage to teach any that are curious in those studies, the particular composition of Talismanic Rings; whereby they may be enabled to judge themselves of the effects that are to be produced by them.

96:1 We have above shewn the power and virtue of magical rings; but the particular characters, inscriptions, and images to be made in, or upon them, we refer the student to that chapter treating of "The Composition of various Talismans" in which we have described exactly the express methods of perfecting them.

CHAPTER 12. THAT THE PASSIONS OF THE MIND ARE ASSISTED BY CELESTIALS...

THAT THE PASSIONS OF THE MIND ARE ASSISTED BY CELESTIALS--AND THAT CONSTANCY OF MIND IS IN EVERY WORK NECESSARY.

THE passions of the mind are much helped, and are helpful, and become most powerful, by virtue of the heaven, as they agree with the heaven--either by any natural agreement, or voluntary election; for, as Ptolemy says, he who chuseth that which is the better, seems to differ nothing from him who hath this of Nature. It conduceth, therefore, very much for the receiving the benefit of the heavens, in any work, if we shall, by the heaven, make ourselves suitable to it in our thoughts, affections, imaginations, elections, deliberations, contemplations, and the like. For such like passions vehemently stir up our spirit to their likeness, and suddenly expose us, and our's, to the superior significators of such like passions; and also, by reason of their dignity and nearness to the superiors, do partake more of the celestials than any material things; for our mind can, through imaginations or reason by a kind of imitation, be so conformed to any star, as suddenly to be filled with the virtues of that star, as if we were a proper receptacle of the influence thereof. Now the contemplating mind, as it withdraws itself from all sense, imagination, nature, and deliberation, and calls itself back to things separated, effects divers things by faith, which is a firm adhesion, a fixed intention, and vehement application of the worker or receiver to him that co-operates in any thing, and gives power to the work which we intend to do. So that there is made, as it were, in us the image of the virtue to be received, and the thing to be done in us, or by us. We must, therefore, in every work and application of things, affect vehemently, imagine, hope, and believe strongly, for that will be a great help. And it is verified amongst physicians, that a strong belief, and an undoubted hope, and love towards the physician, conduce much to health, yea more sometimes than the medicine itself; for the same that the efficacy and virtue of the medicine works, the same doth the strong imagination of the physician work, being able to change the qualities of the body of the sick, especially when the patient places much confidence in the physician, by that means disposing himself for the receiving the virtue of the physician, and physic. Therefore, he that works in magic must be of a constant belief, be credulous, and not at all doubt of the obtaining of the effect; for as a firm and strong belief doth work wonderful things, although it be in false works--so distrust and doubting doth dissipate and break the virtue of the mind of the worker, which is the medium betwixt both extremes; whence it happens that he is frustrated of the desired influence of the superiors, which could not be enjoined and united to our labours without a firm and solid virtue of our mind.

CHAPTER 13. HOW MAN'S MIND MAY BE JOINED WITH THE MIND OF INTELLIGENCES AND CELESTIALS...

HOW MAN'S MIND MAY BE JOINED WITH THE MIND OF INTELLIGENCES AND CELESTIALS AND TOGETHER WITH THEM, IMPRESS CERTAIN WONDERFUL VIRTUES UPON INFERIOR THINGS.

THE philosophers, especially the Arabians, say, that man's mind, when it is most intent upon any work, through its passion and effects, is joined with the mind of the stars and intelligences, and, being so joined, is the cause that some wonderful virtue be infused into our works and things; and this, as because there is in it an apprehension and power of all things, so because all things have a natural obedience to it, and of necessity an efficacy, and more to that which desired them with a strong desire. And according to this is verified the art of characters, images, enchantments, and some speeches, and many other wonderful experiments, to every thing which the mind affects. By this means, whatsoever the mind of him that is in vehement love affects, hath an efficacy to cause love; and whatsoever the mind of him that strongly hates, dictates, hath an efficacy to hurt and destroy. The like is in other things which the mind affects with a strong desire; for all those things which the mind acts, and dictates by characters, figures, words, speeches, gestures, and the like, help the appetite of the soul, and acquire certain wonderful virtues, from the soul of the operator, in that hour when such a like appetite doth invade it; so from the opportunity and celestial influence, moving the mind in this or that manner: for our mind, when it is carried upon the great excess of any passion or virtue, oftentimes takes to itself a strong, better and more convenient hour or opportunity; which Thomas Aquinas, in his third book against the Gentiles, allows. So, many wonderful virtues both cause and follow certain admirable operations by great affections, in those things which the soul doth dictate in that hour to them. But know, that such kind of things confer nothing, or very little, but to the author of them, and to him who is inclined to them, as if he were the author of them; and this is the manner by which their efficacy is found out. And it is a general rule in them, that every mind, that is more excellent in its desire and affection, makes such like things more fit for itself, as also efficacious to that which it desires. Every one, therefore, that is willing to work in magic, must know the virtue, measure, order, and degree of his own soul in the power of the universe.

CHAPTER 14. SHEWING THE NECESSITY OF MATHEMATICAL KNOWLEDGE...

SHEWING THE NECESSITY OF MATHEMATICAL KNOWLEDGE, AND OF THE GREAT POWER AND EFFICACY OF NUMBERS IN THE CONSTRUCTION OF TALISMANS, &c.

THE doctrines of mathematics are so necessary to and have such an affinity with magic, that they who profess it without them are quite out of the way, and labour in vain, and shall in no wise obtain their desired effect. For whatsoever things are, and are done in these inferior natural virtues, are all done and governed by number, weight, measure, harmony, motion, and light: and all things which we see in these inferiors have root and foundation in them; yet, nevertheless, without natural virtues of mathematical doctrines, only works like to naturals can be produced: as Plato saith--a thing not partaking of truth or divinity, but certain images akin to them (as bodies going, or speaking, which yet want the animal faculty), such as were those which, amongst the ancients, were called Dedalus's images, and αυτοματα, of which Aristotle makes mention, viz. the three-footed images of Vulcan and Dedalus moving themselves; which, Homer saith, came out of their own accord to the exercise; and which, we read, moved themselves at the feast of Hiarba, the philosophical exerciser. So there are made glasses (some concave, others of the form of a column) making the representation of things in the air seem like shadows at a distance; of which sort Apollonius and Vitellius, in their books, "De Prospectiva," and "Speculis," taught the making and the use. And we read that Magnus Pompeius brought a certain glass, amongst the spoils from the East, to Rome, in which were seen armies of armed men. And there are made certain transparent glasses, which (being dipped in some certain juices of herbs, and irradiated with an artificial light) fill the whole air round about with visions. And we know how to make reciprocal glasses, in which the sun shining, all things which were illustrated by the rays thereof are apparently seen many miles off. Hence a magician (expert in natural philosophy and mathematics, and knowing the middle sciences, consisting of both these, viz. arithmetic, music, geometry, optics, astronomy, and such sciences that are of weights, measures, proportions, articles, and joints; knowing, also, mechanical arts resulting from these) may, without any wonder, if he excel other men in the art and wit, do many wonderful things, which men may much admire. There are some relics now extant of the antients, viz. Hercules and Alexander's pillars; the gate of Caspia, made of brass, and shut with iron beams, that it could by no art be broken; and the pyramids of Julius Cæsar, erected at Rome, near the hill Vaticanus; and mountains built by art in the middle of the sea; and towers, and heaps of stones, such as I have seen in England, put together by incredible art. But the vulgar seeing any wonderful sight, impute it to the Devil as his work; or think that a miracle which, indeed, is a work of natural or mathematical philosophy. But here it is convenient that you know, that, as by natural virtues we collect natural virtues, so by abstracted, mathematical, and celestial, we receive celestial virtues; as motion, sense, life, speech, soothsaying, and divination even in matter less disposed, as that which is not made by nature, but only by art. And so images that speak, and foretel things to come, are said to be made: as William of Paris relates of a brazen-head, made under the rising of Saturn, which, they say, spake with a man's voice. But he that will chuse a disposed matter, and most fit to receive, and a most powerful agent, shall undoubtedly produce more powerful effects. For it is a general opinion of the Pythagoreans, that, as mathematical are more formal than natural, so also they are more efficacious; as they have less dependance in their being, so also in their operation. But amongst all mathematical things, numbers, as they have more of form in them, so also are more efficacious, as well to affect what is good as what is bad. All things, which were first made by the nature of things in its first age, seem to be formed by the proportion of numbers; for this was the principal pattern in the mind of the Creator. Hence is borrowed the number of the elements--hence the courses of times--hence the motion of the stars, and the revolution of the heavens, and the state of all things subsist by the uniting together of numbers. Numbers, therefore, are endowed with great and sublime virtues. For it is no wonder, seeing there arc so many occult virtues in natural things, although of manifest operations, that there should be in numbers much greater and more occult, and also more wonderful and efficacious; for as much as they are more formal, more perfect, and naturally in the celestials, not mixed with separated substances; and, lastly, having the greatest and most simple commixion with the ideas in the mind of God, from which they receive their proper and most efficacious virtues; wherefore they also are of most force, and conduce most to the obtaining of spiritual and divine gifts--as, in natural things, elementary qualities are powerful in the transmuting of any elementary thing. Again, all things that are, and are made, subsist by and receive their virtue from numbers:--for time consists of numbers--and all motion and action, and all things which are subject to time and motion. Harmony, also, and voices have their power by and consist of numbers and their proportions; and the proportion arising from numbers do, by lines and points, make characters and figures; and these are proper to magical operations--the middle, which is betwixt both, being appropriated by declining to the extremes, as in the use of letters. And lastly, all species of natural things, and of those which are above Nature, are joined together by certain numbers; which Pythagoras seeing, says, that number is that by which all things subsist, and distributes each virtue to each number. And Proclus says, number hath always a being: yet there is one in voice--another in proportion of them--another in the soul and reason--and another in divine things. But Themistius, Boetius, and Averrois (the Babylonian), together with Plato, do so extol numbers, that they think no man can be a true philosopher without them. By them there is a way made for the searching out and understanding of all things knowable;--by them the next access to natural prophecying is had--and the Abbot Joachim proceeded no other way in his prophecies, but by formal numbers.

CHAPTER 15. THE GREAT VIRTUES OF NUMBERS, AS WELL IN NATURAL THINGS AS IN SUPERNATURAL

THAT there lies wonderful efficacy and virtue in numbers, as well to good as to bad, the most eminent philosophers unanimously teach; especially Hierom, Austin, Origen, Ambrose, Gregory of Nazianzen, Athanasius, Basilius, Hilarius, Rubanas, Bede, and many more conform. Hence Hilarius, in his commentaries upon the Psalms, testifies that the seventy elders, according to the efficacy of numbers, brought the Psalms into order. The natural number is not here considered; but the formal consideration that is in the number;--and let that which we spoke before always be kept in mind, viz. that these powers are not in vocal numbers of merchants buying and selling; but in rational, formal, and natural;--these are the distinct mysteries of God and Nature. But he who knows how to join together the vocal numbers and natural with divine, and order them into the same harmony, shall be able to work and know wonderful things by numbers; in which, unless there was a great mystery, John had not said, in the Revelation--"He that hath understanding, let him compute the number of the name of the beast, which is the number of a man;"--and this is the most famous manner of computing amongst the Hebrews and Cabalists, as we shall shew afterwards. But this you must know, that simple numbers signify divine things, numbers of ten; celestial numbers of an hundred; terrestrial numbers of a thousand--those things that shall be in a future age. Besides, seeing the parts of the mind are according to an arithmetical mediocrity, by reason of the identity, or equality of excess, coupled together; but the body, whose parts differ in their greatness, is, according to a geometrical mediocrity, compounded; but an animal consists of both, viz. soul and body, according to that mediocrity which is. suitable to harmony. Hence it is that numbers work very much upon the soul, figures upon the body, and harmony upon the whole animal.

CHAPTER 16. OF THE SCALE OF UNITY

NOW let us treat particularly of numbers themselves; and, because number is nothing else but a repetition of unity, let us first consider unity itself; for unity doth most simply go through every number, and is the common measure, fountain, and original of all numbers; contains every number joined together in itself entirely; the beginner of every multitude, always the same, and unchangeable; whence, also, being multiplied into itself, produceth nothing but itself: it is indivisible, void of all parts. Nothing is before one, nothing is after one, and beyond it is nothing; and all things which are, desire that one, because all things proceed from one; and that all things may be the same, it is necessary that they partake of that one: and as all things proceed of one into many things, so all thins endeavour to return to that one, from which they proceeded; it is necessary that they should put off multitude. One, therefore, is referred to the most high God, who, seeing he is one and innumerable, yet creates innumerable things of himself, and contains them within himself. There is, therefore, one God--one world of the one God--one sun of the one world--also one phœnix in the world--one king amongst bees--one leader amongst flocks of cattle--one ruler amongst herds of beasts--and cranes follow one, and many other animals honour unity. Amongst the members of the body there is one principal, by which all the rest are guided; whether it be the head, or (as some will) the heart. There is one element, overcoming and penetrating all things, viz. fire. There is one thing created of God, the subject of all wondering which is in earth or in heaven--it is actually animal, vegetable, and mineral; every where found, known by few, called by none by its proper name, but covered with figures and riddles, without which neither Alchymy, nor Natural Magic can attain to their complete end or perfection. From one man, Adam, all men proceeded--from that One, all became mortal--from that one, Jesus Christ, they are regenerated; and, as saith St. Paul., one Lord, one faith, one baptism, one God and Father of all, one Mediator betwixt God and man, one most high Creator, who is over all, by all, and in us all, For there is one Father, God, from whence all, and we in him; one Lord Jesus Christ, by whom all, and we by him; one God Holy Ghost, into whom all, and we into him.

THE SCALE OF UNITY.

In the Exemplary World,	Jod.	One Divine Essence, the fountain of all virtues and power whose name is expressed with one most simple letter.
In the Intellectual World,	The Soul of the World	One Supreme Intelligence, the first creature, the fountain of life.
In the Celestial World,	The Sun.	One King of Stars, the fountain of life.
In the Elemental World,	The Philosophers' Stone.	One subject, and instrument of all virtues, natural and supernatural.
In the Lesser World,	The Heart.	One first living and last dying.
In the Infernal World,	Lucifer.	One Prince of Rebellion, of Angels, and Darkness.

114

CHAPTER 17. OF THE NUMBER TWO, AND SCALE

THE first number is two, because it is the first multitude; it can be measured by no number besides unity alone, the common measure of all numbers; it is not compounded of numbers, but of one unity only; neither is it called a number uncompounded, but more properly not compounded. The number three, is called the first number uncompounded. But the number two is the first branch of unity, and the first procreation; and it is called the number of science, and memory, and of light, and the number of man, who is called another, and the lesser world: it is also called the number of charity, and of mutual love; of marriage, and society: as it is said by the Lord--"Two shall be one flesh."--And Solomon saith, "It is better that two be together than one, for they have a benefit by their mutual society: if one shall fall, he shall be supported by the other. Woe to him that is alone; because, when he falls, he hath not another to help him. And if two sleep together, they shall warm one another; how shall one be hot alone?--And if any prevail against him, two resist him." And it is called the number of wedlock, and sex; for there are two sexes--masculine and feminine. And two doves bring forth two eggs; out of the first of which is hatched the male, out of the second the female, It is also called the middle, that is capable, that is good and bad, partaking; and the beginning of division, of multitude, and distinction; and signifies matter. This is also, sometimes, the number of discord, of confusion, of misfortune, and uncleanness; whence St. Hierom, against Jovianus, saith--"that therefore it was not spoken in the second day of the creation of the world."--"And God said, that it was good;"--because the number of two is evil. Hence also it was, that God commanded that all unclean animals should go into the ark by couples; because, as I said, the number of two is a number of uncleanness. Pythagorus, as Eusebius reports, said, that unity was God, and a good intellect; but that duality was a devil, and an evil intellect, in which is a material multitude: wherefore the Pythagorians say, that two is not a number, but a certain confusion of unities. And Plutarch writes, that the Pythagorians called unity, Apollo; and two, strife and boldness; and three, justice, which is the highest perfection, and is not without many mysteries. Hence there were two tables of the law in Sinai--two cherubims looking to the propitiatory in Moses--two olives dropping oil, in Zachariah--two natures in Christ, divine and human: hence Moses saw two appearances of God, viz. his face, and back parts;--also two Testaments--two commands of love--two first dignities--two first people--two kinds of spirits, good and bad--two intellectual creatures, an angel and soul--two great lights--two solstitia--two equinoctials--two poles--two elements, producing a living soul, viz. earth and water.

THE SCALE OF THE NUMBER TWO.

In the Exemplary World,	יה Jah אל El		The names of God, expressed with two Letters.
In the Intellectual World,	An Angel,	The Soul;	Two Intelligible Substances.
In the Celestial World,	The Sun,	The Moon;	Two great Lights.
In the Elementary World,	The Earth,	The Water;	Two Elements producing a living Soul.
In the Lesser World,	The Heart,	The Brain;	Two principal Seats of the Soul.
In the Infernal World,	Beemoth, weeping,	Leviathan, gnashing of teeth;	Two Chiefs of the Devils. Two things Christ threatens to the damned.

116

CHAPTER 18. OF THE NUMBER THREE AND SCALE

THE number Three, is an uncompounded number, a holy number, a number of perfection, a most powerful number:--for there are three persons in God; there are three theological virtues in religion. Hence it is that this number conduceth to the ceremonies of God and religion, that by the solemnity of which, prayers and sacrifices are thrice repeated; for corporeal and spiritual things consist of three things, viz. beginning, middle, and end. By three, as Trismegistus saith, the world is perfected--harmony, necessity, and order, i. e. concurrence of causes (which many call fate), and the execution of them to the fruit, or increase, or a due distribution of the increase. The whole measure of time is concluded in three, viz. past, present, and to come;--all magnitude is contained in three--line, superfices, and body;-- every body consists of three intervals,--length, breadth, and thickness. Harmony contains three consents in time--diapason, hemiolion, diatesseron. There are also three kinds of souls--vegetative, sensitive, and intellectual. And as such, saith the Prophet, God orders the world by number, weight, and measure; and the number three is deputed to the ideal forms thereof, as the number two is the procreating matter, and unity to God the maker of it.--Magicians do constitute three Princes of the world--Oromasis, Mithris, Araminis; i. e. God, the mind, and the spirit. By the three-square or solid, the three numbers of nine, of things produced, are distributed, viz. of the supercelestial into nine orders of intelligences; of celestial, into nine orbs; of inferiors, into nine kinds of generable and corruptible things. Lastly, into this eternal orb, viz. twenty-seven, all musical proportions are included., as Plato and Proclus do at large discourse; and the number three hath, in a harmony of five, the grace of the first voice. Also, in intelligences, there are three hierarchies of angelical spirits. There are three powers of intellectual creatures--memory, mind, and will. There are three orders of the blessed, viz. martyrs, confessors, and innocents. There are three quaternions of celestial signs, viz. of fixed, moveable, and common; as also of houses, viz. centres, succeeding, and falling. There are, also, three faces and heads in every sign, and three Lords of each triplicity. There are three fortunes amongst the planets. In the infernal crew, three judges, three furies, three-headed Cerberus: we read, also, of a thrice-double Hecate. Three months of the Virgin Diana. Three persons in the super-substantial Divinity. Three times--of nature, law, and grace. Three theological virtues--faith, hope, and charity. Jonah was three days in the whale's belly; and so many was Christ in the grave.

THE SCALE OF THE NUMBER THREE.

In the Original World,	The Father,	Adai, The Son,	The Holy Ghost;	The Name of God with three Letters
In the Intellectual World,	Supreme Innocents,	Middle Martyrs,	Lowest of all Confessors;	Three hierarchies of Angels. Three degrees of the Blessed.
In the Celestial World,	Moveable, Corners, Of the Day,	Fixed, Succeeding, Nocturnal,	Common; Falling; Partaking;	Three quaternions of Signs. Three quaternions of houses. Three Lords of triplicities.
In the Elementary World,	Simple,	Compounded,	Thrice compounded;	Three degrees of elements.
In the Lesser World,	The head, in which the intellect grows, answering to the intellectual world,	The breast, where is the heart, the seat of life, answering to the celestial world,	The belly, where the faculty of generation is, and the genital members, answering the elemental world;	Three parts, answering to the threefold world.
In the Infernal World,	Alecto, Minos, Wicked,	Megera, Acacus, Apostates,	Ctesiphone; Rhadamantus; Infidels;	Three infernal Furies. Three infernal Judges. Three degrees of the damned.

CHAPTER 19. OF THE NUMBER FOUR AND SCALE

THE Pythagorians call the number Four, Tectractis, and prefer it before all the virtues of numbers, because it is the foundation and root of all other numbers; Whence, also, all foundations, as well in artificial things, as natural and divine, are four square, as we shall shew afterwards; and it signifies solidity, which also is demonstrated by a four-square figure; for the number four, is the first four-square plane, which consists of two proportions, whereof the first is of one to two, the latter of two to four; and it proceeds by a double procession and proportion, viz. of one to one, and of two to two--beginning at a unity, and ending at a quaternity: which proportions differ in this, that, according to Arithmetic, they are unequal to one another, but according to Geometry, are equal. Therefore a four-square is ascribed to God the Father; and also contains the mystery of the whole Trinity: for by its single proportion, viz. by the first of one to one, the unity of the paternal substance is signified, from which proceeds one Son, equal to Him;--by the next procession, also simple, viz. of two to two, is signified (by the second procession) the Holy Ghost; from both--that the Son be equal to the Father, by the first procession; and the Holy Ghost be equal to both, by the second procession. Hence that superexcellent and great name of the Divine Trinity in God is written with four letters, viz. Jod, He, and Vau. He, where it is the aspiration He, signifies the proceeding of the Spirit from both; for He, being duplicated, terminates both syllables, and the whole name, but is pronounced Jova, as some will whence that Jove of the heathen, which the antients did picture with four cars; whence the number four, is the fountain and head of the whole, Divinity. And the Pythagorians call it the perpetual fountain of Nature: for there are four degrees in the scale of Nature, viz. to be, to live, to be sensible, to understand. There are four motions in Nature, viz. ascendant, descendant, going forward, circular. There are four corners in Heaven, viz. rising, falling, the middle of the Heaven, the bottom of it. There are four elements under Heaven, viz. fire, air, water, and earth; according to these there are four triplicities in Heaven. There are four first qualities under Heaven, viz. cold, heat, dryness, and moisture; from these are the four humours--blood, phlegm, choler, melancholy. Also, the year is divided into four parts, which are the spring, summer, autumn, and winter:--also

119

the wind is divided into eastern, western, northern, and southern. There are, also, four rivers in Paradise; and so many infernal. Also, the number four makes up all knowledge: first, it fills up every simple progress of numbers with four terms, viz. with one, two, three, and four, constituting the number ten. It fills up every difference of numbers: the first even, and containing the first odd in it. It hath in music, diatesseron--the grace of the fourth voice; also it contains the instrument of four strings; and a Pythagorian diagram, whereby are found out first of all musical tunes, and all harmony of music: for double, treble, four times double, one and a half, one and a third part, a concord of all, a double concord of all, of five, of four, and all consonancy is limited within the bounds of the number four. It doth also contain the whole of Mathematics in four terms, viz. point, line, superfices, and profundity. It comprehends all Nature in four terms, viz. substance, quality, quantity, and motion; also all natural philosophy, in which are the seminary virtues of Nature, the natural springing, the growing form, and the compositum. Also metaphysics is comprehended in four bounds, viz. being, essence, virtue, and action. Moral philosophy is comprehended with four virtues, viz. prudence, justice, fortitude, and temperance. It hath also the power of justice: hence a four-fold law--of providence, from God; fatal, from the soul of the world; of Nature, from Heaven; of prudence, from man. There are also four judiciary powers in all things being, viz. the intellect, discipline, opinion, and sense. Also, there are four rivers of Paradise. Four Gospels, received from four Evangelists, throughout the whole Church. The Hebrews received the chiefest name of God written with four letters. Also the Egyptians, Arabians, Persians, Magicians, Mahometans, Grecians, Tuscans, and Latins, write the name of God with four letters, viz. thus--Thet, Alla, Sire, Orsi, Abdi, θεòς, Esar, Deus. Hence the Lacedemonians were wont to paint Jupiter with four wings. Hence, also, in Orpheus's Divinity, it is said that Neptune's chariots are drawn with four horses. There are also four kinds of divine furies proceeding from several deities, viz. from the Muses, Dionysius, Apollo, and Venus. Also, the Prophet Ezekiel saw four beasts by the river Chobar, and four cherubims in four wheels. Also, in Daniel, four great beasts did ascend from the sea; and four winds did fight. And in the Revelations, four beasts were full of eyes, before and behind, standing round about the throne of God and for angels, to whom was given power to hurt the earth and the sea, did stand upon the four corners of the earth, holding the four winds, that they should not blow upon the earth, nor upon the sea, nor upon any tree.

THE SCALE OF THE NUMBER FOUR

The name of God with four letters,	יהוה				In the original world, whence the law of Providence.
Four triplicities, or intelligible hierarchies,	Seraphim, Cherubim, Thrones,	Dominations, Powers, Virtues,	Principalities, Archangels, Angels,	Innocents, Martyrs, Confessors.	In the intellectual world, whence the fatal law.
Four angels ruling over the four corners of the world,	מיכאל Michael,	רפאל Raphael,	גבריאל Gabriel,	אוריאל Uriel.	
Four rulers of the elements,	שרף Seraph,	כרוב Cherub,	תרשיש Tharsis,	אריאל Ariel	
Four consecrated animals,	The Lion,	The Eagle,	Man,	A Calf.	
Four triplicities of the tribes of Israel,	Dan, Asser, Naphthalin,	Jehuda, Isachar, Zebulun,	Manasse, Benjamin, Ephraim,	Reuben, Simeon, Gad.	
Four triplicities of the Apostles,	Matthias, Peter, Jacob the elder,	Simon, Bartholomew, Matthew,	John, Philip, James the younger	Thaddeus, Andrew, Thomas.	
Four Evangelists:	Mark,	John,	Matthew,	Luke.	
Four triplicities of signs,	Aries, Leo, Sagittarius,	Gemini, Libra, Aquarius,	Cancer, Scorpion, Pisces,	Taurus, Virgo, Capricornus.	In the celestial world, where is the law of Nature.

The stars and planets related to the elements,	Mars, and the Sun,	Jupiter, and Venus,	Saturn, and Mercury,	The fixed Stars, and the Moon.	
Four qualities of the celestial elements,	Light,	Diaphanousness,	Agility,	Solidity.	
Four elements,	אש Fire,	ריה Air,	מים Water,	עפר Earth	In the elementary, where the law of generation and corruption is.
Four seasons,	Summer,	Spring,	Winter,	Autumn.	
Four corners of the world,	East,	West,	North,	South.	
Four perfect kinds of mixed bodies,	Animals,	Plants,	Metals,	Stones.	
Four kinds of animals,	Walking,	Flying,	Swimming,	Creeping	
What answers the elements in plants,	Seeds,	Flowers,	Leaves,	Roots.	
What in metals,	Gold and iron,	Copper and tin,	Quicksilver,	Lead and silver.	
What in stones,	Bright and burning,	Light and transsparent,	Clear and congealed,	Heavy and dark.	

Four elements of man,	The Mind,	Spirit,	Soul,	Body.	In the lesser world, viz. man from whom is the law of prudence.
Four powers of the soul,	The Intellect,	Reason,	Phantasy,	Sense.	
Four judiciary powers,	Faith,	Science,	Opinion,	Experience.	
Four moral virtues	Justice,	Temperance,	Prudence,	Fortitude.	
The senses answering to the elements,	Sight,	Hearing,	Taste and smell,	Touch.	
Four elements of man's body,	Spirit,	Flesh,	Humours,	Bones.	
A fourfold spirit,	Animal,	Vital,	Generative,	Natural.	
Four humours,	Choler,	Blood,	Phlegm,	Melancholy.	
Four manners of complexion,	Violence,	Nimbleness,	Dulness,	Slowness.	
Four princes of devils, offensive in the elements,	סמאל Samael,	עזאזל Azazel,	עזאל Azael,	מהזאל Mahazael.	In the infernal world, where is the law of wrath and punishment.
Four infernal rivers	Phlegethon,	Cocytus,	Styx,	Acheron.	
Four princes of spirits, upon the four angles of the world,	Oriens,	Paymon,	Egyn,	Amaymon.	

CHAPTER 20. OF THE NUMBER FIVE, AND ITS SCALE

THE number Five is of no small force; for it consists of the first even and the first odd; as of a female and male: for an odd number is the male, and the even the female; whence arithmeticians call that the father, and this the mother. Therefore the number five is of no small perfection or virtue, which proceeds from the mixtion of these numbers; it is, also, the just middle of the universal number, viz. ten: for if you divide the number ten, there will be nine and one, or eight and two, and seven and three, or six and four, and every collection makes the number ten, and the exact middle is always the number five, and its equadistant; and therefore it is called, by the Pythagorians, the number of wedlock, as also of justice, because it divides the number ten in an even scale. There are five senses in man--sight, hearing, smelling, tasting, and feeling; five powers in the soul--vegetative, sensitive, concupiscible, irascible, and rational; five fingers on the hand; five wandering planets in the heavens, according to which there are fivefold terms in every sign. In elements there are five kinds of mixed bodies, viz. stones, metals, plants, plant-animals, animals; and so many kinds of animals--as men, four-footed beasts, creeping, swimming, and flying. And there are five kinds by which all things are made of God, viz. essence, the same, another, sense, and motion. The swallow brings forth but five young, which she feeds with equity, beginning with the eldest, and so the rest according to their age. For in this number the father Noah found favour with God, and was preserved in the flood of waters. In the virtue of this number, Abraham, being an hundred years old, begat a son of Sarah (Sarah being ninety years old, and a barren woman, and past childbearing), and grew up to be a great people. Hence, in time of grace, the name of Divine Omnipotency is called upon in five letters; in time of nature, the name of God was called upon with three letters שׁדי, Sadai; in time of the law, the ineffable name of God was expressed with four letters יהוה instead of which the Hebrews express אדני Adonai; in time of grace, the ineffable name of God was written with five letters יהשוה, Jhesu, which is called upon with no less mystery than that of three letters יֹשֶׁךְ.

THE SCALE OF THE NUMBER FIVE.

The Names of God with five letters. The Name of Christ with five letters,		אליון אלהים יהשוה	Eloim, Elohi, Jhesu,			In the exemplary world.
Five intelligible substances,	Spirits of the first hierarchy, called Gods, or the sons of God	Spirits of the second hierarchy, called Intelligences,	Spirits of the third hierarchy, called Angels which are sent,	Souls of celestial bodies,	Heroes and blessed souls.	In the intellectual world.
Five wandering stars, lords of the terms,	Saturn,	Jupiter,	Mars,	Venus,	Mercury.	In the celestial world.
Five kinds of corruptible things,	Water,	Air,	Fire,	Earth,	A mixed body.	In the elementary world.
Five kinds of mixed bodies,	Animal,	Plant,	Metal,	Stone,	Plant-animal.	
Five senses,	Taste,	Hearing,	Seeing,	Touching,	Smelling.	In the lesser world.
Five corporeal torments,	Deadly bitterness,	Horrible howling,	Terrible darkness,	Unquenchable heat,	A piercing stink.	In the infernal world.

CHAPTER 21. OF THE NUMBER SIX, AND THE SCALE

SIX is a number of perfection, because it is the most perfect in nature, in the whole course of numbers, from one to ten; and it alone is so perfect that in the collection of its parts, it results the same, neither wanting nor abounding; for if the parts thereof, viz. the middle, third, and sixth part, which are three, two, one, be gathered together, they perfectly fill up the whole body of six, which perfection all the other numbers want. Hence, by the Pythagorians, it is said to be altogether to be applied to generation and marriage, and is called the scale of the world; for the world is made of the number six--neither doth it abound, nor is defective: hence that is, because the world was finished by God the sixth day; for the sixth day God saw all things which he had made, and they were [116:1] very good; therefore the heaven, and the earth, and all the host thereof, were finished. It is also called the number of man, because the sixth day [116:2] man was created. And it is also the number of our redemption; for on the sixth day Christ suffered for our redemption; whence there is a great affinity between the number six and the cross, labour, and servitude. Hence it is commanded in the law, that in six days the manna is to be gathered, and work to be done. Six years the ground was to be sown; and that the Hebrew servant was to serve his master six years. Six days the glory of the Lord appeared upon Mount Sinai, covering it with a cloud. The Cherubims had six wings. Six circles in the firmament: Artic, Antartic, two Tropics, Equinoctial and Ecliptical. Six wandering planets: Saturn, Jupiter, Mars, Venus, Mercury, the Moon, running through the latitude of the Zodiac on both sides the Ecliptic. There are six substantial qualities in the elements, viz. sharpness, thinness, motion; and the contrary to these--dulness, thickness, and rest. There are six differences of position: upwards, downwards, before, behind, on the right side, and on the left side. There are six natural offices, without which nothing can be, viz. magnitude, colour, figure, interval, standing, motion. Also, a solid figure of any four-square thing hath six superfices. There are six tones of all harmony, viz. five tones, and two half tones which make one tone, which is the sixth.

THE SCALE OF THE NUMBER SIX.

In the Exemplary World.							Names of six letters.
In the Intelligible World,	Seraphim,	Cherubim,	Thrones,	Dominations,	Powers,	Virtues;	Six orders of Angels, which are not sent to inferiors.
In the Celestial World.	Saturn,	Jupiter,	Mars,	Venus,	Mercury,	The Moon;	Six planets wandering through the latitude of the Zodiac from the Ecliptic.
In the Elemental World,	Rest,	Thinness,	Sharpness,	Dulness,	Thickness,	Motion;	Six substantial qualities of the elements.
In the Lesser World,	The Intellect,	Memory,	Sense,	Motion,	Life,	Essence;	Six degrees of the mind.
In the Infernal World,	Acteus,	Megalesius,	Ormenus,	Lycus,	Nicon,	Mimon;	Six Devils, the authors of all calamities.

116:1 The sixth day, the Eternal Wisdom pronounced all things created by his divine hand to be "very good."

116:2 Hence arose the mystery of the number of the beast, six hundred three score and six, being the number of a man--DCLXVI.

CHAPTER 22. OF THE NUMBER SEVEN, AND THE SCALE

THE number Seven is of various and manifold power; for it consists of one and six, or of two and five, or of three and four; and it hath a unity, as it were the coupling together of two threes: whence if we consider the several parts thereof, and the joining together of them, without doubt we shall confess that it is, as well by the joining together of the parts thereof as by its fulness apart, most full of all majesty. And the Pythagorians call it the vehiculum of man's life, which it doth not receive from its parts so, as it perfects by its proper right of its whole--for it contains body and soul; for the body consists of four elements, and is endowed with four qualities: also, the number three respects the soul, by reason of its threefold power, viz. rational, irascible, and concupiscible. The number seven, therefore, because it consists of three and four, joins the soul to the body; and the virtue of this number relates to the of men, and it causes man to be received, formed, brought forth, nourished, live, and indeed altogether to subsist: for when the genital seed is received in the womb of the woman, if it remains there seven hours after the effusion of it, it is certain that it will abide there for good; then the first seven days it is coagulated, and is fit to receive the shape of a man; then it produces mature infants, which are called infants of the seventh month, i. e. because they are born the seventh month; after the birth, the seventh hour tries whether it will live or no--for that which will bear the breath of the air after that hour, is conceived will live; after seven days, it casts off the relics of the navel; after twice seven days, its sight begins to move after the light; in the third seventh, it turns its eyes and whole face freely; after seven months, it breeds teeth; after the second seventh month, it sits without fear of falling; after the third seventh month, it begins to speak; after the fourth seventh month, it stands strongly and walks; after the fifth seventh month, it begins to refrain sucking its nurse; after seven years, its first teeth fall, and new are bred, fitter for harder meat, and its speech is perfected; after the second seventh year, boys wax ripe, and then it is a beginning of generation at the third seventh year, they grow to men in stature, and begin to be hairy, and become able and strong for generation; at the fourth seventh year, they cease to grow taller; in the fifth seventh year, they attain to the perfection of their strength; the sixth seventh year, they keep their strength; the seventh seventh year, they attain to their utmost discretion and wisdom, and the perfect age of men; but when they come to the tenth seventh year, where the number seven is taken for a complete number, then they come to the common term of life--the Prophet saying, our age is seventy years. The utmost height of a man's body is seven feet. There are, also, seven degrees in the body, which complete the dimension of its altitude from the bottom to the top, viz. marrow, bone, nerve, vein, artery, flesh, and skin. There are seven, which, by the Greeks, are called black members: the tongue, heart, lungs, liver, spleen, and the two kidnies. There are, also, seven principal parts, of the body: the head, breast, hands, feet, and the privy members. It is manifest, concerning breath and meat, that, without drawing of the breath, the life doth not remain above seven hours; and they that are starved with famine, live not above seven days. 1 The veins, also, and arteries, as physicians say, are moved by the seventh number. Also, judgments in diseases are made with greater manifestation upon the seventh day, which physicians call critical, i. e. judicial. Also, of seven portions God creates the soul;--the soul, also, receives the body by seven degrees. All difference of voices proceeds to the seventh degree, after which there is the same revolution. Again, there are seven modulations of the voices: ditonus, semiditonus, diatesseron, diapente with a tone, diapente with a half tone, and diapason. There are also, in celestials, a most potent power of the number seven; for seeing there are four corners of the Heaven diametrically looking one towards the other, which indeed is accounted a most full and powerful aspect, and consists of the number seven; for it is made with the seventh sign, and makes a cross, the most powerful figure of all, of which we shall speak in its due place;--but this you must not be ignorant of, that the number seven hath a great communion with the cross. By the same radiation and number the solstice is distant from winter, and the winter equinoctium from the summer, all which are done by seven signs. There are also seven circles in the Heavens, according to the longitudes of the axle-tree. There are seven stars about the Arctic Pole, greater and lesser, called Charles Wain; also seven stars called the Pleiades; and seven planets, according to those seven days constituting a week. The Moon is the seventh of the planets, and next to us, observing this number more than the rest, this number dispensing the motion and light thereof; for in twenty-eight days, it runs round the compass of the whole Zodiac; which number of days, the number seven with its seven terms, viz. from one to seven, doth make and fill up as much as the several numbers, by adding to the antecedents, and makes four times seven days, in which the Moon runs through and about all the longitude and latitude of the Zodiac, by measuring and measuring again: with the like seven days it dispenses its light, by changing it; for the first seven days, unto the middle as it were of the divided world, it increases; the second seven days it fills its whole orb with light; the third, by decreasing, is again contracted into a divided orb; but, after the fourth seven days, it is renewed with the last diminution of its light; and by the same seven days, it disposes the increase and decrease of the sea: for in the first seven of the increase of the moon, it is by little and little lessened; in the second, by degrees increased; but the third is like the first, and the fourth does the same as the second. It is also applied to Saturn, which ascending from the lower, is the seventh planet, which betokens rest; to which the seventh day is ascribed, which signifies the seven thousandth, wherein, as St. John says, the dragon (which is the devil) and satan being bound, men shall be quiet, and lead a peaceable life. And the leprous person that was to be cleansed, was sprinkled seven times with the blood of a sparrow; and Elisha the Prophet, as it is written in the second book of Kings, saith unto the leprous person--"Go, and wash thyself seven times in Jordan, and thy flesh shall be made whole, and thou shalt be cleansed."--Also, it is a number of repentance and remission. And Christ, with seven petitions, finished his speech of our satisfaction. It is called the number of liberty, because the seventh year the Hebrew servant did challenge liberty for himself. It is also most suitable to divine praises; whence the Prophet saith--"Seven times a day do I praise thee, because of thy righteous judgments."--It is moreover called the number of revenge, as says the Scripture--"And Cain shall be revenged sevenfold."--And the Psalmist says-- "Render unto our neighbours sevenfold into their bosom their reproach."--Hence there are seven wickednesses, as saith Solomon; and seven wickeder spirits taken, are read of in the Gospel. It signifies, also, the time of the present circle, because it is finished in the space of seven days. Also it is consecrated to the Holy Ghost, which the Prophet Isaiah describes to be sevenfold, according to his gift, viz. the spirit of wisdom and understanding, the spirit of counsel and strength, the spirit of knowledge and holiness, the spirit of fear of the Lord, which we read in Zachariah to be the seven eyes of God. There are also seven angels, spirits standing in the presence of God, as is read in Tobias, and in the Revelation: seven lamps did burn before the throne of God, and seven golden candlesticks, and in the middle thereof was one like unto the Son of Man, and he had in his right hand seven stars. Also, there were seven spirits before the throne of God, and seven angels stood before the throne, and there were given to them seven trumpets. And he saw a Lamb, having seven horns and seven eyes; and he saw the book sealed with seven seals; and when the seventh seal was opened, there was made silence in Heaven.

Now, by all that has been said, it is apparent that the number seven, amongst the other numbers, may be deservedly said to be most full of efficacy. Moreover, the number seven hath great conformity with the number twelve; for as three and four make seven, so thrice four makes twelve, which are the numbers of the celestial planets and signs resulting from the same root; and by the number three partaking of the Divinity, and by the number four of the nature of inferior things. There is in sacred writ a very great observance of this number before all others, and many, and very great are the mysteries thereof: many we have decreed to reckon up here, repeating them out of holy writ, by which it will easily appear that the number seven doth signify a certain fulness of sacred mysteries for we read, in Genesis, that the seventh was the day of rest of the Lord that Enoch, a pious holy man, was the seventh from Adam; and that there was another seventh man from Adam, a wicked man, by name Lamech, that had two wives; and that the sin of Cain should be abolished the seventh generation, as it is written--Cain shall be punished sevenfold; and that he who shall slay Cain, shall be revenged sevenfold; to which the master of the history collects that there were seven sins of Cain. Also, of all clean beasts seven, and seven were brought into the ark, as also of fowls; and after seven days the Lord rained upon the earth; and upon the seventh day the fountains of the deep were broken up, and the waters covered the earth. Also, Abraham gave to Abimelech seven ewe lambs; and Jacob served seven years for Leah, and seven more for Rachel; and seven days the people of Israel bewailed the death of Jacob. Moreover we read, in the same place, of seven kine; and seven years of corn; seven years of plenty, and seven years of scarcity. And in Exodus, the Sabbath of Sabbaths, the holy rest to the Lord, is commanded to be on the seventh day; also, on the seventh day Moses ceased to pray. On the seventh day there shall be a solemnity of the Lord; the seventh year the servant shall go out free; seven days let the calf and the lamb be with its dam; the seventh year, let the ground that hath been sown six years be at rest; the seventh day shall be a holy Sabbath, and a rest; the seventh day, because it is the Sabbath, shall be called holy. In Leviticus, the seventh day also shall be more observed, and be more holy; and the first day of the seventh month shall be a Sabbath of memorial; seven days shall the sacrifices be offered to the Lord; seven days shall the holy days of the Lord be celebrated; seven days in a year everlastingly in the generations. In the seventh month you shall celebrate feasts, and shall dwell in tabernacles seven days; seven times he shall sprinkle himself before the Lord that hath dipped his finger in blood; he that is cleansed from the leprosy, shall dip seven times in the blood of a sparrow; seven days shall she be washed with running water that is menstruous; seven times he shall dip his finger in the blood of a bullock; seven times I will smite you for your sins. In Deuteronomy, seven people possessed the Land of Promise. There is also read, a seventh year of remission; and seven candles set up on the south side of the candlesticks. And in Numbers it is read, that the sons of Israel offered up seven ewe lambs without spot; and that seven days they did eat unleavened bread; and that sin was expiated with seven lambs and a goat; and that the seventh day was celebrated, and holy; and the first day of the seventh month was observed, and kept holy; and the seventh month of the Feast of Tabernacles; and seven calves were offered on the seventh day; and Baalam erected seven altars; seven days Mary, the sister of Aaron, went forth leprous out of the camp; seven days he that touched a dead carcass was unclean. And in Joshua, seven priests carried the ark of the covenant before the host; and seven days they went round the cities; and seven trumpets were carried by the seven priests; and on the seventh day, the seven priests sounded the trumpets. And in the book of judges, Abessa reigned in Israel seven years; Sampson kept his nuptials seven days, and the seventh day he put forth a riddle to his wife; he was bound with seven green withes; seven locks of his head were shaved off; seven years were the children of Israel oppressed by the King of Maden. And in the books of the Kings, Elias prayed seven times, and at the seventh time beheld a little cloud; seven days the children of Israel pitched over against the Syrians, and in the seventh day of the battle were joined: seven years' famine was threatened to David, for the people's murmuring; and seven times the child sneezed that was raised by Elisha; and seven men were crucified together, in the days of the first harvest; Naaman was made clean with seven washings, by Elisha; the seventh month Goliah was slain. And in Hester we read, that the King of Persia had seven eunuchs. And in Tobias, seven men were coupled with Sarah, the daughter of Raguel. And, in Daniel, Nebuchadnezzar's furnace was heated seven times hotter than it was used to be; and seven lions were in the den, and the seventh day came Nebuchadnezzar. In the book of Job, there is mention of seven sons of Job; and seven days and nights Job's friends sat with him on the earth; and, in the same place--"In seven troubles no evil shall come near thee." In Ezra, we read of Artaxerxes's seven counsellors; and in the same place, the trumpet sounded; the seventh month of the Feast of Tabernacles was, in Ezra's time, whilst the children of Israel were in the cities; and on the first day of the seventh month, Esdras read the law to the people. And in the Psalms, David praised the Lord seven times in the day; silver is tried seven times; and he renders to his neighbours sevenfold into their bosoms. And Solomon saith, that Wisdom hath hewn herself seven pillars; seven men that can render a reason; seven abominations which the Lord abhors; seven abominations in the heart of an enemy; seven overseers; seven eyes beholding. Isaiah numbers up seven gifts of the Holy Ghost; and seven women shall take hold on a man. And in Jeremiah, if she that hath borne seven, languishes, she has given up the ghost. In Ezekiel, the Prophet continued sad for seven days. In Zachariah, seven lamps, and seven pipes to those seven lamps; and seven eyes running to and fro through the whole earth; and seven eyes on one stone; and the fast of the seventh day is turned into joy. And in Micah, seven shepherds are raised against the Assyrians. Also, in the Gospel, we read of seven blessings; and seven virtues, to which seven vices are opposed; seven petitions of the Lord's Prayer; seven words of Christ upon the cross; seven words of the blessed Virgin Mary; seven loaves distributed by the Lord; seven baskets of fragments; seven brothers having one wife; seven disciples of the Lord who were fishers; seven water pots in Cana of Galilee; seven woes which the Lord threatens to hypocrites; seven devils cast out of the unclean woman, and seven wickeder devils taken in after that which was cast out; also, seven years Christ was fled into Egypt; and the seventh hour the fever left the governor's son. And in the canonical epistles, James describes seven degrees of wisdom; and Peter, seven degrees of virtues. And in the Acts, we reckon seven deacons, and seven disciples chosen by the Apostles. Also, in the Revelation, there are many mysteries relating to this number; for there we read of seven candlesticks, seven stars, seven crowns, seven churches, seven spirits before the throne, seven rivers of Egypt, seven seals, seven marks, seven horns, seven eyes, seven spirits of God, seven angels with seven trumpets, seven horns of the dragon, seven heads of the dragon which had seven diadems, also seven plagues, and seven vials which were given to every one of the seven angels, seven heads of the scarlet beast, seven mountains and seven kings sitting upon them, and seven thunders uttered their voices.

Moreover, this number hath much power; as in natural so in sacred ceremonial, and also in other things; therefore the seven days are related hither; also the seven planets, the seven stars called Pleiades, the seven ages of the world, the seven changes of man, the seven liberal arts, and as many mechanic, and so many forbidden; seven colours, seven metals, seven holes in the head of a man, seven pair of nerves, seven mountains in the city of Rome, seven Roman kings, seven civil wars, seven wise men in the time of Jeremiah, seven wise men of Greece; also Rome did burn seven days by Nero; by seven kings were slain ten thousand martyrs: there were seven sleepers; and seven principal churches of Rome.

THE SCALE OF THE NUMBER SEVEN.

In the Original World,	Ararita, אאריתא				Asser Eheie,	אשר אהיה		The name of God with seven letters.
In the Intelligible World	צפקיאל Zaphiel,	צדקיאל Zadkiel.	כמאל Camael.	רפאל Raphael,	האניאל Haniel.	מיכאל Michael.	גבריאל Gabriel;	Seven angels which stand in the presence of God.
In the Celestial World,	שבתאי Saturn,	צדק Jupiter,	מאדים Mars,	שמש The Sun	נוגה Venus,	כוכב Mercury,	לבנה The Moon;	Seven planets.
In the Elementary World.	The lapwing, The cuttle fish, The mole, Lead, The onyx.	The eagle, The dolphin, The hart, Tin, The saphire.	The vulture, The puke, The wolf, Iron, The diamond.	The swan, The sea calf, The lion, Gold, The carbuncle.	The dove, Thimallus, The goat, Copper, The emerald.	The stork, The mullet, The ape, Quicksilver, The achates.	The owl, The sea cat, Cat, Silver, Chrystal;	Seven birds of the planets. Seven fish of the planets. Seven animals of the planets. Seven metals of the planets. Seven stones of the planets.
In the Lesser World,	The right foot, The right ear,	The head, The left ear.	The right hand, The right nostril,	The heart, The right eye,	The privy members, The left nostril,	The left hand, The mouth,	The left foot, The left eye;	Seven integral members distributed to the planets. Seven holes of the head distributed to the planets.
In the Infernal World,	Hell, גיהנם	The gates of death, שערי מות	The shadow of death, צלמות	The pit of destruction, באראבדון	The Clay of death, טיט היון	Perdition, אבדון	The depth of the earth, שאול	Seven habitations of infernals, which Rabbi Joseph of Castilia, the Cabalist, describes in the garden of nuts.

119:1 There have been some exceptions to this affirmation, one of which fell under my notice of late years: Doctor Edward Spry, of Plymouth Dock, Philosopher, Cabalist, and Physician, lived upwards of two years upon a gooseberry a day in summer, and an oat cake and three glasses of white wine the rest of the season, per day: this gentleman was particularly abstemious in his diet.

CHAPTER 23. OF THE NUMBER EIGHT, AND THE SCALE

THE Pythagorians call Eight the number of justice, and fulness: first, because it is first of all divided into numbers equally even, viz. into four; and that division is, by the same reason, made into twice two, viz. twice two twice; and by reason of this equality of division it took to itself the name of justice. But the other received the name of fulness, by reason of the contexture of the corporeal solidity, since the first makes a solid body. Hence that custom of Orpheus swearing by the eight deities, if at any time he would beseech Divine justice, whose names are these:-- Fire, Water, Earth, the Heaven, Moon, Sun, Phanes, and the Night. There are only eight visible spheres of the heavens. Also, by it the property of corporeal nature is signified, which Orpheus comprehends in eight of his sea songs: this is also called the. covenant, or circumcision, which was commanded to be done by the Jews the eighth day.

There were also, in the old law, eight ornaments of the priest, viz. a breastplate, a coat, a girdle, a mitre, a robe, an ephod, a girdle of the ephod, and a golden plate. Hither belongs the number to eternity, and the end of the world, because it follows the number seven, which is the mystery of time. Hence, also, the number of blessedness, as you may see in Matthew. It is also called the number of safety, and conservation; for there were so many souls of the sons of Jesse, from which David was the eighth.

THE SCALE OF THE NUMBER EIGHT.

The Magus

The name of God with eight letters,	Eloa Vedaath עדעת אלוה Jehova Vedaath עדעת יהוה								In the original world.
Eight rewards of the blessed,	Inheritance,	Incorruption,	Power,	Victory,	The vision of God,	Grace,	A kingdom,	Joy;	In the intelligible world.
Eight visible heavens,	The starry heaven,	The heaven of Saturn,	The heaven of Jupiter,	The heaven of Mars,	The heaven of the Sun,	The heaven of Venus,	The heaven of Mercury,	The heaven of the Moon;	In the celestial world.
Eight particular qualities,	The dryness of the earth,	The coldness of water,	The moisture of air,	The heat of fire,	The heat of air,	The moisture of water,	The dryness of fire,	The coldness of earth	In the elementary world.
Eight kinds of blessed men,	The peace makers,	They that hunger and thirst after righteousness,	The meek,	They which are persecuted for righteousness sake,	Pure in heart,	Merciful,	Poor in spirit,	Mourners;	In the lesser world.
Eight punishments of the damned.	Prison,	Death,	Judgment,	The wrath of God,	Darkness,	Indignation,	Tribulation,	Anguish;	In the infernal world.

CHAPTER 24. OF THE NUMBER NINE, AND THE SCALE

THERE are nine orders of blessed angels, viz. Seraphim, Cherubim, Thrones, Dominations, Powers, Virtues, Principalities, Archangels, and Angels, which Ezekiel figures out by nine stones, which are the sapphire, emerald, carbuncle, beryl, onyx, chrysolite, jasper, topaz, and sardis. This number hath also a great and occult mystery of the cross; for the ninth hour our Lord Jesus Christ breathed out his spirit. The astrologers also take notice of the number nine in the ages of men, no otherwise than they do of seven, which they call climacterical years, which are eminent for some remarkable change. Yet sometimes it signifies imperfectness and incompleteness, because it does not attain to the perfection of the number ten, but is less by one, without which it is deficient, as Austin interprets it of the ten lepers. Neither is the longitude of nine cubits of Og, King of Basan, who is a type of the devil without a mystery.

THE SCALE OF THE NUMBER NINE.

The name of God with nine letters,	Jehovah Sabbaoth, יהוה צבאות			Jehovah Zidkenu, יהוה צדקנו			Elohim Giber, אלהים גבור			In the original world.
Nine quires of angels, Nine angels ruling the heavens,	Seraphim, Merattron,	Cherubim; Ophaniel,	Thrones, Zaphkiel,	Dominations, Zadkiel,	Powers Camael	Virtues, Raphael,	Principalities, Haniel,	Archangels, Michael,	Angels; Gabriel	In the intelligible world.
Nine moveable spheres,	The primum mobile,	The starry heaven,	The sphere of Saturn,	The sphere of Jupiter,	The sphere of Mars,	The sphere of the Sun,	The sphere of Venus,	The sphere of Mercury,	The sphere of the Moon;	In the celestial world.
Nine stones representing the nine quires of angels,	Saphire	Emerald,	Carbuncle,	Beryl,	Onyx,	Chrysolne,	Jasper,	Topaz,	Sardis;	In the elementary world.
Nine senses, inward and outward together,	Memory,	Cogitative,	Imaginative,	Common sense,	Hearing,	Seeing,	Smelling,	Tasting,	Touching;	In the lesser world.
Nine orders of devils,	False Spirits,	Spirits of lying,	Vessels of iniquity,	Avengers of wickedness,	Jugglers,	Airy Powers	Furies sowing mischief,	Sifters or triers,	Tempters, or ensnarers;	In the infernal world.

CHAPTER 25. OF THE NUMBER TEN, AND THE SCALE

THE number Ten is called every number, or an universal number, complete, signifying the full course of life; for beyond that we cannot number but by replication; and it either implies all numbers within itself, or explains them by itself, and its own, by multiplying them; wherefore it is accounted to be of manifold religion and power, and is applied to the purging of souls. Hence the antients called ceremonies Denary, because they were to be expiated and to offer sacrifices, and were to abstain from some certain things for ten days.

There are ten sanguine parts of man: the menstrues, the sperm, the plasonatic spirit, the mass, the humours, the organical body, the vegetative part, the sensitive part, reason, and the mind. There are, also, ten simple integral parts constituting man: the bone, cartilage, nerve, fibre, ligament, artery, vein, membrane, flesh, and skin. There are, also, ten parts of which a man consists intrinsically: the spirit, the brain, the lungs, the heart, the liver, the gall, the spleen, the kidnies, the testicles, and the matrix. There are ten curtains in the temple, ten strings in the psaltery, ten musical instruments with which the psalms were sung, the names whereof were-- neza, on which their odes were sung; nablum, the same as organs; mizmor, on which the Psalms; sir, on which the Canticles; tehila, on which orations; beracha, on which benedictions; halel, on which praises; hodaia, on which thanks; asre, on which the felicity of any one; hallelujah, on which the praises of God only, and contemplations. There were also ten singers of psalms, viz. Adam, Abraham, Melchisedeck, Moses, Asaph, David, Solomon, and the three sons of Chora. There are, also, ten commandments. And then tenth day after the ascension of Christ, the Holy Ghost came down. Lastly, this is the number, in which Jacob, wrestling with the Angel all night, overcame, and, at the rising of the sun, was blessed, and called by the name of Israel. In this number, Joshua overcame thirty-one kings; and David overcame Goliah and the Philistines; and Daniel escaped the danger of the lions. This number is also circular, as unity; because, being heaped together, returns into a unity, from whence it had its beginning; and it is the end and perfection of all numbers, and the beginning of tens. As the number ten flows back into a unity, from whence it proceeded, so every thing that is flowing is returned back to that from which it had the beginning of its flux: so water returns to the sea, from whence it had its beginning; the body returns to the earth, from whence it was taken; time returns into eternity, from whence it flowed; the spirit shall return to God, who gave it; and, lastly, every creature returns to nothing, from whence it was created. [133:1] Neither is it supported but by the word of God, in whom all things are hid, and all things with the number ten, and by the number ten, make a round, as Proclus says, taking their beginning from God, and ending in him. God, therefore (that first unity, or one thing), before he communicated himself to inferiors, diffused himself first into the first of numbers, viz. the number three; then into the number ten, as into ten ideas and measures of making all numbers and all things, which the Hebrews call ten attributes, and account ten divine names; from which cause there cannot be a further number. Hence all tens have some divine thing in them, and in the law are required as his own, together with the first fruits, as the original of all things and beginning of numbers, and every tenth is as the end given to him, who is the beginning and end of all things.

SCALE OF THE NUMBER TEN.

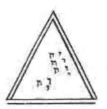

THE SCALE OF THE NUMBER TEN.

In the original	The name of Jehovah of ten letters collected,	The name of Jehovah of ten letters		Extended,		The name Elohim Sabaoth				The name of God with ten letters,
	Eheie, Kether	Jod Jehovah, Hochmah	Jehovah Elohim, Binah	El, Hesed	Elohim Gibor, Geburah	Eloha, Tiphereth	Jehovah Sabaoth, Nezah	Elohim Sabaoth, Hod	Sadai, Jesod	Adonai melech, Malchuth	Ten names of God. Ten Sephiroth.
In the intelligible world,	Seraphim, Hajothhakados, Meratton,	Cherubim, Orphanim, Jophiel,	Thrones, Aralim, Zaphiel,	Dominations, Hasmalim, Zadkiel,	Powers, Seraphim, Camael,	Virtues, Malachim, Raphael,	Principalities, Elohim, Haniel,	Archangels, Ben Elohim, Michael,	Angels, Ben Elohim, Gabriel,	Blessed souls; Isim; The soul of Messiah,	Ten orders of the blessed, according to Dionysius. Ten orders of the blessed, according to the traditions of men. Ten angels ruling.
In the celestial world,	Reschith hagalalim, the primum mobile,	Masloth, the sphere of the Zodiac,	Sabbathi, the sphere of Saturn,	Zedeck, the sphere of Jupiter,	Madim, the sphere of Mars,	Schemes, the sphere of the Sun,	Noga, the sphere of Venus,	Cochab, the sphere of Mercury,	Levanah, the sphere of the Moon,	Holom Jesodoth, the sphere of the elements,	Ten spheres of the world.
In the elementary world,	A dove,	A lizard,	A dragon,	An eagle,	A horse,	Lion,	Man,	The fox,	Bull,	Lamb,	Ten animals consecrated to the gods.
In the lesser world,	Spirit,	Brain,	Spleen,	Liver,	Gall,	Heart,	Kidneys,	Lungs,	Genitals,	Matrix,	Ten parts intrinsical of man.
In the infernal world,	False gods,	Lying spirits,	Vessels of iniquity,	Revengers of wickedness,	Jugglers,	Aiery powers,	Furies, the seminaries of evil,	Sifters, or triers,	Tempters, or ensnarers,	Wicked souls bearing rule;	Ten orders of the damned.

133:1 At the last, the elements give up what they have ever received; the sea gives up her dead, the fire gives up its fuel; the earth gives up the seminal virtue, &c.; and the air gives up whatever voice, sound, or impression it has received, so that not an oath, lie, or secret blasphemy, but what will appear as clear as noon daylight at the great day of God.

CHAPTER 26. OF THE NUMBERS ELEVEN AND TWELVE, WITH THE CABALISTICAL SCALE

THE number Eleven, as it exceeds number ten, which is the number of the commandments, so it falls short of the number Twelve, which is of grace and perfection; therefore it is called the number of sins, and the penitent. Now the number twelve is divine, and that whereby the celestials are measured; [136:1] it is, also, the number of signs in the Zodiac, over which there are twelve angels as chief, supported by the irrigation of the great name of God. In twelve years, also, Jupiter perfects his course, and the Moon daily runs through twelve degrees. There are, also, twelve chief joints in the body of man, viz. in hands, elbows, shoulders, thighs, knees, and vertebræ of the feet. There is, also, a great power of the number twelve in divine mysteries. God chose twelve families of Israel, and set over them twelve princes; so many stones were placed in the midst of Jordan; and God commanded that so many should be set on the breast of the priest. Twelve lions did bear the brazen sea that was made by Solomon; there were so many fountains in Helim; and so many Apostles of Christ set over the twelve tribes; and twelve thousand people were set apart and chosen.

THE NUMBER TWELVE.

The names of God with twelve letters,			אל Holy,	ברוך Blessed,	הוא Ha,				קדוש Father, Son, Holy Ghost.				In the original world
The great name returned back into twelve banners,	יהוה	יהוה	יהוה	יוהה	יההו	הוהי	הוהי	יהוה	יוהי	ויהה	היוה	ההיו	
Twelve orders of blessed spirits,	Seraphim,	Cherubim,	Thrones,	Dominations,	Powers,	Virtues,	Principalities,	Archangels,	Angels,	Innocents,	Martyrs,	Confessors.	In the intelligible world
Twelve angels ruling over the twelve signs,	Malchidiel,	Asmodel,	Ambriel,	Muriel,	Verchiel,	Hamaliel,	Zuriel,	Barbiel,	Adnachiel,	Hanael,	Gabriel,	Barchiel.	
Twelve tribes,	Dan,	Reuben,	Judah,	Manasseh,	Asher,	Simeon,	Issachar,	Benjamin,	Naphthalim,	Gad,	Zabulon,	Ephraim.	
Twelve prophets,	Malachi,	Haggai,	Zachariah,	Amos,	Hosea,	Micha,	Jonah,	Obadiah,	Zephaniah,	Nahum,	Habakkuk,	Joel.	
Twelve apostles,	Matthias,	Thaddeus,	Simon,	John,	Peter,	Andrew,	Bartholomew,	Philip,	James the elder,	Thomas,	Matthew,	James the younger.	
Twelve signs of the Zodiac,	Aries,	Taurus,	Gemini,	Cancer,	Leo,	Virgo,	Libra,	Scorpius,	Sagittarius,	Capricorn,	Aquarius,	Pisces.	In the celestial world
Twelve months,	March,	April,	May,	June,	July,	August,	September,	October,	November,	December,	January,	February.	In the elemental world
Twelve plants,	Sang,	Upright vervain,	Bending vervain,	Comfrey,	Ladie's seal,	Calamint,	Scorpion grass,	Mugwort,	Pimpernel,	Dock,	Dragonwort,	Aristolochy.	
Twelve stones,	Sardonius,	A cornelian,	Topaz,	Calcedony,	Jasper,	Emerald,	Beryl,	Amethyst,	Hyacinth,	Chrysoprasus,	Chrystal,	Sapphire.	
Twelve principal members,	Head,	Neck,	Arms,	Breast,	Heart,	Belly,	Kidneys,	Genitals,	Haunch,	Knees,	Legs,	Feet.	In the elementary world
Twelve degrees of the damned, and of devils,	False gods,	Lying Spirits,	Vessels of iniquity,	Revengers of wickedness,	Jugglers,	Airy powers,	Furies, the sowers of evil,	Sifters, or triers,	Tempters, or ensnarers,	Witches,	Apostates,	Infidels.	In the infernal world

136:1 The use of these Scales, in the composition of Talismans, Seals, Rings, &c., must be obvious to every student upon inspection, and are indispensably necessary to the producing of any effect whatever that the artist may propose to himself; for, as we have before observed, all things were formed according to the proportion of numbers, this seeming to be the principal pattern in the mind of the Creator; therefore, when at any time we set about any work or experiment in Celestial Magic, we are to have especial regard to the rule of numbers and proportions. For example, if we would obtain the celestial influence of any star, we are, first of all, to observe at what time that star is powerful in the heavens, I mean in good aspect with the benefices, and ruling in the day and hour appropriated to the planet, and in fortunate places of the figure; then we are to observe what divine names are ruling the intelligences, or spirits, to which the said planets are subject with their characters (which you may see at large in the Magical Tables of Numbers); then, by referring to the above Tables of the Scales, we may see, by inspection, to what numbers are attributed divine names, and, under them, the orders of the intelligences--the heavenly spheres--elements and their properties--animals, metals, and stones--powers of the soul--senses of man-virtues--the princes of the evil spirits--places of punishment--degrees of the damned souls--degrees of torments hereafter--and every thing that is either in heaven, or earth, or hell;--all our senses, motions, qualities, virtues, words, or works, are submitted to the proportions of numbers, as you may see fully exemplified in the different Scales of the Numbers; and all things that are knowable are demonstrable by them, and are attributed to them; therefore great is the knowledge and wisdom to be derived from numbers. Therefore the artist must be well acquainted with their virtues and properties-by them there is a way open for the knowing and understanding of all things; therefore let him diligently contemplate these Scales, and likewise what we have set down in our fourteenth and fifteenth Chapters preceding the Scales, where we have, upon good authority, explained sufficiently the extent and force of formal numbers, which ought to be well understood and attentively considered, as the ground and foundation of all our operations in this science, without which we are defrauded of the desired effect: therefore whenever we intend to set about any experiment, whether it be an image, or ring, or tablet, or mirror, or amulet, or any other instrument, we are to note first the site, order, number, and government of the intelligence and his planet, his measure of time, revolution in the heavens, &c.; likewise we are to engrave or write upon it its number, intelligence, or spirit, either for a good or bad effect, with the suitable characters and tables; likewise the effect desired, with the divine names congruent thereto; so that our operations may be strong, powerful, and suitable to the constellation and star, both in time, number, and proportion; with a due and attentive observation of all that we have written p. 137 concerning this, without which all our operations could never be brought to have the effect desired; and we are to mind that whenever such an instrument is perfected, that it is the more powerful when the planet or constellation (under

144

which it was constructed) is ruling and potent in the Heavens; for at that time, whatever we desire to bring to perfection by the said Talisman, as a medium and instrument, shall by no means be prevented or hindered. Therefore take this as a general rule, that all magical instruments whatsoever have no power in themselves, further than as they are formed under the influences, and according to the times and numbers of their proper stars and constellations; hence is derived the title we give this Book, viz. the Constellatory Art, or Talismanic Magic. Those who would further consider the power, virtue, extent, and harmony of numbers, let them read Pythagoras, Plato, Averroena, Averroes, &c., who all agree in the virtues lying hid in numbers; and without the knowledge of which, no man can be a true philosopher.

CHAPTER 27. OF THE NOTES OF THE HEBREWS AND CHALDEANS, AND OTHER NOTES OF MAGICIANS

THE Hebrew characters have marks of numbers attributed to them far more excellent than any other language, since the greatest mysteries lie in the Hebrew letters, as is handled concerning these in that part of Cabala which we call Notariacon. Now the principal Hebrew letters are in number twenty-two, whereof five have various other certain figures in the end of a word, which, therefore, they call the five ending letters, which, being added to them aforesaid, make twenty-seven; which being then divided into three degrees, signify units, which are in the first degree--tens, which are in the second--and hundreds, which are in the third degree. Now every one, if they are marked with a great character, signifies so many thousands, as here--

The classes of the Hebrew numbers are these which follow:--

9	8	7	6	5	4	3	2	1
90	80	70	60	50	40	30	20	10
900	800	700	600	500	400	300	200	100

Sometimes the final letters are not used, but we write thus:

1000	900	800	700	600	500

And by those simple figures, and by the joining them together, they describe all other compound numbers: as eleven, twelve, an hundred and ten, an hundred and eleven, by adding to the number ten those which are units; and in the like manner to the rest, after their manner; yet we describe the fifteenth number not by ten

146

and five, but by nine and six, viz. טו and that out of honour to the Divine name הי, which signifies fifteen, lest that sacred name should be abused to profane things. Likewise the Egyptians, Æthiopians, Chaldeans, and Arabians, have their marks of numbers, which serve for the making of magical characters; but the Chaldeans mark their numbers with the letters of their alphabet, after the manner of the Hebrews. I found, in a very antient book of Magic, some very elegant characters, which I have figured in the following manner

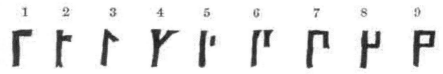

Now of these characters, turned towards the left hand, are made tens.

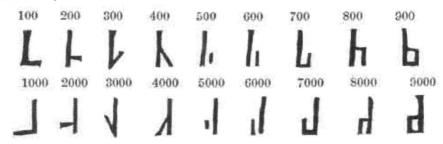

And those marks being downwards, to the right hand, make hundreds; to the left, thousands, viz.

And by the composition and mixture of these characters, other compound numbers are most elegantly made, as you may perceive by these few:--

1510   1511   1471   1486   2421

1801

CHAPTER 28. THE MAGIC TABLES OF THE PLANETS...

THE MAGIC TABLES OF THE PLANETS--THEIR FORM AND VIRTUE--WHAT DIVINE NAMES, INTELLIGENCES, AND SPIRITS, ARE SET OVER THEM.

THERE are certain magic tables of numbers distributed to the seven planets, which they call the sacred tables of the planets; because, being rightly formed, they are endued with many great virtues of the heavens, insomuch that they represent the divine order of the celestial numbers, impressed upon them by the ideas of the divine mind, by means of the soul of the world, and the sweet harmony of those celestial rays; signifying, according to proportion, supercelestial. intelligences, which can no other way be expressed than by the marks of numbers, letters, and characters; for material numbers and figures can do nothing in the mysteries of hidden things, but representatively by formal numbers and figures, as they are governed and informed by intelligences and divine enumerations, which unite the extremes of the matter and spirit to the will of the elevated soul, receiving (through great affection, by the celestial power of the operator) a virtue and power from God, applied through the soul of the universe; and the observation of celestial constellations to a matter fit for a form, the mediums being disposed by the skill and industry of the magician.

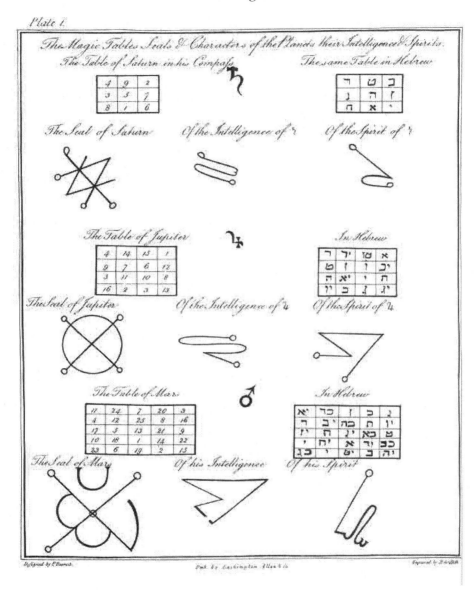

But now we will hasten to explain each particular table. [143:1] The first table is assigned to the planet Saturn, and consists of a square of three, containing the particular numbers of nine, and in every line three every way, and through each diameter making fifteen--the whole sum of numbers forty-five; over this are set such divine names as fill up the numbers with an intelligence, to what is good, and a spirit to bad; and out of the same numbers are drawn the seal and character of Saturn, and of the spirits thereof, such as is beneath ascribed to the table.

Now this table being with a fortunate Saturn, engraven on a plate of lead, helps child-birth; and to make any man safe or powerful; and to cause success of petitions with princes and powers; but if it be done, Saturn being unfortunate, it hinders buildings, planting, and the like, and casts a man from honours and dignities, causes discord, quarrelling, and disperses an army.

The second is the table of Jupiter, which consists of a square drawn into itself; it contains sixteen particular numbers, and in every line and diameter four, making thirty-four; the sum of all is one hundred and thirty-six. There are over it divine names, with an intelligence to that which is good, and a spirit to bad; and out of it is drawn the character of Jupiter and the spirits thereof; if this is engraven on a plate of silver, with Jupiter being powerful and ruling in the heavens, it conduces to gain riches and favour, love, peace, and concord, and to appease enemies, and to confirm honours, dignities, and counsels; and dissolves enchantments if engraven on a coral.

The third table belongs to Mars, which is made of a square of five, containing twenty-five numbers, and of these, in every side and diameter, five, which makes sixty-five, and the sum of all is three hundred and twenty-five; and there are over it divine names with an intelligence to good, and a spirit to evil, and out of it is drawn the characters of Mars and of his spirits. These, with Mars fortunate, being engraven on an iron plate, or sword, makes a man potent in war and judgment, and petitions, and terrible to his enemies; and victorious over them; and if engraven upon the stone correola, it stops blood, and the menstrues; but if it be engraven, with Mars being unfortunate, on a plate of red brass, it prevents and hinders buildings--it casts down the powerful from dignities, honours, and riches--causes discord and hatred amongst men and beasts--drives away bees, pigeons, and fish--and hinders mills from working, i. e. binds them;--it likewise renders hunters and fighters unfortunate--causes barrenness in men and women--and strikes a terror into our enemies, and compels them to submit.

The fourth table is of the Sun, and is made of a square of six, and contains thirty-six particular numbers, whereof six in every side and diameter produce one hundred and eleven, and the sum of all is six hundred and sixty-six; there are over it divine names, with an intelligence to what is good, and a spirit to what is evil, and out of it is drawn the character of the Sun and of his spirits. This being engraven on a plate of pure gold, Sol being fortunate, renders him that wears it renowned, amiable, acceptable, potent in all his works, and equals him to a king, elevating his fortunes, and enabling him to do whatever he will. But with an unfortunate Sun, it makes one a tyrant, proud, ambitious, insatiable, and finally to come to an ill ending.

The fifth table is of Venus; consisting of a square of seven, drawn into itself, viz. of forty-nine numbers, whereof seven on each side and diameter make one hundred and seventy-five, and the sum of all is one thousand two hundred and twenty-five; there are, likewise, over it divine names, with an intelligence to good, and a spirit to evil; and there is drawn out of it the character of Venus, and her spirits. This being engraven on a plate of silver, Venus being fortunate, promotes concord, ends strife, procures the love of women, helps conception, is good against barrenness, gives ability for generation, dissolves enchantments, causes peace between man and woman, and makes all kinds of animals fruitful, and likewise cattle; and being put into a dove or pigeon house, causes an increase; it likewise drives away, melancholy distempers, and causes joyfulness; and this being carried about travellers, makes them fortunate. But if it be formed upon brass, Venus being unfortunate, it acts contrary to all that has been said.

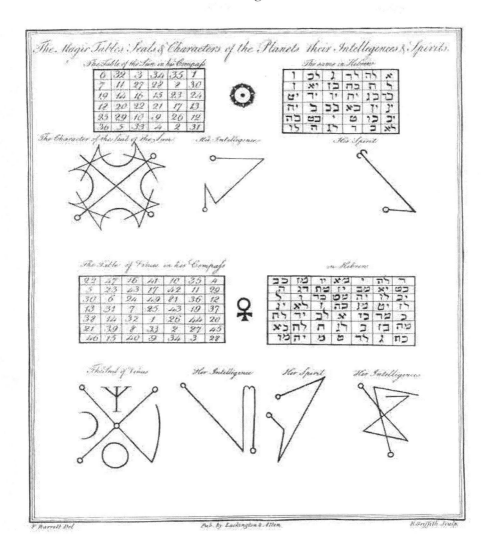

Plate 3.

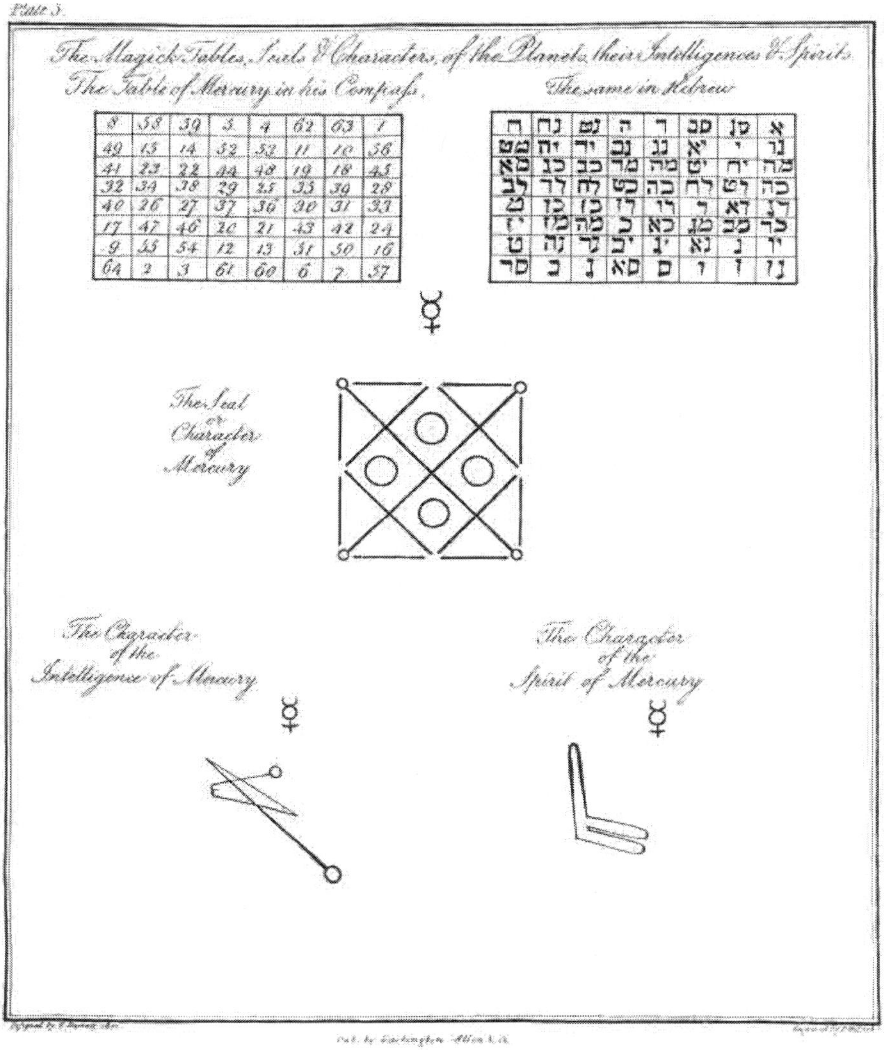

The Magick Tables, Seals & Characters, of the Planets, their Intelligences & Spirits.
The Table of Mercury in his Compass.
8 58 59 5 4 62 63 1
49 15 14 52 53 11 10 56
41 23 22 44 48 19 18 45
32 34 38 29 25 35 39 28
40 26 27 37 36 30 31 33
17 47 46 20 21 43 42 24
9 55 54 12 13 51 50 16
64 2 3 61 60 6 7 57
The same in Hebrew
The Seal or Character of Mercury
The Character of the Intelligence of Mercury
The Character of the Spirit of Mercury

The sixth table is of Mercury, resulting from a square of eight drawn into itself, containing sixty-four numbers, whereof eight on every side and by both diameters make two hundred and sixty, and the sum of all is two thousand and eighty; and over it are set divine names, with an intelligence to good, with a spirit to bad, and from it is drawn a character of Mercury, and the spirits thereof; and if, with

155

Mercury being fortunate, you engrave it upon silver, tin, or yellow brass, or write it upon virgin parchment, it renders the bearer thereof grateful, acceptable, and fortunate to do what he pleases: it brings gain, and prevents poverty; helps the memory, understanding, and divination, and to the understanding of occult things by dreams; but with an unfortunate Mercury does every thing contrary to this.

The seventh and last table is of the Moon: it consists of a square of nine, having eighty-one numbers in every side, and diameter nine, producing three hundred and sixty-nine; and the sum of all is three thousand three hundred and twenty-one. There are over it divine names, with an intelligence to what is good, and a spirit to evil; and from it are drawn the characters of the Moon and the spirits thereof. This, the Moon being fortunate, engraven on silver, makes the bearer amiable, pleasant, cheerful, and honoured, removing all malice and ill-will; it causes security in a journey, increase of riches, and health of body, drives away enemies, and other evil things from what place soever thou shalt wish them to be expelled. But if the Moon be unfortunate, and it be engraven on a plate of lead, wherever it shall be buried it makes that place unfortunate, and the inhabitants thereabouts, as also ships, rivers, fountains, and mills; and it makes every man unfortunate against whom it shall be directly done, making him fly his place of abode (and even his country) where it shall be buried; and it hinders physicians and orators, and all men whatsoever in their office, against whom it shall be made.

Now how the seals and characters of the planets are drawn from these tables, the wise searcher, and he who shall understand the verifying of these tables, shall easily find out.

Here follow the divine names corresponding with the numbers of the planets, with the names of the intelligences and dæmons, or spirits, subject to those names.

It is to be understood that the intelligences are the presiding good angels that are set over the planets; but that the spirits or dæmons, with their names seals, or characters, are never inscribed upon any Talisman, except to execute any evil effect, and that they are subject to the intelligences, or good spirits; and again, when the spirits and their characters are used, it will be more conducive to the effect to add some divine name appropriate to that effect which we desire.

Names answering to the Numbers of Saturn.

ħ

Numbers.	Divine Names.	Divine Names in Hebrew.
3	Ab	אב
9	Hod	הד
15	Jah	יה
15	Hod	היד
45	Jehovah extended	יורהאואהא
45	Agiel, the Intelligence of Saturn	אגיאל
45	Zazel, the Spirit of Saturn	זאזל

Names answering to the Numbers of Jupiter.

♃

4	Aba	אבא
16		הוה
16		אהי
34	El Ab	אלאב
136	Johphiel, the Intelligence of Jupiter	יהפיאל
136	Hismæl, the Spirit of Jupiter	הסמאל

157

Names answering to the Numbers of Mars.

♂

5	He, the letter of the holy name	ה
25		יהי
65	Adonai	אדני p. 147
325	Graphiel, the Intelligence of Mars	גראפיאל
325	Barzabel, the Spirit of Mars	ברצאבאל

Names answering to the Numbers of the Sun.

☉

6	Vau, the letter of the holy name	ו
6	He extended, the letter of the holy name	הא
36	Eloh	אלה
111	Nachiel, the Intelligence of the Sun	נכיאל
666	Sorath, the Spirit of the Sun	סורה

Names answering to the Numbers of Venus.

♀

7	Aha	אהא
49	Hagiel, the Intelligence of Venus	הגיאל
175	Kedemel, the Spirit of Venus	קדמאל
1225	Bne Seraphim, the Intelligence of Venus	בני שרפים

Names answering to the Numbers of Mercury.

☿

8	Asboga, eight extended	אזבגה
64	Din	דין
64	Doni	דני
260	Tiriel, the Intelligence of Mercury	טיריאל
2080	Tapthartharath, the Spirit of Mercury	תפתרתרת

Names answering to the Numbers of the Moon.

☽

9	Hod	הד
81	Elim	אלים
369	Hasmodai, the Spirit of the Moon	השמודאי
3321	Schedbarschemoth Schartathan, the Spirit of the Spirits of the Moon	שדבשהמעחשרתתי
3321	Malcha betharsisim hed beruah schehalim, the Intelligence of the Intelligences of the Moon	קלכאבתדשימימערברויחשהקים

143:1 For the figure of the Tables, Seals, Characters, &c. of the seven Planets, see the following Plates.

CHAPTER 29. OF THE OBSERVATION OF THE CELESTIALS NECESSARY IN EVERY MAGICAL WORK

EVERY natural virtue works things far more wonderful when it is not only compounded of a natural proportion, but also is informed by a choice observation of the celestials opportune to this (viz. when the celestial power is most strong to that effect which we desire, and also helped by many celestials), by subjecting inferiors to the celestials, as proper females, to be made fruitful by their males.

Also, in every work there are to be observed the situation, motion, and aspect of the stars and planets, in signs and degrees, and how all these stand in reference to the length and latitude of the climate; for by this are varied the qualities of the angles, which the rays of the celestial bodies upon the figure of the thing describe, according to which celestial virtues are infused. So when you are working any thing which belongs to any planet, you must place it in its dignities fortunate, and powerful, and ruling in the day hour, and in the figure of the heavens.

Neither must you expect the signification of the work to be powerful, but you must observe the Moon opportunely directed to this; for you shall do nothing without the assistance of the Moon. And if you have more patterns of your work, observe them all, being most powerful, and looking upon one another with a friendly aspect; and if you cannot have such aspects, it will be convenient at least that you take them angular.

But you shall take the Moon either when she looks upon both, or is joined to one, and looks upon the other, or when she passes from the conjunction or aspect of one, to the conjunction or aspect of the other; for that, I conceive, must in no wise be omitted. Also, you shall in every work observe Mercury, for he is a messenger between the higher gods and the infernal gods: when he goes to the good, he increases their goodness--when to the bad, he hath influence on their wickedness.

We call it an unfortunate sign or planet, when it is, by the aspect of Saturn or Mars especially, opposite or quadrant, for these are the aspects of enmity; but a conjunction, a trine, and a sextile aspect, are of friendship; between these there is a greater conjunction; but yet if you do already behold it through a trine, and the planet be received, it is accounted as already conjoined. Now all planets are afraid of the conjunction of the Sun, rejoicing in the trine, and sextile aspect thereof.

CHAPTER 30. WHEN THE PLANETS ARE OF MOST POWERFUL INFLUENCE

NOW we shall have the planets powerful when they are ruling in a house, or in exaltation, or triplicity, or term, or face, without combustion of what is direct in the figure of the heavens, viz. when they are in angles, especially of the rising, or tenth, or in houses presently succeeding, or in their delights; but we must take heed that they are not in the bounds or under the dominion of Saturn or Mars, lest they be in dark degrees, in pits, or vacuities. You shall observe that the angles of the ascendant, and tenth, and seventh be fortunate; as also the lord of the ascendant, and place of the Sun and Moon, and place of the part of fortune, and the lord thereof, the lord of the foregoing conjunction and prevention. But that they of the malignant planet fall unfortunate; unless happily they be significators of thy work, or can be of any advantage to thee, or in thy revolution or birth they had the predominance, for then they are not at all to be depressed. Now we shall have the Moon powerful if she be in her house, or exaltation, or triplicity, or face, or in degree convenient for the desired work; and if it hath a mansion of these twenty-eight, suitable to itself and the work, let her not in the way be burnt up,[149:1] nor slow in course--let her not be in the eclipse, or burnt by the Sun, unless she be in unity with the Sun--let her not descend in the southern latitude, when she goeth out of the burning--neither let her be opposite to the Sun, nor deprived of light--let her not be hindered by Mars or Saturn.

149:1 Via Combusta.

CHAPTER 31. OBSERVATIONS ON THE FIXED STARS, AND THEIR NAMES AND NATURES

THERE is the like consideration to be had in all things concerning the fixed stars. Know this, that all the fixed stars are of the signification and nature of the seven planets; but some are of the nature of one planet, and some of two. Hence, as often as any planet is joined with any of the fixed stars of its own nature, the signification of that star is made more powerful, and the nature of the planet augmented; but if it be a star of two natures, the nature of that which shall be the stronger with it, shall overcome in signification: as for example, if it be of the nature of Mars and Venus, if Mars shall be the stronger to with it, the nature of Mars shall overcome; but if Venus, the nature of Venus shall overcome. Now the natures of fixed stars are discovered by their colours, as they agree with certain planets, and are ascribed to them. Now the colours of the planets are these:--of Saturn, blue, and leaden, and shining with this; of Jupiter, citrine, near to a paleness, and clear with this; of Mars, red and fiery; of the Sun, yellow, and when it rises red, afterwards glittering; of Venus, white and shining--white in the morning, and reddish in the evening; of Mercury, glittering; of the Moon, fair. Know, also, that of the fixed stars, by how much the greater, and brighter, and apparent they are, so much the greater and stronger is the signification: such are those stars called by the astrologers of the first and second magnitude. I will tell thee some of these which are more potent to this faculty, viz. the navel of Andromeda, in the twenty-second degree of Aries of the nature of Venus and Mercury--some call it jovial and saturnine; the head of Algol, in the eighteenth degree of Taurus, of the nature of Saturn and Jupiter; the Pleiades are also in the twenty-second degree, a lunary star by nature, and complexion martial; also Aldeboram, in the third degree of Gemini, is of the nature of Mars, and complexion of Venus--but Hermes places this in the twenty-fifth degree of Aries; the Goat star, in the thirteenth degree of Gemini, is of the nature of Jupiter and Saturn; the Great Dog star is in the seventh degree of Cancer and Venereal; the Little Dog star is in the seventeenth degree of the same, and is of the nature of Mercury, and complexion of Mars; the King star, which is called the Heart of the

Lion, is in the twenty-first degree of Leo, and of the nature of Jupiter and Mars; the tail of the Great Bear is in the nineteenth degree of Virgo, and is venereal and lunary. The star which is called the Right Wing of the Crow, is in the seventh degree of Libra; and in the thirteenth degree of the same, is the left wing of the same, and both of the nature of Saturn and Mars. The star called Spica, is in the sixteenth degree of the same, and is venereal and mercurial. In the seventeenth degree of the same is Alcameth, of the nature of Mars and Jupiter; but of this, when the Sun's aspect is full towards it--of that, when on the contrary. Elepheia, in the fourth degree of Scorpio, of the nature of Venus and Mars. The heart of the Scorpion is in the third degree of Sagittarius, of the nature of Mars and Jupiter. The falling Vulture is in the seventh degree of Capricorn, temperate, mercurial, and venereal. The tail of Capricorn is in the sixteenth degree of Aquarius, of the nature of Saturn and Mercury. The star called the Shoulder of the Horse, is in the third degree of Pisces, of the nature of Jupiter and Mars.-

-And it shall be a general rule for you to expect the proper gifts of the stars, whilst they rule--to be prevented of them, they being unfortunate, as is above shewed; for celestial bodies, inasmuch as they are affected fortunately or unfortunately, so much do they affect us, our works, and those things which we use, fortunately or unhappily. And although many effects proceed from the fixed stars, yet they are attributed to the planets as because being more near to us, and more distinct and known, so because they execute whatever the superior stars communicate to them.

CHAPTER 32. OF THE SUN AND MOON, AND THEIR MAGICAL CONSIDERATIONS

THE Sun and Moon have obtained the administration of ruling the heavens, and all bodies under the heavens. The Sun is the lord of all elementary virtues; and the Moon, by virtue of the Sun, is mistress of generation, increase or decrease. Albumsar says, that by the Sun and Moon, life is infused into all things; which Orpheus calls the enlivening eyes of Heaven. The Sun giveth light to all things of itself, and gives it plentifully, not only to all things in heaven and air, but earth and deep. Whatever good we have, Jamblicus says, we have it from the Sun alone; or from it through other things. Heraclitus calls the Sun, the fountain of celestial light; and many of the Platonists placed the soul of the world chiefly in the Sun, as that which, filling the whole globe of the Sun, doth send forth its rays on all sides, as it were a spirit through all things, distributing life, sense, and motion to the universe. Hence the antient naturalists called the Sun the very heart of Heaven; and the Chaldeans put it as the middle of the Planets. The Egyptians also placed it in the middle of the world, viz. between the two fives of the world; i. e. above the Sun they place five planets, and under him, the Moon and four elements. For it is, amongst the other stars, the image and statue of the great Prince of both worlds, viz. terrestrial and celestial; the true light, and the most exact image of God himself: whose essence resembles the Father--light, the Son--heat, the Holy Ghost. So that the Platonists have nothing to hold forth the divine essence more manifestly by than this.

The Sun disposes even the very spirit and mind of man, which Homer says, and is approved by Aristotle, that there are in the mind such like motions as the Sun, the prince and moderator of the planets, brings to us every day; but the Moon, the nearest to the earth, the receptacle of all the heavenly influences, by the swiftness of her course, is joined to the Sun, and the other planets and stars, every month; and receiving the beams and influences of all the other planets and stars, as a conception, bringing them forth to the inferior world, as being next to itself; for all the stars have influence on it, being the last receiver, which afterwards communicates the influence of all the superiors to these inferiors, and pours them forth on the earth; and it more manifestly disposes these inferiors than others. Therefore her motion is to be observed before the others, as the parent of all conceptions, which it diversely issues forth in these inferiors, according to the diverse complexion, motion, situation, and different aspects to the planets and other stars; and though it receives powers from all the stars, yet especially from the Sun, as oft as it is in conjunction with the same, it is replenished with vivifying virtue; and, according to the aspect thereof, it borrows its complexion. From it the heavenly bodies begin that series of things which Plato calls the golden chain; by which every thing and cause, being linked one to another, do depend on the superior, even until it may be brought unto the supreme cause of all, from which all things depend; hence it is, that, without the Moon intermediating, we cannot at any time attract the power of the superiors; therefore, to obtain the virtue of any star, take the stone and herb of that planet, when the Moon fortunately comes under, or has a good aspect on, that star.

CHAPTER 33. OF THE TWENTY-EIGHT MANSIONS OF THE MOON, AND THEIR VIRTUES

AND seeing the Moon measures the whole space of the Zodiac in the time of twenty-eight days, hence it is that the wise men of the Indians, and most of the antient astrologers have granted twenty-eight mansions to the Moon, which, being fixed in the eighth sphere, do enjoy (as Alpharus says) divers names and properties, from the various signs and stars which are contained in them; through which, while the Moon wanders, it obtains many other powers and virtues; but every one of these mansions, according to the opinion of Abraham, contained twelve degrees, and fifty-one minutes, and almost twenty six seconds, whose names, and also their beginnings in the Zodiac, of the eighth sphere, are these:-- The first is called Alnath; that is, the horns of Aries: his beginning is from the head of Aries, of the eighth sphere: it causes discords and journies. The second is called Allothaim, or Albochan; that is, the belly of Aries; and his beginning is from the twelfth degree of the same sign, fifty-one minutes, twenty-two seconds complete: it conduces to the finding of treasures, and to the retaining captives. The third is called, Achaomazon, or Athoray; that is, showering, or Pleiades: his beginning is from the twenty-fifth degree of Aries complete, forty-two minutes, and fifty-one seconds; it is profitable to sailors, huntsmen, and alchymists. The fourth mansion is called Aldebaram, or Aldelamen; that is, the eye or head of Taurus: his beginning is from the eighth degree of Taurus, thirty-four minutes and seventeen seconds of the same, Taurus being excluded: it causes the destruction and hindrances of buildings, fountains, wells, gold mines, the flight of creeping things, and begets discord. The fifth is called Alchatay, or Albachay; the beginning of it is after the twenty-first degree of Taurus, twenty-five minutes, forty seconds: it helps to the return from a journey, to the instruction of scholars; it confirms edifices, it gives health and good-will. The sixth is called Athanna, or Alchaya; that is, the little star of great light: his beginning is after the fourth degree of Gemini, seventeen minutes, and nine seconds; it conduces to hunting and besieging towns, and revenge of princes: it destroys harvest and fruits, and hinders the operation of the physician. The seventh is called Aldimiach, or

Alarzach; that is, the arm of Gemini, and begins from the seventeenth degree of Gemini, eight minutes, and thirty-four seconds, and lasts even to the end of the sign; it confirms gain and friendship; it is profitable to lovers, and destroys magistracies: and so is one quarter of the heaven completed in these seven mansions, and in the like order and number of degrees, minutes, and seconds the remaining mansions, in every quarter, have their several beginnings namely, so that in the first sign of this quarter three mansions take their beginnings; in the other two signs, two mansions in each; therefore the seven following mansions begin with Cancer, whose names are Alnaza Anatrachya; that is, misty or cloudy, viz. the eighth mansion; it causes love, friendship, and society of fellow travellers: it drives away mice, and afflicts captives, confirming their imprisonment.

After this is the ninth, called Archaam, or Arcaph; that is, the eye of the Lion: it hinders harvest and travellers, and puts discord between men. The tenth is called Algelioche, or Albgebh; that is, the neck or forehead of Leo: it strengthens buildings, promotes love, benevolence, and help against enemies. The eleventh is called Azobra, or Ardaf; that is, the hair of the lion's head: it is good for voyages, and gain by merchandise, and for redemption of captives. The twelfth is called Alzarpha, or Azarpha; that is the tail of Leo: it gives prosperity to harvest and plantations, but hinders seamen; and is good for the bettering of servants, captives, and companions. The thirteenth is named Alhaire; that is, Dog stars, or the wings of Virgo: it is prevalent for benevolence, gain, voyages, harvests, and freedom of captives. The fourteenth is called Achureth, or Arimet; by others, Azimeth, or Athumech, or Alcheymech; that is, the spike of Virgo, or flying spike: it causes the love of married folks; it cures the sick, is profitable to sailors, but hinders journies by land; and in these the second quarter of the heaven is completed. The other seven follow: the first of which begins in the head of Libra, viz. the fifteenth mansion, and its name is Agrapha, or Algrapha; that is, covered, or covered flying: it is profitable for extracting treasures, for digging of pits, it assists divorce, discord, and destruction of houses and enemies, and hinders travellers.

The sixteenth is called Azubene, or Ahubene; that is, the horns of Scorpio: it hinders journies and wedlock, harvest and merchandise; it prevails for redemption of captives. The seventeenth is called Alchil; that is, the crown of Scorpio: it betters a bad fortune, makes love durable, strengthens buildings, and helps seamen. The eighteenth is called Alchas, or Altob; that is, the heart of Scorpio: it causes, discord, sedition, conspiracy against princes and mighty ones, and revenge from enemies; but it frees captives, and helps edifices. The nineteenth is called Allatha, or Achala; by others, Hycula, or Axala, that is, the tail of Scorpio: it helps in besieging of cities, and taking of towns, and in the driving of men from their places, and for the destruction of seamen and perdition of captives. The twentieth is called Abnahaya; that is, a beam: it helps for the taming of wild beasts, for strengthening of prisons; it destroys the wealth of societies; it compels a man to come to a certain place. The twenty-first is called Abeda, or Albeldach, which is a desert: it is good for harvest, gain, buildings, and travellers, and causes divorce; and in this is the third quarter of heaven completed. There remains the seven last mansions completing the last quarter of Heaven: the first of which, being in order to the twenty-second, beginning from the head of Capricorn, called Sadahacha, or Zodeboluch, or Zandeldena; that is, a pastor: it promotes the flight of servants and captives, that they may escape; and helps the curing of diseases. The twenty-third is called Zabadola, or Zobrach; that is, swallowing: it is for divorce, liberty of captives and health to the sick. The twenty-fourth is called Sadabath, or Chadezoad; that is, the star of fortune: it is prevalent for the benevolence of married people, for the victory of soldiers; it hurts the execution of government, and prevents its being exercised. The twenty- fifth is called Sadalabra, or Sadalachia; that is, a butterfly, or a spreading forth: it favours besieging and revenge; it destroys enemies, and causes divorce; confirms prisons and buildings, hastens messengers; it conduces to spells against copulation, and so binds every member of man that it cannot perform its duty. The twenty-sixth is called Alpharg, or Phragal Mocaden; that is, the first drawing: it causes union, health of captives, destroys building and prisons. The twenty-seventh is called Alchara Alyhalgalmoad, or the second drawing: it increases harvests, revenues, gain, and heals infirmities, but hinders buildings, prolongs prisons, causes danger to seamen, and helps to infer mischiefs on whom you shall please. The twenty-eighth and last is called Albotham, or Atchalcy; that is, Pisces: it increases harvest and merchandise; it secures travellers through dangerous places; it makes for the joy of married people; but it strengthens prisons, and causes loss of treasures. And in these twenty-eight mansions lie hid many secrets of the wisdom of the antients, by which they wrought wonders on all things which are under the circle of the Moon; and they attributed to every mansion his resemblances, images, and seals, and his president intelligences, and worked by the virtue of them after different manners.

CHAPTER 34. HOW SOME ARTIFICIAL THINGS...

HOW SOME ARTIFICIAL THINGS (AS IMAGES, SEALS, AND SUCH LIKE) MAY OBTAIN SOME VIRTUE FROM THE CELESTIAL BODIES.

SO great is the extent, power, and efficacy of the celestial bodies, that not only natural things, but also artificial, when they are rightly exposed to those above, do presently suffer by that most potent agent, and obtain a wonderful life. The magicians affirm, that not only by the mixture and application of natural things, but also in images, seals, rings, glasses, and some other instruments, being opportunely framed under a certain constellation) some celestial illustrations may be taken, and some wonderful thing may be received; for the beams of the celestial bodies being animated, living, sensual, and bringing along with them admirable gifts, and a most violent power, do, even in a moment, and at the first touch, imprint wonderful powers in the images, though their matter be less capable. Yet they bestow more powerful virtues on the images if they be framed not of any, but of a certain matter, namely, whose natural, but also specifical virtue is agreeable with the work, and the figure of the image is like to the celestial; for such an image, both in regard to the matter naturally congruous to the operation and celestial influence, and also for its figure being like to the heavenly one, is best prepared to receive the operations and powers of the celestial bodies and figures, and instantly receives the heavenly gift into itself; though it constantly worketh on another thing, and other things yield obedience to it.

CHAPTER 35. OF THE IMAGES OF THE ZODIAC...

OF THE IMAGES OF THE ZODIAC--WHAT VIRTUES, THEY BEING ENGRAVEN, RECEIVE FROM THE STARS.

BUT the celestial images, according to whose likeness images of this kind are framed, are many in the heavens; some visible arid conspicuous, others only imaginary, conceived and set down by the Egyptians, Indians, and Chaldeans; and their parts are so ordered, that even the figures of some of them are distinguished from others; for this reason they place in the circle of the Zodiac twelve general images, according to the number of the signs; of these, they constituting Aries, Leo, and Sagittarius, for the fiery and oriental triplicity, report that it is profitable against fevers, palsy, dropsy, gout, and all cold and phlegmatic infirmities; and that it makes him who carries it to bc acceptable, eloquent, ingenious and honourable; because they are the houses of Mars, Sol, and Jupiter. They made, also, the image of a lion against melancholy phantasies, dropsy, plague and fevers, and to expel diseases; at the hour of the Sun, the first degree of the sign Leo ascending, which is the face and decanate of Jupiter; but against the stone, and diseases of the reins, and against hurts of beasts, they made the same image when Sol, in the heart of the lion, obtained the midst of heaven. And again, because Gemini, Libra, and Aquarius, do constitute the ærial and occidental triplicity, and are the houses of Mercury, Venus, and Saturn, they are said to put to flight diseases, to conduce to friendship and concord, to prevail against melancholy, and to cause health; and they report that Aquarius especially frees from the quartan.

Also, that Cancer, Scorpio, and Pisces, because they constitute the watery and northern triplicity, do prevail against hot and dry fevers, also against the hectic, and all choleric passions; but Scorpio, because among the members it respects the privy parts, doth provoke to lust; but these did frame it for this purpose, his third face ascending, which belongs to Venus; and they made the same, against serpents and scorpions, poisons and evil spirits, his second face ascending, which is the face of the Sun, and decanate of Jupiter; and they report that it maketh him

172

who carries it wise, of a good colour; and they say that the image of Cancer is most efficacious against serpents and poison, when Sol and Luna are in conjunction in it, and ascend in the first and third face; for this is the face of Venus, and the decanate of Luna; but the second face of Luna the decanate of Jupiter. They report, also, that serpents are tormented when the Sun is in Cancer; also, that Taurus, Virgo, and Capricorn, because they constitute the earthly and southern triplicity, do cure hot infirmities, and prevail against the synocal fever; it makes those who carry it grateful, acceptable, eloquent, devout and religious; because they are the houses of Venus, Mars, and Saturn, Capricorn also is reported to keep men in safety, and also places in security, because it is the exaltation of Mars.

CHAPTER 36. OF THE IMAGES OF SATURN

BUT now what images they did attribute to the planets. Although of these things very large volumes have been written by the antient wise men, so that there is no need to declare them here, notwithstanding I will recite a few of them; for they made, from the operations of Saturn, Saturn ascending in a stone, which is called the load-stone, the image of a man, having the countenance of a hart, and camel's feet, and sitting upon a chair or else a dragon, holding in his right hand a scythe, in his left a dart, which image they hoped would be profitable for prolongation of life; for Albumasar, in his book Sadar, proves that Saturn conduces to the prolongation of life; where, also, he says that certain regions of India being subject to Saturn, there men are of a very long life, and die not unless by extreme old age.

They made, also, an image of Saturn, for length of days, in a sapphire, at the hour of Saturn, Saturn ascending or fortunately constituted; whose figure was an old man sitting upon a high chair, having his hands lifted up above his head, and in them holding a fish or sickle, and under his feet a bunch of grapes, his head covered with a black or dusky coloured cloth, and all his garments black or dark. They also make this same image against the stone, and disease of the kidnies, viz. in the hour of Saturn, Saturn ascending with the third face of Aquarius. They made also, from the operations of Saturn, an image for the increasing of power Saturn ascending in Capricorn; the form of which was an old man leaning on a staff, having in his hand a crooked sickle, and clothed in black.

They also made an image of melted copper, Saturn ascending in his rising, viz. in the first degree of Aries, or the first degree of Capricorn; which image they affirm to speak with a man's voice. They made also, from the operations of Saturn, and also Mercury, an image of cast metal, like a beautiful man, which, they said, would foretel things to come; and made it on the day of Mercury, on the third hour of Saturn, the sign of Gemini ascending, being the house of Mercury, signifying prophets; Saturn and Mercury being in conjunction in Aquarius, in the ninth house of heaven, which is also called God. Moreover, let Saturn have a trine aspect on the ascendant, and the Moon in like manner, and the Sun have an aspect on the place of conjunction; Venus, obtaining some angle, may be powerful and occidental; let Mars be combust by the Sun, but let it not have an aspect on Saturn and Mercury; for they said that the splendour of the powers of these stars was diffused upon this image, and it did speak with men, and declare those things which are profitable for them.

CHAPTER 37. OF THE IMAGES OF JUPITER

FROM the operations of Jupiter they made, for prolongation of life, an image in the hour of Jupiter, Jupiter being in his exaltation fortunately ascending, in a clear and white stone; whose figure was a man crowned clothed with garments of a saffron colour, riding upon an eagle or dragon, having in his right hand a dart, about, as it were, to strike it into the head of the same eagle or dragon. They made, also, another image of Jupiter, at the same convenient season, in a white and clear stone, especially in crystal; and it was a naked man crowned, having both his hands joined together and lifted up, as it were, deprecating something sitting in a four-footed chair, which is carried by four winged boys; and they affirm that this image increases felicity, riches, honours, and confers benevolence and prosperity, and frees from enemies. They made, also, another image of Jupiter, for a religious and glorious life, and advancement of fortune; whose figure was a man having the head of a lion or a ram, and eagle's feet, and clothed in saffron coloured clothes.

CHAPTER 38. OF THE IMAGES OF MARS

FROM the operations of Mars, they made an image in the hour of Mars (Mars ascending in the second face of Aries), in a martial stone, especially in a diamond; the form of which was a man armed, riding upon a lion, having in his right hand a naked sword erect, carrying in his left hand the head of a man. They report that an image of this kind renders a man powerful in good and evil, so that he shall be feared by all; and whoever carries it, they give him the power of enchantment, so that he shall terrify men by his looks when he is angry, and stupify them.

They made another image of Mars, for obtaining boldness, courage, and good fortune, in wars and contentions; the form of which was a soldier, armed and crowned, girt with a sword, carrying in his right hand a long lance; and they made this at the hour of Mars, the first face of Scorpio ascending with it.

CHAPTER 39. OF THE IMAGES OF THE SUN

FROM the operations of the Sun they made an image at the hour of the Sun, the first face of Leo ascending with the Sun; the form of which was a king crowned, sitting in a chair, having a raven in his bosom, and under his feet a globe: he is clothed in saffron coloured clothes. They say that this image renders men invincible and honourable, and helps to bring their business to a good end, and to drive away vain dreams; also to be prevalent against fevers, and the plague; and they made it in a balanite stone, or a ruby, at the hour of the Sun, when he, in his exaltation, fortunately ascends. They made another image of the Sun in a diamond, at the hour of the Sun ascending in his exaltation; the figure of which was a woman crowned, with the gesture of one, dancing and laughing, standing in a chariot drawn by four horses, having in her right hand a looking-glass or buckler, in the left a staff, leaning on her breast, carrying a flame of fire on her head. They say that this image renders a man fortunate, and rich, and beloved of all; and they made this image on a cornelian stone, at the hour of the Sun ascending in the first face of Leo, against lunatic passions, which proceed from the combustion of the Moon.

CHAPTER 40. OF THE IMAGES OF VENUS

FROM the operations of Venus they made an image, which was available for favour and benevolence, at the very hour it ascended into Pisces; the form of which was the image of a woman, having the head of a bird, the feet of an eagle, and holding a dart in her hand. They made another image of Venus, to obtain the love of women, in the lapis lazuli, at the hour of Venus, Venus ascending in Taurus; the figure of which was a naked maid, with her hair spread abroad, having a looking-glass in her hand, and a chain tied about her neck--and near her a handsome young man, holding her with his left hand by the chain, but with his right hand doing up her hair, and both looking lovingly on one another--and about them is a little winged boy, holding a sword or dart. They made another image of Venus, the first face of Taurus, Libra, or Pisces, ascending with Venus; the figure of which was a little maid, with her hair spread abroad, clothed in long and white garments, holding a laurel apple, or flowers, in her right hand, in her left a comb: it is said to make men pleasant, jocund, strong, cheerful, and to give beauty.

CHAPTER 41. OF THE IMAGES OF MERCURY

FROM the operations of Mercury they made an image of Mercury, Mercury ascending in Gemini; the form of which was a handsome young man, bearded, having in his left hand a rod, round which a serpent was entwined--in the right he carried a dart; having his feet winged. They say that this image confers knowledge, eloquence, diligence in merchandise, and gain; moreover, to obtain peace and concord, and cure fevers. They made another image of Mercury, ascending in Virgo, for good will, wit, and memory; the form of which was a man sitting upon a chair, or riding on a peacock, having eagle's feet, and on his head a crest, and in his left hand holding a cock of fire.

CHAPTER 42. OF THE IMAGES OF THE MOON

FROM the operations of the Moon they made an image for travellers against weariness, at the hour of the Moon, the Moon ascending in its exaltation; the figure of which was a man leaning on a staff, having a bird on his head, and a flourishing tree before him. They made another image of the Moon for the increase of the fruits of the earth, and against poisons, and infirmities of children, at the hour of the Moon, it ascending in the first face of Cancer; the figure of which was a woman cornuted, riding on a bull, or a dragon with seven heads or a crab, and she hath in her right hand a dart, in her left a looking glass, clothed with white or green, and having on her head two serpents with horns twined together, and to each arm a serpent twined about, and to each foot one in like manner. And thus much spoken concerning the figures of the planets, may suffice.

CHAPTER 43. OF THE IMAGES OF THE HEAD AND TAIL OF THE DRAGON OF THE MOON

THEY made, also, the image of the head. and tail of the Dragon of the Moon, namely, between an ærial and fiery circle, the likeness of a serpent, with the head of a hawk, tied about them after the manner of the great letter Theta; they made it when Jupiter, with the head, obtained the mid heaven; which image they affirm to avail much for the success of petitions, and would signify by this image a good and fortunate genius, which they would represent by this image of the serpent; for the Egyptians and Phoenicians do extol this creature above all others, and say it is a divine creature, and hath a divine nature; for in this is a more acute spirit, and a greater fire than in any other, which thing is manifest both by his swift motion without feet, hands, or any other instruments; and also that it often renews its age with his skin, and becomes young again; but they made the image of the tail like as when the Moon was eclipsed in the tail, or ill affected by Saturn or Mars, and they made it to introduce anguish, infirmity, and Misfortune: we call it an evil genius.

THE TALISMAN OF THE DRAGON'S HEAD.

183

CHAPTER 44. OF THE IMAGES OF THE MANSIONS OF THE MOON

THEY made, also, images for every mansion of the Moon as follows:--

In the first, for the destruction of some one, they made, in an iron ring, the image of a black man, in a garment of hair, and girdled round, casting a small lance with his right hand: they sealed this in black wax, and perfumed it with liquid storax, and wished some evil to come.

In the second, against the wrath of the prince, and for reconciliation with him, they sealed, in white wax and mastich, the image of a king crowned, and perfumed it with lignum aloes.

In the third, they made an image in a silver ring, whose table was square; the figure of which was a woman, well clothed, sitting in a chair, her right hand being lifted up on her head; they sealed it, and perfumed it with musk, camphire, and calamus aromaticus. They affirmed that this gives happy fortune, and every good thing.

In the fourth, for revenge, separation, enmity, and ill-will, they sealed, in red wax, the image of a soldier sitting on a horse, holding a serpent in his right hand: they perfumed it with red myrrh and storax.

In the fifth, for the favour of kings and officers, and good entertainment, they sealed, in silver, the head of a man, and perfumed it with red sanders.

In the sixth, to procure love between two, they sealed, in white wax, two images, embracing one another, and perfumed them with lignum aloes and amber.

In the seventh, to obtain every good thing, they scaled, in silver, the image of a man, well clothed, holding up his hands to Heaven, as it were, praying and supplicating, and perfumed it with good odours.

In the eighth, for victory in war, they made a seal in tin, being an image of an eagle, having the face of a man, and perfumed it with brimstone.

In the ninth, to cause infirmities, they made a seal of lead, being the image of a man wanting his privy parts, covering his eyes with his hands; and they perfumed it with rosin of the pine.

In the tenth, to facilitate child bearing, and to cure the sick, they made a seal of gold, being the head of a lion, and perfumed it with amber.

In the eleventh, for fear, reverence, and worship, they made a seal of a plate of gold, being the image of a man riding on a lion, holding the ear thereof in his left hand, and in his right holding forth a bracelet of gold; and they perfumed it with good odours and saffron.

In the twelfth, for the separation of lovers, they made a seal of black lead, being the image of a dragon fighting with a man; and they perfumed it with the hairs of a lion, and assafœtida.

In the thirteenth, for the agreement of married people, and for dissolving of all the charms against copulation, they made a seal of the images of both (of the man in red wax, and the woman in white), and caused them to embrace one another; perfuming it with lignum aloes and amber.

In the fourteenth, for divorce and separation of the man from the woman, they made a seal of red copper, being the image of a dog. biting his tail; and they perfumed it with the hair of a black dog and a black cat.

In the fifteenth, to obtain friendship and good will, they made the image of a man sitting, and inditing letters, and perfumed it with frankincense and nutmegs.

In the sixteenth, for gaining much merchandising, they made a seal of silver, being the image of a man, sitting on a chair, holding a balance in his hand; and they perfumed it with well smelling spices.

In the seventeenth, against thieves and robbers, they sealed with an iron seal the image of an ape, and perfumed it with the air of an ape.

In the eighteenth, against fevers and pains of the belly, they made a seal of copper, being the image of a snake with his tail above his head; and they perfumed it with hartshorn; and said this same seal put to flight serpents, and all venomous creatures, from the place where it is buried.

In the nineteenth, for facilitating birth, and provoking the menstrues, they made a seal of copper, being the image of a woman holding her hands upon her face; and they perfumed it with liquid storax.

In the twentieth, for hunting, they made a seal of tin, being the image of Sagittary, half a man and half a horse; and they perfumed it with the head of a wolf.

In the twenty-first, for the destruction of some body, they made the image of a man, with a double countenance before and behind; and they perfumed it with brimstone and jet, and put it in a box of brass, and with it brimstone and jet, and the hair of him whom they would hurt.

In the twenty-second, for the security of runaways, they made a seal of iron, being the image of a man, with wings on his feet, bearing a helmet on his head; and they perfumed it with argent vive.

In the twenty-third, for destruction and wasting, they made a seal of iron, being the image of a cat, having a dog's head; and they perfumed it with dog's hair taken from the head, and buried it in the place where they intended the hurt.

In the twenty-fourth, for multiplying herds of cattle, they took the horn of a ram, bull, or goat, or of that sort of cattle they would increase, and sealed in it, burning, with an iron seal, the image of a woman giving suck to her son; and they hanged it on the neck of that cattle who was the leader of the flock, or they sealed it in his horn.

In the twenty-fifth, for the preservation of trees and harvest, they sealed, in the wood of a fig tree, the image of a man planting and they perfumed it with the flowers of the fig tree, and hung it on the tree.

In the twenty-sixth, for love and favour, they sealed, in white wax and mastich, the figure of a woman washing and combing her hair; and they perfumed it with good odours.

In the twenty-seventh, to destroy fountains, pits, medicinal waters, and baths, they made, of red earth, the image of a man winged, holding in his hand an empty vessel, and perforated; and the image being burnt, they put in the vessel assafœtida and liquid storax, and they buried it in the pond or fountain which they would destroy.

In the twenty-eighth, for getting fish together, they made a seal of copper, being the image of a fish; and they perfumed it with the skin of a sea fish, and cast it into the water where they would have the fish gathered.

Moreover, together with the aforesaid images, they wrote down also the names of the spirits, and their characters, and invoked and prayed for those things which they pretended to obtain.

CHAPTER 45. THAT HUMAN IMPRECATIONS NATURALLY IMPRESS THEIR POWERS UPON EXTERNAL THINGS...

THAT HUMAN IMPRECATIONS NATURALLY IMPRESS THEIR POWERS UPON EXTERNAL THINGS--AND HOW MAN'S MIND, THROUGH A DEGREE OF DEPENDENCIES, ASCENDS INTO THE INTELLIGIBLE WORLD, AND BECOMES LIKE TO THE MORE SUBLIME SPIRITS AND INTELLIGENCES.

THE celestial souls send forth their virtues to the celestial bodies, which transmit them to this sensible world; for the virtues of the terrene orb proceed from no other cause than celestial. Hence the magician, that will work by them, uses a cunning invocation of the superiors, with mysterious words and a certain kind of ingenious speech, drawing the one to the other; yet by a natural force, through a certain mutual agreement between them, whereby things follow of their own accord, or sometimes are drawn unwillingly. Hence says Aristotle, in his sixth book of his Mystical Philosophy, "that when any one, by binding or bewitching, calls upon the Sun or other stars, praying them to assist the work desired, the Sun and other stars do not hear his words; but are moved, after a certain manner, by a certain conjunction and mutual series, whereby the parts of the world are mutually subordinate the one to the other, and have a mutual consent, by reason of their great union: as in a man's body, one member is moved by perceiving the motion of another; and in a harp, one string is moved by the motion of another. So when any one moves any part of the world, other parts are moved by the perceiving of that motion."--The knowledge, therefore, of the dependency of things following one the other, is the foundation of all wonderful operation, which is necessarily required to the exercising the power of attracting superior virtues. Now the words of men are certain natural things; and because the parts of the world mutually draw one the other; therefore a magician invocating by words, works by powers fitted to Nature, by leading some by the love of one to the other; or drawing others, by reason of the one following after the other; or by repelling, by reason of the enmity of one to the other, from the contrariety and difference of things, and multitude of virtues; which, although they are contrary and different, yet perfect one part. Sometimes, also, he compels things by way of authority, by the celestial virtue, because he is not a stranger to the heavens. A man, therefore, if he receives the impression of a ligation, or fascination, doth not receive it according to the rational soul, but sensual; and if he suffers in any part, he suffers according to the animal part; for they cannot draw a knowing and intelligent man by reason, but by receiving that impression and force by sense; inasmuch as the animal spirit of man is, by the influence of the celestials, and co-operation of the things of the world, affected beyond his former and natural disposition. As the son moves the father to labour, although unwilling, to keep and maintain him, although he be wearied; and the desire to rule, is moved by anger and other labours to get the dominion; and the indigency of nature, and fear of poverty, moves a man to desire riches; and the ornaments and beauty of women, is an incitement to concupiscence; and the harmony of a wise musician moves his hearers with various passions, whereof some do voluntary follow the consonancy of art, others conform themselves by gesture, although unwilling, because their sense is captivated, their reason not being intent to these things. Hence they fall into errors, who think those things to be above nature, or contrary to nature--which indeed are by nature, and according to nature. We must know, therefore, that every superior moves its next inferior, in its degree and order, not only in bodies, but also in spirits: so the universal soul moves the particular soul; the rational acts upon the sensual, and that upon the vegetable; and every part of the world acts upon another, and every part is apt to be moved by another. And every part of this inferior world suffers from the heavens, according to their nature and aptitude, as one part of the animal body suffers for another.

And the superior intellectual world moves all things below itself; and, after a manner, contains all the same beings, from the first to the last, which are in the inferior world. Celestial bodies, therefore, move the bodies of the elementary world, compounded, generable, sensible (from the circumference to the centre), by superior, perpetual, and spiritual essences, depending on the primary intellect, which is the acting intellect; but upon the virtue put in by the word of God; which word the wise Chaldeans of Babylon call, the Cause of Causes; because from it are produced all beings: the acting intellect, which is the second, from it depends; and that by reason of the union of the word with the First Author, from whom all things being are truly produced: the word, therefore, is the image of God--the acting intellect, the image of the word--the soul is the image of this intellect--and our word is the image of the soul, by which it acts upon natural things naturally, because nature is the work thereof. And every one of those perfects his subsequent: as a father his son; and none of the latter exists without the former; for they are depending among themselves by a kind of ordinate dependency--so that when the latter is corrupted, it is returned into that which was next before it, until it come to the heavens; then to the universal soul; and, lastly, into the acting intellect, by which all other creatures exist; and itself exists in the principal author, which is the creating word of God, to which, at length, all things are returned. Our soul, therefore, if it will work any wonderful thing in these inferiors, must have respect to their beginning, that it may be strengthened and illustrated by that, and receive power of acting through each degree, from the very first Author. Therefore we must be more diligent in contemplating the souls of the stars--then their bodies, and the super-celestial and intellectual world-- then the celestial, corporeal, because that is more noble; although, also, this be excellent, and the way to that, and without which medium the influence of the superior cannot be attained to. As for example: the Sun is the king of stars, most full of light; but receives it from the intelligible world, above all other stars, because the soul thereof is more capable of intelligible splendour. Wherefore he that desires to attract the influence of the Sun, must contemplate upon the Sun; not only by the speculation of the exterior light, but also of the interior. And no man can do this, unless he return to the soul of the Sun, and become like to it, and comprehend the intelligible light thereof with an intellectual sight, as the sensible light with the corporeal eye; for this man shall be filled with the light thereof, and the light whereof, which is an under type impressed by the supernal orb, it receives into itself; with the illustration whereof his intellect being endowed, and truly like to it, and being assisted by it, shall at length attain to that supreme brightness, and to all forms that partake thereof; and when he hath received the light of the supreme degree, then his soul shall come to perfection, and be made like to spirits of the Sun, and shall attain to the virtues and illustrations of the supernatural virtue, and shall enjoy the power of them, if he has obtained faith in the First Author. In the first place, therefore, we must implore assistance from the First Author; and praying, not only with mouth, but a religious gesture and supplicant soul, also abundantly, incessantly, and sincerely, that he would enlighten our mind, and remove darkness, growing upon our souls by reason of our bodies.

CHAPTER 46. THE CONCLUSION OF THE CONSTELLATORY PRACTICE...

THE CONCLUSION OF THE CONSTELLATORY PRACTICE, OR TALISMANIC MAGIC; IN WHICH IS INCLUDED THE KEY OF ALL THAT HAS BEEN WRITTEN UPON THIS SUBJECT; SHEWING THE PRACTICE OF IMAGES, &C. BY WAY OF EXAMPLE, AND LIKEWISE THE NECESSARY OBSERVATIONS OF THE CELESTIALS, TOWARDS THE PERFECTION OF TALISMANICAL OPERATIONS.

WE will now shew thee the observations of celestial bodies, which are required for the practice of these things, which are briefly as follow: --

To make any one fortunate, we make an image at that time in which the significator of life, the giver of life, or Hylech, the signs and planets, are fortunate: let the ascendant and mid-heaven, and the lords thereof, be fortunate; and also the place of the Sun and Moon; part of fortune and lord of conjunction or prevention, make before their nativity, by depressing the malignant planets, i.e. taking the times when they are depressed. But if we would make an image to procure misery, we must do contrary to this; and those which we before placed fortunate, we must now make unfortunate, by taking the malignant stars when they rule.

And the same means we must take to make any place, region, city, or house unfortunate.

But if you would make any one unfortunate who hath injured you, let there be an image made under the ascension of that man whom thou wouldst make unfortunate; and thou shalt take, when unfortunate, the lord of the house of his life, the lord of the ascendant and the Moon, the lord of the house of the Moon, the lord of the house of the lord ascending, and the tenth house and the lord thereof Now, for the building, success, or fitting of any place, place fortunes in the ascendant thereof; and in the first and tenth, the second and eighth house, thou shalt make the lord of the ascendant, and the lord of the house of the Moon, fortunate.

But to chase away certain animals (from any place) that are noxious to thee, that they may not generate or abide there, make an image under the ascension of that animal which thou wouldst chase away or destroy, and after the likeness thereof; for instance, now, suppose thou wouldst wish to chase away scorpions from any place: let an image of a scorpion be made, the sign Scorpio ascending with the Moon; then thou shalt make unfortunate the ascendant, and the lord thereof, and the lord of the house of Mars; and thou shalt make unfortunate the lord of the ascendant in the eighth house; and let them be joined with an aspect malignant, as opposite or square, and write upon the image the name of the ascendant, and of the lord thereof, and the Moon, the lord of the day and hour; and let there be a pit made in the middle of the place from which thou wouldst drive them, and put into it some earth taken out of the four corners of the same place, then bury the image there, with the head downwards, saying--"This is the burying of the Scorpions, that they may be forced to leave, and come no more into this place."-- And so do by the rest.

Now for gain, make an image under the ascendant of that man to whom thou wouldst appoint the gain; and thou shalt make the lord of the second house, which is the house of substance, to be joined with the lord of the ascendant, in a trine or sextile aspect, and let there be a reception amongst them; thou shalt make fortunate the eleventh, and the lord thereof, and the eighth; and, if thou canst, put part of fortune in the ascendant or second; and let the image be buried in that place, or from that place, to which thou wouldst appoint the gain or fortune. Likewise, for agreement or love, let be made an image in the day of Jupiter, under the ascendant of the nativity of him whom you would wish to be beloved; make fortunate the ascendant and the tenth, and hide the evil from the ascendant; and you must have the lords of the tenth, and planets of the eleventh, fortunate, joined to the lord of the ascendant, from the trine or sextile, with reception; then proceed to make another image, for him whom thou wouldst stir up to love; whether it be a friend, or female, or brother, or relation, or companion of him whom thou wouldst have favoured or beloved, if so, make an image under the ascension of the eleventh house from the ascendant of the first image; but if the party be a wife, or a husband, let it be made under the ascension of the seventh; if a brother, sister, or cousin, under the ascension of the third house; if a mother, of the tenth, and so on:--now let the significator of the ascendant of the second image be joined to the significator of the ascendant of the first, and let there be between them a reception, and let the rest be fortunate, as in the first image; afterwards join both the images together in a mutual embrace, or put the face of the second to the back of the first, and let them be wrapped up in silk, and cast away or spoiled.

Also, for the success of petitions, and obtaining of a thing denied, or taken, or possessed by another, make an image under the ascendant of him who petitions for the thing; and cause the lord of the second house to be joined with the lord of the ascendant, from a trine or sextile aspect, and let there be a reception betwixt them; and, if it can be so, let the lord of the second be in the obeying signs, and the lord of ascendant in the ruling: make fortunate the ascendant and the lord thereof; and beware that the lord of the ascendant be not retrograde, or combust, or cadent, or in the house of opposition, i. e. in the seventh from his own house; let him not be hindered by the malignant planets, but let him be strong and in an angle; thou shalt make fortunate the ascendant, and the lord of the second, and the Moon: and make another image for him that is petitioned to, and begin it under the ascendant belonging to him: as if he is a king, or prince, &c. begin it under the ascendant of the tenth house from the ascendant of the first image; if a father, under the fourth, if a son, under the fifth, and so of the like; then put the significator of the second image, joined with the lord of the ascendant of the first image from a trine or sextile, and let him receive it; and put them both strong and fortunate, without any hinderance; make all evil fall from them; thou shalt make fortunate the tenth and the fourth, if thou canst, or any of them; and when the second image shall be perfect, join it with the first, face to face, and wrap them in clean linen, and bury them in the middle of his house who is the petitioner, under a fortunate significator, the fortune being strong; and let the face of the first image be towards the north, or rather towards that place where the thing petitioned for doth remain; or, if it happens that the petitioner goes forward to obtain the thing desired or petitioned for, let him carry the said images with him.

Thus we have given, in a few examples, the key of all Talismanical operations whatsoever, by which wonderful effects may be wrought either by images, by rings, by glasses, by seals, by tables, or any other magical instruments whatsoever; but as these have their chief grounds in the true knowledge of the effects of the planets, and the rising of the constellations, we recommend an earnest attention to that part of Astrology [175:1] which teaches of the power, influences, and effects of the celestial bodies amongst themselves generally; likewise, we would recommend the artist to be expert in the aspects, motions, declinations, risings, &c. &c. of the seven planets, and perfectly to understand their natures, either mixed or simple; also, to be ready and correct in the erecting of a figure, at any time, to shew the true position of the heavens; there being so great a sympathy between the celestials and ourselves; and to observe all the other rules which we have plentifully recited: and, without doubt, the industrious student shall receive the satisfaction of bringing his operations and experiments to effect that which he ardently desires.

With which, wishing all success to the contemplator of the creature and the Creator, we will here close up this Second Part of our Work, and the conclusion of our Book of Talismanical Magic.

THE END OF THE FIRST BOOK

175:1 Those who would be perfect in the necessary knowledge of Astrology, ought to study from Coley, his book, called Clavis Astrologiæ Elimata, or his Key new filed--Salmon's Soul of Astrology--Lilley's, or Partridge's, Vade Mecum--or Middleton's Astrology.

THE MAGUS, BOOK II

CONTAINING MAGNETISM, AND CABALISTICAL MAGIC;
DISCOVERING THE SECRET MYSTERIES OF CELESTIAL MAGIC.

WITH THE ART OF CALCULATING BY THE DIVINE NAMES OF
GOD; SHEWING THE RULE, ORDER, AND GOVERNMENT OF
ANGELS, INTELLIGENCES, AND BLESSED SPIRITS, HOLY
TABLES AND SEALS, TABLES OF THE CABALA, &C.

LIKEWISE TREATING OF CEREMONIAL MAGIC, INVOCATION
OF SPIRITS, CONSECRATIONS, CIRCLES, &C. ALSO OF DREAMS,
PROPHECY, MIRACLES, &C.

BY FRANCIS BARRETT

TO WHICH IS ADDED,
A TRANSLATION OF THE WORKS OF TRITEMIUS OF SPANHEIM,
VIZ.
HIS BOOK OF SECRET THINGS, AND OF SPIRITS

INTRODUCTION

IN our following Treatise of Magnetism we have collected and arranged in order some valuable and secret things out of the writings of that most learned chemist and philosopher Paracelsus, who was the ornament of Germany and the age he lived in. Likewise we have extracted the very marrow of the science of Magnetism out of the copious and elaborate works of that most celebrated philosopher (by fire) Van Helmont, who, together with Paracelsus, industriously promulgated all kinds of magnetic and sympathetic cures, which, through the drowsiness, ignorance, unbelief, and obstinacy of the present age, have been so much and so totally neglected and condemned; yet, however impudent in their assertions, and bigotted to their own false opinions, some of our modern philosophers may be, yet we have seen two or three individuals, who, by dint of perseverance, have proved the truth and possibility of Magnetism, by repeated and public experiments. Indeed the ingenious invention of the Magnetic Tractors prove at once that science should never be impeded by public slander or misrepresentation of facts that have proved to be of general utility. And we do not doubt but that we shall be able to shew, by the theory and practice delivered in the sequel, that many excellent cures may be performed by a due consideration and attentive observance of the principles upon which sympathy, antipathy, magnetic attraction, &c. are founded; and which will be fully illustrated in the following compendium:

We shall hasten to explain the first principles of Magnetism, by examining the magnetic or attractive power.

CHAPTER 1. THE MAGNETIC, OR ATTRACTIVE POWER OR FACULTY

AS concerning an action locally at a distance, wines do suggest a demonstration unto us: for, every kind of wine, although it be bred out of co-bordering provinces, and likewise more timely blossoming elsewhere, yet it is troubled while our country vine flowereth; neither doth such a disturbance cease as long as the flower shall not fall off from our vine; which thing surely happens, either from a common motive-cause of the vine and wine, or from a particular disposition of the vine, the which indeed troubles the wine, and doth shake it up and down with a confused tempest: or likewise, because the wine itself doth thus trouble itself of its own free accord, by reason of the flowers of the vine: of both the which latter, if there be a fore-touched conformity, consent, co-grieving, or congratulation; at least, that cannot but be done by an action at a distance: to wit, if the wine be troubled in a cellar under ground, whereunto no vine perhaps is near for some miles, neither is there any discourse of the air under the earth, with the flower of the absent vine; but, if they will accuse a common cause for such an effect, they must either run back to the stars, which cannot be controuled by our pleasures and liberties of boldness; or, I say, we return to a confession of an action at a distance: to wit, that some one and the same, and as yet unknown spirit, the mover, doth govern the absent wine, and the vine which is at a far distance, and makes them to talk and suffer together. But, as to what concerns the power of the stars, I am unwilling, as neither dare I, according to my own liberty, to extend the forces, powers, or bounds of the stars beyond or besides the authority of the sacred text, which faith (it being pronounced from a divine testimony) that the stars shall be unto us for signs, seasons, days, and years: by which rule, a power is never attributed to the stars, that wine bred in a foreign soil, and brought unto us from far, doth disturb, move, or render itself confused: for, the vine had at some time received a power of encreasing and multiplying itself before the stars were born: and vegetables were before the stars, and the imagined influx of these: wherefore also, they cannot be things conjoined in essence, one whereof could consist without the other. Yea, the vine in some places flowereth more timely;

and, in rainy, or the more cold years, our vine flowereth more slowly, whose flower and stages of

flourishing the wine doth, notwithstanding, imitate; and so neither doth it respect the stars, that it should disturb itself at their beck.

In the next place, neither doth the wine hearken unto the flourishing or blossoming of any kind of capers, but of the wine alone: and therefore we must not flee unto an universal cause, the general or universal ruling air of worldly successive change; to wit, we may rather run back unto impossibilities and absurdities, than unto the most near commerces of resemblance and unity, although hitherto unpassable by the schools.

Moreover, that thing doth as yet far more manifestly appear in ale or beer: when, in times past, our ancestors had seen that of barley, after whatsoever manner it was boiled, nothing but an empty ptisana or barley-broth, or also a pulp, was cooked; they meditated, that the barley first ought to bud (which then they called malt) and next, they nakedly boiled their ales, imitating wines: wherein, first of all, some remarkable things do meet in one; to wit, there is stirred up in barley, a vegetable bud, the which when the barley is dried, doth afterwards die, and loseth the hope of growing, and so much the more by its changing into meal, and afterwards by an after-boiling, it despairs of a growing virtue; yet these things nothing hindering, it retains the winey and intoxicating spirit of aqua vitæ, the which notwithstanding it doth not yet actually possess: but at length, in number of days, it attaineth it by virtue of a ferment: to wit, in the one only bosom of one grain one only spirit is made famous with diverse powers, and one power is gelded, another being left: which thing indeed, doth as yet more wonderfully shine forth; when as the ale or beer of malt disturbs itself while the barley flowereth, no otherwise than as wine is elsewhere wont to do: and so a power at a far absent distance is from hence plain to be seen: for truly there are cities from whom pleasant meadows do expel the growing of barley for many miles, and by so much the more powerfully do ales prove their agreement with the absent flowering barley; in as much as the gelding of their power hath withdrawn the hopes of budding and increasing: and at length the aqua vitae being detained and shut up within the ale, hogshead, and prison of the cellar, cannot with the safety of the ale or beer wandering for some leagues unto the flowering ear of barley, that thereby, as a stormy retainer, it may trouble the remaining ale with much confusion.

Certainly there is a far more quiet passage for a magnetical or attractive agreement among some agents at a far distance from each other, than there is to dream an aqua vitæ wandering out of the ale of a cellar, unto the flowering barley, and from thence to return unto the former receptacles of its pen-case, and ale: But the sign imprinted by the appetite of a woman great with child, on her young, doth fitly, and alike clearly confirm a magnetism or attractive faculty and its operation at a distance: to wit, let there be a woman great with child, which desires another cherry, let her but touch her forehead or any other place with her finger; without doubt, the young is signed in its forehead with the image of the cherry, which afterwards doth every year wax green, white, yellow, and at length looks red, according to the tenor of the trees: and it much more wonderfully expresses the same successive alteration of maturities in Spain than in Germany: and so hereby an action at a distance is not only confirmed, but also a conformity or agreement of the essences of the cherry tree, in its wooden and fleshly trunk; a consanguinity or near affinity of a being impressed upon the part by on instantaneous imagination, and by a successive course of the years of its kernel: surely the more learned ought not to impute those things unto evil spirits, which, through their own weakness, they are ignorant of; for these things do on all sides occur in nature, the which, through our slenderness, we are not able to unfold; for to refer whatsoever gifts of God are in nature (because our dull capacity does not comprehend the same rightly) to the devil, shews both ignorance and rashness, especially when, as all demonstration of causes from a former thing or cause is banished from us, and especially from Aristotle, who was ignorant of all nature, and deprived of the good gifts which descends from the Father of Lights; unto whom be all honour and glory.

Note. We may, by the aforesaid chapter, see the wonderful working power of the attractive or universal spirit, which can by no other means be so clearly demonstrated as by the sympathies in natural things, which are inherent throughout all nature; and, upon this principle of sympathy and antipathy, we say is founded that spiritual power which tends to things and objects remote one from the other, i. e. a magnetic attraction, which does actually exist, as we shall clearly prove by experiment, where we fully shew the action and passion that is between natural spirits, by which means wonderful effects are produced which have ignorantly been attributed to divers superstitions, as Sorcery, Inchantment, Nigromancy, or the Black Art, &c.

4:1 Van HELMONT.

CHAPTER 2. OF SYMPATHETIC MEDICINES

IN the year 1639, a little book came forth, whose title was, 'The Sympathetical Powder of Edricius Mohynus, of Eburo,' whereby wounds are cured without application of the medicine unto the part afflicted, and without superstition; it being sifted by the sieve of the reasons of Galen and Aristotle; wherein it is Aristotetically, sufficiently, proved, whatsoever the title of it promises; but it hath neglected the directive faculty, or virtue, which may bring the virtues of the sympathetical powder, received in the bloody towel or napkin, unto the distant wound.

Truly, from a wound, the venal blood, or corrupt pus, or sanies, from an ulcer, being received in the towel, do receive, indeed, a balsam from a sanative or healing being; I say, from the power of the vitriol, a medicinal power connected and limited in the aforesaid mean; but the virtues of the balsam received are directed unto the wounded object, not indeed by an influential virtue of the stars, and much less do they fly forth of their own accord unto the object at a distance: therefore the ideas of him that applieth the sympathetical remedy are connected in the mean, and are made directresses of the balsam unto the object of his desire: even as we have above also minded by injections concerning ideas of the desire.

Mohyns supposed that the power of sympathy depends upon the stars, because it is an imitator of influences: but I draw it out of a much nearer subject: to wit, out of directing ideas, begotten by their mother Charity, or a desire of goodwill: for, from hence does that sympathetic powder operate more successfully, being applied by the hand of one than another: therefore I have always observed the best process where the remedy is instituted by a desire of charity; but, that it doth succeed, with small success, if the operator be a careless or drunken person; and, from hence, I have more esteemed the stars of the mind, in sympathetical remedies, than the stars of heaven: but that images, being conceived, are brought unto an object at a distance, a pregnant woman is an example of, because she is she who presently transfers all the ideas of her conception on her young, which dependeth no otherwise on the mother than from a communion of universal nourishment. Truly, seeing such a direction of desire is plainly natural, it is no wonder that the evil spirit doth require the ideas of the desires of his imps to be annexed unto a mean offered by him. Indeed, the ideas of the desire are after the manner of the influences of heaven cast into a proper object how locally remote soever; that is, they are directed by the desire, especially pointing out an object for itself, even as the sight of the basilisk, or touch of the torpedo, is reflected on their willed object; for I have already shewn in its place, that the devil doth not attribute so much as any thing in the directions of things injected; but that he hath need of a free, directing, and operative power or faculty. But I will not disgrace sympathetical remedies because the devil operates something about things injected into the body: for what have sympathetical remedies in common? Although Satan doth co- operate in injections by wicked natural means required from his bond slaves; for every thing shall be judged guilty, or good, from its ends and intents: and it is sufficient that sympathetical remedies do agree with things injected in natural means, or medicines.

CHAPTER 3. OF THE MAGNETIC OR SYMPATHETIC UNGUENT...

OF THE MAGNETIC OR SYMPATHETIC UNGUENT, THE POWDER OF SYMPATHY, ARMARY UNGUENT, CURING OF WOUNDS, ECSTASIES, WITCHCRAFT, MUMMIES, &C.

WE shall now show some remarkable operations that are effected by magnetism, and founded upon natural sympathy and antipathy, likewise how by these means some extraordinary cures may be performed.

The goodness of the Creator every where extended, created every thing for the use of ungrateful man; neither did he admit any of the theologists, or divines, as assistants in council, how many or how great virtues he should infuse into things natural. But there are those who venture to measure the wonderful works of God by their own sharpened and refined wit, whereby they deny God to have given such virtue to things; as though man (a worm) was able, by his narrow and limited capacity, to comprehend Omniscience; he therefore measures the minds of all men by his own, who think that cannot be done, which they cannot understand. They therefore can only develope the mysteries of nature, who being versed in the art of Cabala, Fire, and Magic, examined the properties of things, and draw, from darkness into light, the lurking powers of Man, Animals, Vegetables, Minerals, and Stones, and, separating the crudities, dregs, poisons, heterogenities, that are the thorns implanted in virgin nature from the curse. For an observer of nature sees daily she doth distil, sublime, calcine, ferment, dissolve, coagulate, fix, &c. therefore we who are the ministers of nature do separate, &c. finding out the causes and effects of every phenomena she produces.

Now, as magnetism is ordained for the use of man, and for the curing of the various disorders incident to human nature, we shall first touch upon the grand subject of magnetism, known to possess wonderful properties, and which are not only evident to every eye, but shew us sufficient grounds for our admitting the possibility and reality of magnetism in general.

The loadstone possesses an eminent medicinal faculty, against many violent and implacable disorders. Helmont says, that the back of the loadstone, as it repulses iron, so also it removes gout, swellings, rheum, &c. that is of the nature or quality of iron. The iron attracting faculty, if it be joined to the mummy of a woman, and the back of the loadstone be put within her thigh, and the belly of the loadstone on her loins, it safely prevents a miscarriage, already threatened; but the belly of the loadstone applied within the thigh and the back to her loins, it doth wonderfully facilitate her delivery.

Likewise the wearing the loadstone cases and prevents the cramp, and such like disorders and pains.

Uldericus Balk, a dominican friar, published a book at Frankfort in the year 1611, concerning the lamp of life; in which we shall find (taken from Paracelsus) the true magnetical cure of many diseases, viz. the dropsy, gout, jaundice, &c. For if thou shalt enclose the warm blood of the sick in the shell and white of an egg, which is exposed to a nourishing warmth, and this blood, being mixed with a piece of flesh, thou shalt give to a hungry dog, the disorder departs from thee into the dog; no otherwise than the leprosy of Naaman passed over into Gehazi through the execration of the prophet.

If women, weaning their infants, shall milk out their milk upon hot burning coals, the breast soon dries.

If any one happens to commit nuisance at thy door, and thou wilt prevent that beastly trick in future, take the poker red-hot, and put it into the excrement, and, by magnetism, his posteriors shall become much scorched and inflamed.

Make a small table of the lightest, whitest, and basest kind of lead; and at one end put a piece of amber, and, three spans from it, lay a piece of green vitriol; this vitriol will soon lose its colour and acid: both which effects are found in the preparation of amber. The root of the Caroline thistle being plucked up when full of juice and virtue, and tempered with the mummy of a man, will exhaust the powers and natural strength out of a man, on whose shadow thou shalt stand, into thyself.

CHAPTER 4. OF THE ARMARY UNGUENT, OR WEAPON SALVE, &C

THE principal ingredient in this confection, is the moss of a dead man's skull, which Van Helmont calls the excrescencies or superfluities of the stars. Now the moss growing on the skull of a dead man, seeing it has received its seed from the heavens, but its increase from the mummial marrow of the skull of man, or tower of the microcosm, has obtained excellent astral and magnetic powers beyond the common condition of vegetables, although herbs, as they are herbs, want not their own magnetism.

Now, the magnetism of this unguent draws out that strange disposition from the wound (which otherwise, by a disunion of the parts that held together, and by which, I say, strange disposition and foreign quality is produced) from whence it slips, not being overburdened or oppressed by any accident, suddenly grow together; and this is effected by the armary unguent, or weapon salve. From this it appears that the unguent, or weapon salve, its property is to heal suddenly and perfectly without pain, costs, peril, or loss of strength; hence it is manifest that the magnetical virtue is from God.

It is now seasonable to discover the immediate cause of magnetism in the unguent.

First of all, by the consent of mystical divines, we divide man into the external and internal man, assigning to both the powers of a certain mind, or intelligence: for so there doth a will belong to flesh and blood, which may not be either the will of man or the will of God; and the heavenly Father also reveals some things unto the more inward man, and some things flesh and blood reveals, that is, the outward and sensitive, or animal man. For, how could the service of idols, envy, &c. be rightly numbered among the works of the flesh, seeing they consist only in the imagination, if the flesh had not also its own imagination and elective will?

Furthermore, that there are miraculous ecstasies belonging to the more inward man, is beyond dispute. That there are also ecstasies in the animal man, by reason of an intense, or heightend imagination, is, without doubt. Martin del Ris, an elder of the society of Jesus, in his Magical Disquisitions or Enquiries, makes mention of a certain young man in the city Insulis that was transported with so violent a desire of seeing his mother, that through the same intense desire, as if being rapt up by an ecstasy, he saw her perfectly, although many miles absent from thence; and, returning again to himself, being mindful of all that he had seen, gave many true signs of his true presence with his mother.

Now that desire arose from the more outward man, viz. from blood and sense, or flesh, is certain; for, otherwise, the soul being once dislodged, or loosened from the bonds of the body, cannot, except by miracle, be reunited to it; there is therefore in the blood a certain ecstatical or transporting power, which, if at any time shall be excited or stirred up by an ardent desire and most strong imagination, it is able to conduct the spirit of the more outward man even to some absent and far distant object, but then that power lies hid in the more outward man, as it were, in potentia, or by way of possibility; neither is it brought into act, unless it be roused up by the imagination, inflamed and agitated by a most fervent and violent desire.

CHAPTER 5. OF THE IMAGINATIVE POWER AND THE MAGNETISM OF THE NATURAL SPIRITS...

OF THE IMAGINATIVE POWER AND THE MAGNETISM OF THE NATURAL SPIRITS, MUMMIAL ATTRACTION, SYMPATHIES OF ASTRAL SPIRITS, WITH THEIR BODIES, UPON WHICH THE WHOLE ART OF NECROMANCY IS FOUNDED.

MOREOVER, when as the blood is after some sort corrupted, then indeed all the powers thereof which, without a foregoing excitation of the imagination, were before in possibility, are of their own accord, drawn forth into action; for, through corruption of the grain, the seminal virtue, otherwise drowsy, and barren, breaks forth into act; because, that seeing the essences of things, and their vital spirits, know not how to putrify by the dissolution of the inferior harmony, they sprung up as surviving afresh. For, from thence it is that every occult property, the compact of their bodies being by foregoing digestion, (which we call putrifaction) now dissolved, comes forth free to hand, dispatched, and manifest for action.

Therefore when a wound, through the entrance of air, hath admitted of an adverse quality, from whence the blood forthwith swells with heat or rage in its lips, and otherwise becomes mattery, it happens, that the blood in the wound just made, by reason of the said foreign quality, doth now enter into the beginning of some kind of corruption (which blood being also then received on the weapon or splinter thereof, is besmeared with the magnetic unguent) the which entrance of corruption, mediating the ecstatical power lurking potentially in the blood, is brought forth into action; which power, because it is an exiled returner unto its own body, by reason of the hidden ecstasy; hence that blood bears an individual respect unto the blood of its whole body. Then indeed the magnetic or attractive faculty is busied in operating in the unguent, and through the mediation of the ecstatical power (for so I call it for want of an etymology) sucks out the hurtful quality from the lips of the wound, and at length, through the mummial,

211

balsamical, and attractive virtue, attained in the unguent, the magnetism is perfected.

So thou hast now the positive reason of the natural magnetism in the unguent, drawn from natural magic, whereunto the light of truth assents; saying, "where the treasure is there is the heart also."

For if the treasure be in heaven, then the heart, that is, the spirit of the internal man, is in God, who is the paradise, who alone is eternal life.

But if the treasure be fixed or laid up in frail and mortal things, then also the heart and spirit of the external man is in fading things; neither is there any cause of bringing in a mystical sense, by taking not the spirit, but the cogitation and naked desire, for the heart; for that would contain a frivolous thing, that wheresoever a man should place his treasure in his thought or cogitation, there his cogitation would be.

Also truth itself doth not interpret the present text mystically, and also by an example adjoined, shews a local and real presence of the eagles with the dead carcass, so also that the spirit of the inward man is locally in the kingdom of God in us, which is God himself; and that the heart or spirit of the animal or outward sensitive man is locally about its treasure.

What wonder is it, that the astral spirits of carnal or animal men should, as yet, after their funerals, shew themselves as in a bravery, wandering about their buried treasure, whereunto the whole of Necromancy (or art of divination by the calling of spirits) of the antients hath enslaved itself?

I say, therefore, that the internal man is an animal or living creature, making use of the reason and will of blood: but, in the mean time, not barely an animal, but moreover the image of God.

Logicians therefore may see how defectively they define a man from the power of rational discourse. But of these things more elsewhere.

I will therefore adjoin the magnetism of eagles to carcasses; for neither are flying fowls endowed with such an acute smelling, that they can, with a mutual consent, go from Italy into Africa unto carcasses.

For neither is an odour so largely and widely spread; for the ample latitude of the interposed sea hinders it, and also a certain elementary property of consuming it nor is there any ground that thou shouldest think these birds do perceive the dead carcasses at so far a distance, with heir sight, especially if those birds shall lie southwards behind a mountain.

But what need is there to enforce the magnetism of fowls by many arguments, since God himself, who is the becoming and end of philosophy, doth expressly determine the same process to be of the heart and treasure, with these birds and the carcass, and so interchangeably between these and them?

For if the eagles were led to their food, the carcasses, with the same appetite whereby four-footed beasts are brought on to their pastures, certainly he had said, in one word, that living creatures flock to their food even as the heart of man to his treasure; which would contain a falsehood: for neither doth the heart of man proceed unto its treasure, that he may be filled therewith as living creatures do to their meat; and therefore the comparison of the heart of man and of the eagle lies not in the end for which they tend or incline to a desire, but in the manner of tendency; namely that they are allured and carried on by magnetism, really and locally.

Therefore the spirit and will of the blood fetched out of the wound, having intruded itself into the ointment by the weapon being anointed therewith, do tend towards their treasure, that is, the rest of the blood as yet enjoying the life of the more inward man: but he saith by a peculiar testimony, that the eagle is drawn to the carcass, because she is called thereunto by an implanted and mummial spirit

213

of the carcass, but not by the odour of the putrifying body: for indeed that animal, in assimilating, appropriates to himself only this mummial spirit: for from thence it is said of the eagle, in a peculiar manner, "my youth shall be renewed as the eagle's."

For truly the renewing of her youth proceeds from an essential extraction of the mummial spirit being well refined by a certain singular digestion proper to that fowl, and not from a bare eating of the flesh of the carcass; otherwise dogs also and pies would be renewed, which is false.

Thou wilt say, that it is a reason far-fetched in behalf of magnetism; but what wilt thou then infer hereupon? If that which thou confesseth to be far remote for thy capacity of understanding, that shall also with thee be accounted to be fetched from far. Truly the book of Genesis avoucheth, that in the blood of all living creatures doth their soul exist.

For there are in the blood certain vital powers 1, the which, as if they were soulified or enlivened, do demand revenge from Heaven, yea, and judicial punishment from earthly judges on the murderer; which powers, seeing they cannot be denied to inhabit naturally in the blood, [16:1] see not why they can reject the magnetism of the blood, as accounting it among the ridiculous works of Satan.

This I will say more, to wit, that those who walk in their sleep, do, by no other guide than the spirit of the blood, that is, of the outward man, walk up and down, perform business, climb walls, and manage things that are otherwise impossible to those that are awake. I say, by a magical virtue, natural to the more outward man; that Saint Ambrose, although he was for distant in his body, yet was visibly present at the funeral solemnities of Saint Martin; yet was he spiritually present at those solemnities, in the visible spirit of the external man, and no otherwise: for inasmuch as in that ecstasy which is of the more internal man, many of the saints have seen many and absent things. This is done without time and place, through the superior powers of the soul being collected in unity, and by an intellectual vision, but not by a visible presence; otherwise the soul is not separated from the body, but in good earnest, or for altogether; neither is it re-connected thereunto, which re-connexion, notwithstanding, is otherwise natural or familiar to the spirit of the more outward man.

It is not sufficient in so great a paradox, to have once, or by one single reason, touched at the matter; it is to be further propagated, and we must explain how a magnetical attraction happens also between inanimate things, by a certain perceivance or feeling; not indeed animal or sensitive, but natural.

Which thing, that it may be the more seriously done, it behoves us first to shew what Satan can, of his own power, contribute to, and after what manner he can co-operate in the merely wicked and impious actions of witches: for, from thence it will appear unto what cause every effect may be attributed.

In the next place, what that spiritual power may be which tends to a far remote object; or what may be the action, passion, and skirmishing between. natural spirits, or what may be the superiority of man as to other inferior creatures; and, by consequence, why indeed our unguent, being compounded of human mummies, do thoroughly cure horses also. We will explain the matter in the following chapter.

16:1 This singular property of the blood, which Helmont calls Vital Powers, is no less wonderful than true, having been myself a witness of this experiment while in South Wales. It was tried upon a body that was maliciously murdered, through occasion of a quarrel over-night at an alehouse. The fellow who was suspected of the murder appeared the next day in public seemingly unconcerned. The Coroner's jury sat upon the body within twenty-four hours after this notable murder was committed; when the suspected was suddenly taken into custody, and conveyed away to the same public-house where the inquisition was taken. After some debate, one Dr. Jones desired the suspected to be brought into the room; which done, he desired the villain to lay his left hand under the wound, which was a deep gash on the neck, and another on the breast; the villain plainly confessed his guilt by his trepidation; but as soon as he lightly laid his finger on the body, the blood immediately ran, about six or seven drops, to the admiration of all present. If any one doubts the truth of this narrative, however learned and profound he may think himself, let him call personally upon me, and I will give him such reference, and that truly respectable and fair, as shall convince him of the fact. FRANCIS BARRETT.

CHAPTER 6. OF WITCHCRAFT

LET a witch therefore be granted, who can strongly torment an absent man by an image of wax, by imprecation or cursing, by enchantment, or also by a foregoing touch alone, (for here we speak nothing of Sorceries, because they are those which kill only by poison, inasmuch as every common apothecary can imitate those things) that this act is diabolical, no man doubts: however, it is profitable to discern how much Satan and how much the witch can contribute hereunto.

The First Supposition.

First of all, thou shalt take notice, that Satan is the sworn and irreconcileable enemy of man, and to be so accounted by all, unless any one had rather have him to be his friend; and therefore he most readily procures whatsoever mischief he is able to cause or wish unto us, and that without doubt and neglect.

The Second Supposition.

And then although he be an enemy to witches themselves, forasmuch as he is also a most malicious enemy to all mankind in general; yet, in regard they are his bond-slaves, and those of his kingdom, he never, unless against his will betrays them, or discovers them to judges, &c.

From the former supposition I conclude, that if Satan were able of himself to kill a man who is guilty of deadly sin, he would never delay it; but he doth not kill him, therefore he cannot.

Notwithstanding, the witch doth oftentimes kill; hence also she can kill the same man, no otherwise than as a privy murderer at the liberty of his own will slays any one with a sword.

There is therefore a certain power of the witch in this action, which belongs not to Satan, and consequently Satan is not the principal efficient and executor of that

217

murder; for otherwise if he were the executioner thereof, he would in nowise stand in need of the witch as his assistant; but he alone had soon taken the greatest part of men out of the way.

Surely most miserable were the conditions of mortals who should be subject to such a tyrant, and stand liable to his commands; we have too faithful a God, than that he should subject the work of his own hands to the arbitrary dominion of Satan.

Therefore in this act, there is a certain power plainly proper and natural to the witch which belongs not to Satan.

Moreover, of what nature, extent, and quality that power may be, we must more exactly sift out.

In the first place, it is manifest that it is no corporeal strength of the male sex; for neither doth there concur any strong touching of the extreme parts of the body, and witches are for the most part feeble, impotent, and malicious old women, therefore there must needs be some other power, far superior to a corporeal attempt, yet natural to man.

This power therefore was to be seated in that part wherein we most nearly resemble the image of God; and although all things do also, after some sort, represent that venerable image, yet because man doth most elegantly, properly, and nearly do that, therefore the image of God in man doth far outshine, bear rifle over, and command the images of God in all other creatures; for, peradventure, by this prerogative, all things are put under his feet.

Wherefore if God act, per nutum, or by a beck, namely by his word, so ought man to act some things only by his beck or will, if he ought to be called his true image: for neither is that new, is that troublesome, is that proper to God alone: for Satan, the most vile abject of creatures, doth also locally move bodies per nutum, or by his beck alone, seeing he hath not extremities or corporeal organs, whereby to touch, move, or also to snatch a new body to himself

That privilege therefore ought no less to belong to the inward man, as he is a spirit, if he ought to represent the image of God, and that indeed not all idle one; if we call this faculty magical, and thou being badly instructed, art terrified at this word, thou mayest, for me, call it a spiritual strength or efficacy: for, truly, we are nothing solicitous about names. I always, as immediately as I can, cast an eye upon the thing itself.

That magical power, therefore, is in the inward man, whether thou, by this etymology, or true word, understandest the soul or the vital spirit thereof, it is now indifferent to us; since there is a certain proportion of the internal man towards the external in all things, glowing or growing after its own manner, which is an appropriated disposition, and proportioned property.

Wherefore the power or faculty must needs be dispersed throughout the whole man; in the soul, indeed, more vigorous, but in the flesh and blood far more remiss.

CHAPTER 7. OF THE VITAL SPIRIT, &C

THE vital spirit in the flesh and blood performs the office of the soul; that is, it is the same spirit in the outward man, which, in the seed, forms the whole figure, that magnificent structure and perfect delineation of man, and which hath known the ends of things to be done, because it contains them; and the which as president accompanies the new framed young, even unto the period of its life; and the which, although it depart therewith, some smacks or small quantity, at least, thereof remains in a carcass slain by, violence, being as it were most exactly co-fermented with the same. But, from a dead carcass that was extinct of its own accord, and from nature failing, as well the implanted as inflowing spirit passed forth at once.

For which reason, physicians divide this spirit into the implanted or mummial, and inflowing or acquired spirit, which departs; to wit, with the former life and this influxing spirit they afterwards subdivide into the natural, vital, and animal spirit; but, we likewise, do here comprehend them all at once in one single word.

The soul therefore being wholly a spirit could never move or stir up the vital spirit, (being indeed corporeal), much less flesh and bones, unless a certain natural power, yet magical and spiritual, did descend from the soul into the spirit and body.

After what sort, I pray, could the corporeal spirit obey the commands of the soul, unless there should be a command from her for moving of the spirit, and afterwards the body?

But against this magical motive faculty thou will forthwith object, that that power is limited within her composed body, and her own natural inn: therefore although we call this soul a magicianness, yet it shall be only a wresting and abuse of the name; for truly the true and superstitious magic draws not its foundation from the soul; seeing this same soul is not able to move, alter, or exite any thing out of its own body.

I answer, that this power, and that natural magic of the soul which she exerciseth not of herself, by virtue of the image of God, doth now lie hid as obscure in man, and as it were lie asleep since the fall or corruption of Adam, and stands in need or stirring up; all which particulars we shall anon in their proper place prove; which same power, how drowsy and as it were drunk soever, it otherwise remains daily in us, yet it is sufficient to perform its offices in its own body.

CHAPTER 8. OF THE MAGICAL POWER, &C

THEREFORE the knowledge and power magical, and that faculty in man which acteth only per nutum, sleeps since the knowledge of the apple was eaten; and as long as this knowledge (which is of the flesh and blood, gross and material belonging to the external man and darkness) flourishes, the more noble magical power is lying dormant.

But because in sleep this outward or sensual knowledge is sometimes dormant, hence it is that our dreams are sometimes prophetical, and God himself is therefore nearer unto man in dreams, through that effect, viz. when the more inward magic of the soul being uninterrupted by the flesh, diffuses itself on every side into the understanding; even as when it sinks itself into the inferior powers thereof it safely leads those who walk in their sleep by moving or conducting them, whither those that were awake could not surmount or climb.

Therefore we establish this point, viz. that there is inherent in the soul a certain magical virtue given her by God, naturally proper and belonging to her, in asmuch as we are his image and engravement; and in this respect she acts also in a peculiar manner, i. e. spiritually on an object at a distance, and that more powerfully than by any corporeal assistance; for seeing the soul is the principal part of the body, therefore all action belonging to her is spiritual, magical, and of the greatest validity.

Which power man is able, by the Art of the Cabala, to excite in himself at his own pleasure, and these, as we have before said, are called Adepts; who are governed by the Spirit of God.

Thus we have endeavoured to shew that man predominates over all other creatures that are corporeal, and that by his magical faculty he is able to subdue the magical virtues of all other things; which predominance of man, or the soul's natural magic, some have ignorantly attributed solely to verses, charms, signs, characters, &c. by which hierarchy or holy dominion inherent in man, those effects, whatever they may be, are wrought, which some (who but too corporeally philosophize) have attributed to the dominion of Satan.

High and sacred is the force of the microcosmical spirit, which, as is evident in pregnant women, stamps upon the young the image and properties of a thing desired, as we have before instanced in a cherry, which, without the trunk of a tree, brings forth a true cherry, that is flesh and blood, enobled with the properties and power of the more inward or real cherry, by the conception of the imagination alone; from whence are two necessary consequences.

First, that all the spirits, and as it were the essences of all things, lie hid in us, and are born and brought forth only by the working, power, and phantasy of the microcosm.

The second is, that the soul, in conceiving, generates a certain idea of the thing conceived; the which, as it before lay hid unknown, like fire in a flint, so by the stirring up of the phantasy there is produced a certain real idea, which is not a naked quality, but something like a substance, hanging in suspense between a body and a spirit, that is the soul.

That middle being is so spiritual, that it is not plainly exempted from a corporeal condition, since the actions of the soul are limited on the body, and the inferior orders of faculties de ending upon it, nor yet so corporeal that it may be inclosed by dimensions, the which we have also related to be only proper to a seminal being. This ideal entity, therefore, when it falls out of the invisible and intellectual world of the microcosm, it puts on a body, and then it is first inclosed by the limitation of place and numbers.

The object of the understanding is in itself a naked and pure essence, not an accident, by the consent of practical, that is, mystical divines; therefore this Proteus or transferable essence, the understanding doth, as it were, put on and clothe itself, with this conceived essence.

But because every body, whether external or internal, hath its making in its own proper image, the understanding knows or discerns not, the will loves and wills not, the memory recollects not, but by images or likenesses: the understanding therefore puts on this same image of its object; and because the soul is the pure simple form of the body, which turns itself about to every member, therefore the acting understanding cannot have two images at once, but first one and then the other. He, who is wholly the life, created all things and hath said, nothing is to be expected as dead out of his hand. Likewise nothing can come to our view wherein himself is not clearly apparent or present; for it is said, "the spirit of the Lord hath filled the whole globe of the earth:" and, again, "that he containeth or comprehendeth all things," therefore there is nothing in being, no creature but what possesses a certain degree of divine fire and life, yet lying dormant or unexcited, till stirred up by the art, power, and operation of man.

CHAPTER 9. OF THE EXCITING OR STIRRING UP THE MAGICAL VIRTUE

EVERY magical virtue therefore stands in need of an excitement, by which a certain spiritual vapour is stirred up, by reason whereof the phantasy which profoundly sleeps is awakened, and there begins an action of the corporeal spirit, as a medium, which is that of Magnetism, and is excited by a fore-going touch.

There is a magical virtue, being as it were abstracted from the body, which is wrought by the stirring up of the power of the soul, from whence there are made most potent procreations, and most famous impressions, and strong effects, so that nature is on every side a magicianness, and acts by her own phantasy; and by how much the more spiritual her phantasy is, so much the more powerful it is, therefore the denomination of magic is truly proportionable or concordant.

Now the highest sort of magic is that which is stirred up from an intellectual conception, and indeed that of the inward man is only to be excited by the Holy Spirit, and by his gift the Cabala; but that of the external man is stirred up by a strong imagination, by a daily and heightened speculation, and, in witches, by the devil.

But the magical virtue of the exhaled spirituous vapour, or subtil spirits sent from the body, which before lay in potentia, or by way of possibility only, is either excited by a more strong imagination, the magician making use of the blood as a medium, and establishing his kindled entity thereon, or by the ascending phantasy of the weapon salve, the exciteress of the property lying in the blood; else by a foregoing appointment or disposition of the blood unto corruption, viz. whereby the elements are disposed unto a separation, and the essences (which cannot putrify) and the essential phantasies, which lay hid in the properties come forth into action.

The phantasy therefore, of any subject whatsoever has obtained a strong appetite to the spirit of another thing, for the moving of some certain thing in place, for the attracting, repelling, or expulsion thereof; and there and not elsewhere we acknowledge magnetism as the natural magical endowment of that thing firmly planted in it by God.

There is therefore a certain formal property separated from sympathetical and abstruse qualities; because the motive phantasy of these qualities do not directly fly unto a local motion, but only to an alternative motion of the object. Now it is sufficient that (if a man happens to receive many wounds in his body) blood be had only from one of these wounds, and from this one the rest are cured also, because that blood keeps a concordant harmony with the spirit of the whole, and draws forth from the same the offensive quality communicated, not only to the lips of the wound, but to the whole man, for from one wound only the whole man is liable to grow feverish.

Therefore the outchased blood being received on the weapon is introduced into the magnetic unguent.

For then the phantasy of the blood, being otherwise as yet drowsy and slow to action, being stirred up by the virtue of the magnetic unguent, and there finding the balsamic virtue of it, desires the quality induced into it, to be bestowed on itself throughout, and from thence by a spiritual magnetism to draw out all the strange tincture of the wound, which, seeing it cannot fitly enough effect by itself, it implores the aid of the moss, blood, fat, and mummy, which are conjoined together into such a balsam, which not but by its own phantasy becomes also medicinal, magnetical, and is also a tractor of all the strange qualities out of the body, whose fresh blood, abounding with spirit, is carried unto it, whether it shall be that of a man or any other living creature. The phantasy therefore is a returner, or reducible and ecstatical, from part of the blood that is fresh and newly brought unto the unguent; but the magnetic attraction began in the blood is perfected by the medicinal virtue of the unguent; not that the unguent draws the infirmity of the wound unto itself, but it alters the blood newly brought unto it, in its spirit, and makes it medicinal, and stirs up the power thereof: from thence it contracts a certain medicinal virtue, which returns unto its whole body to correct the spirit of the blood throughout the whole man. Now, to manifest a great mystery, viz. to shew that in man there is placed a great efficacy whereby he may be able only by his beck, (as we before mentioned) nod or phantasy, to act out of himself, and to imprint a virtue, a certain influence which afterwards perseveres, or constantly subsists by itself, and acts upon objects at a very great distance; by which only mystery, those things which we have spoken (relative to ideal entity conveyed in a spiritual fewel, and departing far from home to execute its offices, concerning the magnetism of all things begotten in the imagination of man, as in that which is proper to every thing, and also concerning the magical superiority of men over all other bodies,) will plainly and conspicuously appear.

CHAPTER 10. OF THE MAGICAL VIRTUE OF THE SOUL, AND THE MEDIUMS BY WHICH IT ACTS

SOMETHING more we will add, before we dismiss the present subject, which is that if a nail, dart, knife, or sword, or any other iron instrument be thrust into the heart of a horse, it will bind and withhold the spirit of a witch, and conjoin it with the mummial spirit of the horse, whereby they may be burnt in the fire together, and by that the witch is tormented, as by a sting or burning, by which means she may be known so that she who is offensive to God, and destructive to mortal men, may be taken away from society according to the law of God "thou shalt not suffer a witch to live;" for if the work be limited to any outward object, that work the magical soul never attempts without a medium or mean: therefore it makes use of the nail, or sword, or knife, or any other thing as aforesaid.

Now this being proved, that man hath a power of acting, per nutum, or by his nod, or of moving any object remotely placed; it has also been sufficiently confirmed by the same natural example, that this efficacy was also given unto man by God.

And as every magical faculty lies dormant, and has need of excitement, or stirring up; which is always true, if the object whereon it is to act is not nearly disposed, if its internal phantasy doth not wholly confirm to the impression of the agent, or also if the patient be equal in strength, or superior to the agent therein.

But, on the contrary, where the object is plainly and nearly disposed, as steel is, for the receiving of magnetism, then the patient without much stirring up, the alone phantasy of the more outward man being drawn out to the work and bound up to any suitable mean, yields to the magnetism.

Therefore we repeat, the magician must always make use of a medium for then the words or forms of sacraments do always operate, because from the work performed. But the reason why exorcisms, conjurations, charms, incantations, &c.

do sometimes fail of their desired effect, is because the unexcited mind, or spirit of the exorcist, renders the words dull or ineffectual.

Therefore no man can be a happy or successful magician, but him who knows how to stir up the magical virtue of his soul, or can do it practically without science.

And there can be no nearer medium of magnetism, than human blood with human blood.

And no sympathetic remedies, magnetical or attractive, but from the idea or phantasy of the operator impressing upon it a virtue and efficacy from the excited power in his own soul.

And now to bring our Magnetic Treatise to a total conclusion, we have to say, that whoever, through ignorance or obstinacy, will say there is no validity or reason, or reality in the science of magnetism, proves himself unworthy the sacred name of philosopher, because he condemns what he knows nothing at all about.

For those who will give themselves the leisure to examine the truth of those things which we have taught, will not find their expectation deceived, therefore will not condemn.

But whoever should be so superstitious as to attribute a natural effect so created by God, and bestowed on the creature, unto the power and craft of the devil, he filches the honour due to the Omnipotent Creator, and reproachfully applies the same unto Satan; the which (under favour) will be found to be express idolatry and blasphemy.

"There are three" (as says the Scripture) "who bear record in heaven; the Father, the Word, and the Holy Spirit; and these three are only one."

There are three that bear record on earth; the blood, the spirit, and the water; and these three are only one.

We therefore, who have the like humanity, contain blood and spirit of a co-like unity; and the action of the blood is merely spiritual. Therefore, in Genesis, it is not called by the etymology of blood, but is made remarkable by the name of a red spirit.

Therefore, let those who would attain knowledge in these things, and be perfect in what we have set before them, constantly meditate and desire that the First Cause and Archetype of all things would graciously and mercifully illuminate their minds; without which, they grope but in darkness and uncertainty, and are subject to the delusions of impure spirits and devils, who are only to be put to flight by putting on the whole armour of God, in whom we all live, move, breathe, and have our being.

END OF MAGNETISM

THE CABALA; OR THE SECRET MYSTERIES OF CEREMONIAL MAGIC

ILLUSTRATED. SHEWING

THE ART OF CALCULATING BY DIVINE NAMES;

The Rule, Order, and Government of ANGELS, INTELLIGENCES, AND BLESSED SPIRITS;

Holy Seals, Pentacles, Tales of the Cabala, Divine Numbers, Characters and Letters Of Miracles, Prophecy, Dreams, &c. &c. &c.

Embellished and beautified with a vast Number of RARE FIGURES, PENTACLES, CHARACTERS, &,c. &c. &c.

Used in the CABALISTIC ART.

By FRANCIS BARRETT

STUDENT OF CHEMISTRY, NATURAL AND OCCULT PHILOSOPHY, THE CABALA, &c.

CHAPTER 1. OF THE CABALA, ETC

WE shall now turn our pen to the explaining of the high and mysterious secrets of the Cabala, by which only we can know the truth; and likewise how to prepare our mind and spirit for the contemplation of the greatest and best part of magic, which we call intellectual and divine, because it chiefly takes God and the good spirits for its object; and as the cabalistic art opens many and the chiefest mysteries and secrets of ceremonial magic.

But in respect of explaining or publishing those few secrets in the Cabala, which are amongst a few wise men, and communicated by word of mouth only, I hope the student will pardon me if I pass over these in silence, because we are not permitted to divulge some certain things; but this we shall do; we will open all those secrets which are necessary to be known; and by the close reading of which, you shall find out, of your own head, to be both profitable and delightful.

Therefore, all we solicit is, that those who perceive those secrets should keep them together as secrets, and not expose or babble them to the unworthy; but reveal them only to faithful, discreet, and chosen friends. And we would caution you in this beginning, that every magical experiment flies from the public, seeking to be hid, is strengthened and confirmed by silence, but is destroyed by publication; never does any complete effect follow after: likewise all the virtue of thy works will suffer detriment when poured into weak, prating, and incredulous minds; therefore, if thou would be a magician, and gain fruit from this art, to be secret, and to manifest to none, either thy work, or place, or time, nor thy desire, or will, except it be to a master or partner, or companion, who should likewise be faithful, discreet, silent, and dignified by nature and education; seeing that even the prating of a companion, his unbelief, doubting, questioning, and, lastly, unworthiness, hinders and disturbs the effect in every operation.

CHAPTER 2. WHAT DIGNITY AND PREPARATION IS ESSENTIALLY NECESSARY TO HIM WHO WOULD BECOME A TRUE MAGICIAN

IT is fit that we who endeavour to attain so great a height should first study two things: viz. First, how we should leave vain and carnal affections, frail sense and material passions; Secondly, by what ways and means we may ascend to an intellect pure, and joined with the powers of the celestials, without which we shall never happily ascend to the scrutiny of secret things, and to the power of working wonderful effects, &c. Now, if thou art a man perfect in thy understanding, and constantly meditating upon what we have in this book written, and without doubting, believeth, thou shalt be able, by praying, consecrating, deprecating, invocating, &c. to attract spiritual and celestial gifts, and to imprint them on whatever things thou shalt please; and by it to vivify every magical work.

CHAPTER 3. THAT THE KNOWLEDGE OF THE TRUE GOD IS NECESSARY FOR A MAGICIAN

SEEING that the being and operation of all things depend on the Most High God, Creator of all things, and from thence on the other divine powers, to whom also is granted a power of fashioning and creating, not principally indeed, but instrumentally, by virtue of the First Great Creator, (for the beginning of every thing is the first cause; but what is produced by the second cause, is much more produced by the first, which is the producer of the second cause, which therefore we call secondaries.) It is necessary, therefore, that every magician should know that very God, which is the first cause and creator of all things, and likewise the other divine powers, (which we call the second causes,) and not to be ignorant of them, and likewise what holy rites, ceremonies, &c. are conformable to them; but, above all, we are to worship in spirit and truth, and place our firm dependance upon that one only God who is the author and promoter of all good things, the Father of all, most bountiful and wise; the sacred light of justice, and the absolute and sole perfection of all nature, and the contriver and wisdom thereof.

CHAPTER 4. OF DIVINE EMANATIONS...

OF DIVINE EMANATIONS, AND TEN SEPHIROTHS, AND TEN MOST SACRED NAMES OF GOD WHICH RULE THEM, AND THE INTERPRETATION OF THEM.

GOD himself, although he is trinity in persons, yet he is but one only simple essence; yet we doubt not but that there are in him many divine powers, which emanate or flow from him.

The Cabalists most learned in divine things have received the ten principal names of God, as certain divine powers, Or, as it were, members of God; which, by ten numerations, which we call Sephiroth, as it were vestiments, instruments, or exemplars of the Archetype, have an influence upon all created things, from the highest to the lowest; yet by a certain order: for first and immediately they have influence upon the nine orders of angels and quire of blessed souls, and by them into the celestial spheres, planets and men; by the which Sephiroth every thing receiveth power and virtue.

The first of these is the name Eheia, the name of the divine essence; his numeration is called Cether, which is interpreted a crown or diadem, and signifies the most simple essence of the divinity; and it is called that which the eye seeth not; and is attributed to God the Father, and hath its influence by the order of seraphims, or Hajoth Hakados, that is, creatures of holiness; and then by the primum mobile, it bestows the gift of being upon all things, and filleth the whole universe, both through the circumference and center; whose particular intelligence is called Merattron, that is the prince of faces, whose duty it is to bring others to the face of the Prince; and by him the Lord spake to Moses.

The second name is Jod, or Tetragrammaton joined with Jod; his numeration is Hochma, that is, wisdom, and signifies the divinity full of ideas, and the First Begotten; and is attributed to the Son, and has its influence by the order of cherubins, or that the Hebrews call Orphanim, i. e. forms or wheels; and from

235

thence into the starry heavens, where he frames so many figures as he hath ideas in himself, and distinguishes the very chaos of the creatures, by a particular intelligence called Raziel, who was the ruler of Adam.

The third name is called Tetragrammaton Elohim; his numeration is named Prina, viz. providence and understanding; and signifies remissness, quietness, the jubilee, penitential conversion, a great trumpet, redemption of the world, and the life of the world to come: it is attributed to the Holy Spirit, and hath his influence by the order of thrones, or which the Hebrews call Abalim, that is great angels, mighty and strong; and from thence, by the sphere of Saturn, administers form to the unsettled matter, whose particular intelligence is Zaphkiel, the ruler of Noah, and another intelligence named Jophiel, the ruler of Sem; and these are the three supreme and highest numerations, as it were, seats of the divine persons, by whose command all things are made; but are executed by the other seven, which are therefore called numerations framing.

The fourth name is El, whose numeration is Hesed, which signifies clemency or goodness; likewise grace, mercy, piety, magnificence, the scepter, and right-hand; and hath its influx by the order of dominations, which the Hebrews called Hasmalim; and so through the sphere of Jupiter fashions the images of bodies, bestowing clemency and pacifying justice on all: his particular intelligence is Zadkiel, the ruler of Abraham.

The fifth name is Elohim Gibor, that is, the mighty God, punishing the sins of the wicked; and his numeration is called Gebusach, which is to say, power, gravity, fortitude, security, judgment, punishing by slaughter and war; and it is applied to the tribunal of God, the girdle, the sword, the left hand of God: it is also called Pachad, which is fear; and hath his influence through the order of powers, which the Hebrews call Seraphim, and from thence through the sphere of Mars, to whom belongs fortitude, war, and affliction. It draweth forth the elements; and his particular intelligence is Camael, the ruler of Samson.

The sixth name is Eloha, or a name of four letters joined with Vaudahat; his numeration is Tiphereth, that is, apparel, beauty, glory, pleasure, and signifies the tree of life, and hath his influence through the order of virtues, which the Hebrews call Malachim, that is, angels, into the sphere of the sun, giving brightness and life to it, and from thence producing metals; his particular intelligence is Raphael, who was the ruler of Isaac and Toby the younger, and the angel Peliel, the Ruler of Jacob.

The seventh name is Tetragrammaton Sabaoth, or Adonai Sabaoth, that is, the God of Hosts; and his numeration is Nezah, that is, triumph and victory: the right column is applied to it, and it signifies the justice and eternity of a revenging God; it hath its influence through the orders of principalities, whom the Hebrews call Elohim, i. e. Gods, into the sphere of Venus, gives zeal and love of righteousness, and produces vegetables; his intelligence is Haniel, and the angel Cerviel, the ruler of David.

The eighth is called also Elohim Sabaoth, which is likewise the God of Hosts, not of war and justice, but of piety and agreement, for this name signifies both, and precedeth his army; the numeration of this is called Hod, which is, praise, confession, honour and fame; the left column is attributed to it; it hath his influence through the order of the archangels, which the Hebrews call Ben Elohim, that is, the sons of God, into the sphere of Mercury, and gives elegancy, and consonancy of speech, and produces living creatures; his intelligence is Michael, who was the ruler of Solomon.

The ninth name is called Sadai, that is, Omnipotent, satisfying all, and Elhai, which is the Living God; his numeration is Jesod, that is, foundation, and signifies a good understanding, a covenant, redemption and rest; and hath his influence through the order of angels, whom the Hebrews name Cherubim, into the sphere of the moon causing the increase and decrease of all things, and provideth for the genii and keepers of men, and distributeth them; his intelligence is Gabriel, who was the keeper of Joseph, Joshua, and Daniel. The tenth name is Adonai Melech, that is, lord and king; his numeration is Malchuth, that is, kingdom and empire, and signifies a church, the temple of God, and a gate; and hath his influence through the order of Animastic, viz.

of blessed souls, which, by the Hebrews, is called Issim, that is, nobles, lords, and princes; they are inferior to the hierarchies, and have their influences on the sons of men, and give knowledge and the wonderful under standing of things, also industry and prophecy; and the soul of the Messiah is president amongst them, or the intelligence Merattron, which is called the first creature, or the soul of the world, who was the ruler of Moses.

CHAPTER 5. OF THE POWER AND VIRTUE OF THE DIVINE NAMES

GOD himself, though he be one only essence, yet hath divers names, which expound not his divers essences or deities; but certain properties flowing from him; by which names he pours down upon us, and all his creatures, many benefits; ten of those names we have above described. The Cabalists, from a certa in text of Exodus, derive seventy-two names, both of the angels and of God, which they call the name of seventy-two letters and Schemhamphores, that is, the expository. From these therefore, besides those which we have reckoned up before, is the name of the divine essence, Eheia, היהא which Plato translates ὄν, from hence they call God τοὄν, others ὄων, that is, the Being. Hu, אוה, is another name revealed to Esay, signifying the abyss of the godhead, which the Greeks translate ταυτὸν, the Latins, himself the same. Esch, שא, is another name received from Moses, which soundeth fire, and is the name of God; Na, אנ, is to be invocated in perturbations and troubles.

There is also the name Ja, הי, and the name Elion, עלווג, and the name Macom, מוקם, the name Caphu, כפכ the name Innon, ונוי and the name Emeth, which is interpreted truth, and is the seal of God; and there are two other names, Zur, רוז and Aben, אבנ, both of these signify a solid work, and one of them expresseth the Father with the Son; and many names we have placed in the scale of numbers; and many names of God and the angels, are extracted out of the Holy Scriptures by our Cabala, and the Notarian and Gimetrian arts, where many words retracted by certain of their letters, make up one name; or one name dispersed by each of its letters, signifies or renders more. Sometimes they are gathered from the heads of words, as the name Agla, אגלא, from this verse of the Holy Scripture, viz.אתהגיכר לעולמאראכי, that is, the Mighty God for ever. In like manner the name Iaia, יאיא, from this verse, viz. ההואלהינ יהוההא that is, God our God is one God; in like manner the name Java, אואי, from this verse, יהי רוא זייהאיזר, that is, let there be light and there was light: in like manner the name Ararita, אראריתא from this verse, אהר שאר תזרהא ורוהיי שאר תזרהא ותמורהואזהאהר, that is, one principal of his unity,

239

one beginning of his individuality, his vicissitude is one thing; and this name Hacaba, אבקה is extracted from this verse, אוהרבכאאורקהי the holy and blessed One; in like manner this name, Jesu, ושי is found in the heads of these two verses, viz., ולוהולשאיבי, that is until the Messiah shall come; and the other verse, תיזומש ינון, that is, his name abides till the end. Thus also is the name Amen, נמא, extracted from this verse, וטאנ רלמינרא, that is, the Lord is the faithful King. Sometimes these names are extracted from the ends of words, as the same Amen from this verse, מיעשרהו באל , that is, the wicked not so; but the letters are transposed: so, by the final letters of this verse, המיל חמזמא that is, to me what? or what is his name? is found the name Tetragrammaton: in all these a letter is put for a word, and a letter extracted from a word, either from the beginning, end, or where you please; and sometimes these names are extracted from all the letters, one by one, even as those seven-two names of God are extracted from those three verses of Exodus, beginning from these three words, טי ואדי ועסזי, the first and the last verses being written from the right to the left; but the middle contrariwise, from the left to the right, as we shall shew hereafter; and so sometimes a word is extracted from a word, or a name from a name, by the transposition of letters, as Messia, הישמ, from Ismah, המשי, and Michael from Malachi, יכאלמ but sometimes by changing the alphabet, which the Cabalists call Ziruph, צוריץ so from the name Tetragrammaton, הוהי, are drawn forth צפצמ, Maz-Paz, וזוכ, Kuzu. Sometimes, by reason of the equality of the numbers, names are changed, as Merattron, זורטטמ, pro Sadai שדי, for both of them make three hundred and fourteen; so Jiai, יאיי and El, לאֹ, are equal in number, for both make thirty-one; and these are the hidden secrets, concerning which it is most difficult to judge, or to deliver a perfect science; neither can they be understood or taught in any other language but the Hebrew. Therefore, these sacred words have not their power in magical operations from themselves, as they are words, but from the occult divine powers working by them in the mind of those who by faith adhere to them.

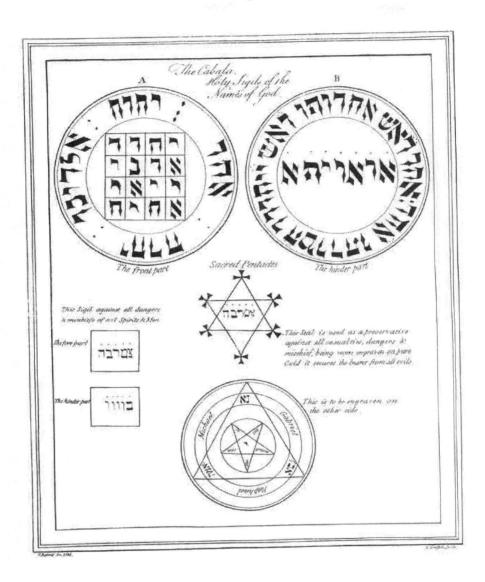

We will here deliver unto thee a sacred seal, efficacious against any disease of man, or any griefs whatsoever, in whose fore-side are the four- squared names of God, so subordinate to one another in a square, that, from the highest to the lowest, those most holy names or seals of the godhead do arise, whose intention is inscribed in the circumference; but on the backside is inscribed the seven-lettered name Araritha, and his interpretation is written about, viz. the verse from which it is extracted, even as you may see in the annexed plate, where A represents the former part, B the hinder; but all this must be done in most pure gold, or virgin parchment, pure, clean, and unspotted; also with ink made of the smoke of consecrated wax-lights, or incense and holy water. The operator must be purified and cleansed, and have an infallible hope, a constant faith, and have his mind lifted up to the Most High God, if he would surely obtain this divine power.

Now, against the depredations of evil spirits and men, and what dangers soever, either of journies, waters, enemies, arms, &c. in the same manner as is above said, these characters on the one side כייי, and these on the other הכפצ, which are the beginnings and ends of the five first verses of Genesis, and representation of the creation of the world; and, by this ligature, they say that a man shall be free from all mischiefs, if that he firmly believes in God, the Creator of all things.

Now these being done on a small plate of gold, as before described, (will be found to have the effect above mentioned); the figure of which you may likewise see in the annexed plate, fig. C and D, where C shows the former part, and B the hinder.

Now let no one distrust or wonder, that sacred words and divine names applied outwardly, can effect wonderful things, seeing, by them, the Almighty created the heavens and the earth; for there is no name of God amongst us (according to Moses the Egyptian) which is not taken from his works, besides the name Tetragrammaton, which is holy, signifying the substance of the Creator in a pure signification.

CHAPTER 6. OF INTELLIGENCES AND SPIRITS...

OF INTELLIGENCES AND SPIRITS, AND OF THE THREE-FOLD KIND OF THEM, AND OF THEIR DIFFERENT NAMES, AND OF INFERNAL AND SUBTERRANEAL SPIRITS.

NOW, consequently, we must discourse of intelligences, spirits, and angels. An intelligence is an intelligible substance, free from all gross and putrifying mass of a body, immortal, insensible, assisting all, having influence over all; and the nature of all intelligences, spirits, and angels is the same. But I call angels here, not those whom we usually call devils, but spirits so called from the propriety of the word, as it were, knowing, understanding, and wise. But of these, according to the tradition of magicians, there are three kinds; the first of which we call super-celestial, and minds altogether separated from a body, and, as it were, intellectual spheres worshipping one only God, as it were, their most firm and stable unity or centre. Wherefore they even call them Gods, by reason of a certain participation of the Divinity, for they are always full of God. These are only about God, and rule not the bodies of the world, neither are they fitted for the government of inferior things, but infuse the light received from God unto the inferior orders, and distribute every one's duty to all of them. The celestial intelligences do next follow these in the second order, which they call worldly angels, viz. being appointed, besides the divine worship for the spheres of the world, and for the government of every heaven and star; whence they are divided into so many orders as there are heavens in the world, and as there are stars in the heavens. And they called these Saturnine, who rule the heaven of Saturn, and Saturn himself; others Jovial, who rule the heaven of Jupiter, and Jupiter himself; and in like manner they name different angels, as well for the name as the virtue of the other stars; and because the old astrologers maintained fifty-five motions, therefore they invented so many intelligences or angels.

Fallen Angels   Plate 1

A Deceiver

Apollion

Scrolls of Iniquity

Belial

They placed also in the starry heaven angels who might rule the signs, triplicities, decans, quinaries, degrees and stars; for although the school of Peripatetics assign one only intelligence to each of the orbs of the stars, yet seeing every star and small part of the heaven hath its proper and different power and influence, it is

244

necessary also that it have its ruling intelligence which may confer power and operate; therefore they have established twelve princes of the angels, who rule the twelve signs of the zodiac, and thirty- six who may rule so many decans, and seventy-two who may rule so many quinaries of heaven, and the tongues of men and nations, and four who may rule the triplicities and elements, and seven governors of the whole world, according to the seven planets; and they have given to all of them names and seals, which they call characters, and used them in their invocations, incantations and carvings, describing them in the instruments of their operations, images, plates, glasses, rings, papers, wax-lights, and such like. And if at any time they operated for the sun, they invoked by the name of the sun and by the names of solar angels, and so of the rest. Thirdly, they established angels as ministers for the disposing of those things which are below, which Origen called certain invisible powers, to which those things which are on earth are committed to be disposed of. For sometimes, they being visible to none do direct our journies and all our business, are often present at battles, and, by secret helps, do give the desired success to their friends; for, at their pleasure, they can procure prosperity, and inflict adversity. In like manner they distribute these into more orders, so as some are fiery, some watery, some aërial, some terrestrial; which four species of angels are computed according to the four powers of the celestial souls, viz. the mind, reason, imagination, and vivifying and moving nature; hence the fiery follow the mind of the celestial souls, whence they concur to the contemplation of more sublime things; but the aërial follow reason, and favour the rational faculty, and, after a certain manner, separate it from the sensitive and vegetative; therefore it serves for an active life, as the fiery the contemplative; but the watery follow the imagination, serve for a voluptuous life; the earthly following nature, favours vegetable nature. Moreover, they distinguish also this kind of angels into saturnine and jovial, according to the names of the stars and the heavens; farther, some are oriental, some Occidental, some meridional, some septentrional. Moreover, there is no part of the world destitute of the proper assistance of these angels, not because they are alone, but because they reign there especially; for they are every where, although some especially operate, and have their influence in this place, some elsewhere; neither truly are these things to be understood as though they were subject to the influence of the stars, but as they have correspondence with the heaven above the world, from whence especially all things are directed, and to which all things ought to be conformable; whence, as these angels are appointed for diverse stars, so also for diverse places and times; not that they are limited to any place or time, neither by the bodies which they are appointed to govern, but because the Divine Wisdom hath so decreed; therefore they favour more, and patronize those bodies, places, times, stars: so they have called some diurnal, some nocturnal, others meridional. In like manner some are called woodmen, some mountaineers, some fieldmen, some domestics: hence the gods of the woods, country gods, satyrs, familiars, fairies of the fountains, fairies of the woods, nymphs of the sea, the Naïades, Nereïdes, Dryades, Piërides, Hamadryades, Patumides, Hinnides Agapte, Pales, Parcades, Dodonæ, Fanilæ, Levernæ, Parcæ, Muses, Aonides, Castalides, Heliconides, Pegasides, Meonides, Phebiades, Carnenæ, the graces, the genii, hobgobblins, and such like; whence the vulgar call them superiors, some the demi-gods and goddesses: some of these are so familiar and acquainted with men, that they are even affected with human perturbations; by whose instructions Plato thinks that men do oftentimes wonderful things, even as by the instruction of men; some beasts which are most nigh to us, apes, dogs, elephants, do often strange things above their species; and they who have written the chronicles of the Danes and Norwegians, do testify that spirits of several kinds in those regions are subject to men's commands; moreover, some of these appear corporeal and mortal, whose bodies are begotten and die; yet to be long-lived is the opinion of the Egyptians and Platonists, and especially approved by Proclus, Plutarch also, and Demetrius the philosopher, and Æmilianus the rhetorician, affirm the same; therefore of these spirits of the third kind, as the opinion of the Platonists is, they report that there are so many legions as there are stars in the heaven, and so many spirits in every legion as in heaven itself stars: but there are, (as Athanasius delivers,) who think, that the true number of the good spirits is according to the number of men, ninety-nine parts, according to the parable of the hundred sheep; others think only nine parts, according to the parable of the ten goats; others suppose the number of the angels equal with men, because it is written, he that hath appointed the bounds of the people according to the number of the angels of God; and concerning their number many have written many things; but the latter theologians, following the masters of the sentences, Austin and Gregory, easily resolve themselves, saying, that the number of the good angels transcendeth human capacity; to the which, on the contrary, innumerable unclean spirits do correspond, there being so many in the inferior world as pure spirits in the superior; and some divines affirm that they have received this by revelation. Under these they place a kind of spirits subterraneous or obscure, which the Platonists call angels that failed, revengers of wickedness and ungodliness, according to the decree of the divine justice; and they call them evil angels and wicked spirits, because they often annoy and hurt, even of their own accord. Of these also they reckon more legions; and, in like manner, distinguishing them according to the names of the stars and elements, and parts of the world, they place over them kings, princes, and rulers; and the names of them: of these, four most mischievous kings rule over the other, according to the four parts of the world. Under these many more princes of legions govern, and many private officers; hence the Gorgones, Statenocte, the Furies; hence Tisiphone, Alecto, Megæra,Cerberus. They of this kind of spirits, Porphyry says, inhabit a place nigh the earth, yea within the earth itself; there is no mischief which they dare not commit; they have altogether a violent and hurtful nature, therefore they plot, and endeavour violent and sudden mischiefs; and when they make incursions, sometimes they lie hid, and sometimes offer open violence, and are very much delighted in all such things done wickedly and mischievously.

CHAPTER 7. OF THE ORDER OF EVIL SPIRITS, AND THEIR FALL, AND DIFFERENT NATURES

THERE are some of the school of theologians, who distribute the evil spirits into nine degrees, as contrary to the nine orders of angels. Therefore, the first of these, which are called false gods, who, usurping the name of God, would be worshipped for gods, and require sacrifices and adorations; as that devil who said to Christ, "If thou wilt fall down and worship me, I will give thee all these things," shewing him all the kingdoms of the world; and the prince of these is he who said, I will ascend above the height of the clouds, and will be like to the Most High, who is called Beelzebub, that is, an old god. In the second place, follow the spirits of lies, of which sort was he who went forth, and was a lying spirit in the mouth of the prophet of Ahab; and the prince of these is the serpent Pytho, from whence Apollo is called Pythius, and that woman a Pythoness, or witch, in Samuel, and the other in the gospel, who had Pytho in her belly. Therefore, these kind of devils join themselves to the oracles, and delude men by divinations and predictions, so that they may be deceived. In the third order, are the vessels of iniquity, which are called vessels of wrath: these are the inventors of evil things, and all wicked arts; as in Plato, that devil Theutus, who taught cards and dice; for all wickedness, malice, and deformity, proceeds from these, of which in Genesis, in the benedictions of Simeon and Levi, Jacob said, "vessels of iniquity are in their habitations, into their counsel let not my soul come;" which the Psalmist calls vessels of death, Isaiah, vessels of fury; and Jeremiah, vessels of wrath; Ezekiel, vessels of destroying and slaying; and their prince is Belial, which signifies, without a yoke, and disobedient, a prevaricator, and an apostate; of whom Paul to the Corinthians says, "what agreement has Christ with Belial?" Fourthly, follow the revengers of evil, and their prince is Asmodeus, viz. causing judgment. After these, in the fifth place, come the deluders, who imitate miracles, and serve conjurers and witches, and seduce the people by their miracles, as the serpent seduced Eve, and their prince is Satan, of whom it is written in the Revelation, "that he seduces the whole world, doing great signs, and causing fire to descend from heaven in the sight of men; seducing the inhabitants of the earth by these signs, which are given him to do." Sixthly, the aerial powers offer themselves and join themselves to thunder and lightning, corrupting the air, causing pestilences, and other evils; in the number of which are the four angels of whom the Revelations speak, to whom it is given to hurt the earth and the sea, holding the four winds from the four corners of the earth and their prince is called Meririm: he is the meridian devil, a boiling spirit, a devil raging in the south, whom Paul, to the Ephesians, calls "the prince of the power of the air, and the spirit which works in the children of disobedience." The seventh mansion the furies possess, who are powers of evil, discords, war, and devastation; whose name in the Revelation is called in Greek, Apollyon; in the Hebrew, Abaddon, that is, destroying and wasting. In the eighth place are the accusers or inquisitors, whose prince is Astaroth, that is, a searcher out; in the Greek language he is called Diabolus, that is, an accuser or calumniator; which in the Revelation is called the "accuser of the brethren, accusing them night and day before the face of God." Moreover, the tempters and ensnarers have the last place; one of which is present with every man, which we call the evil genius, and their prince is Mammon, which is interpreted covetousness.

Ophis.

The Spirit
Antichrist.

F. Barrett Del.   Pub. by Lackington & Allen   G. Griffith Sculp

But we of the Cabala unanimously maintain that evil spirits do wander up and down this inferior world, enraged against, all whom we call devils; of whom Austin, in his first book of the Incarnation of the Word, to Januarius, says, concerning the devils and his angels contrary to virtues, the ecclesiastical

251

preachers have taught that there are such things, but what they are, and who they are, he has not clear enough expounded: yet there is this opinion among them, that this devil was an angel, and being made an apostate, persuaded many of the angels to fall with him, who to this day are called his angels. Greece, notwithstanding, thinks not that these are damned, nor that they are all purposely evil; but that from the creation of the world the dispensation of things is ordained by this means, that the tormenting of sinful souls is made over to them.

The other theologians say, that no devil was created evil, but that they were driven and cast out of heaven from the orders of good angels, for their pride whose fall not only our and the Hebrew theologians, but also the Assyrians, Arabians, Egyptians, and Greeks, do confirm by their tenets. Pherycies, the Assyrian, describes the fall of the devils; and Ophis, that is, the devilish serpent, was the head of that rebelling army; Trismegistus sings the same fall, in his Pimander; and Homer, under the name of Ararus, in his verses; and Plutarch, in his Discourse on Usury, signifies that Empedocles knew that the fall of the devils was in this manner; the devils themselves often confess their fall. They being cast out into this valley of misery, some that are near to us wander up and down in this obscure air; others inhabit lakes, rivers, and seas; others the earth, and terrify earthly things, and invade those who dig wells and metals, cause the gaping of the earth, to strike together the foundations of the mountains, and vex not only men but also other creatures; some being content with laughter and delusion only, do contrive rather to weary men than to hurt them; some heightening themselves to the length of a giant's body, and again shrinking themselves down to the smallest of pigmies, and changing themselves into different forms, to disturb men with vain fear; others study lies and blasphemies, as we read of one in third book of Kings, saying, "I will go forth and be a lying spirit in the mouth of all the prophets of Ahab." But the worst sort of devils are those who lie in wait, and overthrow passengers in their journies, and rejoice in wars and effusion of blood, and afflict men with most cruel stripes: we read of such in Matthew, "for fear of whom no man dare pass that way." Moreover, the Scripture reckons up nocturnal, diurnal, and meridional devils; and describes other spirits of wickedness by different names, as we read in Isaiah of satyrs, screech-owls, sirens, storks, owls; and in the Psalms, of asps, basilisks, lions, dragons; and in the Gospel, we read of scorpions, and Mammon, and the prince of this world, and rulers of darkness, of all whom Beelzebub is the prince, whom the Scripture calls the Prince of wickedness.

CHAPTER 8. OF THE ANNOYANCE OF EVIL SPIRITS, AND THE PRESERVATION WE HAVE FROM GOOD SPIRITS

IT is the opinion of divines, that all evil spirits are of that nature, that they hate God as well as man; therefore Divine Providence has set over us more pure spirits, with whom he hath entrusted us, as with shepherds and governors, that they should daily help us, and drive away evil spirits from us, and curb and restrain them, that they should not hurt us, as they would otherwise; as is read in Tobias, that Raphael did apprehend the demon called Asmodeus, and bound him in the wilderness of the Upper Egypt. Of these, Hesiod says, there are 30,000 of Jupiter's immortal spirits living on the earth, who are the keepers of mortal men, who, that they might observe justice and merciful deeds, having clothed themselves with air, go to and fro every where on the earth. For there is no potentate could be safe, nor any woman continue uncorrupted, no man in this vale of ignorance could come to the end appointed to him by God, if good spirits did not secure us, or if evil spirits should be permitted to satisfy the wills of men; as therefore among the good there is a proper keeper or protector deputed to every one, corroborating the spirit of the man to good; so of evil spirits, there is sent forth an enemy ruling over the flesh and desire thereof; and the good spirit fights for us as a preserver against the enemy and flesh. Now man, between these contenders is in the middle, and left in the hand of his own counsel, to whom he will give victory: we cannot therefore accuse angels, or deny free-will, if they do not bring the nations entrusted to them to the knowledge of the true God and true piety, but suffer them to fall into errors and perverse worship; it is to be imputed to themselves, who have, of their own accord, declined from the right path, adhering to the spirits of error, giving victory to the devil: for it is in the hand of man to adhere to whom he pleases, and overcome whom he will; by whom if once the devil be overcome, he is made his servant, and being overcome, cannot fight any more with another, as a wasp that has lost his sting. To which opinion Origen assents, in his book Periarchon, concluding that the saints fight against evil spirits, and overcoming, do lessen their army; neither can he that is overcome by any molest any more. As therefore there is given to every man a good spirit, so there is given to every man an evil diabolical spirit, whereof each seeks an union with our spirit, and endeavours to attract it to itself, and to be mixed with it, as wine with water; the good indeed, through all good works comformable to itself, change us into angels by uniting us; as it is written of John the Baptist in Malachi, "behold I send my angel before thy face;" of which transmutation and union it is written elsewhere, he that adheres to God is made one spirit with him. An evil spirit also, by evil works, studies to make us conformable to itself, and unite us, as Christ says of Judas, "Have not I chosen twelve, and one of you is a devil?" And this is that which Hermes says, when a spirit hath influence on the soul of man, he scatters the seed of his own notion, whence such a soul, being sown with seeds, and full of fury, brings forth thence wonderful things, and whatsoever are the offices of spirits: for when a good spirit hath influence on a holy soul, it does exalt it to the light of wisdom; but an evil spirit being transfused into a wicked soul, doth stir it up to theft, to man-slaughter, to lust, and whatsoever are the offices of evil spirits. Good spirits, as Jamblicus says, purge the souls most perfectly, and some bestow upon us other good things: they being present, do give health to the body, virtue to the soul, and security; what is mortal in us they take away, cherish heat, and make it more efficacious to life; and, by an harmony, do always infuse light into an intelligible mind. But whether there be many keepers of a man, or one alone, theologians differ among themselves: we think there are more, the prophet saying, "he hath given his angels a charge concerning thee, that they should keep thee in all thy ways," which, as Hierome says, is to be understood of any man, as well as of Christ. All men, therefore, are governed by the ministry of different angels, and are brought to any degree of virtue, deserts, and dignity, who behave themselves worthy of them; but they who carry themselves unworthy of them, are deposed and thrust down, as well by evil spirits as good spirits, unto the lowest degree of misery, as their evil merits shall require; but they that are attributed to the sublimer angels are preferred before other men; for angels having the care of them, exalt them, and subject others to them by a certain occult power, which, although neither of them perceive, yet he that is subjected feels a certain yoke of presidency, of which he cannot easily quit himself; yea, he fears and reverences that power, which the superior angels make to flow upon inferiors, and with a certain terror bring the inferiors into a fear of presidency. This did Homer seem to be sensible of, when he says, that the Muses begot of Jupiter, did always, as inseparable companions, assist the kings begot of Jupiter, speaking figuratively, who by them were made venerable and magnificent: so we read that M. Antoninus being formerly joined in singular friendship with Octavius Augustus, were accustomed always to play together; but when, as always, Augustus always went away Conqueror, a certain magician counselled M. Antoninus thus: "O Anthony, what dost thou do with that young man? Shun and avoid him, for although thou art older than he, and art more skilful than he, and art better descended than he, and hath endured the wars of more emperors, yet thy Genius doth much dread the Genius of this young man, and thy fortune flatters his fortune; unless thou shalt shun him, it seems wholly to decline to him." Is not the prince like other men? how should other men fear and reverence him, unless a divine terror should exalt him, and striking a fear into others, depress them, that they should reverence him as a prince? Wherefore we must endeavour, that, being purified by doing well, and following sublime things, and choosing opportune times and seasons, we be entrusted or committed to a degree of sublimer and more potent angels, who taking care of us we may deservedly be preferred before others.

CHAPTER 9. THAT THERE IS A THREEFOLD KEEPER OF MAN, AND FROM WHENCE EACH OF THEM PROCEED

EVERY man hath a threefold good demon as a proper keeper or preserver, the one whereof is holy, another of the nativity, and the other of profession. The holy demon is one, according to the doctrine of the Egyptians, assigned to the rational soul, not from the stars or planets, but from a supernatural cause--from God himself, the president of demons, being universal and above nature.

This directs the life of the soul, and does always put good thoughts into the mind, being always active in illuminating us, although we do not always take notice of it; but when we are purified and live peaceably, then it is perceived by us, then it does, as it were, speak with us, and communicates its voice to us, being before silent, and studies daily to bring us to a sacred perfection.

So it falls out that some profit more in any science, or art, or office, in a less time and with little pains, when another takes much pains and studies hard, and all in vain; and although no science, art or virtue, is to be contemned, yet that you may live prosperously, carry on thy affairs happily, in the first place, know thy good genius, and his nature, and what good the celestial disposition promises thee, and God the distributer of all these, who distributes to each as he pleases, and follow the beginnings of these, profess these, be conversant in that virtue to which the most high distributer doth elevate and lead thee; who made Abraham excel in justice and clemency, Isaac with fear, Jacob with strength, Moses with meekness and miracles, Joshua in war, Phineas in zeal, David in religion and victory, Solomon in knowledge and fame, Peter in faith, John in charity, Jacob in devotion, Thomas in prudence, Magdalen in contemplation, Martha in officiousness.

Therefore in what virtue you think you can most easily be a proficient in, use diligence to attain to the height thereof, that you may excel in one, when in many you cannot, but in the rest endeavour to be as great a proficient as you can; but if thou shalt have the overseers of nature and religion agreeable, thou shalt find a double progress of thy nature and profession; but if they shall be disagreeing, follow the better, for thou shalt better perceive at some time a preserver of an excellent profession than of nativity.

CHAPTER 10. OF THE TONGUE OF ANGELS, AND OF THEIR SPEAKING AMONGST THEMSELVES AND WITH US

WE might doubt whether angels or demons, since they are pure spirits, use any vocal speech or tongue among themselves or to us; but that Paul, in some place says, "if I speak with the tongue of men or angels;"--but what their speech or tongue is, is much doubted by many. For many think that if they use any idiom, it is Hebrew, because that was first of all, and came from heaven, and was before the confusion of languages in Babylon, in which the law was given by God the Father, and the gospel was preached by Christ the Son, and so many oracles were given to the prophets by the Holy Ghost; and seeing all tongues have and do undergo various mutations and corruptions, this alone does always continue inviolated. Moreover, an evident sign of this opinion is, that though this demon and intelligence do use the speech of those nations with whom they do inhabit, yet, to them who understand it, they never speak in any idiom but in this alone, viz. Hebrew. But now, how angels speak, it is hid from us, as they themselves are. Now, to us, that we may speak, a tongue is necessary with other instruments; as the jaws, palate, lips, teeth, throat, lungs, the aspera artertia, and muscles of the breast, which have the beginning of motion from the soul. But if I speak at a distance to another, he must use a louder voice; but, if near, he whispers in my ear, as if he should be coupled to the hearer, without any noise, as an image in the eye or glass. So souls going out of the body, so angels, so demons speak; and what man does with a sensible voice, they do by impressing the conception of the speech in those to whom they speak after a better manner than if they should express it in an audible voice. So the Platonist says, that Socrates perceived his demon by sense, indeed, but not of this body, but by the sense of the etherial body concealed in this; after which manner. Avicen believes the angels were wont to be seen and heard by the prophets. That instrument, whatsoever the virtue be, by which one spirit makes known to another spirit what things are in his mind, is called by the apostle Paul, the tongue of angels. Yet oftentimes they send forth an audible voice, as they that cried at the ascension of the Lord, Ye men of Galilee, why stand ye here gazing unto the heaven? And in the old law they spake with divers of the fathers with a sensible voice; but this never but when they assumed bodies. But with what senses these spirits and demons hear our invocations and prayers, and see our ceremonies, we are altogether ignorant.

For there is a spiritual body, of demons every where sensible by nature, so that it touches, sees, hears without any medium, and nothing can be an impediment to it; yet they do not perceive after the same manner as we do, with different organs, but haply as sponges drink in water, so do they all sensible things with their body or some other way unknown to us; neither are all animals endowed with those organs, for we know that many want ears, yet we know they perceive a sound, but after what manner we know not.

CHAPTER 11. OF THE NAMES OF SPIRITS...

OF THE NAMES OF SPIRITS, AND THEIR VARIOUS IMPOSITION, AND OF THE SPIRITS THAT ARE SET OVER THE STARS, SIGNS, CORNERS OF THE HEAVEN, AND THE ELEMENTS.

MANY and different are the names of good and bad spirits; but their proper and true names, as those of the stars, are known to God alone, who only numbers the multitude of stars, and calls them by their names, whereof none can be known by us but by divine revelation; very few are expressed to us in sacred writ. But the masters of the Hebrews think, that the names of angels are imposed on them by Adam, according to that which is written, "the Lord brought all things which he had made unto Adam, that he should name them, and as he called any thing, so the name of it was." Hence the Hebrew Mecubals think, together with Magicians and Cabalists, that it is in the power of man, to impose names upon spirits, but of such a man only who is dignified and elevated to this virtue by some divine gift or sacred authority: but because a name that may express the nature of divinity, or the whole virtue of angelical essences, cannot be made by any human voice, therefore names for the most part are put upon them from their works, signifying some certain office or effect which is required by the quire of spirits; which name then, and not otherwise, obtains efficacy and virtue to draw any spiritual substance from above, or beneath, to make any desired effect.

I have seen and known some writing on virgin parchment the name and seal of some spirit in the hour of the moon, which afterwards he gave to be devoured by a water-frog, and had muttered over some verse; the frog being let go into the water, rains and showers presently followed. I saw also the same man inscribing the name of another spirit with the seal thereof in the hour of Mars, which was given to a crow, who, being let go, after a verse muttered over, there followed from that part of the heaven whither it flew, lightnings, shaking, and horrible thunders, with thick clouds; neither were those names of spirits of an unknown tongue, neither did they signify any thing else but their offices; of this kind are the names of those angels, Raziel, Gabriel, Michael, Raphael, Haniel, which is as

262

much as to say the vision of God, the virtue of God, the strength of God, the medicine of God, the glory of God. In like manner, in the offices of evil demons are read their names, viz. a player, a deceiver, a dreamer, a fornicator, and many such like. So we receive from many of the ancient fathers of the Hebrews the names of angels set over the planets and signs; over Saturn, Zaphiel; over Jupiter, Zadkiel; over Mars, Camael; over the Sun, Raphael; over Venus, Haniel; over Mercury, Michael; over the Moon, Gabriel. These are those seven spirits which always stand before the face of God, to whom is entrusted the disposing the whole celestial and terrene kingdoms which are under the moon: for these (as the more curious theologians say) govern all things by a certain vicissitude of hours, days, and years; as the astrologers teach concerning the planets which they are set over, which Mercurius Trismegistus calls the seven governors of the world, who, by the heavens as by instruments, distribute the influences of all the stars and signs upon their inferiors. There are some who ascribe them to the stars by names somewhat differing, saying, that over Saturn is set an intelligence called Oriphael, over Jupiter Zachariel, over Mars Zamael, over the Sun Michael, over Venus Anael, over Mercury Raphael, over the Moon Gabriel. And every one of these governs the world 354 years and four months; and the government begins from the intelligence of Saturn; afterwards, in order, the intelligences of Venus, Jupiter, Mercury, Mars, the Moon, and the Sun reign, and the government returns to the spirit of Saturn.

Tritemius writ to Maximilian Cæsar a special treatise concerning these, which he that will thoroughly examine may from thence draw great knowledge of future times. [56:1] Over the twelve signs are set these, viz. over Aries, Malahidael; over Taurus, Asmodel; over Gemini, Ambriel; over Cancer, Muriel; over Leo, Verchiel; over Virgo, Hamaliel; over Libra, Zuriel; over Scorpio, Barchiel; over Sagittarius, Advachiel; over Capricorn, Hanael; over Aquarius, Cambiel; over Pisces, Barchiel. Of these spirits set over the planets and signs, signs, John made mention of in the Revelation, speaking of the former in the beginning; and the seven spirits which are in the presence of the throne of God, which I find are set over the seven planets, in the end of the book, where he describes the platform of the heavenly city, saying, that on the twelve orates thereof are twelve angels. There are again twenty-eight angels, who rule in the twenty-eight mansions of the moon, whose names are these; Geniel, Enediel, Anixiel, Azariel, Gabriel, Dirachiel, Scheliel, Amnediel, Barbiel, Ardefiel, Neciel, Abdizuel, Jazeriel, Ergediel, Atliel, Azeruel, Adriel, Egibiel, Amutiel, Kyriel, Bethnael, Geliel, Requiel, Abrinael, Agiel, Tagriel, Atheniel, Amnixiel. There are also four princes of the angels, which are set over the four winds, and over the four parts of the world. Michael is placed over the east-wind, Raphael over the west, Gabriel over the north, Nariel, who by some is called Ariel, is over the south. There are also assigned to the elements these, viz. to the air Cherub, to the water Tharsis, to the earth Ariel, to the fire Seraph. Now every one of these spirits is a great prince, and has much power and freedom in the dominion of his own planets and signs, and in their times, years, months, days and hours: and in their elements, and parts of the world, and winds. And every one of them rules over many legions; and after the same manner, among evil spirits, there are four, who, as most potent kings, are set over the rest, according to the four parts of the world, whose names are these, viz.

Urieus, king of the east; Amaymon, king of the south; Paymon, king of the west; Egin, king, of the north; which the Hebrew doctors perhaps call more rightly thus, Samuel, Azazel, Azael, and Mahazuel, under whom many others rule as princes of legions and rulers. Likewise there are innumerable demons of private offices. Moreover, the ancient theologians of the Greeks reckon up six demons, which they call Telchines, others Alastores; which bearing ill-will to men, take up water out of the river Styx with their hands, sprinkle it upon the earth, whence follow calamities, plagues, and famines; and these are said to be Acteus, Megalezius, Ormenus, Lycus, Nicon, Mimon. But he that desires to know exactly the distinct names, offices, places, and times of angels, and evil demons, let him inquire into the book of Rabbi Simon of the Temples, and in his book of Lights, and in his treatise of the Greatness of Stature, and in the treatise of the Temples of Rabbi Ishmael, and in almost all the commentaries of his book of Formation, and he shall find it written at large concerning them.

56:1 TRITEMIUS on Spirits.

The Magus

CHAPTER 12. THE CABALISTS DRAW FORTH THE SACRED NAMES OF ANGELS...

THE CABALISTS DRAW FORTH THE SACRED NAMES OF ANGELS FROM SACRED WRIT, AND OF THE SEVENTY-TWO ANGELS, WHO BEAR THE NAMES OF GOD; WITH THE TABLES OF ZIRUPH AND THE COMMUTATIONS OF NAMES AND NUMBERS.

THERE are also other sacred names of good and evil spirits deputed to each office of much greater efficacy than the former, which the Cabalists draw from sacred writ, according to that art which we teach concerning them; as also certain names of God are drawn forth out of certain places: the general rule of these is, that wheresoever any thing of divine essence is expressed in the Scripture, from that place the name of God may be gathered; but in what place soever in the Scripture the name of God is found expressed, then mark what office lies under that name; wheresoever therefore the Scripture speaks of the office or work of any spirit, good or bad, from thence the name of that spirit, whether good or bad, may be gathered; this unalterable rule being observed, that of good spirits we receive the names of good spirits, of evil the names of evil: and let us not confound black with white, nor day with night, nor light with darkness, which, by these verses as by an example, is manifest:

"Let them be as dust before the face of the wind; and let the angel of the Lord scatter them: let their ways be darkness and slippery and let the angel of the Lord pursue them."

יהוהדההה ומאלאף דות ינפל במוץ יהיו
דרפם יהוה לקות והלק הטף יהידרכם

in the xxxvth Psalm with the Hebrews, but with us, the xxxivth; of which the names of those angels are drawn, לאדים Midael, and לארים Miriael, of the order of warriors; so of that verse, "thou shall set over him the wicked, and Satan shall stand at his right-hand," out of Psalm cix. with the Hebrews, but with the Latins, cviii.

ימינו יאמלאל רשמן עליו חפקר

is extracted the name of the evil spirit Schii, עישי which signifies a spirit that is a worker of engines. There is a certain text in Exodus contained in three verses, whereof every one is written with seventy-two letters, beginning thus; the first Vajisa, עסיו, the second Vajabo, אביו the third Vajot, טיו which are extended into one line, viz. the first and the third from the left-hand to the right, but the middle in a contrary order, beginning from the right to the left, is terminated on the left-hand; then each of the three letters being subordinate the one to the other, make one name, which are seventy-two names, which the Hebrews called Schemhamphoræ, to which if the divine name El לא or Jah ההי be added, they produce seventy-two trisyllable names of angels, whereof every one carries the great name of God, as it is written, "my angel shall go before thee; observe him, for my name is in him." And these are those that are set over the seventy-two celestial quinaries, and so many nations and tongues, and joints of man's body, and cooperate with the seventy-two seniors of the synagogue, and so many disciples of Christ: and their names, according to the extraction which the Cabalists make, are manifest in the following table, according to the manner which we have mentioned.

Now there are many other ways of making Schemhamphoræ out of those verses; as when all three are written in a right order, one after the other, from the right to the left, besides those which are extracted by the tables of Ziruph, and the tables of commutations, of which we made mention of before. Because these tables serve for all names, as divine, so angelical, we shall therefore subjoin them to this chapter.

These are the seventy-two angels, bearing the name of God, Schemhamphoræ.

For the tables, &c. see the annexed Plates, No. 1, 2, 3, 4.

CHAPTER 13. OF FINDING OUT THE NAMES OF SPIRITS AND GENII, FROM THE DISPOSITION OF THE CELESTIAL BODIES

THE ancient magicians taught an art of finding out the name of a spirit to any desired effect, drawing it from the disposition of the heavens; as, for example, any celestial harmony being proposed to thee, to make an image or a ring, or any other work to be done under any constellation, if thou wilt find out the spirit that is the ruler of that work, the figure of the heaven being erected, cast forth letters in their number and order, from the degree of the ascendant, according to the succession of signs through each degree, by filling the whole circle of the heavens; then those letters which fall into the places of the stars, the aid of which you would use, being according to the number and power of those stars marked without into number and order, make the name of a good spirit. But if thou wilt do so from the beginning of a degree falling against the progress of the signs, the resulting spirit shall be evil. By this art some of the Hebrews and Chaldean masters teach that the, nature and name of any genius may be found out; as for example, the degree of the ascendant of any one's nativity being known, and the other corners of the heaven being co- equated, then let that which has the most dignities of planets in those four corners, which the Arabians call Almutez, be first observed among the rest; and according to that in the second place, that which shall be next to it in the number of dignities, and so in order the rest of them, which obtain any dignity in the aforesaid corners.

This order being used, you may know the true place and degree of them in the heavens, beginning from the degree of the ascendant through each degree, according to the order of signs, to cast twenty-two of the letters of the Hebrews; then what letters shall fall into the places of the aforesaid stars, being marked and disposed according to the order found out above in the stars, and rightly joined together according to the rules of the Hebrew tongue, make the name of a genius; to which, according to the custom, some monosyllable name of Divine Omnipotence, viz. El or Jah, is subjoined. But if the casting of the letters be made from an angle of the falling, and against the succession of the signs, and the letters which shall fall in the Nadir (that is the opposite point) of the aforesaid stars be after that order, as are said, joined together, shall make the name of an evil genius.

But the Chaldeans proceed another way, for they take not the Almutez of the angles but the Almutez of the eleventh house, and do all things as has been said. Now they find out an evil genius from the Almutez of the angle of the twelfth house, which they call an evil spirit, casting from the degree of the falling against the progress of the signs.

CHAPTER 14. OF THE CALCULATING ART OF SUCH NAMES BY THE TRADITION OF CABALISTS

THERE is yet another art of these kind of names, which they call calculatory; and it is made by the following tables, by entering with some sacred, divine, or angelical name, in the column of letters descending, by taking those letters which thou shalt find in the common angles under their stars and signs, which being reduced into order, the name of a good spirit is made of the nature of that star or sign under which thou didst enter; but if thou shalt enter in the column ascending, by taking the common angles above the stars and signs marked in the lowest line, the name of an evil spirit is made. And these are the names of spirits of any order of heaven ministering, as of good, so of bad, which you may after this manner multiply into nine names of so many orders; inasmuch as you may, by entering with one name, draw forth another of a spirit of a superior order out of the same, as well of a good as a bad one; yet the beginning of this calculation depends upon the names of God; for every word hath a virtue in magic, inasmuch as it depends on the word of God, and is thence framed. Therefore we must know that every angelical name must proceed from some primary name of God. Therefore angels are said to bear the name of God, according to that which is written, "because my name is in him;" therefore that the names of good angels may be discerned from the names of bad, there is wont oftentimes to be added some name of Divine Omnipotence, as El, or On, or Jah, or Jod, and to be pronounced together with it: and because Jah is a name of beneficence, and Jod the name of a deity, therefore these two names are put only to the names of angels; but the name El, because it imports power and virtue, is therefore added, not only to good but bad spirits; for neither can evil spirits either subsist or do any thing without the virtue of El, God. But we must know that common angles of the same star and sign are to be taken, unless entrance be made with a mixt name, as are the names of genii, and those of which it hath been spoken in the preceding chapter, which are made of the dispositions of the heavens, according to the harmony of divers stars. For as often as the table is to be entered with these, the common angle is to be taken under the star or sign of him that enters.

There are moreover some that do so extend those tables that they think also if there be an entrance made with the name of a star, or office, or any desired effect, a demon, whether good or bad, serving to that office or effect may be drawn out; upon the same account they that enter with the proper name of any person can extract the names of the genii under that star which shall appear to be over such a person as they shall, by his physiognomy, or by the passions and inclinations of his mind, and by his profession and fortune, know him to be either martial, or saturnine, or solary, or of the nature of any other star.

And although such kind of primary names have none or little power by their signification, yet such kind of extracted names, and such as are derived from them, are of very great efficacy; as the rays of the sun collected in a hollow glass do most intensely burn, the sun itself being scarce warm.

Now there is an order of letters in those tables under the stars and signs, almost like that which is with the astrologers, of tens, elevens, twelves. Of this calculatory art Alphonsus Cyprius once wrote, and also fitted it to Latin characters; but because the letters of every tongue, as we shewed in the first book, have, in their number, order and figure, a celestial and divine original, I shall easily grant this calculation concerning the names of spirits to be made not only by Hebrew letters, but also Chaldean, Arabick, Egyptian, Greek and Latin, and many others, the tables being rightly made after the imitation of the presidents.

But here it is objected by many, that it falls out that in these tables men of a differing nature and fortune do oftentimes, by reason of the sameness of name, obtain the same genius of the same name. We must know therefore that it must not be thought absurd, that the same daemon may be separated from any one soul, and the same be set over more. Besides, as many men have the same name, so also spirits of divers offices or natures may be noted or marked by one name, and by one and the same seal or character, yet in a different respect; for as the serpent does sometimes typify Christ, and sometimes the devil, so the same names and the same seals may be applied sometimes to the order of a good demon, sometimes of a bad one. Lastly, the very ardent intention of the invocator, by which our intellect is joined to the separated intelligences, is the cause that we have sometimes one spirit, sometimes another, (although called upon under the same name,) made obsequious to us.

See the following Plates for the tables of the calculation of the names of spirits, good and bad, under the presidency of the seven planets, and under the order of the twelve militant signs.

The Cabala

Shewing at one View the Seventy-two Angels bearing the name of God Shemhamphora.

The table of the seventy-two angels, each cell containing Hebrew letters above an angel name:

Row 1: Vehuiah · Ieliel · Sitael · Elemiah · Mahasiah · Lelahel · Achaiah · Cahethel · Haziel · Aladiah · Lauviah · Hahaiah · Ietael · Mebahel · Hariel · Hakamiah · Leviah · Caliel

Row 2: Leuuiah · Pahaliah · Nelchael · Ieiaiel · Melahel · Hahuiah · Nithhaiah · Haaiah · Ierathel · Sehiah · Reiiel · Omael · Lecabel · Vasariah · Iehuiah · Lehahiah · Chavakiah · Menadel

Row 3: Aniel · Haamiah · Rehael · Ieiazel · Hahahel · Mihael · Veualiah · Ielahiah · Sealiah · Ariel · Asaliah · Mihael · Vehuel · Daniel · Hahasiah · Imamiah · Nanael · Nithael

Row 4: Mebahiah · Poiel · Nemamaiah · Ieialel · Harahel · Mizrael · Umabel · Iahhel · Anauel · Mehiel · Damabiah · Menkl · Eiael · Habuiah · Rochel · Iabamiah · Haiaiel · Neremaiah

The Cabala

Table 2d The Right Table of the Commutations.

ת	ש	ר	ק	צ	פ	ע	ס	נ	מ	ל	כ	י	ט	ח	ז	ו	ה	ד	ג	ב	א
א	ת	ש	ר	ק	צ	פ	ע	ס	נ	מ	ל	כ	י	ט	ח	ז	ו	ה	ד	ג	ב
ב	א	ת	ש	ר	ק	צ	פ	ע	ס	נ	מ	ל	כ	י	ט	ח	ז	ו	ה	ד	ג
ג	ב	א	ת	ש	ר	ק	צ	פ	ע	ס	נ	מ	ל	כ	י	ט	ח	ז	ו	ה	ד
ד	ג	ב	א	ת	ש	ר	ק	צ	פ	ע	ס	נ	מ	ל	כ	י	ט	ח	ז	ו	ה
ה	ד	ג	ב	א	ת	ש	ר	ק	צ	פ	ע	ס	נ	מ	ל	כ	י	ט	ח	ז	ו
ו	ה	ד	ג	ב	א	ת	ש	ר	ק	צ	פ	ע	ס	נ	מ	ל	כ	י	ט	ח	ז
ז	ו	ה	ד	ג	ב	א	ת	ש	ר	ק	צ	פ	ע	ס	נ	מ	ל	כ	י	ט	ח
ח	ז	ו	ה	ד	ג	ב	א	ת	ש	ר	ק	צ	פ	ע	ס	נ	מ	ל	כ	י	ט
ט	ח	ז	ו	ה	ד	ג	ב	א	ת	ש	ר	ק	צ	פ	ע	ס	נ	מ	ל	כ	י
י	ט	ח	ז	ו	ה	ד	ג	ב	א	ת	ש	ר	ק	צ	פ	ע	ס	נ	מ	ל	כ
כ	י	ט	ח	ז	ו	ה	ד	ג	ב	א	ת	ש	ר	ק	צ	פ	ע	ס	נ	מ	ל
ל	כ	י	ט	ח	ז	ו	ה	ד	ג	ב	א	ת	ש	ר	ק	צ	פ	ע	ס	נ	מ
מ	ל	כ	י	ט	ח	ז	ו	ה	ד	ג	ב	א	ת	ש	ר	ק	צ	פ	ע	ס	נ
נ	מ	ל	כ	י	ט	ח	ז	ו	ה	ד	ג	ב	א	ת	ש	ר	ק	צ	פ	ע	ס
ס	נ	מ	ל	כ	י	ט	ח	ז	ו	ה	ד	ג	ב	א	ת	ש	ר	ק	צ	פ	ע
ע	ס	נ	מ	ל	כ	י	ט	ח	ז	ו	ה	ד	ג	ב	א	ת	ש	ר	ק	צ	פ
פ	ע	ס	נ	מ	ל	כ	י	ט	ח	ז	ו	ה	ד	ג	ב	א	ת	ש	ר	ק	צ
צ	פ	ע	ס	נ	מ	ל	כ	י	ט	ח	ז	ו	ה	ד	ג	ב	א	ת	ש	ר	ק
ק	צ	פ	ע	ס	נ	מ	ל	כ	י	ט	ח	ז	ו	ה	ד	ג	ב	א	ת	ש	ר
ר	ק	צ	פ	ע	ס	נ	מ	ל	כ	י	ט	ח	ז	ו	ה	ד	ג	ב	א	ת	ש
ש	ר	ק	צ	פ	ע	ס	נ	מ	ל	כ	י	ט	ח	ז	ו	ה	ד	ג	ב	א	ת

Publ. by Lackington & Allen

Cabala
The Averse Table of Commutations.

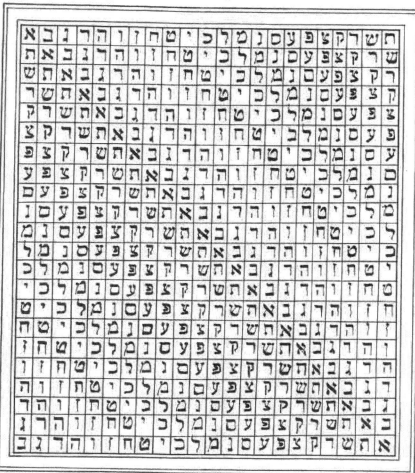

F. Barrett Del.   T. Griffith Sculp.

Pub. by Lackington & Allen.

The Cabala.

Table 4 & 5 The Table of the Combinations of Tziruph.

The Rational Table of Tziruph.

F. Barrett del.   Pub. by Lackington & Allen   R. Griffith Sc.

CHAPTER 15. OF THE CHARACTERS AND SEALS OF SPIRITS

WE must now speak of the characters and seals of spirits. Characters are nothing else than certain unknown letters and writings, preserving the secrets of spirits and their names from the use and reading of prophane men, which the ancient called hieroglyphical, or sacred letters, because devoted to the secrets of God only. They accounted it unlawful to write the mysteries of God with those characters which prophane and vulgar things were wrote. Whence Porphyry says, "that the ancients were willing to conceal God and divine virtues, by sensible figures and by those things which are visible, yet signifying invisible things;" as being willing to deliver great mysteries in sacred letters, and explain them in certain symbolical figures; as when they dedicated all round things to the world, the sun and the moon, hope and fortune; a circle to the heavens, and parts of a circle to the moon; pyramids and obelisks to the fire, a cylinder to the sun and earth.--See the plate.

CHAPTER 16. ANOTHER WAY OF MAKING CHARACTERS, ACCORDING TO THE CABALISTS

AMONG the Hebrews I find more fashions of characters, whereof one is most ancient, viz. an ancient writing which Moses and the prophets used, the form of which is not rashly to be discovered to any; for those letters which they use at this day were instituted by Esdras. There is among them a writing which they call celestial, because they shew it placed and figured among the stars. There is also a writing which they call Malachim, or Melachim, i. e. of angels, or regal; there is also another, which they call the passing through the river, and the characters and figures of all which you may see in the following Plates.

The Cabala

The Tables for the calculations of the names of Spirits good & bad & under the presidency of the 7 Planets & 12 militant Signs

The entrance of the Evil Angels — The entrance of the good Angels

	☽	☿	♀	☉	♂	♃	♄	The Line of Good
ת	ו	י	ה	ד	ג	ב	א	א
ש	נ	מ	ל	כ	י	ט	ח	ב
ר	ש	ר	ק	צ	פ	ע	ס	ג
ק	ו	ה	ד	ג	ב	א	ת	ד
צ	מ	ל	כ	י	ט	ח	ז	ה
פ	ר	ק	צ	פ	ע	ס	נ	ו
ע	ה	ד	ג	ב	א	ת	ש	ז
ס	ל	כ	י	ט	ח	ז	י	ח
נ	ק	צ	פ	ע	ס	נ	מ	ט
מ	ר	ג	ב	א	ת	ש	ר	י
ל	כ	י	ט	ח	ז	ו	ה	כ
כ	צ	פ	ע	ס	נ	מ	ל	ל
י	ג	ב	א	ת	ש	ר	ק	מ
ט	י	ט	ח	ז	ו	ה	ר	נ
ח	פ	ע	ס	נ	מ	ל	כ	ס
ז	ב	א	ת	ש	ר	ק	צ	ע
ו	ט	ח	ז	ו	ה	ד	י	פ
ה	פ	ס	נ	מ	ל	כ	י	צ
ד	א	ת	ש	ר	ק	צ	פ	ק
ג	ח	ז	ו	ה	ד	ג	ב	ר
ב	ס	נ	מ	ל	כ	י	ט	ש
א	ת	ש	ר	ק	צ	פ	ע	ת
The Line of Evil	♄	♃	♂	☉	☽	♀	☿	

The entrance of the Evil Angels — The entrance of the good Angels

	♓	♒	♑	♐	♏	♎	♍	♌	♋	♊	♉	♈	The Line of Good
ת	ל	כ	י	ט	ח	ז	ו	ה	ד	ג	ב	א	א
ש	א	ב	ג	ד	ה	ו	ז	ח	ט	י	כ	ל	ב
ר	ב	א	ת	ש	ר	ק	צ	פ	ע	ס	נ	מ	ג
ק	מ	נ	ס	ע	פ	צ	ק	ר	ש	ה	א	ב	ד
צ	נ	מ	ל	כ	י	ט	ח	ז	ו	ה	ד	ג	ה
פ	ג	ד	ה	ו	ז	ח	ט	י	כ	ל	מ	נ	ו
ע	ד	ג	ב	א	ת	ש	ר	ק	צ	פ	ע	ס	ז
ס	ס	ע	פ	צ	ק	ר	ש	ת	א	ב	ג	ר	ח
נ	ע	ס	נ	מ	ל	כ	י	ט	ח	ז	ו	ה	ט
מ	ה	ו	ז	ח	ט	י	כ	ל	מ	נ	ס	ע	י
ל	י	ה	ד	ג	ב	א	ת	ש	ר	ק	צ	פ	כ
ל	פ	צ	ק	ר	ש	ת	א	ב	ג	ד	ה	ו	ל
י	צ	פ	ע	ס	נ	מ	ל	כ	י	ט	ח	ז	מ
ט	ז	ח	ט	י	כ	ל	מ	נ	ס	ע	פ	צ	נ
ח	ח	ז	ו	ה	ד	ג	ב	א	ת	ש	ר	ק	ס
ז	ק	ר	ש	ת	א	ב	ג	ד	ה	ו	ז	ח	ע
ו	ר	ק	צ	פ	ע	ס	נ	מ	ל	כ	י	ט	פ
ה	ט	י	כ	ל	מ	נ	ס	ע	פ	צ	ק	ר	צ
ד	י	ט	ח	ז	ו	ה	ד	ג	ב	א	ת	ש	ק
ג	ש	ת	א	ב	ג	ד	ה	ו	ז	ח	ט	י	ר
ב	ה	ש	ר	ק	צ	פ	ע	ס	נ	מ	ל	כ	ש
א	כ	ל	מ	נ	ס	ע	פ	צ	ק	ר	ש	ת	ת
The Line of Evil	ל	כ	י	ט	ח	ז	ו	ה	ד	ג	ב	א	

There is another manner among the Cabalists, formerly held in great esteem, but now it is so common that it is placed among prophane things, viz. the twenty-seven characters of the Hebrews may be divided into three classes, whereof every one contains nine letters. The

281

first, viz. תחזוההדגבא which are the seals or marks of simple numbers and of intellectual things distributed into nine orders of angels. The second hath צפעסנמלכי, the marks of tens and celestial things in the nine orbs of the heavens. The third hath the other four letters, with the five final, viz. ץןםףךתשרק which are marks of hundreds, and inferior things, viz. four simple elements, and five kinds of perfect com pounds. They do now and then distribute these three classes into nine chambers, the first is of units, vi-,. intellectual, celestial and elemental. The second is of two's, the third of three's, and so of the rest; these chambers are framed by the intersection of four parallel lines intersecting themselves into right angles, as is expressed in the following Plate, fig. A.

Out of which, being dissected into parts, proceed nine particular figures (See Plate, fig. B.) which are of the nine chambers, characterizing their letters by that Notariacon, which, if it be of one point, shews the first letter of that chamber; if of two, the second; if of three, the third letter; as if you would frame the character, Michael, לאכימ, that comes forth extended with five figures (for which see the Plate C.) which are contracted to three figures, which then are contracted into one, yet the points Notariacon are usually omitted, and then there comes forth such a character of Michael. See fig. D.

There is yet another fashion of characters common to almost all letters and tongues, and very easy, which is by gathering together of letters; as if the name of the angel Michael be given, the characters thereof shall be framed according to the fig. E. And this fashion among the Arabians is most received; neither is there any writing which is so readily and elegantly joined to itself as the Arabick.

You must know that angelical spirits, seeing they are of a pure intellect, and altogether incorporeal, are not marked with any marks or characters, or any other human signs; but we, not otherwise knowing their essence or quality, do, from their names, or works, or otherwise, devote and consecrate to them figures and marks, by which we cannot any way compel them to us, but by which we rise up to them, as not to be known by such characters and figures, and, first of all, we do set our senses, both inward and outward, upon them; then, by a certain admiration of our reason, we are induced to a religious veneration of them; and then are wrapt with our whole mind into an ecstatical adoration; and then with a wonderful belief, an undoubted hope, and quickening love, calling upon them in spirit and truth by true names and characters, do obtain from them that virtue or power which we desire.

CHAPTER 17. THERE IS ANOTHER KIND OF CHARACTERS, OR MARKS OF SPIRITS, WHICH ARE RECEIVED ONLY BY REVELATION

THERE is another kind of character received by revelation only, which can be found out no other way; the virtue of which characters is from the Deity revealing; of whom there are some secret works breathing out a harmony of some divinity, or they are, as it were, some certain agreements or compacts of a league between us and them. Of this kind there was a sign shewed to Constantine, which was this, in hoc vince; there was another revealed to Antiochus in the figure of a Pentangle, which signifies health; for, being resolved into letters, it speaks the word ὑγίεια i. e. health: in the faith and virtue of which signs, both kings obtained a great victory against their enemies. So Judas, who by reason of that, was afterwards surnamed Machabeus, being to fight with the Jews against Antiochus Eupator, received from an angel a notable sign, יבכמ in the virtue of which they first slew 11,000, with an infinite number of elephants, then again 35,000 of their enemies: for that sign did represent the name of Jehovah, and was a memorable emblem of the name of seventy-two letters by the equality of number; and the exposition thereof is חיהימ ילאב דיטב ימ i. e. who is there among thee strong as Jehovah? See Plate, fig. F.

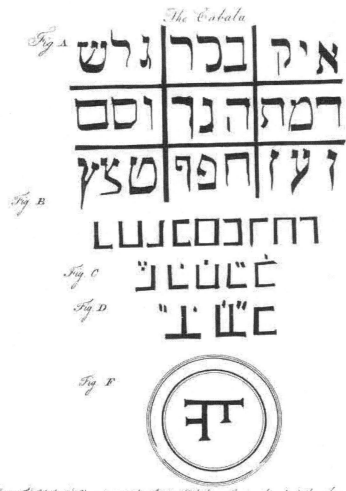

The Cabala

Fig A

Fig B

Fig C

Fig D

Fig F

Fig F. The Cabalistic Character of the Spirit Michæl as Composed out of the above Tables A B C D

CHAPTER 18. ON THE BONDS OF SPIRITS, AND THEIR ADJURATIONS, AND CASTINGS OUT

THE bond by which spirits are bound, besought, or cast out, are three; some of them are taken from the elemental world, as when we adjure a spirit by an inferior and natural thing of affinity with or adverse to them; inasmuch as we would call up or cast them out, as by fumigations of flowers, herbs, animals, snow, ice, or by hell, fire, and such like; and these also are often mixt with. divine praises, and blessings, and consecrations, as appears in the song of the Three Children, and in the psalm, Praise ye the Lord from the heavens, and in the consecration and blessing of the paschal taper. This bond works upon the spirits by an apprehensive virtue, under the account of love or hatred, inasmuch as the spirits are present with, or favour, or abhor any thing that is natural or against nature, as these things themselves love or hate one another.

The second bond is taken from the celestial world, viz. when we adjure them by their heaven, by the stars, by their motions, rays, light, beauty, clearness, excellency, fortitude, influence and wonders, and such like; and this bond works upon spirits by way of admonition and example. It hath also some command, especially upon the ministering spirits, and those who are of the lowest orders.

The third bond is from the intellectual and divine world, which is perfected by religion; that is to say, when we swear by the sacraments, miracles, divine names, sacred seals, and other mysteries of religion; wherefore this bond is the highest of all and the Strongest, working upon the spirits by command and power; but this is to be observed, that as after the universal Providence there is a particular one, and after the universal soul, particular souls; so, in the first place, we invocate by the superior bonds, and by the names and powers which rule the things, then by the inferior and the things themselves. We must know further, that by these bonds, not only spirits, but also all creatures are bound, as tempests, burnings, floods, plagues, diseases, force of arms, and every animal, by assuming them, either by adjuration or deprecation, or benediction, as in the charming of serpents;

besides the natural and celestial, by rehearsing out of the mysteries and religion, the cure of the serpent in terrestrial paradise, the lifting up of the serpent in the wilderness; likewise by assuming that verse of the 91st Psalm, thou shall walk upon the asp and the basilisk, and shall tread upon the lion and the dragon.

CHAPTER 19. BY WHAT MEANS MAGICIANS AND NECROMANCERS CALL FORTH THE SOULS OF THE DEAD

BY the things which have been already spoken it is manifest, that souls after death do as yet love their body which they left, as those souls do whose bodies want due burial or have left their bodies by violent death, and as yet wander about their carcasses in a troubled and moist spirit, being, as it were, allured by something that hath an affinity with them, the means being known, by which in times past, they were joined to their bodies, they may be easily called forth and allured by the like vapours, liquors and savours, certain artificial lights being also used, songs, sounds, and such like, which moves the imaginative and spiritual harmony of the soul; and sacred invocations, and such like, as belong to religion, ought not to be neglected by reason of the portion of the rational soul which is above nature.

Necromancy has its name because it works on the bodies of the dead, and gives answers by the ghosts and apparitions of the dead, and subterraneous spirits, alluring them into the carcasses of the dead by certain hellish charms, and infernal invocations, and by deadly sacrifices and wicked oblations.

There are two kinds of necromancy: raising the carcasses, which is not done without blood; the other sciomancy, in which the calling up of the shadow only suffices. To conclude, it works all its experiments by the carcasses of the slain and their bones and members, and what is from them; for there is in these things a spiritual power friendly to them: therefore they easily allure the flowing down of wicked spirits, by reason of the similitude and property of every familiar, by whom the necromancer, strengthened by their help, can do much in human and terrestrial things, and kindle unlawful lusts, cause dreams, diseases, hatred, and such like passions; to which also they can confer the powers of the soul, which as yet being involved in a moist and turbid spirit, wandering about their cast bodies, can do the same things that the wicked spirits commit, seeing therefore they, experimentally find, that the wicked and impure souls violently plucked from their bodies, and of men not expiated, and wanting burial, do stray about carcasses, and are drawn to them by affinity. The witches easily abuse them for effecting witchcraft, alluring these unhappy souls, by the opposition of their body, or by the taking of some parts thereof, and compelling them by their devilish charms, by entreating them by the deformed carcasses dispersed through the wide fields, and the wandering shadows of those who want burials, and by the ghosts sent back from Acheron, and the guests of hell, whom untimely death has precipitated into hell, and by the horrible desires of the damned and proud devils, revengers of wickedness. But he who could restore the souls truly to their bodies, must first know what is the proper nature of the soul from whence it went forth, with how many and how great degrees of perfection it is replenished, with what intelligence it is strengthened, by what means diffused into the body, by what harmony it shall be compacted with it, what affinity it hath with God, with the intelligences, with the heavens, elements, and all other things, whose image and resemblance it holds, To conclude, by what influences the body may be knit together again for the raising of the dead, requires all these things which belong not to men, but to God only, and to whom he will communicate them.

CHAPTER 20. OF PROPHETICAL DREAMS

I CALL that a dream which proceeds either from the spirit of the phantasy and intellect united together, or by the illustration of the agent intellect above our souls, or by the true revelation of some divine power in a quiet and purified mind; for by this our soul receives true oracles, and abundantly yields prophecies to us; for in dreams we seem both to ask questions, and learn to find them out; also many doubtful things, many policies, many things unknown, unwished for, and never attempted by our minds, are manifested to us in dreams: also the representation of things unknown, and unknown places appear to us; and the images of men, both alive and dead, and of things to come, are foretold; and also things which at any time have happened are revealed, which we know not by any report. And these dreams need not any art of interpretation, as those of which we have before spoken, which belong to divination, not to foreknowledge; and it comes to pass that they who see dreams, for the most part, understand them not: for as to see dreams is from the strength of imagination, so to understand them is from the strength of the understanding. They, therefore, whose intellect being overwhelmed by too much commerce of the flesh is in a dead sleep, or its imaginative or phantastic power or spirit is too dull and unpolished, that it cannot receive the species and representation which flow from the superior intellect; this man, I say, is altogether unfit for the receiving of dreams and prophesying by them.

Therefore it is necessary that he who would receive true dreams should keep a pure undisturbed, and an undisquieted imaginative spirit, and so compose it that it may be made worthy of the knowledge and government by the mind and understanding; for such a spirit is most fit for prophesying, and is a most clear glass of all the images which flow (every where) from all things. When therefore we are sound in body, not disturbed in mind, our intellect not dulled by meats and drinks, not sad through poverty, not provoked through lust, not incited by any vice, not stirred up by wrath or anger, not being irreligiously and prophanely inclined, not given to levity, not lost in drunkenness, but chastely going to bed, fall asleep; then our pure and divine soul, being free from all the evils above recited, and separated from all hurtful thoughts, and now freed by dreaming, is endowed with this divine spirit as an instrument, and doth receive those beams and representations which are darted down, as it were, and shine forth from the Divine Mind into itself; and, as it were in a deifying glass, it does more certain, more clear and efficaciously behold all things than by the vulgar inquiry of the intellect, and by the discourse of reason. The divine powers instructing the soul, being invited to their society by the opportunity of the nocturnal solitariness, neither will that genius be wanting to him when he is awake, which rules all his actions.

Whosoever therefore, by quiet and religious meditation, and by a diet temperate and moderate according to nature, preserves his spirit pure shall very much prepare himself, and by this means become (in a degree) divine and knowing all things, justly merits the same. But whosoever, on the contrary, languishes with a fantastic spirit, he receives not perspicuous and distant visions; but even as the divine sight, by reason of its vision, being weakened and impaired, judges confusedly and indistinctly, so also when we are overcome with wine and drunkenness, then our spirit, being oppressed with noxious vapours (as a troubled water is apt to appear in various forms) is deceived, and waxes dull; therefore those who would receive oracles by dreams, and those oracles true and certain, I would advise him to abstain one whole day from meat, and three days from wine or any strong liquors, and drink nothing but pure water; for, to sober and religious minds, the pure spirits are adherent, but fly those who are drowned in drunkenness and surfeiting. Although impure spirits do very often administer notable secrets to those who are apparently besotted with wine or liquors; yet all such communications are to be contemned and avoided.

But there are four kinds of true dreams, viz. the first, matutine, i.e. between sleeping and waking; the second that which one sees concerning another, the third, that whose interpretation is shewn to the same dreamer in the nocturnal vision; and, lastly, the fourth, that which is repeated to the same dreamer in the nocturnal vision.

END OF PART FIRST

THE PERFECTION AND KEY OF THE CABALA, OR CEREMONIAL MAGIC

INTRODUCTION

IN this last book, which we have made the Perfection and Key of all that has been written, we have given thee the whole and entire practice of Ceremonial Magic, shewing what is to be done every hour of the day; so that as by reading what we have heretofore written, thou shalt contemplate in theory, here thou shalt be made perfect by experiment and practice: for in this Key you may behold, as in a mirror, the distinct functions of the spirits, and how they are to be drawn into communication in all places, seasons, and times.

This then is to be known, that the names of the intelligent presidents of every one of the planets are constituted after this manner; that it to say, by collecting together the letters out of the figures of the world from the rising of the body of the planet, according to the succession of the signs through the several degrees, and out of the several degrees, from the aspects of the planet himself, the calculation being made from the degree of the ascendant.

In like manner are constituted the names of the princes of the evil spirits; they are taken under all the planets of the presidents in a retrograde order, the projection being made contrary to the succession of the signs, from the beginning of the seventh house. Now the name of the supreme and highest intelligence, which many suppose to be the soul of the world, is collected out of the four cardinal points of the figure of the world, after the manner already delivered; and by the opposite and contrary way is known the name of the great demon or evil spirit, upon the four cadent angles.

In like manner you shall understand the names of the great presidential spirits ruling in the air, from the four angles of the succedent houses, so as to obtain the names of the good spirits: the calculation is to be made according to the succession of the signs, beginning from the degree of the ascendant, and to attain the names of the evil spirits by working the contrary way.

You must also observe, that the names of the evil spirits are extracted as well from the names of the good spirits as of the evil: so, notwithstanding, that if we enter the table with the name of a good spirit of the second order, the name of the evil shall be extracted from the order of princes and governors; but if we enter the table with the name of a good spirit of the third order, or with the name of an evil spirit, a governor, after what manner soever they are extracted, whether by this table or from a celestial figure, the names which do proceed from hence shall be the names of the evil spirits, the ministers of the inferior order.

It is further to be noted, that as often as we enter this table with the good spirits of the second order, the names extracted are of the second order; and if under them we extract the name of an evil spirit, he is of the superior order of the governors. The same order is, if we enter with the name of an evil spirit of the superior. If therefore we enter this table with the names of the spirits of the third order, or with the names of the ministering spirits, as well of the good spirits as of the evil, the names extracted shall be the names of the ministering spirits of the inferior order.

But many magicians, men of no small authority, will have the tables of this kind to be extended with Latin letters; so that by the same tables also, out of the name of any office or effect, might be found out the name of any spirit, as well good as evil, by the same manner which is above delivered, by taking the name of the office or of the effect in the column of letters, in their own line, under their own star. And of this practice Trismegistus is a great author, who delivered this kind of calculation in Egyptian letters: not improperly also may they be referred to the letters of other tongues, for the reason assigned to the signs; for truly he only is extant of all men who have treated concerning the attaining to the names of spirits.

Therefore the force, secrecy, and power, in what manner the sacred names of spirits are truely and rightly found out, consisteth in the disposing of vowels, which make the name of a spirit, and wherewith is constituted the true name and right word. Now this art is thus perfected and brought to pass. First, we are to take heed to placing the vowels of the letters, which are found by the calculation of the celestial figure, to find the names of the spirits of the second order, presidents and governors: and this, in the good spirits, is thus brought to effect, by considering the stars which do constitute and make the letters, and by placing them according to their order. First, let the degree of the eleventh house be subtracted from the degree of that star which is first in order, and that which remains thereof, let it be projected from the degree of the ascendant; and where the number ends, there is part of the vowel of the first letter.

Begin therefore to calculate the vowels of these letters according to their number and order, and the vowel which falls in the place of the star, which is the first in order, the same vowel is attributed to the first letter; then afterwards thou shalt find the part of the second letter, by subtracting the degree of a star, which is the second in order from the first star; and that which remains cast from the ascendant. And this is the part from which you shall begin the calculation of vowels; and that vowel which falls upon the second star the same is the vowel of the second letter: and so consequently thou mayest search out the vowels of the following letters by always subtracting the degree of the following star from the degree of the star next preceding and going before. And, likewise, all calculations and numerations in the names of the good spirits ought to be made according to the succession of the signs. And whereas in calculating the names of the evil spirits, the names of the good spirits are taken from the degree of the eleventh house; in these ought to be taken the degree of the twelfth house. And all numerations and calculations may be made with the succession of the signs, by taking the beginning from the degree of the tenth house.

But in all extractions by tables, the vowels are placed after another manner. In the first place, is taken the certain number of letters, making the name itself, and is thus numbered from the beginning of the column of the first letter, or whereupon the name is extracted; and the letter on which this number falleth is referred to the first letter of the name extracted, by taking the distance of the one from the other, according to the order of the alphabet. But the number of that distance is projected from the beginning of that column, and where it ends there is part of the first vowel; from thence thou shalt calculate the vowels themselves, in their own number and order in the same column; and the vowel which shall fall upon the first letter of a name, the same shall be attributed to that name.

Now thou shalt find the following vowels, by taking the distance from the preceding vowel to the following, and so consequently according to the succession of the alphabet; and the number of that distance is to be numbered from the beginning of his own column, and where he shall cease, there is part of the vowel sought after. From thence therefore must you calculate the vowels, as we have above said, and those vowels which shall fall upon your own letters, are to be attributed to them. If therefore any vowel should happen to fall upon a vowel, the former must give place to the latter: and this you are to understand only of the good spirits. In the evil spirits likewise you may proceed in the same way; except only that you make the numerations after a contrary and backward order, contrary to the succession of the alphabet, and contrary to the order of the columns (that is to say) ascending.

The name of good angels, and of every man, which we have before taught how to find out, according to that manner, is of no little authority, nor of a mean foundation. But now we will give thee some other ways illustrated with no vain reasons. One whereof is by taking in the nativity the five places of Hylech; which being noted, the characters of the letters are projected in their order and number, beginning from Aries, and those letters which fall upon the degrees of the said places, according to their order and dignity disposed and aspected, make the name of an angel.

There is also another way wherein they take Almutel, which is the ruling and governing star over the aforesaid five places, and the projection is to be made from the degree of the ascendant; which is done by gathering together the letters falling upon Almutel, which being placed in order, according to their dignity, make the name of an angel. There is likewise another way used, and very much had in observation from the Egyptians, by making calculations from the degree of the ascendant, and by gathering together the letters according to the Almutel of the eleventh house; which house they call a good demon; which being placed according to their dignities, the names of the angels are constituted.

Now the names of the evil angels are known after the like manner, except only that the projections must be performed contrary to the course and order of the succession of the signs; so that in seeking the names of good spirits, we are to calculate from the beginning of Aries; contrariwise, in attaining the names of evil, we ought to account from the beginning of Libra. And whereas, in the good spirits, we number from the degree of the ascendant; contrariety, in the evil, we must calculate from the degree of the seventh house.

But according to the Egyptians, the name of this angel is collected according to the Almutel of the twelfth house, which they call an evil spirit. Now all those rites, which are elsewhere already by us delivered in this Book, may be made by the characters of any language. In all which (as we have said before) there is a mystical and divine number, order and figure, from whence it comes to pass, that the same spirit may be called by divers names; but others are discovered from the name of the spirit himself, of the good or evil, by tables formed to this purpose.

Now these celestial characters do consist of lines and heads. The heads are six, according to the six magnitudes of the stars, whereunto the planets likewise are reduced. The first magnitude holds a star with the sun or a cross, the second, with Jupiter, a circular point; the third, with Saturn, a semicircle, a triangle, either crooked, round, or acute; the fourth, with a Mars, a little stroke penetrating the line, either square, straight or oblique; the fifth, with Venus and Mercury, a little stroke or point with a tail ascending or descending; the sixth, with the moon, a point made black, all which you may see in the annexed plate. The heads then being posited according to the site of the stars of the figure of heaven then the lines are to be drawn out according to the congruency or agreement of their natures. And this you are to understand of the fixed stars. But in the erecting of the planets, the lines are drawn out, the heads being posited according to their course and nature among themselves.--See the Plate, No. 1.

So when a character is to be found, of any celestial image ascending in any degree or face of a sign, which consists of stars of the same magnitude and nature, then the number of these stars being posited according to their place and order, the lines are drawn after the similitude of the image signified, as copiously as the same can be done.

But the characters which are extracted according to the name of a spirit are composed by the table following, by giving to every letter that name which agrees to him out of the table; and although it may appear easy to those that apprehend it, yet there is no small difficulty herein; to wit, when the letter of a name falls upon the line of letters or figures, that we may know which figure or which letter is to be taken. And this may thus be known; if a letter falls upon the line of letters, consider of what number this letter may be in the order of the name, as the second or the third; then how many letters that name contains, as five or seven; and multiply these numbers one after another by themselves and treble the product; then cast the whole (being added together) from the beginning of the letters according to the succession of the alphabet; and the letter upon which that number shall happen to fall, ought to be placed for a character of that spirit. But if any letter of a name fall upon the line of figures, it is thus wrought: take the number how many this letter is in the order of the name, and let it be multiplied by the number of which this letter is in the order of the alphabet; and, being added together, divide it by nine, and the remainder will shew the figure or number to be placed in the character, and this may be put either in a geometrical or arithmetrical figure of number; which, notwithstanding, ought not to exceed the number of nine, or nine angels.--See the Plate, No. 2.

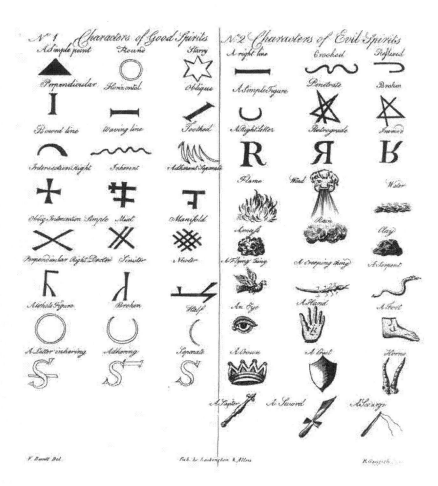

But the characters which are understood by the revelations of spirits take their virtue from thence, because they are, as it were, certain hidden seals, making the harmony of some divinity: either they are signs of a covenant entered into, and of a promised or plighted faith, or of obedience. And those characters cannot by any other means be found out.

Besides these characters there are certain familiar figures and images of evil spirits, under which forms they are wont to appear, and yield obedience to those who invoke them. And all these characters and images may be seen in the considerations of each day's business, according to the course of the letters constituting the names of spirits themselves; so that if in any letter there is found more than the name of one spirit, his image holds the pre-eminence, the others imparting their own orders; so they which are of the first order, to them is attributed the head, the upper part of the body, according to their own figure; those which are lowest possess the thighs and feet; so likewise the middle letters do attribute like to themselves the middle parts of the body, to give the parts that fit; but if there happen any contrariety, that letter which is the strongest in the number shall bear rule; and if they are equal they all impart equal things. Moreover if any name shall obtain any notable character or instrument out of the table, he shall likewise have the same character in the image.

We may also attain to the knowledge of the dignities of the evil spirits, by the same tables of characters and images: for upon whatsoever spirit falls any excellent sign or instrument out of the table of characters, he possesses that dignity. As if there should be a crown, it shows a kingly dignity; if a crest or plume, a dukedom; if a horn, a county: if without these there be a sceptre, sword, or forked instrument, it shows rule and authority. Likewise out of the table of images you shall find them who bear the chief kingly dignity: from the crown judge dignity; and from the instruments, rule and authority.

Lastly, they which bear a human shape and figure have a greater dignity than those which appear under the forms and images of beasts. They likewise who ride do excel them which appear on foot. And thus, according to all their commixtures, you may judge the dignity and excellency of spirits, one before another. Moreover, you must understand that the spirits of the inferior order, of what dignity soever, they are always subject to the spirits of the superior order; likewise that it is not incongruent for their kings and dukes to be subject and minister to the presidents of the superior order.

OF MAGIC PENTACLES AND THEIR COMPOSITION

WE now proceed to speak of the holy and sacred Pentacles and Seals. For these pentacles are certain holy signs and characters, preserving us from evil chances and events, helping and assisting us to bind, exterminate, and drive away evil spirits, alluring the good spirits, and reconciling them to us. These pentacles consist either of characters of good spirits of the superior order, or of sacred pictures of holy letters or revelations, with apt and proper versicles, which are composed either of geometrical figures and holy names of God, according to the course and manner of many of them, or they are compounded of all of them, or many of them mixed. The characters which are useful for us to constitute and make the pentacles are the characters of the good spirits, chiefly of the good spirits of the first and second order, and sometimes of the third order. These kind of characters are especially to be named holy.

Whatsoever characters of this kind are to be instituted, we must draw about him a double circle, wherein we must write the name of his angel; and if we will add some divine name congruent with his spirit and office, it will be of greater force and efficacy; and if we draw about him any angular figure, according to the manner of his numbers that is lawful to be done. But the holy pictures which make the pentacles are they which every where are delivered to us in the prophets and sacred writings, both in the Old and New Testaments; even as the figure of the serpent hanging on the cross, and such like; whereof many may be found in the visions of the prophets, as in Isaiah, Daniel, Esdras, and others, and likewise in the revelations of the Apocalypse. And we have before spoken of them in our First Part, where we have made mention of holy things, therefore where any picture is posited of any of these holy images, let the circle be drawn round it on each side; wherein let there be written some divine name that is apt and conformed to the effect of that figure, or else there may be written around it some versicle taken out of part of the body of holy Scripture, which may ascertain or deprecate the desired effect.

If a pentacle were to be made to gain a victory, or revenge against one's enemies, as well visible as invisible, the figure may be taken out of the Second book of the Maccabees, that is to say, a hand holding a golden sword drawn, about which let there be written the versicle there contained, to wit, take the holy sword, the gift of God, wherewith thou shall slay the adversaries of my people Israel. Or else there may be written about a versicle of the fifth Psalm; in this is the strength of thy arm: before they face there is death; or some other such like versicle. But if you will write a divine name about the figure, then let some name be taken that signifies fear; a sword, wrath, the revenge of God, or some such like name congruent and agreeing with the effect desired. And if there shall be written any angular figure, let it be taken according to the rule of the numbers, as we have taught where we have treated of numbers, and the like operations. And of this sort there are two pentacles of sublime virtue and great power, very useful and necessary to be used in the consecration of experiments and spirits; one whereof is that in the first chapter of the Apocalypse, to wit, a figure of the majesty of God sitting. upon a throne, having in his mouth a two-edged sword, as there is described; about which let there be written, "I am Alpha and Omega, the Beginning and the End, which is, and which was, and which is to come, the Almighty. I am the First and the Last, who am living, and was dead, and behold I live for ever and ever; and I have the keys of death and hell." Then there shall be written about it these three versicles:

Munda Deus virtuti tuæ &c.--Give commandment, O God, to thy strength; confirm, O God, thy strength in us. Let them be as dust before the face of the wind: and let the angel of the Lord scatter them. Let all their ways be darkness and uncertain: and let the angel of the Lord persecute them.

Moreover, let there be written about it the ten general names, which are El, Elohim, Elohe, Zebaoth, Elion, Escerchie, Adonay, Jah, Tetragrammaton, Saday.

There is another pentacle, the figure whereof is like a lamb slain, having seven eyes and seven horns; and under his feet a book sealed with seven seals, as it is in the fifth chapter of the Apocalypse. Round about let be written this versicle, behold the lion hath overcome of the tribe of Judah, the root of David. I will open the book and unloose the seven seals thereof. And another versicle, I saw Satan like lightning fall down from heaven. Behold I have given you power to tread upon serpents and scorpions, and over all the power of your enemies, and nothing shall be able to hurt you. And let there be also written about it the ten general names as aforesaid.

But those pentacles which are thus made of figures and names, let them keep this order; for when any figure is posited, conformable to any number, to produce any certain effect or virtue, there must be written thereupon, in all the several angles, some divine name obtaining the force and efficacy of the thing desired; yet so nevertheless, that the name which is of this sort do consist of just so many letters as the figure may constitute a number; or of so many letters of a name, as, joined together among themselves, may make the number of a figure; or by any number which may be divided without any superfluity or diminution. Now such a name being found, whether it be only one name or more, or divers names, it is to be written in all the several angles in the figure; but in the middle of the figure let the revolution of the name be wholly and totally placed, or at least principally.

We likewise constitute pentacles by making the revolution of some kind of name, in a square table, and by drawing about it a single or double circle, and writing therein some holy versicle competent and befitting this name, or from which that name is extracted. And this is the way of making the pentacles, according to their several distinct forms and fashions, which we may, if we please, either multiply or commix together by course among themselves, to work the greater efficacy, extension and enlargement of force and virtue.

As, if a deprecation would be made for the overthrow and destruction of one's enemies, we are to mind, and call to remembrance how God destroyed the face of the whole earth in the deluge of waters, and the destruction of Sodom and Gomorrah, by raining down fire and brimstone; likewise, how God overthrew Pharaoh and his host in the Red Sea; and to call to mind if any other malediction

303

or curse be found in holy writ. And thus in things of the like sort. So likewise in deprecating and praying against perils and dangers of waters, we ought to call to remembrance the saving of Noah in the deluge of waters, the passing of the children of Israel through the Red Sea; and also we are to mind how Christ walked on the waters, and how he saved the ship in danger from being cast away by the tempest; and how he commanded the winds and the waves, and they obeyed him; and also, that he drew Peter out of the water, being in danger of drowning, and the like. And, lastly, with these we invoke and call upon some certain holy names of God; to wit, such as are significative to accomplish our desire and accommodated to the desired effect; as if it be to overthrow enemies; we are to invoke and call upon names of wrath, revenge, fear, justice, and fortitude of God; and if we would avoid and escape any evil or danger, we then call upon the names of mercy, defence, salvation, fortitude, goodness, and such like names of God. When likewise we pray to God that he would grant us our desires, we are likewise to intermix therewith the name of some good spirit, whether one only, or more, whose office it is to execute our desires; and sometimes also we require some evil spirit to restrain or compel, whose name likewise we intermingle, and that rightly, especially if it be to execute any evil work; as revenge, punishment, or destruction. Furthermore, if there be any versicle in the Psalms, or any other part of the holy Scripture, that shall seem congruent and agreeable to our desire, the same is to be mingled with our prayers. Now, after prayer has been made to God, it is expedient afterwards to make an oration to that executioner, whom, in our precedent prayer to God, we have desired should administer to us, whether one or more, or whether he be an angel, or star, or soul, or any of the noble angels. But this kind of oration ought to be composed according to the rules which we have delivered in the former part of our work, where we have treated of the manner of the composition of enchantments, &c.

You may know farther, that these kind of bonds have a threefold difference; for the first bond is when we conjure by natural things; the second is compounded of religious mysteries, by sacraments, miracles, and things of this sort; and the third is constituted by divine names and holy seals. With these kind of bonds we may bind not only spirits, but also other creatures whatsoever, as animals, tempests, burnings, floods of waters, the force and power of arms. Also we use these bonds aforesaid, not only by conjuration, but sometimes also using the means of deprecation and benediction. Moreover it conduces much to this purpose to join some sentence of holy Scripture, if any shall be found convenient thereto, as in the conjuration of serpents, by commemorating the curse of the serpent in the earthly paradise, and the setting up the serpent in the wilderness; and further, adding that versicle, thou shall walk upon the asp and the basilisk, &c. Superstition is also of much prevelancy herein, by the translation of some sacramental rites, to bind that which we intend to hinder; as, the rites of excommunication, of sepulchres, funerals, buryings, and the like sort.

OF THE CONSECRATION OF ALL MAGICAL INSTRUMENTS AND MATERIALS WHICH ARE USED IN THIS ART

THE virtue of consecrations chiefly consists in two things, viz. the power of the person consecrating, and the virtue of the prayer by which the consecration is made. For in the person consecrating, there is required firmness, constancy, and holiness of life; and that the consecrator himself shall, with a firm and undubitable faith, believe the virtue, Power, and effect thereof.

Then in the prayer by which the consecration is made it derives its virtue either from divine inspiration, or else by composing it from sundry places in the holy Scriptures, in the commemoration of some of the wonderful miracles of God, effects, promises, sacraments and sacramental things, of which we have abundance in holy writ.

There must likewise be used the invocation of divine names, that are significative of the work in hand; likewise a sanctifying and expiation which s wrought by sprinkling with holy water, unctions with holy oil, and odoriferous suffumigations. Therefore in every consecration there is generally used a benediction and consecration of water, earth, oil, fire, and suffumigations, &c. with consecrated wax-lights or lamps burning; for without lights no consecration is duly performed. You must therefore particularly observe this, that when any thing (which we call prophane) is to be used, in which there is any defilement or pollution, it must, first of all, be purified by an Exorcism composed solely for that purpose, which ought to precede the consecration; which things being so made pure are most apt to receive the influences of the divine virtue. We must also observe that at the end of any consecration after the prayer is rightly performed, as we have mentioned, the operator ought to bless the thing consecrated, by breathing out some sentence with divine virtue and power of the present consecration, with a commemoration of his virtue and authority, that so it may be the more duly performed, and with an earnest and attentive mind. Now I shall mention here some examples, that, by these, a path may be made to the whole perfection thereof.

THE CONSECRATION OF WATER

SO in the consecration of water, we must commemorate that God has placed the firmament in the midst of the waters, and likewise that God placed the fountain of waters in the earthly paradise, from whence sprang four holy rivers that watered the whole earth; likewise we are to remember that God caused the waters to be an instrument of his justice in destroying the giants, by bringing on the deluge which covered the face of the whole earth; and in the overthrow of the host of Pharaoh in the Red Sea, and that God led the children of Israel through on dry land, and through the midst of the river Jordan, and likewise his marvellously drawing water out of the stony rock in the wilderness; and that, at the prayer of Samson, he caused water to flow out of the jaw-bone of an ass; and likewise that God has made water the instrument of his mercy and salvation for the expiation of original sin; also that Christ was baptized in the river Jordan, and hath thereby sanctified and cleansed the waters.

Likewise certain divine names are to be invoked which are conformable hereto; as, that God is a living fountain, living water, the fountain of mercy, and names of the like sort.

CONSECRATION OF FIRE

AND likewise, in the consecration of fire, we are to commemorate that God hath created the fire to be an instrument to execute his justice, for punishment, vengeance, and the expiation of sins; also, when God comes to judge the world that he will command a conflagration of fire to go before him; likewise we are to mention that God appeared to Moses in a burning bush; and also how he went before the children of Israel in a pillar of fire; and that nothing can be duly offered, sanctified, or sacrificed, without fire; and how that God instituted fire to be kept in continually in the tabernacle of the covenant; and how miraculously he re-kindled the same, being extinct, and preserved it elsewhere from going out being hidden under the waters; and things of this sort; likewise the names of God are to be called upon which are consonant to this; as we read in the law and prophets, that God is a consuming fire; and likewise if there are any divine names which signify fire, as the glory of God, the light of God, the splendor and brightness of God,. &c.

THE CONSECRATION OF OIL

AND likewise in the consecration of oil and perfumes we are to mention such things as are consonant to this purpose, as of the holy anointing oil mentioned in Exodus, and divine names significant thereunto; such as is the name Christ, which signifies anointed; and whatever mysteries there are relative to oil in the Scriptures, as the two olive-trees distilling holy oil into the lamps that burn before the face of God, mentioned in Revelations.

OF THE BENEDICTION OF LIGHTS, LAMPS, WAX, &C

NOW, the blessing of the lights, lamps, wax, &c. is taken from the fire, and whatever contains the substance of the flame, and whatever similitudes are in the mysteries, as the seven candlesticks which burn before the face of God.

Therefore we have here given the manner of composing the consecrations, which first of all are necessary to be used in every kind of ceremony, and ought to precede every experiment or work, and without which nothing in magic rites can be duly performed.

In the next place, we will shew thee the consecration of places, instruments, and the like things.

THE CONSECRATION OF PLACES, GROUND, CIRCLE, ETC

THEREFORE when you would consecrate any place or circle, you should take the prayer of Solomon used in the dedication and consecration of the temple; you must likewise bless the place by sprinkling with holy water and with suffumigations, and commemorate in the benediction holy mysteries; such as these, the sanctification of the throne of God, of Mount Sinai, of the tabernacle of the covenant, of the holy of holies, of the temple of Jerusalem; also the sanctification of Mount Golgotha, by the crucifixion of Christ; the sanctification of the temple of Christ; of Mount Tabor, by the transfiguration and ascension of Christ, &c. And by, invoking all divine names which are significant to this; such as the place of God, the throne of God, the chair of God, the tabernacle of God, the altar of God, the habitation of God, and the like divine names of this sort, which are to be written about the circle, or place to be consecrated.

And, in the consecration of instruments, and every other thing that is used in this art, you must proceed after the same manner, by sprinkling with holy water the same, by fumigation, by anointing with holy oil, sealing it with some holy seal, and blessing it with prayer, and by commemorating holy things out of the sacred Scriptures, collecting divine names which are agreeable to the things to be consecrated; as for example, in the consecration of the sword we are to remember in the gospel, "he that hath two coats," &c. and that in the second of the Maccabees, it is said that a sword was divinely and miraculously sent to Judas Maccabeus; and if there is any thing of the like in the prophets, as "take unto you two-edged swords," &c. And you shall also, in the same manner, consecrate experiments and books, and whatever of the like nature, as writings, pictures, &c. by sprinkling, perfuming, anointing, scaling, blessing, with holy commemorations, and calling to remembrance the sanctification of mysteries; as the table of the ten commandments, which were delivered to Moses by God in mount Sinai, the sanctification of the Old and New Testaments, and likewise of the law, prophets, and Scriptures, which were promulgated by the Holy Ghost: and again, there are to be mentioned such divine names as are convenient to this; as these are, viz. the testament of God, the book of God, the book of life, the knowledge of God, the wisdom of God, and the like. And with such kind of rites as these is the personal consecration performed.

There are beside these another rite of consecration of great power and efficacy; and this is one of the kinds of superstition, viz. when the rite of consecration or collection of any sacrament in the church is transferred to that thing which we would consecrate.

It must be noted that vows, oblations, and sacrifices, have the power of consecration also, as well real as personal; and they are, as it were, certain conventions between those names with which they are made and us who make them, strongly cleaving to our desire and wished effects, as when we sacrifice with certain names., or things; as fumigations, unctions, rings, images, mirrors; and some things less material, as characters, seals, pentacles, enchantments, orations, pictures, Scriptures, of which we have largely spoken before.

OF THE INVOCATION OF EVIL SPIRITS, AND THE BINDING, OF, AND CONSTRAINING OF THEM TO APPEAR

NOW, if thou art desirous of binding any spirit to a ready obedience to thee, we will shew you how a certain book may be made by which they may be invoked; and this book is to be consecrated a book of Evil Spirits, ceremoniously to be composed in their name and order, whereunto they bind with a certain holy oath, the ready and present obedience of the spirit. This book is therefore to be made of the most pure and clean paper, which is generally called virgin paper; and this book must be inscribed after this manner, viz. let there be drawn on the left side of the book the image of the spirit, and on the right side thereof his character, with the oath above it, containing the name of the spirit, his dignity and place, with his office and power. Yet many magicians do compose this book otherwise, omitting the characters and images; but I think that it is much more efficacious not to neglect any thing above mentioned in the forms.

There is likewise to be observed the circumstances of places, times, hours, according to the stars which these spirits are under, and are seen to agree to; with their site, rite, and order, being applied.

Which book being so written, is to be well bound, adorned, garnished, embellished and kept secure, with registers and seals, lest it should happen after the consecration to open in some part not designed, and endanger the operator. And, above all, let this book be kept as pure and reverent as possible; for irreverence of mind causes it to lose its virtue by pollution and prophanation.

Now this sacred book being thus composed according to the form and manner we have delivered, we are to consecrate it after a two-fold way; the first is, that all and singularly each of the spirits who are written in the book be called to the circle, according to the rites magical, which we have before taught, and place the book which is to be consecrated in a triangle on the outside of the circle; then read, in the presence of the spirits, all the oaths which are contained and written in that book; then the book to be consecrated being already placed without the circle in a triangle there drawn, compel all the spirits to impose their hands where their images and characters are drawn, and to confirm and consecrate the same with a special and common oath. This being done, let the book be shut and preserved as we have spoken before; then licence the spirits to depart according to due rite and magical order.

There is another method extant among us of consecrating a general book of spirits which is more easy, and of as much efficacy to produce every effect, except that in opening this book, the spirits do not always appear visible. And this way is thus: let be made a book of spirits, as we have before shewn, but in the end thereof write invocations, bonds, and strong conjurations, wherewith every spirit may be bound; then bind this book between two lamens or tables, and on the inside thereof draw or let be drawn two holy pentacles of the divine Majesty, which we have before set forth, out of the Apocalypse. Then let the first of them be placed in the beginning, of the book, and the second at the end of the same.

This book being thus perfected, let it be brought, in a clear and fair night, to a circle prepared in a cross-way, according to the art which we have before delivered; and there, in the first place, the book is to be opened, and to be consecrated according to the rites and ways which we have before delivered concerning consecration, which being done, let all the spirits be called which are written in the book, in their own order and place, conjuring them thrice by the bonds described in the book that they come to that place within the space of three days, to assure their obedience and confirm the same, to the book so to be consecrated; then let the book be wrapped up in a clean linen cloth, and bury it in the midst of the circle, and stop the hole so as it may not be perceived or discovered: the circle being destroyed after you have licensed the spirits, depart before sun-rise; and on the third day, about the middle of the night, return and make the circle anew and on thy knees make prayer unto God, and give thanks to him; and let a precious perfume be made, open the hole in which you buried your book and take it out, and so let it be kept, not opening the same. Then after licensing the spirits in their, order and destroying the circle, depart before sunrise. And this is the last rite and manner of consecrating, profitable to whatever writings, experiments, &c. that direct the spirits, placing the same between two holy lamens or pentacles, as is before mentioned.

But when the operator would work by the book thus consecrated he should do it in a fair and clear season, when the spirits are least troubled; and let him turn himself towards the region of the spirits; then let him open the book under a due register, and likewise invoke the spirits by their oaths there described and confirmed, and by the name of their character and image, to whatever purpose you desire, and if there be need conjure them by the bonds placed in the end of the book.[92:1] And having attained thy desired effect license them to depart.

And now we proceed to speak of the Invocation of good as well as bad Spirits.

The good spirits may be invocated of us, or by us, divers ways, and they in sundry shapes and manners offer themselves to us, for they openly speak to those that watch, and do offer themselves to our sight, or do inform us by dreams and by oracle of those things which we have a great desire to know. Whoever therefore would call any good spirit to speak or appear in sight, he must particularly observe two things; one whereof is about the disposition of the invocant, the other concerning those things which are outwardly to be adhibited to the invocation for the conformity of the spirit to be called.

It is necessary therefore that the invocant religiously dispose himself for the space of many days to such a mystery, and to conserve himself during the time chaste, abstinent, and to abstract himself as much as he can from all manner of foreign and secular business; likewise he should observe fasting, as much as shall seem convenient to him, and let him daily, between sun-rising and setting, being clothed in pure white linen, seven times call upon God, and make a deprecation to the angels to be called and invocated, according to the rule which we have before taught. Now the number of days of fasting and preparation is commonly one month, i. e. the time of a whole lunation. Now, in the Cabala, we generally prepare ourselves forty days before.

Now concerning the place, it must be chosen clean, pure, close, quiet, free from all manner of noise, and not subject to any stranger's sight. This place must first of all be exorcised and consecrated; and let there be a table or altar placed therein, covered with a clean white linen cloth, and set towards the east: and on each side thereof place two consecrated wax-lights burning, the flame thereof ought not to go out all these days. In the middle of the altar let there be placed lamens, or the holy paper we have before described, covered with fine linen, which is not to be opened until the end of the days of consecration. You shall also have in readiness a precious perfume and a pure anointing oil.--And let them both be kept consecrated. Then set a sensor on the head of the altar, wherein you shalt kindle the holy fire, and make a precious perfume every day that you pray.

Now for your habit, you shall have a long garment of white linen, close before and behind, which may come down quite over the feet, and gird yourself about the loins with a girdle. You shall likewise have a veil made of pure white linen on which must be wrote in a gilt lamen, the name Tetragrammaton; all which things are to be consecrated and sanctified in order. But you must not go into this holy place till it be first washed and covered with a cloth new and clean, and then you may enter, but with your feet naked and bare; and when you enter therein you shall sprinkle with holy water, then make a perfume upon the altar; and then on thy knees pray before the altar as we have directed.

Now when the time is expired, on the last day, you shall fast more strictly; and fasting on the day following, at the rising of the sun, enter the holy place, using the ceremonies before spoken of, first by sprinkling thyself, then, making a perfume, you shall sign the cross with holy oil in the forehead, and anoint your eyes, using prayer in all these consecrations. Then, open the lamen and pray before the altar upon your knees; and then ail invocation may be made as follows:

92:1 I have given an example of the book of spirits, by which you may see the method in which the characters, &c. are placed as above described. See the Plate.

AN INVOCATION OF THE GOOD SPIRITS

IN the name of the blessed and Holy Trinity, I do desire thee, strong, and mighty angels (here name the spirits you would have appear) that if it be the divine will of him who is called Tetragrammaton, &c. the holy God, the Father, that thou take upon thee some shape as best becometh thy celestial nature, and appear to us visibly here in this place, and answer our demands, in as far as we shall not transgress the bounds of the divine mercy and goodness, by requesting unlawful knowledge; but that thou wilt graciously shew us what things are most profitable for us to know and do to the glory and honour of his divine Majesty who liveth and reigneth, world without end. Amen.

Lord thy will be done on earth as it is in heaven--make clean our hearts within us, and take not thy holy spirit from us. O Lord, by thy name we have called them, suffer them to administer unto us.

And that all things may work together for thy honour and glory, to whom with thee, the Son and blessed Spirit, be ascribed all might, majesty, and dominion world without end. Amen.

THE PARTICULAR FORM OF THE LAMEN

THE invocation being made, the good angels will appear unto you which you desire, which you shall entertain with a chaste communication, and licence them to depart.

Now the lamen which is used to invoke any good spirit must be made after the following manner: either in metal conformable or in new wax mixed with convenient spices and colours; or it may be made with pure white paper with convenient colours, and the outward form of it may be either square, circular, or triangular, or of the like sort, according to the rule of the numbers, in which there must be written the divine names, as well general as special. And in the centre of the lamen draw a hexagon or character of six corners, in the middle thereof write the name and character of the star, or of the spirit his governor, to whom the good spirit that is to be called is subject. And about this character let there be placed so many characters of five corners or pentacles as the spirits we would call together at once. But if we should call only one, nevertheless there must be made four pentagons, wherein the name of the spirit or spirits, with their characters, are to be written. Now this lamen ought to be composed when the moon is in her increase, on those days and hours which agree to the spirit; and if we take a fortunate planet therewith, it will be the better for the producing the effect: which table or lamen being rightly made in the manner we have fully described, must be consecrated according to the rules above delivered.

And this is the way of making the general table or lamen for the invocating of all spirits whatever; the form whereof you may see in the Plates of pentacles, seals, and lamens.

Nevertheless, we make special tables congruent to every spirit by the rule which we have above spoken concerning holy pentacles.

We will yet declare unto you another rite more easy to perform this thing: let the man who wishes to receive an oracle from a spirit be chaste, pure, and sanctified;

320

then a place being chosen pure, clean, and covered every where with clean and white linen, on the Lord's-day in the new of the moon, let him enter into that place clothed with white linen; let him exorcise the place, bless it, and make a circle therein with a consecrated

coal; let there be written in the outer part of the circle the names of the angels; in the inner part thereof write the mighty names of God; and let be placed within the circle, at the four parts of the world, the vessels for the perfumes. Then, being washed and fasting, let him enter the place and pray towards the east this whole Psalm, "Blessed are the undefiled in the way," &c. Psalm cxix. Then make a fumigation, and deprecate the angels by the said divine names, that they will appear unto you, and reveal or discover that which you so earnestly desire; and do this continually for six days, washed and fasting. On the seventh day, being washed and fasting, enter the circle, perfume it, and anoint thyself with holy oil upon the forehead, eyes, and in the palms of both hands, and upon the feet; then, with bended knees, say the Psalm aforesaid, with divine and angelical names. Which being said, arise, and walk round the circle from East to West, until thou shalt be wearied with a giddiness of thy head and brain, then straitway fall down in the circle, where thou mayest rest, and thou wilt be wrapped up in an ecstasy; and a spirit will appear and inform thee of all things necessary to be known. We must observe also, that in the circle there ought to be four holy candles burning at the four parts of the world, which ought not to want light for the space of a week.

And the manner of fasting is this: to abstain from all things having a life of sense, and from those which do proceed from them, let him drink only pure running water; neither is there any food or wine to be taken till the going down of the sun.

Let the perfume and the holy anointing oil be made as is set forth in Exodus, and other holy books of the Bible. It is also to be observed, that as often as he enters the circle he has upon his forehead a golden lamen, upon which there must be written the name Tetragrammaton, in the manner we have before mentioned.

OF ORACLES BY DREAMS

BUT natural things and their own commixtures do likewise belong unto magicians, and we often use such to receive oracles from a spirit by a dream; which are either by perfumes, unctions, meats, drinks, seals, rings, &c.

Now those who are desirous to receive oracles in or through a dream, let him make himself a ring of the sun or Saturn for this purpose. There are likewise images of dreams, which, being put under the head when he goes to sleep, doth effectually give true dreams of whatever the mind hath before determined or consulted upon, the practice of which is as follows:

Thou shalt make an image of the sun, the figure whereof must be, a man sleeping upon the bosom of an angel, which thou shalt make when Leo ascends, the sun being in the ninth house in Aries; thou shalt write upon the figure the name of the effect desired, and in the hand of the angel the name of the intelligence of the sun. Let the same image be made in Virgo ascending, Mercury being fortunate in Aries in the ninth; or Gemini ascending, Mercury being fortunate in the ninth house in Aquarius; and let it be received with Saturn with a fortunate aspect, and let the name of the spirit be written upon it. Let the same likewise be made in Libra ascending, Venus being received from Mercury in Gemini in the ninth house, and write upon it the angel of Venus. Again, you may make the same image Aquarius ascending, Saturn fortunately possessing the ninth in his exaltation, which is Libra; and let there be written upon it the angel of Saturn. The same may be made Cancer ascending, the moon being received by Jupiter and Venus in Pisces, and being fortunately placed in the ninth house, and write upon it the spirit of the moon.

There are likewise made rings of dreams of wonderful efficacy; and there are rings of the sun and Saturn; and the constellation of them is when the sun or Saturn ascend in their exaltations in the ninth, and when the moon is joined to Saturn in the ninth, and in that sign which was the ninth house of the nativity; and write and engrave upon the rings the name of the spirit of the sun or Saturn; and by these rules you may know how and by what means to constitute more of thyself: but know this, that such images work nothing (as they are simply images) unless they are vivified by a spiritual and celestial virtue, and chiefly by the ardent desire and firm intent of the soul of the operator. But who can give a soul to an image, or make a stone, or metal, or clay, or wood, or wax, or paper to live? certainly no man; (for this arcanum doth not enter into an artist of a stiff neck,) he only hath it who transcends the progress of angels, and comes to the very architype himself.

The tables of numbers likewise confer to the receiving of oracles, being duly formed under their own constellations. Holy tables and papers likewise serve to this effect, being especially composed and consecrated; such as the Almutel of Solomon, and the Table of the Revolution of the name Tetragrammaton; and those things which are of this kind, and written to produce these effects, out of various figures, numbers, holy Scriptures, and pictures, with inscriptions of the divine names of God and names of holy angels; the composition whereof is taken out of diverse places of the holy Scriptures, Psalms, and versicles, and other certain promises out of the divine revelations and prophecies. To the same effect do conduce, likewise, holy prayers and deprecations as well to God as to the blessed angels; the deprecations of which prayers are to be composed, as we have before shewn, according to some religious similitude, making mention of those things which we intend to do; as out of the Old Testament of the dream of Jacob, Joseph, Pharaoh, Daniel, and Nebuchadnezzar: if out of the New Testament, of the dream of Joseph; of the three wise men, or magi, of John the evangelist sleeping upon the breast of our Lord; and whatever of the like kind can be found in religion, miracles, and revelation. According to which the deprecation may be composed; if when he goes to sleep it be with a firm intention, and then, without doubt, they will afford a wonderful effect.

Therefore he who is desirous of receiving true oracles by dreams, let him abstain from supper, from drink, and be otherwise well disposed, so his brain will be free from turbulent vapours; let him also have his bed- chamber fair and clean, exorcised and consecrated if he will; then let him perfume the same with some convenient fumigation, and let him anoint his temples with some unguent efficacious hereunto, and put a ring of dreams upon his finger; then let him take one of the images we have spoken of, or some holy table, or paper, and place the same under his head; then, having made a devout prayer, let him address himself to sleep, meditating upon that thing which he desires to know; so shall he receive a most certain and undoubted oracle by a dream, when the moon goes through that sign which was in the ninth house of his nativity, and also when she goes through the sign of the ninth of the revolution of his nativity, and when she is in the ninth sign from the sign of perfection.

This is the way whereby we may obtain all sciences and arts whatsoever, whether alchemy, magic, or else, suddenly and perfectly with a true illumination of our intellect; although all inferior familiar spirits whatsoever conduce to this effect, and sometimes also evil spirits sensibly inform us intrinsically and extrinsically.

OF THE METHOD OF RAISING EVIL OR FAMILIAR SPIRITS...

Of the Method of raising EVIL or FAMILIAR SPIRITS by a CIRCLE; likewise the Souls and Shadows of the Dead.

IT is here convenient that we say something about the means used by exorcists to raise up what are usually termed evil spirits to the circle, and, the methods of calling up the ghosts or souls of those who have died a violent or premature death.

Now, if any one would call any evil spirit to the circle, he must first consider and know his nature, and to which of the planets it agrees, and what offices are distributed unto him from the planet. This being known, let there be sought out a place fit and convenient, and proper for his invocation, according to the nature of the planet and the quality of the offices of the same spirit, as near as it can be done; as if their power be over the sea, rivers or floods, then let the place be the sea-shore, and so of the rest. Then chuse a convenient time both for the quality of the air (being serene, quiet, clear and fitting for the spirits to assume bodies); as also of the quality of and nature of the planet and the spirit, as on his day and time in which he rules; he may be fortunate or unfortunate sometimes of the day, and sometimes of the night, as the stars and spirits do require.

These things being judiciously considered, let the circle be made at the place elected, as well for the defence of the invocant as the confirmation of the spirit. And in the circle write the divine general names, and all those things which do yield defence to us; and, with them, those divine names which do rule his planet, and the offices of the spirit himself; likewise write therein the names of the good spirits which bear rule in the time you do this, and are able to bind and constrain that spirit which we intend to call. And if we will further strengthen and fortify our circle, we may add characters and pentacles agreeing to the work; then also, if we will, we may either, within or without the circle, frame an angular figure with the inscription of such convenient numbers as are congruent amongst themselves to our work, which are to be known according to the manner of numbers and figures delivered in our first Book.

Further we are to be provided with lights, perfumes, unguents, and medicines, compounded according to the nature of the spirit and planet which agree with the spirit by reason of their natural and celestial virtue.

Then we are to be furnished with holy and consecrated things necessary, not only for the defence of the invocant and his companions, but also serving for bonds to bind and constrain the spirits; such as holy papers, lamens, pictures, pentacles, swords, scepters, garments of convenient colour and matter.

Then, with all these things provided, let the exorcist and his companions go into the circle. In the first place, let him consecrate the circle and every thing he uses; which being done in a solemn and firm manner, with convenient gesture and countenance, let him begin to pray with a loud voice after the manner following. First, by making an oration or prayer to God, and then intreating the good spirits; but we should read some prayer, or psalm, or gospel, for our defence in the first place. After those prayers and orations are said, let him begin to invocate the spirit which he desireth, with a gentle and loving enchantment to all the coasts of the world, with a commemoration of his own authority and power.

Then rest and look round to see if any spirit does appear; which if he delays, then let him repeat his invocation, as above said, until he hath done it three times; and if the spirit is obstinate and will not appear, then let the invocator begin to conjure him with divine power; but so that all his conjurations and commemorations do agree with the nature and office of the spirit, and reiterate the same three times, from stronger to stronger, using contumelies, cursings, punishments, suspension from his power and office, and the like.

And after these courses are finished, cease; and if the spirit shall appear, let the invocant turn himself towards the spirit, and courteously receive him, and, earnestly entreating him, let him ask his name, which write down on your holy paper, and then proceed by asking him whatsoever you will; and if in any thing the spirit shall appear to be obstinate, ambiguous, or lying, let him be bound by convenient conjurations; and if you doubt any thing, make, without the circle with the consecrated sword, the figure of a triangle or pentagon, and compel the spirit to enter into it; and if you receive any promise which you would have confirmed with an oath, stretch the sword out of the circle, and swear the spirit by laying his hand on the sword. Then having obtained of the spirit that which you desire, or are otherwise contented, license him to depart with courteous words, giving command that he do no hurt; and if he will not depart, compel him by powerful conjurations; and if need require expel him by exorcisms and by making contrary suffumigations. And when he is departed, go not out of the circle, but make a stay, and use some prayer giving thanks to God and the good angels; and also praying for your future defence and conservation, which being orderly performed you may depart.

But if your hopes are frustrated, and no spirit will appear, yet for this you need not despair; but leaving the circle after licensing to depart (which must never be omitted whether a spirit appears or not [101:1],) return at other times, doing as before. And if you think that you have erred in any thing, then you shall amend by adding or diminishing; for the constancy of repetition encreases your authority and power, and strikes a terror into the spirits, and compels them to obey.

And often the spirits do come although they appear not visible (to cause terror to him who calls them,) either in the thing which he uses, or else in the operation itself. But this kind of licensing is not given simply, but by a kind of dispensation, with suspension, until they shall render themselves obedient: also, without a circle, these spirits may be called to appear, by the way we have delivered in the consecration of a book. But when we intend to execute any effect where an apparition is not needful, then that is to be done, by making and forming that which is to be to us an instrument; as whether it be an image, ring, character, table, writing, candle, sacrifice, or any thing else; then the name of the spirit is to be written therein with his character, according to the exigency of the experiment, either by writing it with blood, or otherwise using a perfume agreeable to the spirit. Likewise we are often to make orations and prayers to God and the good angels before we invoke any evil spirit, conjuring him by divine power.

In some former parts of our work we have taught how and by what means the soul is joined to the body.

We will in this place inform thee farther, that those souls do still love their relinquished bodies after death, a certain affinity alluring them as it were. Such are the souls of noxious men who have violently relinquished their bodies, and souls wanting a due burial, which still wander in a liquid and turbulent spirit about their dead carcasses; but these souls, by the known means by which they were joined to their bodies, by the like vapours, liquors, and savours, are easily drawn into them.

Hence it is that the souls of the dead are not to be called up without blood or by the application of some part of their relict body.

In the raising therefore of these shadows, we are to perfume with new blood the bones of the dead, and with flesh, eggs, milk, honey, and oil, which furnish the soul with a medium apt to receive its body.

It is likewise to be understood, those who are desirous to raise any souls of the dead, ought to select those places wherein these kind of souls are most known to be conversant; or by some alliance alluring the souls into their forsaken bodies, or by some kind of affection in times past impressed in them in their life, drawing the souls to certain places, things, or persons; or by the forcible nature of some place fitted and prepared to purge or punish these souls: which places for the most part, are to be known by the appearance of visions, nightly incursions, and apparitions.

Therefore the places most fitting for these things are church-yards. And better than them are those places devoted to the executions of criminal judgements; and better than these are those places where, of late years, there have been so great and so many public slaughters of men; and that place is still better than those where some dead carcass that came by violent death is not yet expiated, nor was lately buried; for the expiation of those places is likewise a holy rite duly to be adhibited to the burial of the bodies, and often prohibits the soul returning to its body, and expels the same afar off to the place of judgment.

And from hence it is that the souls of the dead are not easy to be raised up, except it be the souls of them whom we know to be evil, or to have perished by a violent death, and whose bodies do want the rite of due burial.

Now although we have spoken concerning such places of this kind, it will not be safe or commodious to go unto them; but it is requisite for us to take to whatsoever place is to be chosen some principal relict of the body, and therewith make a perfume in due manner, and to perform other competent rites.

It is also to be known, that because the souls are certain spiritual lights, therefore artificial lights framed out of certain competent things, compounded according to a true rule, with congruent inscriptions of names and seals, do very much avail to the raising up of departed souls. But those things which are now spoken of are not always sufficient to raise up souls, because of an extra-natural portion of understanding and reason, which is above and known only to the heavenly destinies and their powers.

We should therefore allure the said souls by supernatural and celestial powers duly administered, even by those things which do move the very harmony of the soul, as well imaginative as rational and intellectual, such as voices, Songs, sounds, enchantments; and religious things, as Prayers, conjurations, exorcisms, and other holy rites, which may commodiously be administered hereunto.

END OF PART SECOND

101:1 They who neglect licensing the spirits are in very great danger, because instances have been known of the operator experiencing sudden death.

OF THE PARTICULAR COMPOSITION OF THE MAGICAL CIRCLE

EXORCISMS, BENEDICTIONS, AND THE CONJURATIONS

THE following instructions are the principal and sum total of all we have said, only we have brought it rather into a closer train of experiment and practice than any of the rest; for here you may behold the distinct functions of the spirits; likewise the whole perfection of magical ceremonies is here described, syllable by syllable.

But as the greatest power is attributed to the circles, (for they are certain fortresses,) we will now clearly explain, and shew the composition and figure of a circle.

A Table shewing the names of the Angels governing the 7 days of the week, with their Sigils, Planets, Signs, &c.

Sunday	Monday	Tuesday	Wednesday	Thursday	Friday	Saturday
Michael	Gabriel	Camael	Raphaël	Sachiel	Anaël	Caffiel
☉ ♌	☽ ♋	♂ ♈ ♏	☿ ♎ ♍	♃ ♐ ♓	♀ ♉ ♎	♄ ♑ ♒
Machen.	Shamain.	Machon.	Raquie.	Zebul.	Sagun.	

The Composition of the CIRCLE.--(For the figure of the Circle see the Plate.)

The forms of circles are not always one and the same, but are changed according to the order of spirits that are to be called, their places, times, days, and hours; for in making a circle it ought to be considered in what time of the year, what day, and what hour, what spirits you would call, and to what star or region they belong, and what functions they have: therefore, to begin, let there be made three circles of the latitude of nine feet, distant one from another about a hand's breadth. First, write in the middle circle the name of the hour wherein you do the work; in the second place, write the name of the angel of the hour; in the third place, the seal of the angel of the hour; fourthly, the name of the angel that rules the day in which you work, and the names of his ministers; in the fifth place, the name of the present time; sixthly, the name of the spirits ruling in that part of time, and their presidents; seventhly, the name of the head of the sign ruling in the time; eighthly, the name of the earth, according to the time of working; ninthly, and for the compleating of the middle circle, write the name of the sun and moon, according to the said rule of time: for as the times are changed, so are the names: and in the outer circle let there be drawn, in the four angles, the names of the great presidential spirits of the air that day wherein you would do this work, viz. the name of the king and his three ministers. Without the circle, in four angles, let pentagons be made. In the inner circle write four divine names, with four crosses interposed: in the middle of the circle, viz. towards the east let be written Alpha; towards the west, Omega; and let a cross divide the middle of the circle.

When the circle is thus finished, according to rule, you shall proceed to consecrate and bless it, saying,

In the name of the holy, blessed, and glorious Trinity, proceed we to our work in these mysteries to accomplish that which we desire; we therefore, in the names aforesaid, consecrate this piece of ground for our defence, so that no spirit whatsoever shall be able to break these boundaries, neither be able to cause injury nor detriment to any of us here assembled; but that they may be compelled to stand before this circle, and answer truly our demands, so far as it pleaseth Him who liveth for ever and ever; and who says, I am Alpha and Omega, the Beginning and the End, which is, and which was, and which is to come, the Almighty; I am the First and the Last, who am living and was dead; and behold I live for ever and ever; and I have the keys of death and hell. Bless, O Lord! this creature of earth wherein we stand; confirm, O God! thy strength in us, so that neither the adversary nor any evil thing may cause us to fail, through the merits of Jesus Christ. Amen.

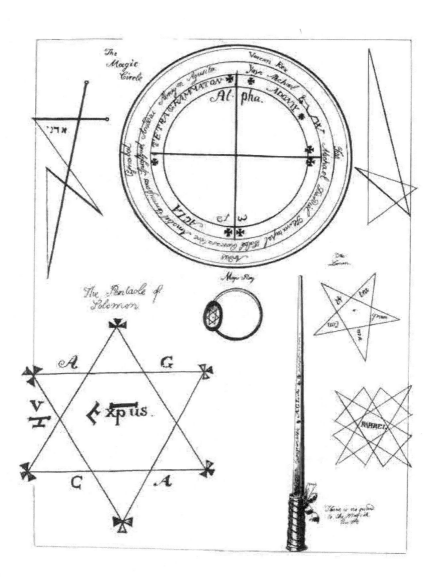

It is also to be known that the angels rule the hours in a successive order, according to the course of the heavens and the planets to which they are subject;

so the same spirit which governeth the day rules also the first hour of the day; the second from this governs the second hour, and so on throughout; and when seven planets and hours have made their revolution it returns again to the first which rules the day. Therefore we shall first speak of the names of the hours, viz.

A TABLE shewing the MAGICAL NAMES of the HOURS, both DAY and NIGHT.

	Names of Hours of the Day.		Names of Hours of the Night.
1	Yain	1	Beron
2	Janor	2	Barol
3	Nasnia	3	Thami
4	Salla	4	Athar
5	Sadedali	5	Methon
6	Thamur	6	Rana
7	Ourer	7	Netos
8	Thamic	8	Tafrac
9	Neron	9	Sassur
10	Jayon	10	Agle
11	Abai	11	Calerva
12	Natalon.	12	Salam

Of the names of the angels and their seals it shall be spoken in their proper places; but here we will shew the names of the times.

A year therefore is four--fold, and is divided into spring, summer, autumn, and winter; the names thereof are these: The spring, Talvi; the summer, Casmaran; autumn, Adarcel; winter, Farlas.

The ANGELS of the SPRING--Caracasa, Core, Amatiel, Commissoros. The head of the sign in spring is called Spugliguel.
The name of the earth in spring, Amadai.
The names of the sun and moon in spring: sun, Abraym; moon, Agusita.

The ANGELS of the SUMMER--Gargatel, Tariel, Gaviel. The head of the sign of the summer, Tubiel.
The name of the earth in summer, Festativi.
The names of the sun and moon in summer: sun, Athemay; moon, Armatus.

The ANGELS of the AUTUMN--Tarquam, Guabarel. The head of the sign of autumn, Torquaret.
The name of the earth in autumn, Rabinnara.
The names of the sun and moon in autumn: the sun, Abragini, the moon, Matasignais.

The ANGELS of the WINTER--Amabael, Cetarari.
The head of the sign of winter, Attarib. The name of the earth in winter, Geremiah.
The names of the sun and moon in winter: the sun, Commutoff; the moon, Affaterim.

These things being known, finish the consecration of the circle by saying,

"Thou shalt purge me with hysop, O Lord, and I shall be clean: thou shalt wash me and I shall be whiter than snow."
Then sprinkle the same with holy water, and proceed with the benediction of the perfumes.

BENEDICTION of PERFUMES.

THE God of Abraham, God of Isaac, God of Jacob, bless here the creatures of these kinds, that they may fill up the power and virtue of their odours; so that neither the enemy nor any false imagination may be able to enter into them; through our Lord Jesus Christ, &c. Then sprinkle the same with holy water.

The EXORCISM of FIRE into which the PERFUMES are to be put.

I EXORCISE thee, O thou creature of fire, by the only true God Jehovah, Adonai, Tetragrammaton, that forthwith thou cast away every phantasm from thee, that it shall do no hurt to any one. We beseech thee, O Lord, to bless this creature of fire, and sanctify it, so that it may be blessed to set forth the praise and glory of thy holy name, and that no hurt may be permitted to come to the exorciser or spectators; through our Lord Jesus Christ. Amen.

Of the HABIT of the EXORCIST.

IT should be made, as we have before described, of fine white linen and clean, and to come round the body loose, but close before and behind.

Of the PENTACLE of SOLOMON.--(For the fig. see the Plate.)

IT is always necessary to have this pentacle in readiness to bind with, in case the spirits should refuse to be obedient, as they can have no power over the exorcist while provided with and fortified by the pentacle, the virtue of the holy names therein written presiding with wonderful influence over the spirits.

It should be made in the day and hour of Mercury upon parchment made of a kidskin, or virgin, or pure, clean, white paper; and the figures and letters wrote in pure gold; and it ought to be consecrated and sprinkled (as before often spoken) with holy water.

When the vesture is put on, it will be convenient to say the following oration:

An ORATION when the HABIT or VESTURE is put on.

ANOOR, Amacor, Amides, Theodonias, Anitor; by the merits of the angels, O Lord! I will put on the garment of salvation, that this which I desire I may bring to effect, through thee, the most holy Adonai, whose kingdom endureth for ever and ever. Amen.

The Manner of Working.

LET the moon be increasing and equal, if it can then be conveniently done; but especially let her not be combust, or in Via Combusta, which is between fourteen degrees of Libra and fourteen degrees of Scorpio.

The operator ought to be clean and purified for nine days before he does the work. Let him have ready the perfume appropriated to the day wherein he does the work; and he must be provided with holy water from a clergyman, or he may make it holy himself, by reading over it the consecration of water of baptism; he must have a new vessel of earth, with fire, the vesture, and the pentacle; and let all these things be rightly and duly consecrated and prepared. Let one of the companions carry the vessel with fire, and the perfumes, and let another bear the book, the garment, and pentacle; and let the operator himself carry the sword, over which should be said a prayer of consecration: and on the middle of the sword on one side let there be engraven Agla ✠, and on the other side, ✠ On, ✠ Tetragrammaton ✠. And the place being fixed upon where the circle is to be erected, let him draw the lines we have before taught, and sprinkle the same with holy water, consecrating, &c. &c.

The operator ought therefore to be prepared with fasting, chastity, and abstinence, for the space of three days before the day of operation; and on the day that he would do this work, being clothed with the fore- mentioned vesture, and furnished with pentacles, perfumes, a sword, bible, paper, pen, and consecrated ink, and all things necessary hereunto, let him enter the circle, and call the angels from the four parts of the world which do rule the seven planets, the seven days of the week, colours, and metals, whose names you will see in their places; and, with bended knees, first let him say the Paternoster or Lord's Prayer, and then let him invoke the said angels, saying,

O angeli! supradicti estote adjutores mihi petitioni & in adjutorum mihi, in meis rebus et petitionibus.

Then call the angels from the four parts of the world that rule the air the same day in which he makes the experiment; and, having employed especially all the names and spirits within the circle, say,

O vos omnes, adjutore atque contestor per sedem Adonai, per Hagios, Theos, Ischyros, Athanatos, Paracletos, Alpha & Omega, & per hæc tria nomina secreta, Agla, On, Tetragrammaton, quod hodie debeatis adimplere quod cupio.

These things being performed, let him read the conjuration assigned for the day; but if they shall be pertinacious or refractory, and will not yield themselves obedient, neither to the conjuration assigned for the day, nor any of the prayers before made, then use the exorcism following:

A GENERAL EXORCISM of the SPIRITS of the AIR.

WE being made after the image of God, endued with power from God and made after his will, do exorcise you, by the most mighty and powerful name of God, El, strong and wonderful, (here name the spirit which is to appear,) and we command you by Him who spoke the word and it was done, and by all the names of God, and by the name Adonai, El, Elohim, Elohe, Zebaoth, Elion, Eserchie, Jah, Tetragrammaton, Sadai, Lord God Most High: we exorcise you, and powerfully command you that you forthwith appear unto us here before this circle in a fair human shape, without any deformity or tortuosity; come ye all such, because we command you by the name Yaw and Vau, which Adam heard and spoke; and by the name of God, Agla, which Lot heard, and was saved with his family; and by the name Joth, which Jacob heard from the angel wrestling with him, and was delivered from the hand of his brother Esau; and by the name Anaphexeton, which Aaron heard and spoke, and was made wise; and by the name Zebaoth, which Moses named, and all the rivers were turned into blood; and by the name Eserchie Oriston, which Moses named, and all the rivers brought forth frogs, and they ascended into the houses of the Egyptians, destroying all things; and by the name Elion, which Moses named, and there was great hail, such as had not been since the beginning of the world; and by the name Adonai, which Moses named, and there came up locusts, which appeared upon the whole land of Egypt, and devoured all which the hail had left; and by the name Schema Amathia, which Joshua called upon, and the sun stayed his course; and by the name Alpha and Omega, which Daniel named, and destroyed Bel and slew the dragon; and in the name Emmanuel, which the three children, Sidrach, Misach, and Abednego, sung in the midst of the fiery furnace, and were delivered; and by the name Hagios; and by the seal of Adonai; and by Ischyros, Athanatos, Paracletos; and by these three secret names, Agla, On, Tetragrammaton, I do adjure and contest you; and by these names, and by all the other names of the living and true God, our Lord Almighty, I exorcise and command you, by Him who spoke the word and it was done, to whom all creatures are obedient; and by the dreadful judgment of God; and by the uncertain sea of glass, which is before the divine Majesty, mighty and powerful; by the four beasts before the throne, having eyes before and behind; and by the fire round about his throne; and by the holy angels of heaven; by the mighty wisdom of God, we do powerfully exorcise you, that you appear here before this circle, to fulfil our will in all things which shall seem good unto us; by the seal of Baldachia, and by this name Primeumaton, which Moses named, and the earth opened and swallowed up Corah, Dathan, and Abiram: and in the power of that name Primeumaton, commanding the whole host of heaven, we curse you, and deprive you of your office, joy, and place, and do bind you in the depth of the bottomless pit, there to remain until the dreadful day of the last judgment; and we bind you into eternal fire, and into the lake of fire and brimstone, unless you forthwith appear before this circle to do our will therefore, come ye, by these names, Adonai, Zebaoth, Adonai, Amioram; come ye, come ye, come ye, Adonai commandeth; Saday, the most mighty King of Kings, whose power no creature is able to resist, be unto you most dreadful, unless ye obey, and forthwith affably appear before this circle, let miserable ruin and fire unquenchable remain with you; therefore come ye, in the name of Adonai, Zebaoth, Adonai, Amioram; come, come, why stay you? hasten! Adonai, Sadai, the King of Kings commands you: El, Aty, Titcip, Azia, Hin, Jen, Minosel, Achadan, Vay, Vaah, Ey, Exe, A, El, El, El, A, Hy, Hau, Hau, Hau, Vau, Vau, Vau, Vau.

A PRAYER to GOD, to be said in the four Parts of the WORLD in the CIRCLE.

AMORULE, Taneha, Latisten, Rabur, Teneba, Latisten, Escha, Aladia, Alpha and Omega, Leyste, Orision, Adonai; O most merciful heavenly Father! have mercy upon me, although a sinner; make appear the arm of thy power in me this day against these obstinate spirits, that 1, by thy will, may be made a contemplator of thy divine works, and may be illustrated with all wisdom, to the honour and glory of thy holy name. I humbly beseech thee, that these spirits which I call by thy judgment may be bound and constrained to come and give true and perfect answers to those things which I shall ask of them; and that they may do and declare those things unto us, which by me may be commanded of them, not hurting any creature, neither injuring or terrifying me or my fellows, nor hurting any other creature, and affrighting no man; and let them be obedient to those things which are required of them.

Then, standing in the middle of the circle, stretch out thy hand towards the pentacle, saying, By the pentacle of Solomon I have called you; give me a true answer.

Then follows this ORATION.

BERALANENSIS, Baldachiensis, Paumachia, and Apologia Sedes, by the most mighty kings and powers, and the most powerful princes, genii, Liachidæ,

341

ministers of the Tartarean seat, chief prince of the seat of Apologia, in the ninth legion, I invoke you, and by invocating, conjure you; and being armed with power from the supreme Majesty, I strongly command you, by Him who spoke and it was done, and to whom all creatures are obedient; and by this ineffable name, Tetragrammaton Jehovah, which being beard the elements are overthrown, the air is shaken, the sea runneth back, the fire is quenched, the earth trembles, and all the host of the celestials, and terrestrials, and infernals do tremble together, and are troubled and confounded: wherefore, forthwith and without delay, do you come from all parts of the world, and make rational answers unto all things I shall ask of you; and come ye peaceably, visibly and affably now, without delay, manifesting what we desire, being conjured by the name of the living and true God, Helioren, and fulfil our commands, and persist unto the end, and according to our intentions, visibly and affably speaking unto us with a clear voice, intelligible, and without any ambiguity.

Of the APPEARANCE of the SPIRITS.

THESE things being duly performed, there will appear infinite visions, apparitions, phantasms, &c. beating of drums, and the sound of all kinds of musical instruments; which is done by the spirits, that with the terror they might force some of the companions out of the circle, because they can effect nothing against the exorcist himself: after this you shall see an infinite company of archers, with a great multitude of horrible beasts, which will arrange themselves as if they would devour the companions; nevertheless, fear nothing.

Then the exorcist, holding the pentacle in his hand, let him say, Avoid hence these iniquities, by virtue of the banner of God. Then will the spirits be compelled to obey the exorcist, and the company shall see them no more.

Then let the exorcist, stretching out his hand with the pentacle, say, Behold the pentacle of Solomon, which I have brought into your presence; behold the person of the exorcist in the middle of the exorcism, who is armed by God, without fear, and well provided, who potently invocateth and calleth you by exorcising; come, therefore, with speed, by the virtue of these names; Aye Saraye, Aye Saraye; defer not to come, by the eternal names of the living and true God, Eloy, Archima, Rabur, and by the pentacle of Solomon here present, which powerfully reigns over you; and by the virtue of the celestial spirits, your lords; and by the person of the exorcist, in the middle of the exorcism: being conjured, make haste and come, and yield obedience to your master, who is called Octinomos. This being performed, immediately there will be hissings in the four parts of the world, and then immediately you shall see great motions; which when you see, say, Why stay you? Wherefore do you delay? What do you? Prepare yourselves to be obedient to your master in the name of the Lord, Bathat or Vachat rushing upon Abrac, Abeor coming upon Aberer.

Then they will immediately come in their proper forms; and when you see them before the circle, shew them the pentacle covered with fine linen; uncover it, and say, Behold your confusion if you refuse to be obedient; and suddenly they will appear in a peaceable form, and will say, Ask what you will, for we are prepared to fulfil all your commands, for the Lord hath subjected us hereunto.

Then let the exorcist say, Welcome spirits, or most noble princes, because I have called you through Him to whom every knee doth bow, both of things in heaven, and things in earth, and things under the earth; in whose hands are all the kingdoms of kings, neither is there any able to contradict his Majesty. Wherefore, I bind you, that you remain affable and visible before this circle, so long and so constant; neither shall you depart without my licence, until you have truly and without any fallacy performed my will, by virtue of his power who hath set the sea her bounds, beyond which it cannot pass, nor go beyond the law of his providence, viz. of the Most High God, Lord, and King, who hath created all things. Amen.

Then let the exorcist mention what he would have done.

After which say, In the name of the Father, and of the Son, and of the Holy Ghost, go in peace unto your places; peace be between us and you; be ye ready to come when you are called. (For the figures of the circle, pentacle, and other instruments, see the Plate.)

Now, that you may have an idea of the manner of composing the circle, we have given the scheme of one for the first hour of the Lord's day, in spring.

CONSIDERATIONS AND CONJURATIONS FOR EVERY DAY IN THE WEEK

Here follow the CONSIDERATIONS and CONJURATIONS for every Day in the Week; and first of

The CONSIDERATIONS, &c. of SUNDAY.

(For the figure of the seals, planets, signs, names of the angels of the several days, and names of the fourth heaven, with the characters and magic book, see the Plate.)

THE angels of the Lord's day--Michael, Dardiel, Huratapel.

The angels of the air ruling on the Lord's day, Varcan, king;--his ministers, Tus, Andas, Cynabal.

The wind which the angels of the air are said to rule, is the north wind.

The angels of the fourth heaven ruling on the Lord's day, which should be called from the four parts of the world, are,--east, Samael, Baciel, Abel, Gabriel, Vionatraba;--from the west, Anael, Pabel, Ustael, Burchat, Suceratos, Capabili;--from the north, Aiel, Ariel, vel Aquiel, Masgabriel, Saphiel, Matuyel,--at the south, Haludiel, Machasiel, Charsiel, Uriel, Naromiel.

The perfume of Sunday is Red Sanders.

The CONJURATION for SUNDAY.

I CONJURE and confirm upon you, ye strong and holy angels of God, in the name Adonai, Eye, Eye, Eya, which is he who was, and is, and is to come, Eye, Abray; and in the name Saday, Cados, Cados, sitting on high upon the cherubim;

and by the great name of God himself, strong and powerful, who is exalted above all the heavens; Eye, Saraye, who created the world, the heavens, the earth, the sea, and all that in them is, in the first day, and scaled them with his holy name Phaa; and by the name of the angels who rule in the fourth heaven, and serve before the most mighty Salamia, an angel great and honourable; and by the name of his star, which is Sol, and by his sign, and by the immense name of the living God, and by all the names aforesaid, I conjure thee, Michael, O great angel! who art chief ruler of this day; and by the name Adonai, the God of Israel, I conjure thee, O Michael! that thou labour for me, and fulfil all my petitions according to my will and desire in my cause and business.

The spirits of the air of the Lord's day are under the north wind; their nature is to procure gold, gems, carbuncles, diamonds, and rubies, and to cause one to obtain favour and benevolence, to dissolve enmities amongst men, to raise to honours, and to take away infirmities. They appear, for the most part, in a large, full and great body, sanguine and cross, in a gold colour, with the tincture of blood. Their motion is like the lighting of heaven; the sign of their becoming visible is that they move the person to sweat that calls them; but their particular forms are as follows; viz.

A king, having a scepter, riding on a lion. A king crowned; a queen with a scepter. A bird; a lion; a cock.

A yellow garment. A scepter.

CONSIDERATIONS, &c. of MONDAY.

(For the angel of Monday, his sigil, planet, sign of the planet, and name of the first heaven, see the Plate.)

THE angels of Monday--Gabriel, Michael, Samael.

The angels of the air ruling Monday, Arcan, king;--his ministers, Bilet, Missabu, Abuhaza. The wind which these are subject to is the west wind.

The angels of the first heaven, ruling on Monday, to be called from the four parts of the world. From the east, Gabriel, Madiel, Deamiel, Janak;--from the west, Sachiel, Zaniel, Habiel, Bachanæ, Corobael;--from the north, Mael, Uvael, Valnum, Baliel, Balay, Humastraw;--from the south,--Curaniel, Dabriel, Darquiel, Hanun, Vetuel.

The perfume of Monday--Aloes.

The CONJURATION of MONDAY.

I CONJURE and confirm upon you, ye strong and good angels, in the name Adonai, Adonai, Adonai, Adonai, Eye, Eye, Eye; Cados, Cados, Cados, Achim, Achim, Ja, Ja, strong Ja, who appeared in mount Sinai with the glorification of king Adonai, Sadai, Zebaoth, Anathay, Ya, Ya, Ya, Maranata, Abim, Jeia, who created the sea, and all lakes and waters, in the second day, which are above the heavens and in the earth, and scaled the sea in his high name, and gave it its bounds beyond which it cannot pass; and by the names of the angels who rule in the first legion, and who serve Orphaniel, a great, precious, and honourable angel, and by the name of his star which is Luna, and by all the names aforesaid, I conjure thee, Gabriel, who art chief ruler of Monday, the second day, that for me thou labour and fulfil, &c.

The spirits of the air of Monday are subject to the west wind, which is the wind of the moon; their nature is to give silver and to convey things from place to place; to make horses swift, and to disclose the secrets of persons both present and future.

Their familiar Forms are as follow:

They appear generally of a great and full stature, soft and phlegmatic, of colour like a black, obscure cloud, having a swoln countenance, with eyes red and full of water, a bald head, and teeth like a wild boar; their motion is like an exceeding great tempest of the sea. For their sign there will appear an exceeding great rain,. and their particular shapes are,

A king, like an archer, riding upon a doe. A little boy.

A woman-hunter with a bow and arrows. A cow; a little doe; a goose.

A green, or silver-coloured garment. An arrow; a creature with many feet.

CONSIDERATIONS of TUESDAY.

(For the angel of Tuesday, his sigil, planet, sign governing the planet, and name of the fifth heaven, see the Plate.)

THE angels of the air on Tuesday--Samael, Satael, Amabiel.

The angels of the air ruling on Tuesday, Samax, king; his Ministers, Carmax, Ismoli, Paffran.

The wind to which the said angels are subject is the east wind.

The angels of the fifth heaven ruling on Tuesday.-At the east, Guel, Damael, Calzas, Arragon;--the west, Lama, Astagna, Lobquin, Soneas, Jazel, Isiael, Irel;-- the north, Rhaumel, Hyniel, Rayel, Seraphiel, Fraciel Maithiel;--the south, Sacriel, Janiel, Galdel, Osael, Vianuel, Zaliel.

The perfume of Tuesday--Pepper.

The CONJURATION of TUESDAY.

I CONJURE and call upon you, ye strong and good angels, in the names Ya, Ya, Ya; He, He, He; Va, Hy, Hy, Ha, Ha, Ha; Va, Va, Va; An, An, An; Aia, Aia, Aia; El, Ay, Elibra, Elohim, Elohim; and by the names of the high God, who hath made the sea and dry land, and by his word hath made the earth, and produced trees, and hath set his seal upon the planets, with his precious, honoured, revered and holy name; and by the name of the angels governing in the fifth house, who are subservient to the great angel Acimoy, who is strong, powerful, and honoured, and by the name of his star which is called Mars, I call upon thee, Samael, by the names above mentioned, thou great angel! who presides over the day of Mars, and by the name Adonai, the living and true God, that you assist me in accomplishing my labours, &c. (as in the conjuration of Sunday.).

The spirits of the air on Tuesday are under the east wind; their nature is to bring or cause war, mortality, death, combustions, and to give two- thousand soldiers at a time; to bring death, infirmity or health.

Familiar Forms of the SPIRITS of MARS.

THEY appear in a tall body and choleric, a filthy countenance, of colour brown, swarthy, or red, having horns like harts, and griffins claws, and bellowing like wild bulls. Their motion is like fire burning: their sign thunder and lightning round about the circle.

Their particular shapes are, a king armed, riding on a wolf; a man armed. A woman with a buckler on her thigh.

A she-goat; a horse; a stag.

A red garment; a piece of wool; a cowslip.

CONSIDERATIONS of WEDNESDAY.

(For the angel of Wednesday his sigil, &c. &c. see the Plate.) THE angels of Wednesday--Raphael, Meil, Seraphiel.

The angels of the air ruling on Wednesday, Mediat, king;

349

Ministers, Suquinos, Sallales; the said angels of the air are subject to the south-west wind.

The angels of the second heaven, governing Wednesday, that are to be called, &c. At the east--Mathlai, Tarmiel, Baraborat--at the west, Jeruscue, Merattron;--at the north, Thiel, Rael, Jarihael, Venahel, Velel, Abuiori, Ucirmiel--at the south, Milliel, Nelapa, Calvel, vel Laquel.

The perfume of Wednesday--Mastic.

The CONJURATION of WEDNESDAY.

I CONJURE and call upon you, ye strong and holy angels, good and powerful, in a strong name of fear and praise, Ja, Adonay, Elohim, Saday, Saday, Saday; Eie, Eie, Eie; Asamie, Asamie; and in the name of Adonay, the God of Israel, who hath made the two great lights, and distinguished day from night for the benefit of his creatures; and by the names of all the discerning angels, governing openly in the second house before the great angel, Tetra, strong and powerful; and by the name of his star which is Mercury; and by the name of his seal, which is that of a powerful and honoured God; and I call upon thee, Raphael, and by the names above mentioned, thou great angel who presidest over the fourth day: and by the holy name which is written in the front of Aaron, created the most high priest, and by the names of all the angels who are constant in the grace of Christ, and by the name and place of Ammaluim, that you assist me in my labours, &c. &c.

The spirits of the air, on Wednesday are subject to the south-west wind; their nature is to give all sorts of metals, to reveal all earthly things past, present, and to come; to pacify judges, to give victory in war, to teach experiments and all sciences decayed, and to change bodies mixt of elements, conditionally, out of one thing into another; to give health or infirmities, to raise the poor and cast down the rich, to bind or loose spirits, to open locks or bolts.

Such kinds of spirits have the operations of others, but not in their perfect power, but in virtue or knowledge.

Forms of the SPIRITS of MERCURY.

THE spirits of Mercury appear in a body of a middle stature, cold, liquid and moist, fair and of an affable speech in a human shape and form, like a knight armed, of colour clear and bright. The motion of them is like silver coloured' clouds: for their sign they cause horror and fear to him that calls them.

Their particular shapes are, a king riding upon a bear. A fair youth; a woman holding a distaff.

A dog, a she-bear, and a magpye.

A garment of various changeable colours. A rod, a little staff.

CONSIDERATIONS of THURSDAY.

(For the angel of Thursday, his sigil, &c. see the Plate.) THE angels of Thursday-- Sachiel, Cassiel, Asasiel.

The angels of the air of Thursday, Suth, king; Ministers, Maguth, Gutrix.

The angels of the air are under the south-wind.--(But because there are no angels of the air to be found above the fifth heaven, therefore, on Thursday, say the prayers following in the four parts of the world:)

At the east--O Deus magne et excelse et honorate, per infinita secula; or, O great and most high God, honoured be thy name, world without end.

At the west--O wise, pure, and just God, of divine clemency, I beseech thee, most holy Father, that this day I may perfectly understand and accomplish my petition,

351

work, and labour; for the honour and glory of thy holy name, who livest and reignest, world without end. Amen.

At the north--O God, strong, mighty, and wonderfuly from everlasting to everlasting, grant that this day I bring to effect that which I desire, through our blessed Lord. Amen.

At the south--O mighty and most merciful God, hear my prayers and grant my petition.

The perfume of Thursday--Saffron.

The CONJURATION of THURSDAY.

I CO NJ U RE and confirm upon you, ye strong and holy angels, by the names Cados, Cados, Cados, Eschercie, Escherei, Eschercie, Hatim, Ya, strong founder of the worlds; Cantine, Jaym, Janic, Anic, Calbot, Sabbac, Berisay, Alnaym; and by the name Adonai, who created fishes and creeping things in the waters, and birds upon the face of the earth, flying towards heaven, in the fifth day; and by the names of the angels serving in the sixth host before Pastor, a holy angel, and a great and powerful prince and by the name of his star, which is Jupiter, and by the name of his seal, and by the name of Adonai, the great God, Creator of all things, and by the name of all the stars, and by their power and virtue, and by all the names aforesaid, I conjure thee, Sachiel, a great Angel, who art chief ruler of Thursday, that for me thou labour, &c.

The spirits of the air of Thursday are subject to the south wind; their nature is to procure the love of women, to cause men to be merry and joyful, to pacify strifes and contentions, to appease, enemies, to heal the diseased, and to disease the whole, and procure losses, or restore things lost.

The familiar Forms of the SPIRITS of JUPITER.

They appear with a body sanguine and choleric, of a middle stature, with a horrible, fearful motion, but with a mild countenance, and a gentle speech, and of the colour of iron: the motion of them is flashings of lightning, and thunder. For their sign there will appear about the circle men who shall seem to be devoured by lions. Their forms are,

A king, with a sword drawn, riding on a stag. A man, wearing a mitre, with long raiment.

A maid, with a laurel crown, adorned with flowers. A bull; a stag; a peacock.

An azure garment; a sword; a box-tree

CONSIDERATIONS of FRIDAY.

(For the seal planet, and sign governing the planet, and name of the third heaven, see the Plate.)

THE angels of Friday--Anael, Rachiel, Sachiel.

The angels of the air ruling on Friday, Sarabotes, king; Ministers, Amahiel, Aba, Abalidoth, Blaef. The wind which the angels of the air are subject to is the west wind.

Angels of the third heaven, which are to be called from the four parts of the world, are

At the east, Setchiel, Chedusilaniel, Corat, Tamuel, Tenaciel;--at the west, Turiel, Coniel, Babiel, Kadie, Maltiel, Huphaltiel;--at the north, Peniel, Penael, Penat, Raphael, Ranie, Doremiel;--at the south, Porosa, Sachiel, Chermiel, Samael, Santanael, Famiel.

The perfume of Friday--Pepperwort.

The CONJURATION of FRIDAY.

I CONJURE and confirm upon you, ye strong and holy angels, by the names On, Hey, Heya, Ja, Je, Saday, Adonai, and in the name Sadai, who created four-footed beasts, and creeping things, and man, in the sixth day, and gave to Adam. power over all creatures; wherefore blessed be the name of the Creator in his place; and by the name of the angels serving in the third host, before Dagiel, a great angel, and a strong and powerful prince, and by the name of his star, which is Venus, and by his seal which is holy; and by all the names aforesaid, I conjure upon thee, Anael, who art the chief ruler this day, that thou labour for me, &c.

The spirits of the air on Friday are subject to the west wind: their nature is to give silver, to incite men, and incline them to luxury, to cause marriages, to allure men to love women, to cause or take away infirmities, and to do all things which have motion.

Their familiar Shapes.

They appear with a fair body, of middle stature, with an amiable and pleasant countenance, of colour white or green, their upper parts golden; the motion of them is like a clear star. For their sign there will appear naked virgins round the circle, which will strive to allure the invocator to dalliance with them: but

Their particular Shapes are,

A king, with a scepter, riding on a camel. A naked girl; a she-goat.

A camel; a dove.

A white or green garment. Flowers; the herb savine.

The CONSIDERATIONS of SATURDAY.

The Magus

(For seal, &c. &c. see the Plate.)

THE angels of Saturday--Cassiel, Machatan, Uriel.

The angels of the air ruling this day, Maymon, king; Ministers, Abumalith, Assaibi, Balidet. The wind they are subject to, the south wind.

The fumigation of Saturday is sulphur.

There are no angels ruling in the air on Saturday above the fifth heaven, therefore in the four corners of the world, in the circle, use those orations which are applied to Thursday.

The CONJURATION of SATURDAY.

I CONJURE and confirm upon you, Caphriel, or Cassiel, Machator, and Seraquiel, strong and powerful angels; and by the name Adonai, Adonai, Adonai; Eie, Eie, Eie; Acim, Acim, Acim; Cados, Cados; Ima, Ima, Ima; Salay, Ja, Sar, Lord and Maker of the World, who rested on the seventh day; and by him who of his good pleasure gave the same to be observed by the children of Israel throughout their generations, that they should keep and sanctify the same, to have thereby a good reward in the world to conic; and by the names of the angels serving in the seventh host, before Booel, a great angel, and powerful prince; and by the name of his star, which is Saturn; and by his holy seal, and by the names before spoken, I conjure upon thee, Caphriel, who art chief ruler of the seventh day, which is the Sabbath, that for me thou labour, &c. &c.

The spirits of the air on Saturday are subject to the south-west wind: the nature of them is to sow discords, hatred, evil thoughts and cogitations, to give leave to kill and murder, and to lame or maim every member.

Their familiar Shapes.

THEY generally appear with a tall, lean, slender body, with an angry countenance, having four faces, one on the back of the head, one in the front, and one on each side, nosed or beaked, likewise there appears a face on each knee of a black shining colour; their motion is the moving of the wind, with a kind of earthquake; their sign is white earth, whiter than snow.

Their particular Shapes are,

127:1 A king, bearded, riding on a dragon. An old man with a beard.

An old woman leaning on a crutch. A hog; a dragon; an owl.

A black garment; a hook or sickle. A juniper tree.

Those are the figures that these spirits usually assume, which are generally, terrible at the first coming on of the visions, but as they have only a limited power, beyond which they cannot pass, so the invocator need be under no apprehensions of danger, provided he is well fortified with those things we have directed to be used for his defence, and above all, to have a firm and constant faith in the mercy, wisdom, and goodness of God.

END OF THE THIRD PART, AND OF CABALISTICAL AND CEREMONIAL MAGIC

127:1 Those spirits who appear in a kingly form, have a much higher dignity than them who take an inferior shape; and those who appear in a human shape, exceed in authority and power them that come as animals; and again, these latter surpass in dignity them who appear as trees or instruments, and the like: so that you are to judge of the power, government, and authority of spirits by their assuming a more noble and dignified apparition.

THE MAGIC AND PHILOSOPHY OF TRITHEMIUS OF SPANHEIM

CONTAINING HIS BOOK OF SECRET THINGS, AND DOCTRINE OF SPIRITS:

With many curious and rare Secrets (hitherto not generally known;) THE ART OF DRAWING SPIRITS INTO CRYSTALS, &c.

With many other Experiments in the Occult Sciences, never yet published in the English Language.

TRANSLATED FROM A VALUABLE LATIN MANUSCRIPT,

By FRANCIS BARRETT,

STUDENT OF CHEMISTRY, NATURAL AND OCCULT PHILOSOPHY, THE CABALA, &c.

PART IV.

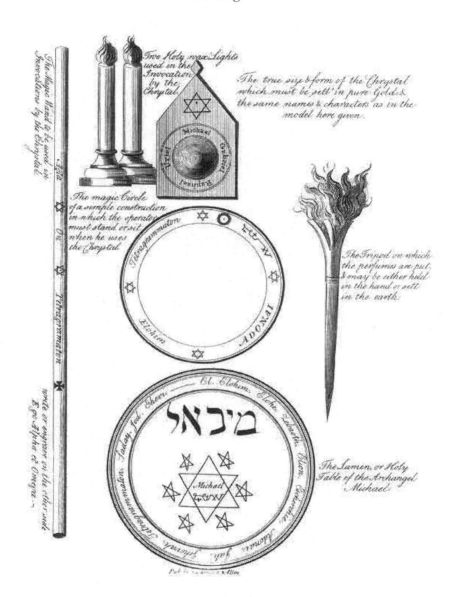

Two Holy wax Lights used in the Invocation by the Chrystal.

The true size & form of the Chrystal which must be sett in pure Gold & the same names & characters as in the model here given.

The magic Circle of a simple construction in which the operator must stand or sit when he uses the Chrystal.

The Tripod on which the perfumes are put & may be either held in the hand or sett in the earth.

The Magic Wand to be used in Invocations by the Chrystal.

Tetragrammaton

write or engrave on the other side Ego Alpha et Omega.

מיכאל

The Lamen, or Holy Table of the Archangel Michael.

THE TRANSLATOR'S LETTER TO A FRIEND OF HIS, A YOUNG STUDENT IN THESE OCCULT SCIENCES

MY FRIEND,

KNOWING thee to be a curious searcher after those sciences which are out of the common track of study, (I mean the art of foretelling events, magic, telismans, &c.) I am moved spiritually to give thee my thoughts upon them, and by these ideas here written, to open to thine eye (spiritual) as much information as it seems necessary for thee to know, by. which thou mayest be led by the hand into the delectable field of nature; and to give thee such documents as, guided by the supreme wisdom of the Highest, thou mayest refresh thy soul with a delicious draught of knowledge; so that after recreating thy spirit with the use of those good gifts which may please God to bestow on thee, thou mayest be wrapped up into the contemplation of the immense wisdom of that great munificent Being who created thee.

Now, art thou a man, in whose soul the image of Divinity is sealed for eternity, think first what is thy desire in the searching after these mysteries! Is it wealth, honour, fame, power, might, aggrandizement, and the like? Perhaps thy heart says, All! all these I would gladly crave! If so, this is my answer,--seek first to know thyself thoroughly, cleanse thy heart from all wicked, vain, and rapacious desires. Thinkest thou, oh man! to attain power to gratify thy lusts, to enrich thy coffers, to build houses, to raise thyself to the pinnacle of human admiration; if these are thy hopes and desires, thou hast reason to lament thy being born: all such desires are immediately from the devil, I mean that Being whose engines (i. e. myriads of demons) are continually in the act of placing sensual delights and luxuries before the depraved minds and hearts of man, and whose chief business and property it is to counteract the benevolent actions and inspirations of those blessed spirits who are the instruments of God our Creator.

Fear God and love thy neighbour; use no deceit, swear not, neither lye; let all thy actions be sincere. Here, O man! is the grand seal of all earthly wisdom, the true talisman of human happiness. When thou shalt accomplish this, behold nothing will be impossible unto thee as far as God permits: then with all speed apply thy mind and heart to attain knowledge and wisdom; with all humility throw thy dependence on God alone, the author of all things that cannot die.

To know thyself is to know God, for it is a spiritual gift from God that enables a man to know himself. This gift but very few possess, as may be daily seen. How many are there tossed about to and fro' upon the perilous sea of contending passions, and who are more light than feathers! how many in this great city who place their chiefest good in debauchery and letchery! See their actions, manners, and dispositions; these poor, unfortunate, miserable wretches, such is their fatal magical infatuation and ignorance, that they think those mad who might even attempt to reason with them on the vanity and misery of their situation. To make myself more intelligible, these are what the world calls men of fashion, a phrase insignificant enough when we consider that the universal fashion of this time is vice, and that so glaring, that it needs no great intellect to discover what is daily open to the view of the observer. But to you, my friend, I have addressed these lines; therefore let it not be supposed that I am reprehending my friend for vices which I cannot suppose him attached to: for I know thou art a young man designed for the receiving of instruction, in much higher and more glorious contemplations than those sons of earth are capable of, therefore I have presented thee with this translation which thou didst desire me to give thee.

But beware of flattery, self-love, and covetousness, so wilt thou thrive; and be diligent in thy occupation, so shall thy body be fed. Idleness is offensive to the Deity, industry shall sweeten thy brown bread, and the fruits of it shall warm thine heart, and inspire thy soul with gratitude to him that blesses thee with enough: seek for no more, for it will damn thee; pray for enough to feed and clothe thy body, but ask no more, lest thou pine away in heart-rending poverty, and spend the remainder of thy days in contumely and beggary. For know a thing most necessary for thee to know, that if by thy study, by thy art, or any other thing, thou couldst command a million of spirits, it should not be lawful for thee to wish to gain riches suddenly, for the Wisdom Eternal has put forth the fiat; and it has been said by him who never spoke in vain, and who cannot lye, that man shall get bread by the sweat of his brow; therefore let us not have in view the enriching of ourselves in worldly goods, by supernatural means, or by a greedy desiring of what we ought to look upon with eyes of contempt, draw upon us the wrath of God. Rather let us cheerfully rely on, and follow in very deed, spirit and truth, these words of the apostle, Seek ye first the kingdom of God, and all these things shall be added unto you fear not but that God shall make thy household as a flourishing tree, and thy wife shall be as a fruitful vine. Farewell, remember my poor counsel, and be happy. From thy true friend, F. B.

N. B. To enable thee the better to comprehend this Book, I have drawn out the various figures, of which mention is made in this work, that thou mayest see the very exact method of working; likewise the images of seals, spirits, and various other rare, and curious instruments, which are necessary for thee to know and see with the eye; therefore in the construction of them thou canst not be liable to error.

Fig. I. The form of the crystal for invocating spirits, with the plate of pure gold. in which the crystal must be fastened, with the divine characters around.

Fig 2. A magical circle (C D E F), of a simple construction, for the operator to stand or sit in when he calleth the spirits.

Fig. 3. The crystal (A), two silver or other candlesticks (G G,) with the wax tapers burning, and tripod or vessel for the oderiferous suffumigation.

Fig 4. A wand of black ebony with golden characters. The characters are explained.

A CAUTION TO THE INEXPERIENCED IN THIS ART, AND A WORD OF ADVICE TO THOSE WHO WOULD BE ADEPTS

BROTHER,

IT is necessary for me to inform thee, that whatever thy desires are in the pursuit of this art, which we call Magic, so wilt thy connexion and answer be. If in the pursuit of revenge, it is but proper thou shouldest know that thou wilt, in any of these experiments here laid down, draw to thyself a revengeful demon, or an infernal furious spirit, serving in the principle of the wrath of God; if worldly riches and aggrandizement, then shalt thou have an earthial or fiery spirit, which will delude thee with the riches of the central world; if fame, or the blaze of glory, then the spirits of pride will be allotted thee, who will gratify thy inordinate desire of vain glory; for all these offices are there spirits allotted and will be eager to mix with thy spirit: it will attract thee to his own nature, and serve all thy purposes according to the extent of God's permission; and as thy desires are and from what principle they proceed, so shalt thou be answered: but if thou desirest to know nothing but for the honour and glory of God, and the help of thy neighbour, and, in great humility, fill thy heart with the love of God, thou shalt then have a pure spirit which will grant (by the Lord's permission) they desires. Therefore seek for that which is good; avoid all evil either in thought, word, or action; pray to God to fill thee with wisdom, and then thou shalt reap an abundant harvest. There are two ways magically set before thee; chuse which thou wilt, thou shalt be sure of thy reward. Farewel.

F. B.
London, 1800.

OF THE MAKING OF THE CRYSTAL AND THE FORM OF PREPARATION FOR A VISION

PROCURE of a lapidary good clear pellucid crystal, of the bigness of a small orange, i. c. about one inch and a half in diameter; let it be globular or round each way alike; then, when you have got this crystal, fair and clear, without any clouds or specks, get a small plate of pure gold to encompass the crystal round one half; let this be fitted on an ivory or ebony pedestal, as you may see more fully described in the drawing, (see the Plate, fig. I.) Let there be engraved a circle (A) round the crystal with these characters around inside the circle next the crystal

   ; afterwards the name "Tetragrammaton". On the other side of the plate let there be engraven "Michael, Gabriel, Uriel, Raphael;" which are the four principal angels ruling over the Sun, Moon, Venus and Mercury; but on the table on which the crystal stands the following names, characters, &c. must be drawn in order.

First, The names of the seven planets and angels ruling them, with their seals or characters. The names of the four kings of the four corners of the earth. Let them be all written within a double circle, with a triangle on a table; on which place the crystal on its pedestal: this being. done, thy table is complete (as in the Fig. D,) and fit for the calling of the spirits; after which thou shalt proceed to experiment, thus:

In what time thou wouldest deal with the spirits by the table and crystal, thou must observe the planetary hour; and whatever planet rules in that hour, the angel governing the planet thou shalt call in the manner following; but first, say this short prayer:

"Oh, God! who art the author of all good things, strengthen, I beseech thee, thy poor servant, that he may stand fast, without fear, through this dealing and work;

363

enlighten, I beseech thee, oh Lord! the dark understanding of thy creature, so that his spiritual eye may be opened to see and know thy angelic spirits descending here in this crystal: (Then lay thy hand on the crystal saying,) and thou, oh inanimate creature of God, be sanctified and consecrated, and blessed to this purpose, that no evil phantasy may appear in thee; or, if they do gain ingress into this, creature, they may be constrained to speak intelligibly, and truly, and without the least ambiguity, for Christ's sake. Amen. And forasmuch as thy servant here standing before thee, oh, Lord! desires neither evil treasures, nor injury to his neighbour, nor hurt to any living creature, grant him the power of descrying those celestial spirits or intelligences, that may appear in this crystal, and whatever good gifts (whether the power of healing infirmities, or of imbibing wisdom, or discovering any evil likely to afflict any person or family, or any other good gift thou mayest be pleased to bestow on me, enable me, by thy wisdom and mercy, to use whatever I may receive to the honour of thy holy name. Grant this for thy son Christ's sake. Amen."

Then taking your ring and pentacle, put the ring on the little finger of your right hand; hang the pentacle round thy neck; (Note, the pentacle may be either wrote on clean virgin parchment, or engraven on a square plate of silver and suspended from thy neck to the breast), then take your black ebony wand, with the gilt characters on it and trace the circle, (Fig.
7. C D E F,) saying, "In the name of the blessed Trinity, I consecrate this piece of ground for our defence; so that no evil spirit may have power to break these bounds prescribed here, through Jesus Christ our Lord." Amen.

Then place the vessel for the perfumes between thy circle and the holy table on which the crystal stands, and, having fire therein, cast in thy perfumes, saying,

"I conjure thee, oh thou creature of fire! by him who created all things both in heaven and earth, and in the sea, and in every other place whatever, that forthwith thou cast away every phantasm from thee, that no hurt whatsoever shall be done in any thing. Bless, oh Lord, this creature of fire, and sanctify it that it may be blessed, and that they may fill tip the power and virtue of their odours; so neither the enemy, nor any false imagination, may enter into them, through our Lord Jesus Christ. Amen."

Now, this being done in the order prescribed, take out thy little book, which must be made about seven inches long, of pure white virgin vellum or paper, likewise pen and ink must be ready to write down the name, character, and office, likewise the seal or image of whatever spirit may appear (for this I must tell you that it does not happen that the same spirit you call will always appear, for you must try the spirit to know whether he be a pure or impure being, and this thou shalt easily know by a firm and undoubted faith in God.)

Now the most pure and simple way of calling the spirits or spirit is by a short oration to the spirit himself, which is more effectual and easy to perform than composing a table of letters; for all celestial operations, the more pure and unmixed they are, the more they are agreable to the celestial spirits: therefore, after the circle is drawn, the book, perfumes, rod, &c. in readiness, proceed as follows:

(After noticing the exact hour of the day, and what angel rules that hour, thou shalt say,)

"In the name of the blessed and holy Trinity, I do desire thee, thou strong and mighty angel [137:1], Michæl, that if it be the divine will of him who is called Tetragrammaton, &c. the Holy God, the Father, that thou take upon thee some shape as best becometh thy celestial nature, and appear to us visibly here in this crystal, and answer our demands in as far as we shall not transgress the bounds of the divine mercy and goodness, by requesting unlawful knowledge; but that thou wilt graciously shew us what things are most profitable for us to know and do, to the glory and honour of his divine Majesty, who liveth and reigneth, world without end. Amen.

"Lord, thy will be done on earth, as it is in heaven;--make clean our hearts within us, and take not thy Holy Spirit from us.

"O Lord, by thy name, we have called him, suffer him to administer unto us. And that all things may work together for thy honour and glory, to whom with thee, the Son, and blessed Spirit, be ascribed all might, majesty and dominion. Amen."

Note, In these dealings, two should always be present; for often a spirit is manifest to one in the crystal when the other cannot perceive him; therefore if any spirit appear, as there most likely will, to one or both, say,

"Oh, Lord! we return thee our hearty and sincere thanks for the hearing of our prayer, and we thank thee for having permitted thy spirit to appear unto us which we, by thy mercy, will interrogate to our further instruction, through Christ. Amen."

Interrog. 1. In the name of the holy and undefiled Spirit, the Father, the begotten Son, and Holy Ghost, proceeding from both, what is thy true name?

If the spirit answers, Michael, then proceed.

Quest. 2. What is thy office? 3. What is thy true sign or character? 4. When are the times most agreeable to thy nature to hold conference with us?

Wilt thou swear by the blood and righteousness of our Lord Jesus Christ, that thou art truly Michael?

(Here let him swear, then write down his seal or character in thy book, and against it, his office and times to be called, through God's name; also write down any thing he may teach thee, or any responses he may make to thy questions or interrogations, concerning life or death, arts or sciences, or any other thing;) and then shalt thou say,

"Thou great and mighty spirit, inasmuch as thou camest in peace and in the name of the ever blessed and righteous Trinity, so in this name thou mayest depart, and return to us when we call thee in his name to whom every knee doth bow down. Fare thee well, Michael; peace be between us, through our blessed Lord Jesus Christ. Amen."

Then will the spirit depart; then say, "To God the Father, eternal Spirit, fountain of Light, the Son, and Holy Ghost, be all honour and glory, world without end. Amen."

I shall here set down the Table of the names of Spirits and Planets governing the Hours; so thou shalt easily know by inspection, what Spirit and Planet governs every Hour of the Day and Night in the Week.

	Angels and Planets ruling SUNDAY.	Angels and Planets ruling MONDAY.	Angels and Planets ruling TUESDAY.	Angels and Planets ruling WEDNESDAY.	Angels and Planets ruling THURSDAY.	Angels and Planets ruling FRIDAY.	Angels and Planets ruling SATURDAY.
Hours Day.	*Day.*	*Day.*	*Day.*	*Day.*	*Day.*	*Day.*	*Day.*
1	☉ Michael	♀ Gabriel	♂ Samael	☿ Raphael	♄ Sachiel	♀ Anael	♃ Cassiel
2	♀ Anael	♃ Cassiel	☉ Michael	♀ Gabriel	♂ Samael	☿ Raphael	♄ Sachiel
3	☿ Raphael	♄ Sachiel	♀ Anael	♃ Cassiel	☉ Michael	♀ Gabriel	♂ Samael
4	♀ Gabriel	♂ Samael	☿ Raphael	♄ Sachiel	♀ Anael	♃ Cassiel	☉ Michael
5	♃ Cassiel	☉ Michael	♀ Gabriel	♂ Samael	☿ Raphael	♄ Sachiel	♀ Anael
6	♄ Sachiel	♀ Anael	♃ Cassiel	☉ Michael	♀ Gabriel	♂ Samael	☿ Raphael
7	♂ Samael	☿ Raphael	♄ Sachiel	♀ Anael	♃ Cassiel	☉ Michael	♀ Gabriel
8	☉ Michael	♀ Gabriel	♂ Samael	☿ Raphael	♄ Sachiel	♀ Anael	♃ Cassiel
9	♀ Anael	♃ Cassiel	☉ Michael	♀ Gabriel	♂ Samael	☿ Raphael	♄ Sachiel
10	☿ Raphael	♄ Sachiel	♀ Anael	♃ Cassiel	☉ Michael	♀ Gabriel	♂ Samael
11	♀ Gabriel	♂ Samael	☿ Raphael	♄ Sachiel	♀ Anael	♃ Cassiel	☉ Michael
12	♃ Cassiel	☉ Michael	♀ Gabriel	♂ Samael	☿ Raphael	♄ Sachiel	♀ Anael

Hours Night	Night.	Night.	Night.	Night.	Night.	Night.	Night.
1	♄ Sachael	♀ Anael	♃ Cassiel	☉ Michael	♀ Gabriel	♂ Samael	☿ Raphael
2	♂ Samiel	☿ Raphael	♄ Sachiel	♀ Anael	♃ Cassiel	☉ Michael	♀ Gabriel
3	☉ Michael	♀ Gabriel	♂ Samael	☿ Raphael	♄ Sachiel	♀ Anael	♃ Cassiel
4	♀ Anael	♃ Cassiel	☉ Michael	♀ Gabriel	♂ Samael	☿ Raphael	♄ Sachiel
5	☿ Raphael	♄ Sachiel	♀ Anael	♃ Cassiel	☉ Michael	♀ Gabriel	♂ Samael
6	♀ Gabriel	♂ Samael	☿ Raphael	♄ Sachiel	♀ Anael	♃ Cassiel	☉ Michael
7	♃ Cassiel	☉ Michael	♀ Gabriel	♂ Samael	☿ Raphael	♄ Sachiel	♀ Anael
8	♄ Sachiel	♀ Anael	♃ Cassiel	☉ Michael	♀ Gabriel	♂ Samael	☿ Raphael
9	♂ Samael	☿ Raphael	♄ Sachiel	♀ Anael	♃ Cassiel	☉ Michael	♀ Gabriel
10	☉ Michael	♀ Gabriel	♂ Samael	☿ Raphael	♄ Sachiel	♀ Anael	♃ Cassiel
11	♀ Anael	♃ Cassiel	☉ Michael	♀ Gabriel	♂ Samael	☿ Raphael	♄ Sachiel
12	☿ Raphael	♄ Sachiel	♀ Anael	♃ Cassiel	☉ Michael	♀ Gabriel	♂ Samael

Note, The day is divided into twelve equal parts, called Planetary Hours, reckoning from sun-rise to sun-set, and, again, from the setting to the rising; and to find the planetary hour, you need but to divide the natural hours by twelve, and the quotient gives the length of the planetary hours and odd minuets, which shews you how long a spirit bears rule in that day. as Michael governs the first and the eighth hour on Sunday, as does the ☉. After you have the length of the first hour, you have only to look in the Table, as if it be the fourth hour, on Sunday, you see in the Table that the ☽ and Gabriel rules; and so for the rest it being so plain and easy you cannot err.

THE CONCLUSION OF THE MAGUS

137:1 Or any other angel or spirit.

ADVERTISEMENT

THE Author of this Work respectfully informs those who are curious in the studies of Art and Nature, especially of Natural and Occult Philosophy, Chemistry, Astrology, &c. &c. that, having been indefatigable in his researches into those sublime Sciences, of which he has treated at large in this Book, that he gives private instructions and lectures upon any of the above mentioned Sciences; in the course of which he will discover many curious and rare experiments. Those who become Students will be initiated into the choicest operations of Natural Philosophy, Natural Magic, the Cabala, Chemistry, the Talismanic Art, Hermetic Philosophy, Astrology, Physiognomy, &c. &c. Likewise they will acquire the knowledge of the Rites, Mysteries, Ceremonies, and Principles of the ancient Philosophers, Magi, Cabalists, Adepts, &c.--The purpose of this School (which will consist of no greater number than Twelve Students) being to investigate the hidden treasures of Nature; to bring the Mind to a Contemplation of the Eternal Wisdom; to promote the discovery of whatever may conduce to the perfection of Man,. the alleviating the miseries and calamities of this life, both in respect of ourselves and others; the study of morality and religion here, in order to secure to ourselves felicity hereafter; and, finally, the Promulgation of whatever may conduce to the general happiness and welfare of mankind.--Those who feel themselves thoroughly disposed to enter upon such a course of studies, as is above recited, with the same principles of philanthropy with which the Author invites the lovers of Philosophy and wisdom, to incorporate themselves in so select, permanent, and desirable a society, may speak with the Author upon the subject, tit any time between the hours of Eleven and Two o'clock, at 99 Norton Street, Mary-le-Bonne.

Letters (post paid) upon any subject treated of in this Book, will be duly answered, with the necessary information.

BIOGRAPHIA ANTIQUA

OR,

AN ACCOUNT OF THE LIVES AND WRITINGS OF THE ANCIENT AND MODERN MAGI, CABALISTS, AND PHILOSOPHERS,

DISCOVERING THE PRINCIPLES AND TENETS OF THE FIRST FOUNDERS OF THE MAGICAL AND OCCULT SCIENCES:

WHEREIN THE MYSTERIES OF THE PYTHAGORIANS, GYMNOSOPHISTS, EGYPTIANS, BRAGMANNI, BABYLONIANS, PERSIANS, ETHIOPIANS, CHALDEANS, &c. ARE DISCOVERED:

Including a particular and interesting Account of ZOROASTER, THE SON OF OROMASIUS
THE FIRST INSTITUTOR OF PHILOSOPHY BY FIRE, AND MAGIC; LIKEWISE, OF HERMES TRISMEGISTUS, THE EGYPTIAN,

And other Philosophers, famous for their Learning, Piety, and Wisdom.
TO WHICH IS ADDED A SHORT ESSAY,

Proving that the First Christians were Magicians, who foretold, acknowledged, and worshipped

THE SAVIOUR OF THE WORLD, AND FIRST FOUNDER OF THE CHRISTIAN RELIGION.

ZOROASTER, THE SON OF OROMASIUS

FIRST INSTITUTOR OF PHILOSOPHY BY FIRE, AND MAGIC.

ZOROASTER, the son of Oromasius, flourished in the reign of Darius, the successor of Cambyses. [143:1] All authors are full of variations in their accounts of this famous person, some making him of a much later date than others; however, we shall give what we have collected from those who appear most authentic, not omitting the traditional history extant amongst the Magi, with which our readers may compare the several stories of biographers, and accept that account which shall seem to them the most rational. Zoroaster, king of the Bactrians, was vanquished by Ninus, and passed for the inventor of magic [143:2]. Eusebius places this victory of Ninus in the seventh year of Abraham:

Abraham; now several authors make Zoroaster appear much earlier. It has been reported that Zoroaster laughed on the same day he was born, and that he was the only one to whom this happened, and that the palpitation of his brain was so strong as to repulse the hand, it being laid to his head, which they say was a presage of his future knowledge and wisdom. It is added, that he passed twenty years in the deserts, and there eat nothing but a sort of cheese which was never the worse for age; that the love of wisdom and justice obliged him to retire from the world to a mountain, where he lived in solitude; but when he come down from thence there fell a celestial fire upon it, which perpetually burned; that the king of Persia, accompanied with the greatest lords of his court, approached it for the purpose of putting up prayers to God; that Zoroaster came out from these flames unhurt; that he comforted and encouraged the Persians, and offered sacrifices for them to God; that, afterwards, he did not live indifferently with all sorts of men, but only those who were born for truth, and who were capable of the true knowledge of God, which kind of people are called among the Persians, Magi; that he desired his end might be this, viz. to be struck with thunder, and consumed by celestial fire; and that he requested the Persians to collect his ashes, after he was consumed in this manner, and to preserve and venerate them as a pledge of the preservation of their monarchy; that they for a length of time paid great veneration to the relics of Zoroaster, but at length, neglecting them, their monarchy fell to ruin and decay [145:1]. The Chronicle of Alexandria adds, that having held this discourse discourse with them he invoked Orion, and was consumed by celestial fire. Many will have it that Ham was the Zoroaster of the eastern nations, and the inventor of magic. Mr. Bochart refutes this falsity. Cedrenus observes that Zoroaster, who became so famous for wisdom among the Persians, was descended from Belus: this imports that he was descended from Nimrod. Some authors have taken him for Nimrod; others for Assur or Japhet. The ancient Persians believe that Zoroaster was before Moses [146:1]. Some maintain he was the prophet Ezekiel, and it cannot be denied that they ground their opinions on the agreement of numerous particulars which belong to the one, and are related of the other. George Hornius foolishly imagines that he was the false prophet Balaam. Huetius shews that he was the Moses of the Jews, and mentions an infinite number of particulars in which the accounts we have of Moses agree with the stories related of Zoroaster.--How near all or any of these come to the probability of truth will appear in the sequel, where we have given the most probable and rational account of him, as far as we have been able to trace, from the tradition of the Magi, which we prefer before the confused and partial accounts vulgarly extant. They who believe that Zoroaster professed and taught a diabolical magic [147:1] are certainly in the wrong; the magic he taught (of which we shall speak more anon) was only the study of the divine nature, and of religious worship. Some have presumed that Zoroaster was the promulgator of a doctrine of two principles [147:2], or two co-eternal causes, one of good good, the other of evil things. of this doctrine Plutarch takes notice: he says, "that Zoroaster the magician, who is said to have lived five thousand years" before the Trojan war, called the good God, Oromazes, and the evil, Arimanius, &c. &c." See Plut. de Iside & Osiride, page 369.

Dr. Hyde, in his excellent treatise on the religion of the ancient Persians, cites some authors who clear him on this head. We shall examine whether they deserve credit. It is affirmed that he was no idolater, either with respect to the worship of fire, or that of Mithra [148:1]. What appears least uncertain, amongst so many things that are related of him is, that he was the introducer of a new religion into Persia, and that he did it about the reign of Darius the successor of Cambyses: he is still in great veneration among those Persians who are not of the Mahometan religion, but still retain the ancient worship of their country. They call him Zardhust, and several believe that he came from China, and relate many miraculous things on that head. Several authors affirm, that all the books published hitherto under Zoroaster's name, some of which are yet extant, are supposititious. Dr. Hyde dissents from this opinion. Suidas affirms, that there were extant four books of Zoroaster: the first, "Of Nature," a book of the Virtues of precious Stones, called de Gemmis; and five books of Astrology and Astronomy, "Prædictiones ex. Inspectione Stellarum." It is very likely that what Pliny relates, as quoted from Zoroaster, was taken from those books, Plin. lib. xviii, cap. 24. Eusebius recites a passage which contains a magnificent description of God, and gives it as the very words of Zoroaster in his sacred commentary on the Persian rites. Clemens Alexandrinus says, that the followers of Prodicus boasted of having the secrets or secret books of Zoroaster. But most likely he meant that they boasted of having the secret books of Pythagoras. They were printed, together with the verses of the Sybils at Amsterdam, in the year 1689, according to Opsopæus's edition, Oracula Magica Zoroastris, cum Scholiis Plethonis & Pselli.

143:1 The Author regrets, that, notwithstanding his laborious researches to obtain an authentic and satisfactory account of Zoroaster to present to his readers that a few generals, and not particulars, can only be given: indeed, the most serious and respectable historians differ so widely in their accounts of him that nothing certain can from thence be deduced however, we have above recited several authorities to which we have annexed various notes and commentations.

143:2 Passed for the inventor of magic. It is to be noted that he was the inventor of it, and the first of the magi. Justin informs us that this victory was the last of Ninus; that Zoroaster philosophized most judiciously upon the nature and influences of the stars, and on the principles of the universe. Thomas Stanleius, Hist. of Philos. Orientalis, lib. I. cap. iii. informs us that Zoroaster, according to Eusebius, was cotemporary with Semiramis; but it is certain, according to

Eusebius, that he was vanquished by king Ninus. Arnobius, lib. I. pa. m. 5. says, "Anciently the Assyrians and Bactrians, the former under the conduct of Ninus, and the latter under Zoroaster, fought against each other, not only with men and weapons, but also by the help of magic, and the secret discipline of the Chaldeans." Hermippus, who has wrote cautiously on every thing relative to magic, and explained twenty thousand verses composed by Zoroaster, relates, that one Azonaces initiated p. 144 him into this art, and that he lived 5,000 years before the Trojan war. St. Augustin and Orosius have followed the tradition mentioned by Justin. Apuleius, in his Catalogue of all the most famous Magicians of Antiquity, with great justice places Zoroaster in the first rank, and proves him the most ancient of all: "Magicarum artium fuisse perhibeter inventor Zoroastres." Augustin. de Civitat. Dei, lib. 21. cap. xiv. Eudoxus, who esteemed the art of magic to be accounted the noblest and most useful of all worldly knowledge, relates that Zoroaster lived six thousand years before the death of Plato. Note, that the same thing is affirmed by Aristotle. Agathias, who lived in the reign of Justinian, informs us, that, according to the Persians of that time, Zoroaster and Hystaspes were cotemporary; but they do not say whether this Hystaspes was father to Darius or any other. Sir John Marsham positively decides that he was the father of Darius; and grounds his opinion on this, that one of the elogies engraven on the tomb makes him the instructor of the Magi; and that the same historian who makes Hystaspes excel in magic, calls him the father of Darius. Ammianus Marcellinus, lib. 23, pag. m. 324. says, "After the time of Zoroaster, reigned Hystaspes, a very prudent king, and the father of Darius. This prince, having boldly penetrated into the remotest parts of the Upper India, came at length to a solitary forest, where there dwelt, in awful and silent tranquility, the Brachmans. In this peaceful solitude they instructed him in the knowledge of the earth's motion, likewise of the stars; and from them he learned the pure and sacred rites of religion. Part of this knowledge he communicated to the Magi, which, together with the art of predicting future events, they delivered down to posterity, each in his own family. The great number of men who have descended from these families, ever since that age down to the present, have all been set apart for cultivating the knowledge of the Gods." But Ammianus Mercellinus was wrong in saying, that this father of Darius was a king; and no doubt he committed this blunder by having read in general that one king Hystaspes was a great magician, and thought there was no other Hystaspes than the father of Darius. But it is beyond dispute, that one Hystaspes, older than the foundation of Rome, and a great prophet, is mentioned by authors. "Hystaspes also, the most ancient king of the Medes, and from whom the river Hystaspes derives its name, is the most admirable of them all; for under the interpretation of the prophecy of a boy, he informed posterity that the Roman empire, nay, even the Roman name, should be utterly destroyed; and this he predicted a long time before the establishment of that colony of Trojans," Lactant. lib. VII. cap. xv. pag. in. 492. Justin Martyr informs us, that he predicted the general conflagration of all perishable things, Justin Apolog. ii. pag. 66. It is affirmed that Pythagoras was Zoroaster's disciple, under the reign of Cambyses, the son of Cyrus: the words of Apuleius inform us of the fact. Some say that Pythagoras having been made a slave in Egypt, was transported into Persia; others will have transported him into Babylon, and there instructed by Zoroaster the Babylonian, whom they distinguish from the Persian. We find no less than five Zoroasters mentioned in history: to these five may be added a sixth, mentioned by Apuleius. This Zoroaster lived in Babylon at the time Pythagoras was brought thither by Cambyses. The same writer calls him "the chief interpreter of all divine mysteries," and says that Pythagoras was chiefly instructed by him. He appears to be the same p. 145 with Zabratus, by whom Diogenes affirms Pythagoras was purged from all his former filth, and instructed in what is essentially necessary for good men to know, viz. God, nature, and philosophy: he is also the same with Nazaratus, the Assyrian, whom Alexander, in his book of the Pythagorical symbols, affirms to have taught Pythagoras. The same person Suidas calls Zares, Cyrillus, Zaranes, and Plutarch, Zarates.

145:1 According to the tradition of the Magi, we shall explain this fabulous and figurative description of Zoroaster's end. The truth is, he enjoined the Persians rigidly to persevere in the laws he had framed, and the doctrine he had been at the labour to establish, which was, to live in the practice of moral virtue, to avoid all species of luxury, to promote the liberal sciences, to govern all their actions with prudence and integrity, and to meet misfortune with resolution, and to encounter it with philosophy, and to endure the unavoidable calamities of life with fortitude: these, his disciplines, he left as a precious relic among them; which while they strictly adhered to, they need be under no apprehension of tyranny and p. 146 oppression:--these they collected, and for some space of time religiously followed the precepts of this great philosopher: at length, human frailty and vice, corrupting their manners, caused them to relax from their duties, upon which their empire fell into ruin and decay. The idolatry falsely imputed to this wise man, viz. his instituting the worshipping of fire, is thus to be interpreted.--Under the celestial symbol of fire was meant truth:--truth he ascribed purely as the great and wonderful attribute of the Godhead, which he acknowledged and worshipped, to wit, one only God, the eternal fire of wisdom and everlasting truth, justice, and mercy!--His magic was the study of the religious worship of that Eternal Being. After Zoroaster, there were four persons chosen to educate the successor of the king of Persia. They chose the wisest, the most just, the most temperate, and the bravest man that could be found. The wisest man (viz. one of the Magi), instructed him in Zoroaster's magic, the just in government, the brave in war, and the temperate in social virtue and temperance. Now observe, that Zoroaster is called the son of Oromasius, and that Oromasius is the name given by Zoroaster and his disciples to the good God, and this title was really bestowed upon him by the Persians; therefore, according to Plato, this Persian Magus, on account of his uncommon learning, religion, and wisdom, was, in an allegorical or figurative manner, called the son of God, or the son of wisdom, truth, &.c.

146:1 Some Magi affirm that he is the same with Abraham, and frequently call him Ibrahim Zerdascht, which is Abraham the friend of fire.

147:1 The preceding note fully explains those erroneous relations of the wisdom of the Magi. Those who desire to see a great many passages which testify that the magic of the Persians, instituted by Zoroaster, was the study of religion, virtue, and wisdom, let them refer to Brissonius de Regno Persarum, lib. ii. p. 178, &. seq. edit. Commel. 1595; likewise Jul. Cæsar, Bullengerus Eclog. ad Arnobium, p. 346, &. seq. Nor are we ignorant that Gabriel Naude hath most learnedly and solidly justified our Zoroaster against the ignorant imputations of necromancy, black art, &c.

147:2 It has been much contended by philosophers whether Zoroaster was the first suggester of this doctrine of the two principles: the one called by the Magi, Oromases the good, and Arimanius the evil principle. It is certain Zoroaster asserted the one, viz. that of the good, or an essential uncreated self-existent principle, the cause of all good, called by him Oromasus, meaning a good God, &c. In respect of the other principle, Arimanius, we must, before we decide either for or against Zoroaster, consider the nature of the thing in its most impartial sense.

Those who ever read Mr. Bernard's journal (Nouvelles de la Republique des Lettres, Feb. 1701, and March 1701, Art. iii. l. i.) needs not be informed that the Historia Religionis veterum Persarum, published by Dr. Hyde (professor of the oriental languages in the university of Oxford) at Oxford, in the year 1700, 4to, is one of the most excellent pieces that could possibly be written on such a subject. The idea which the learned journalist hath given of this performance is sufficient to convince us that it contains a very curious erudition, and profound discussions, which discover many rare and uncommon particulars of a country which we scarce knew any thing of before. But to come to the point: Dr. Hyde affirms, that the ancient Persians acknowledge no more than one uncreated principle, which was the good principle, or, in one word, God: and that they looked upon the evil principle as a created being. One of the names, or attributes, which they gave to God, was Hormizda; and they called the evil principle, Ahariman; and this is the original of the two Greek words, Ὡρομάσδες and Ἀπειμανιος one of which was the name of the good, and the other of the evil, principle, as we have seen above, in a passage of Plutarch. The Persians affirmed that Abraham was the first founder of their religion. Zoroaster afterwards made some alterations in it; but it is said he made no manner of change with relation to the doctrine of one sole uncreated principle, but that the only innovation in this particular was the giving the name of Light to the good principle, and that of Darkness to the evil one.

From a misconstruction put upon the doctrine of the Magi, some considerable misreports of their tenets have been propagated: I think none more curious than the following--"That a war arose betwixt the army of light and that of darkness, which at last ended in an accommodation, of which the angels were mediators, and the conditions were that the inferior world should be wholly left to the government of Arimanius for the space of 7000 years, after which it should be restored to light. Before the peace, Arimanius had exterminated all the inhabitants of the world. Light had called men to its assistance while p. 148 they were yet but spirits; which it did, either to draw them out of Arimanius' territories, or in order to give them bodies to engage against this enemy. They accepted the bodies and the fight, on condition they should be assisted by the light, and should at last overcome Arimanius. The resurrection shall come when he shall be vanquished. This they conclude was the cause of the mixture, and shall be the cause of the deliverance. The Greeks were not ignorant that Zoroaster taught a future resurrection.

148:1 The ancient Persian Magi never did divine honours to the sun or any of the stars. They maintain they do not adore the sun, but direct themselves towards it when they pray to God. It has been found amongst Zoroaster's secret precepts, that we ought to salute the sun, but not that we should adore him with religious worship. He proves that their ceremonies might very justly pass for civil honours, and to this purpose he makes some exceeding curious observations. He applies to the fire what he says of the sun. The bowings and prostrations of the Persians before the holy fire were not a religious observation, but only a civil one. The same thing must be attributed to their reported worship of fire, which, as I have said above, they kept in their Pyrea in imitation of the Jews. For though they paid a certain reverence to the fire, and that by prostration, yet this was not a religious, only a civil, worship; as it is from the force of custom that the eastern people prostrate themselves before any great man; (so they might with as much propriety be said to adore or worship him.) Believe me we ought to be the last to censure the eastern people with such gross idolatry as has been represented. The Persians, who have always been devoted to the highest study of wisdom, performed their duties in life for the honour of their God; and, although unenlightened and

Barbarians, lived as men, and not as irrational creatures: whereas we, who know our duty so well, yet practise it so ill: for I may truly say, that notwithstanding. the great benefits we derive from the divine precepts of Christianity, yet I believe it will be found an incontrovertible fact that man to man is a serpent, a few individuals excepted. But to return to our subject: It was the ancient custom to fall prostrate to angels, as being the messengers and representatives of God. Besides, there are many examples of this kind of worship, not only in the Old, but New Testament, where the women who had been converted to the true faith, upon seeing the angels at the sepulchre of Christ, fell with their faces to the ground and worshipped. Yet they well knew that it was not God they saw, but his angels, as appears from their own confession--"we have seen a vision of angels." Therefore they are wrongfully called Idolaters and worshippers of fire, for Zoroaster was the instrument of their continuation in the true faith. He was a man who had the knowledge of the true God, whom he p. 149 peculiarly worshipped in a natural cave, in which he placed several symbols representing the world; Mithra, representing the sun, filled the master's place. But it was not Mithra, but the true God, that he adored: and, lastly, as he was a true philosopher, a profound alchemist, greatly informed in all the arts of the mathematics, strict and austere in his religion, he struck the Persians with an admiration of him, and by these means made them attentive to his doctrine. The sum of all is, that he lived in a cave, dedicated to the service of God, and the study of all natural and supernatural knowledge; that he was divinely illuminated, knew the courses of the stars, and the occult and common properties of all compounded and earthly things; that by fire and Geometry (i. e. by Chemistry and the Mathematics) he investigated, proved, and demonstrated, the truth and purity, or else the fugacity and vileness, of all things knowable in this mortal state of humanity. So that the fame, sagacity, wisdom, and virtue of Zoroaster induced some certain men wickedly and fraudulently to impose upon the unwary some false magical oracles, and diabolical inventions, written in Greek and Latin, &c. as the genuine works of the divine and illustrious Zoroaster.

HERMES TRISMEGISTUS

OR THE
THRICE GREATEST INTELLIGENCER.

HERMES Trismegistus, (who was the author of the divine Pymander and some other books,) lived some time before Moses. He received the name of Trismegistus, or Mercurius ter Maximus, i. e. thrice greatest Intelligencer, because he was the first intelligencer who communicated celestial and divine knowledge to mankind by writing.

He was reported to have been king of Egypt; without doubt he was an Egyptian; nay, if you believe the Jews, even their Moses; and for the justification of this they urge, 1st, His being well skilled in chemistry; nay, the first who communicated that art to the sons of men; 2dly, They urge the philosophic work, viz. of rendering gold medicinal, or, finally, of the art of making aurum potabile; and, thirdly, of teaching the Cabala, which they say was shewn him by God on Mount Sinai: for all this is confessed to be originally written in Hebrew, which he would not have done had he not been an Hebrew, but rather in his vernacular tongue.

But whether he was Moses or not [150:1], it is certain he was an Egyptian, even as Moses himself also was; and therefore for the age he lived in, we shall not fall short of the time if we conclude he flourished much about the time of Moses; and if he really was not the identical Moses, affirmed to be so by many, it is more than probable that he was king of Egypt; for being chief philosopher, he was, according to the Egyptian custom, initiated into the mysteries of priesthood, and from thence to the chief governor or king.

He was called Ter Maximus, as having a perfect knowledge of all things contained in the world (as his Aureus, or Golden Tractate, and his Divine Pymander shews) which things he divided into three kingdoms, viz. animal, vegetable, and mineral; in the knowledge and comprehension of which three he excelled and transmitted to posterity, in enigmas and symbols, the profound secrets of nature; likewise a true description of the Philosopher's Quintessence, or Universal Elixir, which he made as the receptacle of all celestial and terrestrial virtues.

The Great Secret of the philosophers he discoursed on, which was found engraven upon a Smaragdine table, in the valley of Ebron.

Johannes Functius, in his Chronology says, he lived in the time of Moses, twenty-one years before the law was given in the wilderness. Suidas seems to confirm it by saying, "Credo Mercurium Trismegistum sapientem Egyptium floruisse ante Pharaonem." But this of Suidas may be applied to several ages, for that Pharaoh was the general name of their kings; or possibly it might be intended before the name of Pharaoh was given to their kings, which, if so [151:1], he makes Trismegistus to exist 400 years before Moses, yea, before Abraham's descent into Egypt. There is no doubt but that he possessed the great secret of the philosophic work; and if God ever appeared in man, he appeared in him, as is evident both from his books and his Pymander; in which works he has communicated the sum of the abyss, and the divine knowledge to all posterity; by which he has demonstrated himself to have been not only an inspired divine, but also a deep philosopher, obtaining his wisdom from God and heavenly things, and not from man.

150:1 The Cabalists of the Hebrews affirm that Moses was this Hermes; and although meek, yet was a man possessed of the most serious gravity, and a profound speculator in chemistry and divine magic; that he by divine inspiration on the mount, became acquainted with the knowledge of all the natural and secret operations of nature; that he taught the transmutation of metals per Cabala, i. e. by oral tradition, to the Jews.

151:1 According to the best authorities to be taken, Hermes Trismegistus lived in the time of Pharaoh, Israel's tyrant and oppressor, and was not the same with Moses who opposed Jannes and Jambres.

APPOLLONIUS OF TYANA

WITH SOME ACCOUNT OF HIS
REMARKABLE MIRACLES, PROPHECIES, VISIONS, RELATIONS,
&c. &c.

APPOLLONIUS Tyanæus, was one of the most extraordinary persons that ever appeared in the world. He was born at Tyana in Cappadocia, towards the beginning of the first century. At sixteen years of age he became a rigid disciple of Pythagoras, renouncing wine, flesh, and women, wearing no shoes, and letting his hair and beard grow long, and cloathing himself only in linen: soon after he became a reformer, and fixed his abode in a temple of Æsculapius, where many sick persons resorted to be cured by him. Being come to age, he gave part of his estate to his eldest brother, and distributed another part to his poor relations, and kept back only a very small share to himself. He lived six years without speaking a word, notwithstanding during this silence he quelled several seditions in Cecilia and Pamphilia; that which he put a stop to at Aspenda was the most difficult of all to appease, because the business was to make those hearken to reason whom famine had driven to revolt: the cause of this commotion was, some rich men having monopolized all the corn, occasioned an extraordinary scarcity in the city; Appollonius stopped this popular commotion, without speaking a word to the enraged multitude: Appollonius had no occasion for words; his Pythagoric silence did all that the finest figures of oratory could effect. He travelled much, professed himself a legislator; understood all languages, without having learned them: he had the surprising faculty of knowing what was transacted at an immense distance, and at the time the Emperor Domitian was stabbed, Appollonius being at a vast distance, and standing in the market-place of the city, exclaimed, "Strike! strike!-- 'tis done, the tyrant is no more." He understood the language of birds; he condemned dancing, and other diversions of that sort; he recommended charity and piety; he travelled almost over all the countries of the world; and he died at a very great age. His life has been fully related by Philostratus; but it contains so many fabulous relations that we do not pretend to introduce them in this place. There are many who have very readily opposed the miracles of this man to those of Christ, and drew a parallel between them. It cannot be denied that this philosopher received very great honours, both during his life and after his death; and that his reputation continued long after paganism. He wrote four books of judicial Astrology, and a Treatise on Sacrifices, shewing what was to be offered to the Deity.

We must not omit a circumstance which tends to the honour of this venerable person. It is related that Aurelius had come to a resolution, and had publikly declared his intentions, to demolish the city of Tyana; but that Appollonius of Tyana, an ancient philosopher, of great renown and authority, a true friend of the gods, and himself honoured as a deity, appeared to him in his usual form as he retired into his tent, and addressed him thus:--"Aurelian, if you desire to be victorious, think no more of the destruction of my fellow-citizens!--Aurelian, if you desire to rule, abstain from the blood of the innocent!--Aurelian, if you will conquer, be merciful!" Aurelian being acquainted with the features of this ancient philosopher, having seen his image in several temples, he vowed to erect a temple and statues to him; and therefore altered his resolution of sacking Tyana. This account we have from men of credit, and have met with it in books in the Olpian library; and we are the more inclined to believe it on account of the dignity of Apollonius; for was there ever any thing among men more holy, venerable, noble, and divine than Apollonius? He restored life to the dead, he did and spoke many things beyond human reach; which whoever would be informed of, may meet with many accounts of them in the Greek histories of his life.' See Vopiscus in Aurelian, cap. 24.

Lastly, the inhabitants of Tyana built a temple to their Appollonius after his death; his statue was erected in several temples: the Emperor Adrian collected as many of his writings as he possibly could, and kept them very select, in his superb palace at Antium, with a rare but small book of this philosopher's, concerning the Oracle of Trophonius. This little book was to be seen at Antium during the life of Philostratus; nor did any curiosity whatever render this small town so famous as did this rare and extraordinary book of Appollonius.

It is reported that a wise prince of the Indians, well skilled in magic, made seven rings of the seven planets, which he bestowed upon Appollonius, one of which he wore every day; by which he always maintained the health and vigour of his youth, and lived to a very advanced age. His life was translated from the Greek of Philostratus into French, by Blaise de Vigners, with a very ample commentary by Artus Thomas, Lord of Embry, a Parisian; and some time since there has been made an English translation of his life, which was condemned, prohibited, and anathematized without reason.

PETRUS DE ABANO, OR PETER OF APONA

DOCTOR OF PHILOSOPHY AND PHYSIC, &c. &c. &c.

PETRUS APONENSIS, or APONUS, one of the most famous philosophers and physicians of his time, was born A. D. 1250, in a village, situated four miles from Padua. He studied a long time at Paris, where he was promoted to the degrees of Doctor in philosophy and physic, in the practice of which he was very successful, but his fees remarkably high. Gabriel Naude, in his Antiquitate Scholæ Medicæ Parisiensis, gives the following account of him: "Let us next produce Peter de Apona, or Peter de Abano, called the Reconciler, on account of the famous book which he published during his residence in your university [155:1]."--It is certain that physic lay buried in Italy, scarce known to any one, uncultivated and unadorned, till its tutelar genius, a villager of Apona, destined to free Italy from its barbarism and ignorance, as Camillus once freed Rome from the siege of the Gauls, made diligent enquiry in what part of the world polite literature was most happily cultivated, philosophy most subtilly handled, and physic taught with the greatest solidity and purity; and being assured that Paris alone laid claim to this honour, thither he presently flies; giving himself up wholly to her tutelage, he applied himself diligently to the mysteries of philosophy and medicine; obtained a degree and the laurel in both; and afterwards taught them both with great applause: and after a stay of many years, loaden with the wealth acquired among you, arid, after having become the most famous philosopher, astrologer, physician, and mathematician of his time, returns to his own country, where, in the opinion of the judicious Scardeon, he was the first restorer of true philosophy and physic. Gratitude, therefore, calls upon you to acknowledge your obligations due to Michæl Angelus Blondus, a physician of Rome, who in the last century undertaking to publish the Conciliationes Physiognomicæ of your Aponensian doctor, and finding they had been composed at Paris, and in your university, chose to publish them in the name, and under the patronage, of your society." 'Tis said, that he was suspected of magic [156:1], and persecuted on that account by the Inquisition: and it is probable that, if he had lived to the end of his trial, he would have suffered in person what he was sentenced to suffer in effigy after his death. His apologists observe, that his body, being privately taken out of his grave by his friends, escaped the vigilance of the Inquisitors, who would have condemned it to be burnt. He was removed from place to place, and at last deposited in St. Augustin's Church, without Epitaph, or any other mark of honour. His accusers ascribed inconsistent opinions to him; they charged him with being a magician, and yet with denying the existence of spirits. He had such an antipathy to milk, that the very seeing any one take it made him vomit. He died in the year 1316 [157:1] in the sixty-sixth year of his age. One of his principal books was the Conciliator, already mentioned.

155:1 Naude takes notice of this in a speech in which he extols the ancient glory of the university of Paris. We have, above, recited his words at length, because they incidentally inform us, that Peter de Abano composed that great work at Paris which procured him the appellation of the Reconciler.

156:1 Naude, in his Apology for great Men accused of Magic, says, "The general opinion of almost all authors is, that he was the greatest magician of his time; that by means of seven spirits, familiar, which he kept inclosed in chrystal, he had acquired the knowledge of the seven liberal arts, and that he had the art of causing the money he had made use of to return again into his pocket. He was accused of magic in the eightieth year of his age, and that dying in the year 1305, before his trial was over, he was condemned (as Castellan reports) to the fire; and that a bundle of straw, or osier, representing his person, was publicly burnt at Padua; that by so rigorous an example, and by the fear of incurring a like penalty, they might suppress the reading of three books which he had composed on this subject: the first of which is the noted Heptameron, or Magical Elements of Peter de Abano, Philosopher, now extant, and printed at the end of Agrippa's works; the second, that which Trithemius calls Elucidarium Necromanticum Petri de Abano; and a third, called by the same author Liber experimentorum mirabilium de Annulis secundem, 28 Mansiom Lunæ." Now it is to be noted, that Naude lays no stress upon these seeming strong proofs; he refutes them by immediately after affirming, that Peter of Apona was a man of prodigious penetration and learning, living in an age of darkness which caused everything out of the vulgar track to be suspected as diabolical, especially as he was very much given to study, and acquainted with the harmony of the celestial bodies and the proportions of nature, and addicted to curious and divinatory science. "He was one (says he) who appeared as a prodigy of learning amidst the ignorance of that age, and who, besides his skill in languages and physic, had carried his enquiries so far into the occult sciences of abstruse and hidden nature, that, after having given most ample proofs, by his writings concerning physiognomy, geomancy, and chiromancy, what he was able to perform in each of these, he quitted them all together with his youthful curiosity to addict himself wholly to the study of philosophy, physic, and astrology; which studies proved so advantageous to him, that, not to speak of the two first, which introduced him to all the popes and sovereign pontiffs of his time, and acquired him the reputation which at present he enjoys among learned men, it is certain that he was a great master in the latter, which appears not only by the astronomical figures which he caused to be painted in the great hall of the palace at Padua, and the translations he made of the books of the most learned Rabbi Abraham Aben Ezra, added to those which he himself composed on critical days, and the improvement of astronomy, but by the testimony of the renowned mathematician Regio Montanus, who made a fine panegyric on him, in quality of an astrologer, in the oration which he delivered publicly at Padua when he explained there the book of Alfraganus." Now, many respectable authors are of opinion that it was not on the score of magic that the Inquisition sentenced him to death, but because he endeavoured to account for the wonderful effects in nature by the influences of the celestial bodies, not attributing them to angels or dæmons; so that heresy, instead of magic, seems to have been the ground of his falling under the tyranny of the sage fathers of the Roman Catholic faith, as being one who opposed the doctrine of spiritual beings.

157:1 If this be true as we read in Tomasini, in Elog. Vilor. Illustr. p. 22, Naude must be mistaken where he says, that "Peter Aponus being accused at the age of 80 years, died A. D.1305." Freherus affirms the same upon the authority of Bernardin Scardeon. Gesner is mistaken in making Peter Aponus flourish in the year 1320. Konig has copied this error. But Father Rapin is much more grossly mistaken than any of them when he places him in the sixteenth century, saying, "Peter of Apona, a physician of Padua, who flourished under Clement VII, debauched his imagination so far by reading the Arabian philosophers, and by too much studying the astrology of Alfraganus, that he was put into the Inquisition upon the suspicion of magic, &c." See Rapin Reflex. sur la Philosophiæ, n. 28. p. 360. Vossius has followed Gesner, and makes an observation worthy to be considered. He says, that Peter of Apona sent his book, De Medicina Omnimoda, to Pope John XXII, who was elected in the year 1316, and held the Pontifical Chair seventeen years. By this we know the age of this physician. But if the year 1316 was that of his death, the conclusion is unjust; neither does it clear Vossius of an error.

APULEIUS

THE PLATONIC PHILOSOPHER

LUCIUS APULEIUS, a Platonic philosopher, publicly known by the famous work of the Golden Ass, lived in the second century under the Antonines. He was a native of Madaura, a Roman colony in Africa; his family was considerable; he had been well educated, and possessed a graceful exterior; he had wit and learning; but was suspected of magic. He studied first at Carthage, then at Athens, and afterwards at Rome, where he acquired the Latin tongue without any assistance. An insatiable curiosity to know every thing induced him to make several voyages, and enter himself into several religious fraternities. He would see the bottom of their mysteries. He spent almost all his estate in travelling; insomuch, that being returned to Rome, and having a desire to dedicate himself to the service of Osiris, he lacked money to defray the expence of the ceremonies of his reception, he was obliged to make money of his clothes to complete the necessary sum: after this, he gained his living by pleading; and, as he was eloquent and subtle, he did not want causes, some of which were very considerable. But he improved his fortunes much more by a lucky marriage than by pleading. A widow, whose name was Pudentilla, neither young nor fair, but who had a good estate, thought him worth her notice. He was not coy, nor was he solicitous to keep his fine person, his wit, his neatness, and his eloquence, for some young girl he married this rich widow chearfully (and with the most becoming philosophy overcame all turbulent passions, which might draw him into the snares of beauty,) at a country house near Oëa, a maritime town of Africa. This marriage. drew upon him a troublesome law-suit. The relations of this lady's two sons urged that he had made use of art magic to possess himself of her person and money; they accused him of being worse than a magician, viz. a wizard, before Claudius Maximus, Proconsul of Africa. He defended himself with great vigour [159:1]. His apology, which he delivered before the judges, furnishes us with examples of the most shameful artifices that the villainy of an impudent calumniator is capable of putting in practice [160:1]. Apuleius was extremely laborious, and composed several books, some in verse and others in prose, of which but a small part has resisted the injuries of time. He delighted in making public speeches, in which he gained the applause of all his hearers. When they heard him at Oëa, the audience cried out with one voice, that he ought to be honoured with the freedom of the city. Those of Carthage heard him favourably, and erected a statue in honour of him. Several other cities did him the same honour. It is said that his wife held the candle to him whilst he studied; but this is not to be taken literally; it is rather a figure of Gallic eloquence in Sidonis Apollinaris, Legentibus meditantibusque candelas & candelabra tenuerunt. Several critics have published notes on Apuleius: witness Phillipus Beraldus, who published very large notes on the Golden Ass, at Venice, in folio, ann. 1504, which were reprinted in 8vo, at Paris and at several other places. Godescalk Stewichius, Peter Colvius, John Wiewer, &c. have written on all the works of Apuleius. Precius published the Golden Ass, and the Apology, separately, with a great many observations. The annotations of Casaubon, and those of Scipio Gentilis, on the Apology, are very scarce, and much valued: the first appeared in the year 1594, and the latter in 1607. The Golden Ass may be considered (as Bayle says) as a continued satire on the disorders which the pseudo-magicians, priests, pandars, and thieves filled the world with at that time. This observation occurs in Fleuri's annotations. A person who would take the pains, and had the requisite qualifications, might draw up a very curious and instructive commentary on this romance, and might inform the world of several things which the preceding commentaries have never touched upon. There are some very obscene passages in this book of Apuleius. It is generally believed that this author has inserted some curious episodes in it of his own invention; and amongst others, that of Psyche. Horum certe noster itæ imitator fuit, ut è suo penu enumerabilia protulerit, atque inter cætera venustissimum illud Psyches, Ἐπεισόδιον. This episode furnished Moliere with matter for an excellent Dramatic Piece, and M. de la Fontaine for a fine Romance.

159:1 Besides the accusation of magic, they reproached him with his beauty, his fine hair, his teeth, and his looking-glass. To the two first particulars he answered he was sorry their accusation was false.--"How do I wish," replied he, "that these heavy accusations of beauty, fine hair, &c. were just! I should, without difficulty, reply, as Paris in Homer does to Hector,

--------------- *nor thou despise the charms*
With which a lover golden Venus arms.
Soft moving speech, and pleasing outward show,
No wish can gain them, but the Gods bestow.

POPE

"Thus would I reply to the charge of beauty. Besides that, even philosophers are allowed to be of a liberal aspect; that Pythagoras, the first of philosophers, was the handsomest man of his time; and Zeno--but, as I observed, I am far from pretending to this apology; since, besides that nature has bestowed but a very moderate degree of beauty on me, my continual application to study wears off every bodily grace, and impairs my constitution. My hair, which I am falsely accused of curling and dressing by way of ornament, is, as you see, far from being beautiful and delicate: on the contrary, it is perplexed and entangled like a bundle of flocks or tow, and so knotty through long neglect of combing, and even of disentangling, as never to be reduced to order." As to the third particular, he did not deny his having sent a very exquisite powder for the teeth to a friend, together with some verses, containing an exact description of the effects of the powder. He alleged that all, but especially those who spake in public, ought to be particularly careful to keep their mouths clean. This was a fine field for defence and for turning his adversary into ridicule; though, in all probability, he had given occasion enough for censure by too great an affectation of distinguishing himself from other learned men. Observe with how much ease some causes are defended, although the defendant be a little in the wrong. "I observed that some could scarce forbear laughing when our orator angrily accused me of keeping my mouth clean, and pronounced the word tooth-powder with as much indignation as any one ever pronounced the word poison. But, surely, it is not beneath a philosopher to study cleanliness, and to let no part of the body be foul, or of an ill savour, especially the mouth, the use of which is the most frequent and conspicuous, whether a man converses with another, or speaks in public, or says his prayers in a temple. For speech is previous to every action of a man, and, as an excellent poet says, proceeds from the Wall of the Teeth."

We may make the same observation upon the last head of his accusation. It is no crime in a doctor of what faculty soever, to have a looking-glass; but if he consults it too often in dressing himself, he is justly liable to censure. Morality in Apuleius's time was much stricter than at present as to external behaviour, for he durst not avow his making use of his looking-glass. He maintains that he might do p. 160 it, and proves it by several philosophical reasons, which, to say the truth, are much more ingenious than judiciously applied; but he denies that he ever consulted his looking-glass; for he says, alluding to this ludicrous accusation, "Next follows the long and bitter harangue about the looking-glass; in which, so heinous is the crime, that Pudens almost burst himself with bawling out--'A philosopher to have a looking-glass!'--Suppose I should confess that I have, that you may not believe there is really something in your objection, if I should deny it; it does not follow from hence that I must necessarily make a practice of dressing myself at it. In many things I want the possession but enjoy the use of them. Now, if neither to have a thing be a proof that it is made use of, nor the want of it of the contrary, and as I am not blamed for possessing, but for making use of, a looking-glass, it is incumbent upon him to prove farther at what time, and in what place, and in the presence of whom, I made cc use of it; since you determine it to be a greater crime in a philosopher to see a looking-glass, than for the profane to behold the attire of Ceres."

160:1 I shall instance one to shew that in all ages the spirit of calumny has put men upon forging proofs by . false extracts from what a person has said or written. To convict Apuleius of practising magic, his accusers alledge a letter which his wife had wrote during the time he paid his devoirs to her, and affirmed that she had confessed, in this letter, that Apuleius was a wizard, and had actually bewitched her. It was no hard matter to make the court believe that she had written so, for they only read a few words of her letter, detached from what preceded or followed, and no one pressed them to read the whole. At last

394

Apuleius covered them with confusion by reciting the whole passage from his wife's letter. It appeared, that far from complaining of Apuleius, she justified him, and artfully ridiculed his accusers. These are his words: you will find that precisely the same terms may either condemn or justify Apuleius, according as they are taken with or without what precedes them. "Being inclined to marry, for the reasons which I have mentioned, you yourself persuaded me to make choice of this man, being fond of him, and being desirous, by my means, to make him one of the family. But now, at the instigation of wicked men, Apuleius must be informed against as a magician (or wizard), and I, forsooth, am enchanted by him. I certainly love him: come to me before my reason fails me." He aggravates this kind of fraud as it deserves; his words deserve to be engraved in letters of gold, to deter (if possible) all calumniators from practising the like cheats. He says, "There are many things which, produced alone, may seem liable to calumny. Any discourse may furnish matter of accusation, if what is connected with foregoing words be robbed of its introduction; if some things be suppressed at pleasure, and if what is spoken by way of reproach to others, for inventing a calumny, be pronounced by the reader as an assertion of the truth of it."

ARISTOTLE

THE PERIPATETIC.

ARISTOTLE, commonly called the Prince of Philosophers, or the Philosopher, by way of excellence, was the founder of a sect which surpassed, and at length even swallowed up all the rest. Not but that it has had reverse of fortune in its turn; especially in the seventeenth century, in which it has been violently shaken, though the Catholic divines on the one side, and the Protestant on the other, have run (as to the quenching of fire) to its relief, and fortified themselves so strongly, by the secular arm, against the New Philosophy, that it is not like to lose its dominion. Mr. Moreri met with so many good materials in a work of father Rapin, that he has given a very large article of Aristotle, enough to dispense with any assistance. Accordingly, I design not to enlarge upon it as far as the subject might allow, but shall content myself with observing some of the errors which I have collected concerning this philosopher. It is not certain that Aristotle practised pharmacy in Athens while he was a disciple of Plato, nor is it more certain that he did not. Very little credit ought to be given to a current tradition that he learnt several things of a Jew, and much less to a story of his pretended conversion to Judaism. They who pretend that he was born a Jew, are much more grossly mistaken: the wrong pointing of a certain passage occasioned this mistake. They are deceived who say that he was a disciple of Socrates for three years, for Socrates died 15 years before Aristotle was born. Aristotle's behaviour towards his master Plato is variously related: some will have it that, through prodigious vanity and ingratitude, he set up altar against altar: that is, he erected a school in Athens during Plato's life, and in opposition to him: others say that he did not set up for a professor till after his master's death. We are told some things concerning his amours which are not altogether to his advantage. It was pretended that his conjugal affection was idolatrous, and that, if he had not retired from Athens, the process for irreligion, which the priests had commenced against him, would have been attended with the same consequences as that against Socrates. Though he deserved very, great praise, yet it is certain that most of the errors concerning him are to be found in the extravagant commendations which have been heaped upon him: as, for example, is it not a downright falsehood to say, that if Aristotle spoke in his natural philosophy like a man, he spoke in his moral philosophy like a God; and that it is a question in his moral philosophy whether he partakes more of the lawyer than of the priest; more of the priest than the prophet; more of the prophet than of the God? Cardinal Pallavinci scrupled not in some measure to affirm that, if it had not been for Aristotle, the church would have wanted some of its articles of faith. The Christians are not the only people who have authorized his philosophy; the Mahometans are little less prejudiced in its favour; and we are told, that to this day, notwithstanding the ignorance which reigns among them, they have schools for this sect. It will be an everlasting subject of wonder, to persons who know what philosophy is, to find that Aristotle's authority was so much respected in the schools, for several ages, that when a disputant quoted a passage from this philosopher, he who maintained the thesis durst not say transeat, but must either deny the passage, or explain it in his own way. It is in this manner we treat the Holy Scriptures in the divinity schools. The parliaments which have proscribed all other philosophy but that of Aristotle, are more excusable than the doctors: for whether the members of parliament were really persuaded that this philosophy was the best of any, or was not, the public good might induce them to prohibit new opinions, lest the academical divisions should extend their malignant influence to the disturbance of the tranquillity of the state. What is most astonishing to wise men is, that the professors should be so strongly prejudiced in favour of Aristotle's philosophy. Had this prepossession been confined to his poetry and rhetoric, it had been less wonderful: but they were fond of the weakest of his works; I mean his Logic, and Natural Philosophy [164:1]. This justice, however, must be done to the blindest of his followers, that they have deserted him where he clashes with Christianity; and this he did in points of the greatest consequence, since he maintained the eternity of the world, and did not believe that providence extended itself to sublunary beings. As to the immortality of the soul, it is not certainly known whether he acknowledged it or not [164:2]. In the year 1647, the famous capuchin, Valerian Magni, published a work concerning the Atheism of Aristotle. About one hundred and thirty years before, Marc Antony Venerius published a system of philosophy, in which he discovered several inconsistencies between Aristotle's doctrine, and the truths of religion. Campanella maintained the same in his book de Reductione ad Religionem, which was approved at Rome in the year 1630. It was not long since maintained in Holland, in the prefaces to some books, that the doctrine of this philosopher differed but little from Spinozism. In the mean time, if some Peripatetics may be believed, he was not ignorant of the mystery of the Trinity. He made a very good end, and enjoys eternal happiness. He composed a great number of books; a great part of which is come down to us. It is true some critics raise a thousand scruples about them. He was extremely honoured in his own city, and there were not wanting heretics who worshipped his image with that of Christ. There is extant some book which mentions, that, before the Reformation, there were churches in Germany in which Aristotle's Ethics were read every Sunday morning to the people instead of the Gospel. There are but few instances of zeal for religion which have not been shewn for the Peripatetic philosophy. Paul de Foix, famous for his embassies and his learning, would not see Francis Patricius at Ferrara, because he was informed that that learned man taught a philosophy different from the Peripatetic. This was treating the enemies of Aristotle as zealots treat heretics. After all, it is no wonder that the Peripatetic philosophy, as it has been taught for several centuries, found so many protectors; or that the interests of it are believed to be inseparable from those of theology: for it accustoms the mind to acquiesce without evidence. This union of interests may be esteemed as a pledge to the Peripatetics of the immortality of their sect, and an argument to abate the hopes of the new philosophers.--Considering, withal, that there are some doctrines of Aristotle which the moderns have rejected, and which must, sooner or later, be adopted again. The Protestant divines have very much altered their conduct, if it is true, as we are told, that the first reformers clamoured so loud against the Peripatetic philosophy. The kind of death,. which in some respects does much honour to the memory of Aristotle, is, that which some have reported, viz. that his vexation at not being able to discover the cause of the flux and reflux of the Eurippus occasioned the distemper of which he died. Some say, that being retired into the island of Eubæa, to avoid a process against him for irreligion, he poisoned himself: but why should he quit Athens to free himself from persecution this way? HESYCHIUS affirms, not only that sentence of death was pronounced against him for an hymn which he made in honour of his father-in-law, but also that he swallowed aconite in execution of this sentence. If this were true, it would have been mentioned by more authors.

The number of ancient and modern writers who have exercised their pens on Aristotle, either in commenting on, or translating, him, is endless. A catalogue of them is to be met with in some of the editions of his works, but not a complete one. See a treatise of father Labbé, entitled Aristotelis & Platonis Græcorum Interpretum, typis hactenus editorum brevis conspectus; A short view of the Greek interpreters of Aristotle and Plato hitherto published; printed at Paris in the year 1657, in 4to. Mr. Teissier names four authors who have composed the life of Aristotle; Ammonius, Guarini of Verona, John James Beurerus, and Leonard Aretin. He forgot Jerome Gemusæus, physician and professor of philosophy at Bazil, author of a book, De Vitæ Aristotelis, et eus Operum Censura.--The Life of Aristotle, and a Critique on his Works.

PETER BAYLE.

164:1 To be convinced of the weakness of these works, we need only read Gassendus in his Exercitationes Paradoxicæ adversos Aristoteleos. He says enough there against Aristotle's philosophy in general, to convince every unprejudiced reader that it is very defective; but he particularly ruins this philosopher's Logic. He was preparing, likewise, a criticism on his Natural Philosophy, his Metaphysics, and Ethics, in the same way; when, being alarmed at the formidable indignation of the peripatetic party against him, be chose rather to drop his work, than expose himself to their vexatious persecutions. In Aristotle's Logic and Natural Philosophy, there are many things which discover the elevation and profundity of his genius.

164:2 Pomponatius and Niphus had a great quarrel on this subject. The first maintained, that the immortality of the soul was inconsistent with Aristotle's principles: the latter undertook to defend the contrary. See the discourse of la

Mothe le Vayer on the Immortality of the Soul, and Bodin, in page 15 of Pref. to
Dæmonomania.

ARTEMIDORUS OF EPHESUS

THE SOMNABULIST, OR DREAMER

ARTEMIDORUS (who wrote so largely upon Dreams) was a native of Ephesus. He lived under Antonius Pius, as he informs us himself, where he says, he knew an Athlete, who having dreamt that he had lost his sight, obtained the prize in the games which that Emperor ordered to be celebrated. No author has ever taken more pains upon so useful a subject than Artemidorus has done. He bought up all that had been written upon the subject of dreams, which amounted to several volumes, but he spent many years in travelling to collect them, as well as the different opinions of all the learned who were then living. He kept a continual correspondence with those in the towns and assemblies of Greece, in Italy, and in the most populous islands; and he collected every where all the dreams he could hear of, and the events they had. He despised the censure of those grave and supercilious persons, who treat all pretenders to predictions as sharpers, or impostors, and without regarding the censures of these Catos, he frequented those diviners many years. In a word, he devoted all his time and thoughts to the science of dreams. He thought that his great labour in making so many collections, &c. had enabled him to warrant his interpretations by reason and experience, but unfortunately he ever fixed upon the most trifling and frivolous subjects, such as almost every one is dreaming of: there is no dream which Artemidorus has explained, but will bear a quite different interpretation, with the same probability and with at least as natural resemblances, as those on which that interpreter proceeds. I say nothing of the injury done to intelligences, to whose direction we must necessarily impute our dreams if we expect to find in them any presage of futurity [167:1]. Artemidorus took great pains to instruct his son in the same science, as appears by the two books which he dedicated to him. So eager a pursuit after these studies is the less to be wondered at, when we consider that he believed himself under the inspiration of Apollo. He dedicated his three first books to one Cassius Maximus, and the other two to his son.--They were printed in Greek at Venice in the year 1518. In the year 1603 Rigaultius published them at Paris in Greek and Latin, with notes. The Latin translation he made use of was that published by John Cornarius at Bazil, in the year 1539. Artemidorus wrote a treatise of augury, and another upon chiromancy; but we have no remains of them. Tertullian has not taken notice of him in that passage, where he quotes several onirocritic authors; but Lucian does not forget him, though he names but two writers of this class.

167:1 We find in Artemidorus some of the most trifling incidents in dreams noted by him to presage very extraordinary things; such, as if any one dreams of his nose, or his teeth, or such like trifling subjects, such particular events they must denote.--Now, as we cannot attribute a true and significant dream to any other cause than the celestial intelligences, or an evil dæmon, or else to the soul itself (which possesses an inherent prophetic virtue, as we have fully treated of in our Second Book of Magic, where we have spoken of prophetic dreams),--I say, from which of these causes a dream proceeds, we must ascribe but a very deficient portion of knowledge to either of them, if we do not allow them capable of giving better and plainer information respecting any calamity or change of fortune or circumstances, than by dreaming of one's nose itching, or a tooth falling out, and a hundred other toys like these--I say, such modes of dictating to us a fore-knowledge of events to happen, cannot but be unworthy of their Wisdom, subtilty, or power, and if they cannot instruct us by better signs, how great is their ignorance, and if they will not, how great is their malice? therefore, all such trifling dreams are to be altogether rejected as vain and insignificant, for we must remember that "a dream comes through the multitude of business," and often otherwise; but such dreams as we are to notice, and draw predictions of future accidents and events, are those where the dream is altogether consistent, not depending upon any prior discourse, accidents, or other like circumstances; likewise that the person who would wish to dream true dreams, should so dispose himself as to become a fit recipient of the heavenly powers, but this is only to be done by a temperate and frugal diet, a mind bent on sublime contemplation, a religious desire of being informed of any misfortune, accident, or event, which might introduce misery, poverty, or distraction of mind; so as when we know it, to deprecate the same by prayer to the divine wisdom, that he would be pleased to divert the evil impending, or to enable us to meet the same with fortitude, and endure it with patience till the will of the Deity is accomplished. These are the things which we ought to be desirous to receive information of by dream, vision, or the like, and of which many are often truly forewarned, and thereby foretell things to come, also presage of the death of certain friends; all which I know by experience to be true and probable.

BABYLONIANS

UNDER this article of Babylonians we shall just give the reader a general sketch of the antiquity of occult learning among the Chaldeans of Babylon, so famous for their speculations in astrology. Diodorus Siculus informs us, that the inhabitants of Babylon assert, that their city was very ancient; for they counted four hundred and seventy-three thousand years, from the first observations of their astrologers to the coming of Alexander. Others say, that the Babylonians boasted of having preserved in their archives the observations which their astrologers had made on nativities for the space of four hundred and seventy thousand years; from hence we ought to correct a passage of Pliny, which some authors make use of improperly, either to confute the antiquity of Babylon, or for other purposes. Aristotle knew without doubt that the Babylonians boasted of having a series of astronomical observations comprehending a prodigious number of centuries. He was desirous to inform himself of the truth of this by means of Calisthenes, who was in Alexander's retinue, but found a great mistake in the account; for it is pretended that Calisthenes assured him that the astronomical observations he had seen in Babylon, comprehended no more than 1903 years. Simplicius reports this, and borrows it from Porphyry. If Calisthenes has computed right, it must be agreed, that after the deluge men made very great haste to become astrologers; for according to the Hebrew Bible there is but two thousand years [169:1] to be found from the flood to the death of Alexander. There is reason to question what Simplicius reports, and it is remarkable that all the ancient authors, who have ascribed the building of Babylon to Semiramis, have no authority than that of Ctesias, whose histories abounded in fables. And, therefore, we see that Berosius blames the Greek writers for affirming, that Semiramis built Babylon, and adorned it with the most beautiful structures. The supplement to Moreri quotes Quintus Curtinus, in relation to the immodesty of the Babylonian women [169:2], who prostituted their bodies to strangers for money, under the idea of performing their devotions required by Venus. Observe, that these sums were afterwards applied to religious uses.

169:1 Epigenus tells us, that amongst the Babylonians there were celestial observations for four hundred and seventy thousand years, inscribed on pillars or tables of bricks. Berosius and Critodemus, who make the least of it, say four hundred and ninety years.

169:2 This lascivious ceremony was very ancient. Jeremiah's letter inserted in the book of Baruch touches something on it, but in an obscure manner, and wants a commentary taken out of Herodotus. Jeremiah's text runs thus:--"The women also with cords about them sat in the ways--but if any of them, drawn by some that passeth by, lie with him, she reproacheth her fellow, that she was not thought as worthy as herself, nor her cord broken." Herodotus informs us, that there was a law in Babylon which obliged all the women of the country to seat themselves near the temple of Venus, and there to wait an opportunity of copulating with a stranger, &c. &c.

THE LIFE OF HENRY CORNELIUS AGRIPPA

KNIGHT,DOCTOR OF BOTH LAWS, COUNSELLOR TO CHARLES V. EMPEROR OF GERMANY, AND JUDGE OF THE PREROGATIVE COURT.

HENRY CORNELIUS AGRIPPA, a very learned man and a magician [170:1], flourished in the sixteenth century. He was born at Cologne on the 14th of September, 1486. He descended from a noble and ancient family of Nettesheim. in Belgia; desiring to walk in the steps of his ancestors, who for many generations had been employed by the princes of the house of Austria, he entered early into the service of the Emperor Maximilian. He had at first the employ of Secretary; but as he was equally qualified for the sword as the pen, he afterwards turned soldier, and served the Emperor seven years in his Italian army. He signalized himself on several occasions, and as a reward of his brave actions he was created knight in the field. He wished to add the academical honours to the military, he therefore commenced doctor of laws and physic. He was a man possessed of a very wonderful genius, and from his youth applied his mind to learning, and by his great natural talents he obtained great knowledge in almost all arts and sciences. He was a diligent searcher into the mysteries of nature, and was early in search of the philosopher's stone; and it appears that he had been recommended to some princes as master of the art of alchymy [171:1], and very fit for the grand projection. He had a very extensive knowledge of things in general, as likewise in the learned languages. He was pupil to Trithemius, who wrote upon the nature, ministry, and offices of intelligences and spirits. He was of an unsettled temper, and often changed his situation, and was so unfortunate as to draw upon himself the indignation of the Popish clergy by his writings. We find by his letters that he had been in France before the year 1507, that he travelled into Spain in the year 1508, and was at Dole in the year 1509. He read public lectures there, which engaged him in a contest with the Cordelier Catilinet. The monks in those times suspected whatever they did not understand, of heresy and error; how then could they suffer Agrippa to explain the mysterious works of Reuchlinus de Verbo Mirifico with impunity? It was the subject of the lectures which he read at Dole in

1509 with great reputation. To ingratiate himself the better with Margaret of Austria, governess of the Austrian Netherlands, he composed at that time a treatise on the excellency of women; but the persecution he suffered from the monks prevented him from publishing it; he gave up the cause, and came into England, where he wrote on St. Paul's Epistles, although he had another very private affair upon his bands. Being returned to Cologne, he read public lectures there on the questions of the divinity, which are called Quodlibetales; after which he went to the Emperor Maximilian's army in Italy, and continued there till Cardinal de Sainte Croix sent for him to Pisa. Agrippa would have displayed his abilities there in quality of theologist of the council, if that assembly had continued. This would not have been the way to please the Court of Rome, or to deserve the obliging letter he received from Leo X, and from whence we may conclude, that he altered his opinion. From that time he taught divinity publicly at Pavia, and at Turin. He likewise read lectures on Mercurius Trismegistus at Pavia, in the year 1515. He had a wife who was handsome and accomplished, by whom he had one son; he lost her in 1521; he married again an accomplished lady at Geneva in the year 1522, of whom he gives a very good character; by this wife he had three children, two sons and one daughter, who died. It appears by the second book of his letters, that his friends endeavoured in several places to procure him some honourable settlement, either at Grenoble, Geneva, Avignon, or Metz. He preferred the post which was offered him in this last city; and I find that in the year 1518 he was chosen by the lords of Metz to be their advocate, syndic, and orator. The persecutions which the monks raised against him, as well on account of his having refuted the common opinion concerning the three husbands of St. Anne, as because he had protected a country-woman, who was accused of witchcraft, made him leave the city of Metz. The story is as follows:-- A country-woman, who was accused of witchcraft, was proposed (by the Dominican, Nicholas Savini, Inquisitor of the Faith at Metz) to be put to the torture, upon a mere prejudice, grounded on her being the daughter of a witch, who had been burnt. Agrippa immediately took up the cudgels, and did what he could to prevent so irregular a proceeding, but could not prevent the woman from being put to the question; however, he was the instrument of proving her innocence. Her accusers were condemned in a fine. The penalty was too mild, and far from a retaliation. This country-woman was of Vapey, a town situated near the gates of Metz, and belonging to the chapter of the cathedral. There appeared in Messin, who was the principal accuser of this woman, such sordid passions, and such a total ignorance of literature and philosophy, that Agrippa, in his letter of June 2, 1519, treats the town of Metz as--"The stepmother of learning and virtue." This satyrical reflexion of Agrippa's might give rise to the proverb-- "Metz, the covetous, and step-mother of arts and sciences."--What induced him to treat of the monogamy of St. Anne was his seeing, that James Faber Stapulensis, his friend, was pulled to pieces by the preachers of Metz, for having maintained that opinion. Agrippa retired to Cologne, his native city, in the year 1520, willingly forsaking a city, which the seditious inquisitors had made an enemy to learning and true merit. It is indeed the fate of all cities where such persons grow powerful of whatsoever religion they are of. He again left his own city in the year 1521, and went to Geneva, but his fortunes did not much improve there, for he complained that he was not rich enough to make a journey to Chamberi to solicit the pension which he was led to expect from the Duke of Savoy. This expectation came to nothing, upon which Agrippa went from Geneva to Fribourg in Switzerland in the year 1523, to practise physic there as he had done at Geneva. The year following he went to Lyons, and obtained a pension from Francis I. He was in the service of that prince's mother in quality of her physician, but made no great improvement of his fortune there; neither did he follow that princess when she departed from Lyons in the month of August, 1525, to conduct her daughter to the frontiers of Spain. He danced attendance at Lyons for some time to employ the interest of his friends in vain, to obtain the payment of his pension; and before he received it he had the vexation to be informed that he was struck out of the list. The cause of this disgrace was, that having received orders from his mistress to enquire by the rules of astrology what turn the affairs of France would take, he expressed his disapprobation too freely, that the princess should employ him in such a vain curiosity, instead of making use of his abilities in more important affairs. The lady took this lesson very in, but she was highly incensed when she heard that Agrippa had, by the Rules of Astrology, the Cabala, or some other art, predicted new triumphs to the constable of Bourbon. [173:1]--Agrippa finding himself discarded, murmured, stormed, threatened, and wrote; but, however, he was obliged to look out for another settlement. He cast his eyes on the Netherlands, and having after long waiting obtained the necessary passes, he arrived at Antwerp in the month of July, 1528. One of the causes of these delays was the rough proceeding of the Duke of Vendôme, who instead of signing the pass for Agrippa tore it up, saying, that "he would not sign any passport for a conjuror." In the year 1529 the King of England sent Agrippa a kind invitation to come into his territories, and at the same time he was invited by the Emperor's chancellor, by an Italian marquiss, and by Margaret of Austria, governess of the Netherlands. He accepted the offers of the latter, and was made historiographer to the Emperor, a post procured him by that princess. He published by way of prelude, The History of the Government of Charles V. and soon after he was obliged to compose that princess's funeral oration, whose death was in some manner the life of our Agrippa; for she had been strangely prejudiced against him: the same ill office was done him with his Imperial Majesty. His treatise of the Vanity of the Sciences, which he caused to be printed in 1530, terribly exasperated his enemies. That which he published soon after at Antwerp, viz. of the Occult Philosophy, afforded them a still farther pretence to defame him. It was fortunate for him that Cardinal Campegius, the Pope's legate, and Cardinal De la Mark, Bishop of Liege, were his advocates; but, however, their good offices could not procure him his pension as historiographer, nor prevent his being imprisoned at Brussels, in the year 1531, but he was soon released. The following year he made a visit to the Archbishop of Cologne, to whom he had dedicated his Occult Philosophy, and from whom he had received a very obliging letter. The fear of his creditors, with whom he was much embarrassed on account of his salary being stopped, made him stay longer in the country of Cologne than he desired. He strenuously opposed the inquisitors, who had put a stop to the printing of his Occult Philosophy, when he was publishing a new edition of it corrected, and augmented at Cologne.--See the xxvith, and the following Letters of the viith Book. In spite of them the impression was finished, which is that of the year 1533. He continued at Bonn till the year 1535, and was then desirous of returning to Lyons. He was imprisoned in France for something he had said against the mother of Francis I. but was released at the request of certain persons, and went to Grenoble, where he died the same year, 1535. Some say that he died in the hospital (but this is mere malice, for his enemies reported every thing that envy could suggest to depreciate his worth and character). He died at the house of the Receiver General of the province of Dauphiny, whose son was first president of Grenoble. Mr. Allard, at p. 4, of the Bibliotheque of Dauphiné, says, that Agrippa died at Grenoble, in the house which belonged to the family of Ferrand in Clerk's Street, and was then in the possession of the president Vachon; and that he was buried in the convent of the Dominicans. He lived always in the Roman communion, therefore it ought not to have been said that he was a Lutheran [175:1]. Burnet in his history of the Reformation asserts, that Agrippa wrote in favour of the divorce of King Henry VIII. But if we look into Agrippa's letters we shall find that he was against it, as well in them as likewise in his declamation on the vanity of the sciences, where he says--"I am informed there is a certain king, at this time o'day, who thinks it lawful for him to divorce a wife to whom he has been married these twenty years, and to espouse an harlot." In respect of the charge of magic diabolical being preferred against him by Martin del Rio and others who confidently asserted, that Agrippa paid his way at inns, &c. with pieces of horn, casting an illusion over the senses, whereby those who received them took them for real money; together with the story of the boarder at Louvain, who, in Agrippa's absence, raised the devil in his study, and thereby lost his life; and Agrippa's coming home, and seeing the spirits dancing at the top of the house, his commanding one of them into the dead body, and sending it to drop down at the market-place: all these stories, asserted by Martin del Rio, are too ridiculous to be believed by men of sense or science, they being no way probable even if he had dealt in the Black Art.--As to magic, in the sense it is understood by us, there is no doubt of his being a proficient in it, witness his three books of Occult Philosophy; to say nothing here of the fourth, which we have good authority to say was never wrote by Agrippa, as we shall shew presently, where we shall treat of the history of his Occult Philosophy.--In a word, to sum up the character of Agrippa we must do him the justice to acknowledge, that notwithstanding his impetuous temper which occasioned him many broils, yet from the letters which he wrote to several of his most intimate friends, without any apparent design of printing them, he was a man used to religious reflexions, and the practice of Christianity; that he was well versed in many of the chiefest and most secret operations of nature, viz. the sciences of natural and celestial magic; that he certainly performed strange things (in the vulgar eye) by the application of actives to passives, as which of us cannot? that he was an expert astrologer, physician, and mathematician, by which, as well as by magic, he foretold many uncommon things, and performed many admirable operations. John Wierus, who was his domestic, has given several curious and interesting anecdotes which throw great light upon the mysterious character of Agrippa, and serve to free him from the scandalous imputation of his being a professor of the BLACK ART. Now, because Agrippa continued whole weeks in his study, and yet was acquainted with almost every transaction in several countries of the world, many silly people gave out, that a black dog which Agrippa kept was an evil spirit, by whose means he had all this information, and which communicated the enemies' posts, number, designs, &c. to his master; this is Paul Jovius's account, by which you may see on what sort of reports he founded his opinions of this great man. We wonder that Gabriel Naudé had not the precaution to object to the accusers of Agrippa, the great number of historical falsehoods of which they (his accusers) stand convicted. Naudé supposes that the monks and others of the ecclesiastical order did not think of crying down the Occult Philosophy till a long time after it was published; he affirms that they exclaimed against that work, only in revenge for the injuries they believed they had received in that of the Vanity of the Sciences. 'Tis true, this latter book gave great offence to many. The monks, the members of the universities, the preachers, and the divines, saw themselves drawn to the life in it. Agrippa was of too warm a complexion. "The least taste of his book (of the Vanity of the Sciences) convinced me that he was an author of a fiery genius, extensive reading, and great memory; but sometimes more copious than choice in his subject, and writing in a disturbed, rather than in a composed, style." He lashes vice, and commends virtue, everywhere, and in every person: but there are some with whom nothing but panegyric will go down. See ERASMI Epist. lib. xxvii. p. 1083.

Let us now, in a few words, and for the conclusion of this article, describe the history of the Occult Philosophy. Agrippa composed this work in his younger days, and shewed it to the Abbot Trithemius, whose pupil he had been.

411

Trithemius was charmed with it, as appears by the letter which he wrote to him on the 8th of April, 1510; but he advises him to communicate it only to those whom he could confide in. However, several manuscript copies of it were dispersed almost all over Europe. It is not necessary to observe that most of them were faulty, which never fails to happen in the like cases. They were preparing to print it from one of these bad copies; which made the author resolve to publish it himself, with the additions and alterations with which he had embellished it, after having shewed it to the Abbot Trithemius. Melchior Adam was mistaken in asserting that Agrippa, in his more advanced years, having corrected and enlarged this work, shewed it to the Abbot Trithemius. He had refuted his Occult Philosophy in his Vanity of the Sciences, and yet he published it to prevent others from printing a faulty and mutilated edition. He obtained the approbation of the doctors of divinity, and some other persons, whom the Emperor's council appointed to examine it.

"This book has been lately examined and approved by certain prelates of the church, and doctors, thoroughly versed both in sacred and profane literature, and by commissaries particularly deputed for that purpose by CÆSAR'S council: after which, it was admitted by the whole council, and licensed by the authentic diploma of his Imperial Majesty, and the stamp of the CÆSAREAN EAGLE in red wax; and was afterwards publicly printed and sold at ANTWERP, and then, at PARIS, without any opposition."

After the death of Agrippa a Fourth Book was added to it by another hand. Jo. Wierus de Magis, cap. 5. p. 108, says, "To these (books of Magic) may very justly be added, a work lately published, and ascribed to my late honoured host and preceptor, HENRY CORNELIUS AGRIPPA, who has been dead more than forty years; whence I conclude it is unjustly inscribed to his manes, under the title of THE FOURTH BOOK OF THE OCCULT PHILOSOPHY, OR OF MAGICAL CEREMONIES, which pretends likewise to be a Key to the three former books of the OCCULT PHILOSOPHY, and all kinds of Magical Operations." Thus John Wierus expresses himself; There is an edition in folio of the Occult Philosophy, in 1533, without the place where it was printed. The

412

privilege of Charles V. is prefixed to it, dated from Mechlin, the 12th of January, 1529. We have already mentioned the chief works of Agrippa. It will be sufficient to add, that he wrote A Commentary on the Art of Raimundus Lullius and A Dissertation on the Original of Sin, wherein he teaches that the fall of our first parents proceeded from their unchaste love. He promised a work against the Dominicans, which would have pleased many persons both within and without the pale of the church of Rome [178:1]. He held some uncommon opinions, and never any Protestant spoke more forcibly against the impudence of the Legendaries, than he did. We must riot forget the Key of his Occult Philosophy, which he kept only for his friends of the first rank, and explained it in a manner, which differs but little from the speculations of our Quietists. Now many suppose that the 4th book of the Occult Philosophy is the Key which Agrippa mentions in his letters to have reserved to himself; but it may be answered, with great shew of probability, that he amused the world with this Key to cause himself to be courted by the curious. James Gohory and Vigenere say, that he pretended to be master of the Practice of the Mirror of Pythagoras, and the secret of extracting the spirit of gold from its body, in order to convert silver and copper into fine gold. But he explains what he means by this Key, where he says, in the Epist. 19. lib. v. "This is that true and occult philosophy of the wonders of nature. The key thereof is the understanding: for the higher we carry our knowledge, the more sublime are our attainments in virtue, and we perform the greatest things with more ease and effect." Agrippa makes mention of this Key in two letters which he wrote to a religious who addicted himself to the study of the Occult Sciences, viz. Aurelius de Aqualpendente Austin, friar, where he says, "What surprising, accounts we meet with, and how great writings there are made of the invincible power of the Magic Art, of the prodigious images of Astrologers, of the amazing transmutations of Alchymists, and of that blessed stone by which, MIDAS-like, all metals are transmuted into gold: all which are found to be vain, fictitious, and false, as often as they are practised literally." Yet he says, "Such things it are delivered and writ by great and grave philosophers, whose traditions who dare say are false? Nay, it were impious to think them lies: only there is another meaning than what is writ with the bare letters. We must not, he adds, look for the principle of these grand operations without ourselves: it is an internal spirit within us, which can very well perform whatsoever the monstrous Mathematicians, the prodigious Magicians, the wonderful Alchymists, and the bewitching Necromancers, can effect."

Nos habitat, non tartara; sed nec sidera cœli,
Spiritus in nobis qui viget, illa facit.

See AGRIPPA Epist. dat. Lyons, Sept. 24, 1727.

Note. Agrippa's three books of Magic, with the fourth, were translated into English, and published in London in the year 1651. But they are now become so scarce, as very rarely to be met with, and are sold at a very high price by the booksellers.

170:1 As he himself asserts in his preface to his three books of Occult Philosophy and Magic, where he says, "who am indeed a magician," applying the word magic to sublime and good sciences, not to prophane and devilish arts. Paul Jovius, Thevet, and Martin del Rio, accuse him not of magic, (because we cannot apply that to necromantic arts) but the black art; but we shall shew in some of the following notes, their grounds on which this accusation of Agrippa is founded, and examine how far their information will justify their calumny against this author.

171:1 We have no authority to say, that ever he was in possession of the great secret of transmutation, neither can we gather any such information from his writings; the only circumstance relative to this is what himself says in occult philosophy, that he had made gold, but no more than that out of which the soul was extracted.

173:1 See Agrippa's words in his 29th Epist. lib. iv. p. 854, which are as follow:--"I wrote to the Senechal, desiring him to advise her not to misapply my abilities any longer in so unworthy an art; that I might for the future avoid these follies, since I had it in my power to be of service to her by much happier studies." But the greatest misfortune was, that "this unworthy art," and "these follies," as he called them, predicted success to the opposite party, as you may judge by his own words.--"I remember I told the Seneschal in a letter, that in casting the constable of Bourbon's nativity, I plainly discovered that he would this year likewise gain the victory over your armies."--They who are acquainted with the history of these times, must see plainly that Agrippa could not pay his court worse to Francis 1. than by promising good success to the constable. From that time Agrippa was looked upon as a Bourbonist: to silence this reproach he represented the service he had done to France, by dissuading 4000 foot soldiers from following the Emperor's party, and by engaging them in the service of Francis I. He alledged the refusal of the great advantages which were promised him when he left Fribourg, if he would enter into the constable's service. It appears by the 4th and 6th Letter of Book V. that he held p. 174 a strict correspondence with that prince in 1527. He advised and counselled, yet refused to go and join him, and promised him victory. He assured him that the walls of Rome would fall down upon the first attack; yet he omitted informing him of one point, and that was, that the constable would be killed there.

175:1 Agrippa, in his Apolog. cap. 19, speaks in lofty terms of Luther, and with such contempt of the adversaries of that reformer that it is plain from hence Sixtus Sienensis affirmed that Agrippa was a Lutheran.

178:1 "In the treatise I am composing of the vices and erroneous opinions of the Dominicus, in which I shall expose to the whole world their vicious practices, such as the sacrament often infected with poison--numberless pretended miracles--kings and princes taken off with poison--cities and states betrayed--the populace seduced--heresies avowed--and the rest of the deeds of these heroes and their enormous crimes." See AGRIPPA Opera, T. ii. p. 1037..

ALBERTUS MAGNUS

ALBERTUS MAGNUS, a Dominican, bishop of Ratisbon, and one of the most famous doctors of the XIII century, was born at Lawingen, on the Danube, in Suabia, in the year 1193, or 1205. Moreri's dictionary gives us an account of the several employs which were conferred upon him, and the success of his lectures in several towns. It is likewise said, that he practised midwifery, and that he was in search of the Philosopher's Stone: that he was a famous Magician, and that he had formed a machine in the shape of a man, which served him for an oracle, and explained all the difficulties which he proposed to it. I can easily be induced to believe that, as he understood the mathematics, &c. he made a head, which, by the help of some spirits, might certain articulate sounds.

Though he was well qualified to be the inventor of artillery, there is reason to believe, that they who ascribed the invention of it to him are mistaken. It is said that he had naturally a very dull wit, and that he was upon the point of leaving the cloister, because he despaired of attaining what his friar's habit required of him, but that the Holy Virgin appeared to him, and asked him in which he would chuse to excel, in philosophy or divinity; that he made choice of philosophy, and that the Holy Virgin told him he should surpass all men of his time in that science, but that, as a punishment for not chusing divinity, he should before his death, relapse into his former stupidity.

They add, that, after this apparition, he shewed a prodigious deal of sense, and so improved in all the sciences, that he quickly surpassed his preceptors; but that, three years before his death, he forgot in an instant all that he knew: and that, being at a stand in the middle of a lecture on divinity at Cologne, and endeavouring in vain to recal his ideas, he was sensible that it was the accomplishment of the prediction.

Whence arose the saying, that he was miraculously converted from an ass into a philosopher, and, afterwards, from a philosopher into an ass. Our Albertus was a very little man [181:1] , and, after living eighty-seven years, died in the year of our redemption, 1280, at Cologne, on the 15th of November; his body was laid in the middle quire of the convent of the Dominicans, and his entrails were carried to Ratisbon; his body was yet entire in the time of the Emperor Charles V. and was taken up by his command, and afterwards replaced in its first monument. He wrote such a vast number of books, that they amount to twenty-one volumes in folio, in the edition of Lyons, 1651.

181:1 When he came before the Pope, after standing some time in his presence, his Holiness desired him to rise, thinking he had been kneeling.

ROGER BACON

COMMONLY CALLED FRIAR BACON

ROGER BACON, an Englishman, and a Franciscan friar, lived in the XIII century. He was a great Astrologer, Chymist, Mathematician, and Magician. There runs a tradition in English annals, that this friar made a brazen head, under the rising of the planet Saturn, which spake with a man's voice, and gave responses to all his questions. Francis Picus says, "that he read in a book wrote by Bacon, that a man might foretel things to come by means of the mirror Almuchesi, composed according to the rules of perspective; provided he made use of it under a good constellation, and first brought his body into an even and temperate state by chymistry." This is agreeable to what John Picus has maintained, that Bacon gave himself only to the study of Natural Magic. This friar sent several instruments of his own invention to pope Clement IV. Several of his books have been published (but they are now very scarce,) viz. Specula Mathematica & Perspectiva, Speculum Alchymiæ, De Mirabili Potestate Artis & Naturæ, Epistolæ, cum Notis, &c. In all probability he did not perform any thing by any compact with devils, but has only ascribed to things a surprising efficacy which they could not naturally have. He was well versed in judicial astrology. His Speculum Astrologiæ was condemned by Gerson and Agrippa. Francis Picus and many others have condemned it only because the author maintains in it, that, with submission to better judgments, books of magic ought to be carefully preserved, because the time draws near that, for certain causes not there specified, they must necessarily be perused and made use of on some occasions. Naude adds, "that Bacon was so much addicted to judicial astrology, that Henry de Hassia, William of Paris, and Nicholas Oresmius, were obliged to inveigh sharply against his writings." Bacon was fellow of Brazen- nose college in Oxford in the year 1226. He was beyond all compeer the glory of the age he lived in, and may perhaps stand in competition with the greatest that have appeared since. It is wonderful, considering the age wherein he lived, how he came by such a depth of knowledge on all subjects. His treatises are composed with that elegancy, conciseness, and strength, and abound with such just and exquisite observations on nature, that, among the whole line of chymists, we do not know one that can pretend to contend with him. The reputation of his uncommon learning still survives in England. His cell is shewn at Oxford to this day; and there is a tradition, that it will fall whenever a greater man than Bacon shall enter within it. He wrote many treatises; amongst which, such as are yet extant have beauties enough to make us sensible of the great loss of the rest. What relates to chymistry are two small pieces, wrote at Oxford, which are now in print, and the manuscripts to be seen in the public library at Leiden; having been carried thither among Vossius's manuscripts from England. In these treatises he clearly shews how imperfect metals may be ripened into perfect ones. He entirely adopts Geber's notion, that mercury is the common basis of all metals, and sulphur the cement; and shews that it is by a gradual depuration of the mercurial matter by sublimation, and the accession of a subtle sulphur by fire, that nature makes her gold; and that, if during the process, any other third matter happen to intervene, besides the mercury and sulphur, some base metal arises: so that, if we by imitating her operations ripen lead, we might easily change it into good gold.

Several of Bacon's operations have been compared with the experiments of Monsieur Homberg, made by that curious prince the duke of Orleans; by which it has been found that Bacon has described some of the very things which Homberg published as his own discoveries. For instance, Bacon teaches expressly, that if a pure sulphur be united with mercury, it will commence gold: on which very principle, Monsieur Homberg has made various experiments for the production of gold, described in the Memoire de l'Academie Royale des Sciences. His other physical writings shew no less genius and force of mind. In a treatise 183:1 Of the secrets Works of Nature, he shews that a person who was perfectly acquainted with the manner nature observes in her operations, would not only be able to rival, but to surpass nature herself.

This author's works are printed in 8vo and 12mo, under the title of Frater Rogerius Baco de Secretis Artis & Naturæ, but they are become very rare. From a repeated perusal of them we may perceive that Bacon was no stranger to many of the capital discoveries of the present and past ages. Gunpowder he certainly knew;

thunder and lightning, he tells us, may be produced by art and that sulphur, nitre, and charcoal, which when separate have no sensible effect, when mingled together in a due proportion, and closely confined, yield a horrible crack. A more precise description of gunpowder cannot be given with words: and yet a Jesuit, Barthol. Schwartz, some ages afterwards, has had the honour of the discovery. He likewise mentions a sort of inextinguishable fire, prepared by art, which indicates he knew something of phosphorus. And that he had a notion of the rarefaction of the air, and the structure of the air-pump, is past contradiction. A chariot, he observes, might be framed on the principle of mechanics, which, being sustained on very large globes, specifically lighter than common air, would carry a man aloft through the atmosphere; this proves that he likewise had a competent idea of aerostation.

There are many curious speculations in this noble author, which will raise the admiration of the reader: but none of them will affect him with so much wonder, as to see a person of the most sublime merit fall a sacrifice to the wanton zeal of infatuated bigots. See BOERHAAVE'S Chym. p. 18.

183:1 De Secretis Naturæ Operibus.

RAYMOND LULLY

A FAMOUS ALCHYMIST

RAYMOND LULLY, or Raymon Lull, comes the next in order. He was born in the island of Majorca, in the year 1225, of a family of the first distinction, though he did not assume his chymical character till towards the latter part of his life.

Upon his applying himself to chymistry, he soon began to preach another sort of doctrine; insomuch that, speaking of that art, he says it is only to be acquired by dint of experiment and practice, and cannot be conveyed to the understanding by idle words and sounds. He is the first author I can find, who considers alchymy expressly with a view to the universal medicine: but after him it became a popular pursuit, and the libraries were full of writings in that vein.

Lully, himself, beside what he wrote in the scholastic way, has a good many volumes wrote after his conversion: 'tis difficult to say how many; for it was a common practice with his disciples and followers to usher in their performances under their master's name. "I have perused (says Boerhaave) the best part of his works, and find them, beyond expectation, excellent: insomuch, that I have been almost tempted to doubt whether they could be the work of that age, so full are they of the experiments and observations which occur in our later writers, that either the books must be supposititious, or else the ancient chymists must have been acquainted with a world of things which pass for the discoveries of modern practice. He gives very plain intimations of phosphorus, which he calls the Vestal Fire, the Offa Helmontii, &c. and yet it is certain he wrote 200 years before either Helmont, or my Lord Bacon."

He travelled into Mauritania, where he is supposed to have first met with chymistry, and to have imbibed the principles of his art from the writings of Geber: which opinion is countenanced by the conformity observable between the two. The Spanish authors ascribe the occasion of his journey to an amour: he had fallen in love, it seems, with a maiden of that country, who obstinately refused his addresses. Upon enquiring into the reason, she shewed him a cancered breast.

Lully, like a generous gallant, immediately resolved on a voyage to Mauritania, where Geber had lived, to seek some relief for his mistress. He ended his days in Africa; where, after having taken up the quality of missionary, and preaching the gospel among the infidels, he was stoned to death [185:1].

185:1 The history of this eminent adept is very confused. Mutius, an author, is express, that that good man, being wholly intent upon religion, never applied himself either to chymistry or the philosopher's- stone: and yet we have various accounts of his making gold. Among a variety of authors, Gregory of Thoulouseasserts that "Lully offered EDWARD III, king of England, a supply of six millions to make war against the Infidels." Besides manuscripts, the following printed pieces bear Lully's name, viz. The Theory of the Philosopher's Stone: The Practise: The Transmutation of Metals: The Codicil: The Vade-Mecum: The Book of Experiments: The Explanation of his Testament: The Abridgements, or Accusations: and The Power of Riches.

GEORGE RIPLEY

GEORGE RIPLEY, an Englishman by nation, and by profession a canon or monk of Britlingthon. His writings were all very good in their kind, being wrote exactly in the style of Bacon, only more allegorical. As he was no physician, he does not meddle with any thing of the preparations of that kind; but treats much of the cure of metals, which in his language is the purification and maturation thereof. He rigorously pursued Geber's and Bacon's principles, and maintained, for instance, with new evidence, that mercury is the universal matter of all metals; that this set over the fire, with the purest sulphur, will become gold, but that if either of them be sick or leprous, i. e. infected with any impurity, instead of gold, some other metal will be produced. He adds, that as mercury and sulphur are sufficient for the making of all metals: so of these may an universal medicine, or metal, be produced for curing of all the sick; which some mistakenly understood of an universal metal, efficacious in all the diseases of the human body.

JOHN AND ISAAC HOLLANDUS

THEY were two brothers, both of them of great parts and ingenuity, and wrote on the dry topics of chymistry. They lived in the 13th century, but this is not assured. The whole art of enamelling is their invention, as is also, that of colouring glass, and precious stones, by application of thin metal plates. Their writings are in the form of processes, and they describe all their operations to the most minute circumstances. The treatise of enamelling is esteemed the greatest and most finished part of their works: whatever relates to the fusion, separation, and preparation of metals, is here delivered. They write excellently of distillation, fermentation, putrefaction, and their effects; and seem to have understood, at least, as much of these matters as any of the moderns have done. They furnish a great many experiments on human blood; which Van Helmont and Mr. Boyle have since taken for new discoveries. I have a very large work in folio, under their name, of the construction of chymical furnaces and instruments. Their writings are as easily purchased, as they are worthy of perusal, on account of valuable secrets in them, which may pave the way for greater discoveries. See BOERHAAVE, p. 21.

PARACELSUS

PHILIPPUS AUREOLUS THEOPHRASTUS PARACELSUS BOMBAST DE HOENHEYM,

THE PRINCE OF PHYSICIANS AND PHILOSOPHERS BY FIRE; GRAND PARADOXICAL PHYSICIAN; THE TRISMEGISTUS OF SWITZERLAND; FIRST REFORMER OF CHYMICAL PHILOSOPHY; ADEPT IN ALCHYMY, CABALA, AND MAGIC; NATURE'S FAITHFUL SECRETARY; MASTER OF THE ELIXIR OF LIFE AND THE PHILOSOPHER'S STONE;

AND THE

GREAT MONARCH OF CHYMICAL SECRETS;

Now living in his Tomb, whither he retired disgusted with the Vices and Follies of Mankind, supporting himself with his own

QUINTESSENTIA VITÆ.

PARACELSUS was born, as he himself writes, in the year 1494, in a village in Switzerland called Hoenheym (q. d. ab alto nido) two miles distant from Zurich. His father was a natural son of a great master of the Teutonic order, and had been brought up to medicine, which he practised accordingly in that obscure corner. He was master of an excellent and copious library, and is said to have become eminent in his art, so that Paracelsus always speaks of him with the highest deference, and calls him laudatissimus medicus in eo vico. Of such a father did Paracelsus receive his first discipline. After a little course of study at home he was committed to the care of Trithemius, the celebrated abbot of Spanheim, who had the character of an adept himself, and wrote of the Cabala,

425

being at that time a reputed magician. Here he chiefly learnt languages and letters; after which he was removed to Sigismund Fugger to learn medicine, surgery, and chymistry; all these masters, especially the last, Paracelsus ever speaks of with great veneration; so that he was not altogether so rude and unpolished as is generally imagined. Thus much we learn from his own writings, and especially the preface to his Lesser Surgery, where he defends himself against his accusers. At twenty years of age he undertook a journey through Germany and Hungary, visiting all the mines of principal note, and contracting an acquaintance with the miners and workmen, by which means he learnt every thing, relative to metals, and the art thereof: in this enquiry he shewed an uncommon assiduity and resolution. He gives us an account of the many dangers he had run from earthquakes, falls of stones, floods of water, cataracts, exhalations, damps, heat, hunger, and thirst; and every where takes occasion to insist on the value of an art acquired on such hard terms. The same inclination carried him as far as Muscovy, where as he was in quest of mines near the frontiers of Tartary he was taken prisoner by that people, and carried before the great Cham; during his captivity there he learnt various secrets, till, upon the Cham's sending an embassy to the Grand Signior, with his own son at the head of it, Paracelsus was sent along with him in quality of companion. On this occasion he came to Constantinople in the twenty-eighth year of his age, and was there taught the secret of the philosopher's stone by a generous Arabian, who made him this noble present, as he calls it, Azoth. This incident we have from Helmont only; for Paracelsus himself, who is ample enough on his other travels, says nothing of his captivity. At his return from Turkey he practised as a surgeon in the Imperial army, and performed many excellent cures therein; indeed, it cannot be denied but that he was excellent in that art, of which his great surgery, printed in folio, will ever be a standing monument. At his return to his native country he assumed the title of utriusque medicinæ doctor, or doctor both of external and internal medicine or surgery; and grew famous in both, performing far beyond what the practice of that time could pretend to; and no wonder, for medicine was then in a poor condition; the practice and the very language was all Galenical and Arabic; nothing was inculcated but Aristotle, Galen, and the Arabs; Hippocrates was not read; nay, there was no edition of his writings, and scarce was he ever mentioned. Their theory consisted in the knowledge of the four degrees, the temperaments, &c. and their whole practice was confined to venesection, purgation, vomiting, clysmata, &c. Now, in this age a new disease had broke out, and spread itself over Europe, viz. the venereal disorder; the common Galenic medicines had here proved altogether ineffectual; bleeding, purging, and cleansing medicines were vain; and the physicians were at their wit's end. Jac Carpus, a celebrated anatomist and surgeon at Bolonge, had alone been master of the cure, which was by mercury administered to raise a salivation; he had attained this secret in his travels through Spain and Italy, and practised it for some years, and with such success and applause, that it is incredible what immense riches this one nostrum brought him (it is said upon good authority, that in one year he cleared six thousand pistoles) he acknowledged himself, that he did not know the end of his own wealth; for the captains, merchants, governors, commanders, &c. who had brought that filthy disease from America, were very well content to give him what sums he pleased to ask to free them from it.--Paracelsus about this time having likewise learnt the properties of mercury, and most likely from Carpus, who undertook the same cure but in a very different manner; for whereas Carpus did all by salivation-- Paracelsus making up his preparation in pills attained his ends in a gentler manner. By this he informs us he cured the itch, leprosy, ulcers, Naples disease, and even gout, all which disorders were incurable on the foot of popular practice, and thus was the great basis laid for all his future fame and fortune.

Paracelsus, thus furnished with arts, and arrived at a degree of eminence beyond any of his brothers in the profession, was invited by the curators of the university of Bazil to the chair of professor of medicine and philosophy in that university. The art of printing was now a new thing, the taste for learning and art was warm 190:1 , and the magistracy of Bazil were very industrious in procuring professors of reputation from all parts of the world. They had already got Desid. Erasmus, professor of theology, and J. Oporinus professor of the Greek tongue; and now in 1527 Paracelsus was associated in the 33d year of his age. Upon his first entrance into that province, having to make a public speech before the university, he posted up a very elegant advertisement over the doors inviting every body to his doctrine. At his first lecture he ordered a brass vessel to be brought into the

427

middle of the school, where after he had cast in sulphur and nitre, in a very solemn manner he burnt the books of Galen and Avicenna, alledging that he had held a dispute with them in the gates of hell, and had fairly routed and overcome them. And hence he proclaimed, that the physicians should all follow him; and no longer style themselves Galenists, but Paracelsists.--"Know," says he, "physicians, my cap has more learning in it than all your heads, my beard has more experience than your whole academies: Greeks, Latins, French, Germans, Italians, I will be your king."

While he was here professor he read his book De Tartaro, de Gradibus, and De compsitionibus, in public lectures, to which he added a commentary on the book De Gradibus; all these he afterwards printed at Bazil for the use of his disciples; so that these must be allowed for genuine writings; about the same time he wrote De Calculo, which performance Helmont speaks of with high approbation.

Notwithstanding his being professor in so learned an university he understood but a very little Latin; his long travels, and application to business, and disuse of the language, had very much disqualified him for writing or speaking therein; and his natural warmth rendered him very unfit for teaching at all. Hence, though his auditors and disciples were at first very numerous, yet they very much fell off, and left him preaching to the walls. In the mean time he abandoned himself to drinking at certain seasons; Oporinus, who was always near him, has the good nature to say, he was never sober; but that he tippled on from morning to night, and from night to morning, in a continual round. At length he soon became weary of his professorship, and after three years continuance therein relinquished it, saying, that no language besides the German was proper to reveal the secrets of chymistry in.

After this he again betook himself to an itinerant life, travelling and drinking, and living altogether at inns and taverns, continually flushed with liquor, and yet working many admirable cures in his way. In this manner he passed four years from the 43d to the 47th year of his life, when he died at an inn at Saltzburg, at the sign of the White Horse, on a bench in the chimney-corner. Oporinus relates, that after he had put on any new thing, it never came off his back till he had worn it into rags; he adds, that notwithstanding his excess in point of drinking, he was never addicted to venery.--But there is this reason for it: when he was a child, being neglected by his nurse, a hag gelded him in a place where three ways met, and so made a eunuch of him; accordingly in his writings he omits no opportunity of railing against women.--Such is the life of Paracelsus; such is the immortal man, who sick of life retired into a corner of the world, and there supports himself with his own Quintessence of Life.

In his life time he only published three or four books, but after his death he grew prodigiously voluminous, scarce a year passing but one book or other was published under his name, said to be found in some old wall, ceiling, or the like. All the works published under his name were printed together at Strasburg in the year 1603, in three volumes folio, and again in 1616. J. Oporinus, that excellent professor and printer, before named, who constantly attended Paracelsus for three years as his menial servant, in hopes of learning some of his secrets, who published the works of Vesalius, and is supposed to have put them in that elegant language wherein they now appear: this Oporinus, in an epistle to Monavius, concerning the life of Paracelsus, professes himself surprized to find so many works of his master; for, that in all the time he was with him never wrote a word himself, nor ever took pen in hand, but forced Oporinus to write what he dictated; and Oporinus wondered much how such coherent words and discourse which might even become the wisest persons, should come from the mouth of a drunken man. His work called Archidoxa Medicinæ, as containing the principles and maxims of the art, nine books of which were published at first; and the author in the prolegomena to them, speaks thus:--"I intended to have published my ten books of Archidoxa; but finding mankind unworthy of such a treasure as the tenth, I keep it close, and have firmly resolved never to bring it thence, till you have all abjured ARISTOTLE, AVICEN, and GALEN, and have sworn allegiance to PARACELSUS alone."

However, the book did at length get abroad, though by what means is not known; it is undoubtedly an excellent piece, and may be ranked among the principal productions in the way, of chymistry, that have ever appeared; whether or no it be Paracelsus's we cannot affirm, but there is one thing speaks in its behalf, viz. it contains a great many things which have since been trumped up for great nostrums; and Van Helmont's Lithonthriptic and Alcahest are apparently taken from hence; among the genuine writings of Paracelsus are likewise reckoned, that De Ortu Rerum Naturalium, De Transformatione Rerum Naturalium, and De Vita Rerunt Naturalium. The rest are spurious or very doubtful, particularly his theological works.

The great fame and success of this man, which many attribute to his possessing an universal medicine may be accounted for from other principles. It is certain he was well acquainted with the use and virtue of opium, which the Galenists of those times all rejected as cold in the fourth degree. Oporinus relates that he made up certain little pills of the colour, figure, and size of mouse-turds, which were nothing but opium. These he called by a barbarous sort of name, his laudanum; q.d. laudable medicine; he always carried them with him, and prescribed them in dyssenteries, and all cases attended with intense pains, anxieties, deliriums, and obstinate wakings; but to be alone possessed of the use of so extraordinary and noble a medicament as opium, was sufficient to make him famous.

Another grand remedy with Paracelsus was turbith mineral; this is first mentioned in his Clein Spital Boeck, or Chirurgia Minor, where he gives the preparation. In respect of the philosopher's stone.--Oporinus says, he often wondered to see him one day without a farthing in his pocket, and the next day, full of money; that he took nothing with him when he went abroad. He adds, that he would often borrow money of his companions, the carmen and porters, and pay it again in twenty-four hours with extravagant interest, and yet from what fund nobody but himself knew. In the Theatrum Alchemiæ he mentions a treasure, hid under a certain tree; and from such like grounds they supposed him to possess the art of making gold; but it was hard if such noble nostrums as he possessed would not subsist him without the lapis philosophorum.

190:1 We feel ourselves happy in being able to say, that the taste for learning and arts (notwithstanding the follies of the age) was never more prevalent than in the present time; the year 1801 commences an age of flourishing science, in which even our females seem to wish to bear a part-instance, a lady of quality, who went in her carriage the other day to Foster-lane, Cheapside, and bought a portable blacksmith's forge for her private amusement; her person was strong and athletic, and very fit for the manual practice of handling iron, and working other metallic experiments.

JOHN RUDOLPH GLAUBER

R. GLAUBER, a celebrated chymist of Amsterdam, accounted the Paracelsus of his time: he had travelled much and by that means attained to a great many secrets. He wrote above thirty tracts, in some of which he acted the physician; in others, the adept; and in others, the metallist. He principally excelled in the last capacity, and alchymy.

He was a person of easy and genteel address, and, beyond dispute, well versed in chymistry: being author of the salt, still used in the shops, called Sal Glauberi; as also of all the salts, by oil of vitriol., &c. He is noted for extolling his arcanæ and preparations, and is reported to have traded unfairly with his secrets: the best of them he would sell, at excessive rates, to chymists and others, and would afterwards re-sell them, or make them public, to increase his fame; whence he was continually at variance with them.

The principal of his writings are De Furnis, and De Metallis, which, though wrote in Dutch, have been translated into Latin and English. It was Glauber who shewed, before the States of Holland, that there is gold contained in sand; and made an experiment thereof to their entire satisfaction: but so much lead, fire, and labour, being employed in procuring it, that the art would not pay charges [195:1]. However he plainly demonstrated, that there is no earth, sand, sulphur, or salt, or other matter, but what contains gold in a greater or less quantity. In short, he possessed a great many secrets, which are at this time in the hands of some of our modern chymists.

195:1 It has been asserted by several eminent chymists, that it might be performed to advantage, as the process is very simple, and takes up but little time: all that is requisite is silver, sand, and litharge.

DOCTOR DEE AND SIR EDWARD KELLY

DOCTOR JOHN DEE, and SIR EDWARD KELLY, knight, being professed associates, their story is best delivered together. They have some title to the philosopher's stone in common fame. Dee, besides his being deep in chymistry, was very well versed in mathematics, particularly geometry and astrology: but Sir Edward Kelly appears to have been the leading man in alchymy. In some of Dee's books are found short memoirs of the events of his operations: as, Donum Dei, five ounces. And in another place, "This day Edward Kelly discovered the grand secret to me, sit nomen Domini benedictum." Ashmole says, absolutely, they were masters of the powder of projection, and, with a piece not bigger than the smallest grain of sand, turned an ounce and a quarter of mercury into pure gold: but here is an equivoque; for granting them possessed of the powder of projection, it does not appear they had the secret of making it. The story is, that they found a considerable quantity of it in the ruins of Glastonbury Abbey, with which they performed many notable transmutations for the satisfaction of several persons. Kelly, in particular, is said to have given away rings of gold wire to the tune of 4000l. at the marriage of his servant maid. And a piece of a brass warming-pan being cut out by order of queen Elizabeth, and sent to them when abroad, was returned pure gold. Likewise Dee made a present to the landgrave of Hesse of twelve Hungarian horses, which could never be expected from a man of his circumstances without some extraordinary means.

In the year 1591 they went into Germany, and settled some time at Trebona, in Bohemia; the design of which journey is very mysterious. Some say their design was to visit the alchymists of these countries, in order to get some light into the art of making the powder. Accordingly they travelled through Poland, &c. in quest thereof, and, some say, attained it; others say, not. Others, again, will make them sent by the queen as spies, and that alchymy was only a pretence, or means, to bring them into confidence with the people. But what will give most light upon this subject, is a book, now extant, wrote by Dee, entitled Dee's Conferences with Spirits, but some conjecture it to be with Trithemius's mere Cryptography; which light Doctor Hook takes it in. However, this book is truly curious in respect of the many magical operations there displayed, it being wrote journal-fashion by the Doctor's own hand, and relates circumstantially the conferences he held with some spirits (either good or bad) in company with Sir Edward Kelly.

They were no sooner gone out of England than Dee's library was opened by the queen's order, and 4000 books, and 700 choice manuscripts, were taken away on pretence of his being a conjuror. That princess soon after used means to bring him back again, which a quarrel with Kelly happening to promote, he returned in 1596, and in 1598 was made warden of Manchester college, where he died.[196:1]
Some very curious manuscripts, with the chrystal he used to invoke the spirits into, are at this time carefully laid up in the British Museum. [196:2]

As for Sir Edward Kelly, the Emperor, suspecting he had the secret of the philosophers in his possession, clapped him up in prison, in hopes to become a sharer in the profits of transmutation: however, Kelly defeated his intentions. After having been twice imprisoned, the last time he was shut up endeavouring to make his escape by means of the sheets of his bed tied together, they happened to slip the knots, and so let him fall, by which he broke his leg, and soon after lost his life.

196:1 Authors differ very much in respect of the place where Doctor Dee resigned his life: it appears from the most eminent historians that he died at his house at Mortlake.

196:2 Although Dee's manuscripts, and his Magic Chrystal, are to be seen at the Museum, there are six or seven individuals in London who assert they have the stone in their possession; thereby wishing to deceive the credulous, and to tempt them to a purchase at an enormous price.

THE CONCLUSION

HAVING collected the most interesting and curious accounts of the lives of those great men, so famous for their speculations in philosophic learning, we draw to a conclusion; having only to add, that we have sufficiently discovered in this biographical sketch whatsoever was necessary to prove the authenticity of Our Art, which we have delivered faithfully and impartially, noting, at the same time, the various opinions of different men at different ages; likewise, we have taken sufficient trouble to explain what is meant by the word Magic, and to clear up the term from the imputation of any diabolical association with evil spirits, &c. Also, how nearly it is allied to our religious duties, we refer the reader to the annotations under the, article Zoroaster, where we have spoke of the Magi, or wise men, proving the first who adored Christ were actually magicians. It is enough that we have spoke of the principal characters renowned in past ages for their laborious inquisition into the labyrinth of occult and natural philosophy; there are many other philosophers standing upon ancient and modern record. A copious and general biography falls not within the limits of our work. We have introduced some characters (applicable to the subject before us) most distinguished for occult learning; of which kind of science, whether by a particular influence of planetary configuration, which may have directed and impelled my mind and intellects to the observation and study of nature, and her simple operations, as well as to the more occult, I leave to the judgment of the astrologers, to whose inspection I submit a figure of my nativity, which I shall annex to a sketch of my own history, which I mean to make the subject of a future publication, including a vast number of curious experiments in occult and chymical operations, which have fell either under my own observation, or have been transmitted to me from others. In respect of the astrologic art, (as we have already observed) it has such an affinity with talismanic experiments, &c. that no one can bring any work to a complete effect without a due knowledge and observation of the qualities and effects of the constellations (which occasioned us to give it the title of the Constellatory Art;) likewise, a man must be well acquainted with the nature, qualities, and effects, of the four elements, and of the animal, vegetable, and mineral kingdoms; which knowledge cannot better be obtained than by chymical experience, for it does, as I may say, unlock the secret chambers of nature, and introduces the student into a world of knowledge, which could not be attained but by chymical analyzation, whereby we decompound mixt bodies, and reduce them to their simple natures, and come to a thorough acquaintance with those powerful and active principles, causing the wonderful transmutations of one compound body into another of a different species, as is to be seen in the course of our operations upon salts and metals, giving us clear and comprehensive ideas of the principles of life or generation, and putrefaction or death.

Finally, to conclude, we are chiefly to consider one thing to be attained as the ground of perfection in the rest: i. e. The great First Cause, the Eternal Wisdom, to know the Creator by the contemplation of the creature. This is the grand secret of the philosophers, and the master-key to all sciences both human and divine, for without this we are still wandering in a labyrinth of perplexity and errors, of darkness and obscurity: for this is the sum and perfection of all learning, to live in the fear of God, and in love and charity with all men.

FINIS

The Magus

Made in the USA
Columbia, SC
07 October 2024

43806455R00246